Ernst Kurth as Theorist and Analyst

Ernst Kurth as

Theorist and Analyst

Lee A. Rothfarb

upp

University of Pennsylvania Press
Philadelphia

Studies in the Criticism and Theory of Music

A complete listing of the books in this series appears at the back of this volume

Library of Congress Cataloging-in-Publication Data

Rothfarb, Lee Allen.
   Ernst Kurth as theorist and analyst.

   (Studies in the criticism and theory of music)
   Bibliography: p.
   Includes index.
   1. Kurth, Ernst.   2. Music—Theory.   3. Harmony.
I. Title.   II. Series.
ML423.K98R7   1988   781'.092'4   88-17258
ISBN 0-8122-7562-4

Permission is acknowledged to quote material from the following sources:

Ernst Kurth. *Romantische Harmonik und ihre Krise in Wagners "Tristan."* Bern: Haupt, 1920; Berlin, Hesse, 1922, 1923; repr. Hildesheim: Olms, 1975. All citations are from the 1975 edition. Reprinted by permission of Olms Verlag.

Ernst Kurth. *Grundlagen des linearen Kontrapunkts: Bachs melodische Polyphonie.* Bern: Drechsel, 1917; Berlin: Hesse, 1922, 1927; Bern: Krompholz, 1946, 1956. Reprinted by permission of Krompholz and Company.

Music and translations from Richard Wagner, *Tristan und Isolde* (1934), *Das Rheingold* (1904), *Die Walküre* (1904), *Siegfried* (1904), *Götterdämmerung* (1904), *Die Meistersinger von Nürnberg* (1932), *Parsifal* (1904). Used by arrangement with G. Schirmer, Inc.

The musical examples were prepared by Music Art Company, New York.

The frontispiece photograph was provided courtesy of the Kurth family.

CONTENTS

PREFACE AND ACKNOWLEDGMENTS

Until recently, the writings of Dr. Ernst Kurth have received little attention from the American academic music community. References to his work have largely been bibliographic, or have been limited to quotations of some of his leading ideas as foils for those of other authors. Acknowledgments of this sort cannot possibly do justice to a man whose innovative works have been widely read in Europe since the 1920s. This book provides an opportunity for English-language readers to learn about and benefit from the writings of one of this century's most important and creative musical thinkers.

Writing a book on Kurth today is no easy task. Understanding his works hinges on understanding the fin-de-siècle culture that produced them. Yet this culture is difficult to recall. The vast sociological and cultural-intellectual changes that have come about since the end of World War II have greatly telescoped the passage of time, pushing into the distant past the world and *Weltanschauung* of only fifteen to twenty years before. While reading Kurth, it is important to keep in mind the intellectual climate of his early adulthood. The growth of psychology in particular—the efforts to understand psychic life and cognitive processes—profoundly affected Kurth. Influenced also by neo-Romantic sentiments, he was one of several theorists who challenged the dominant rationalism of music theory in the decades around 1900. In addition to cultural barriers, there are fundamental methodological differences between Kurth's approach to analysis and that of some of his better-known contemporaries. In order to appreciate Kurth's achievements and assess their significance, we must consider his cultural milieu and distinctive analytical approach.

Our study begins with a sketch of Kurth's biography. At appropriate stages of the sketch, I examine his cultural milieu by pointing out some of the philosophical, aesthetic, scientific, and music-theoretical influences that shaped his outlook. In preparing the biographical material, I was fortunate to have had access to archival resources concerning Kurth's personal and professional life. Additionally, I have incorporated information from tape-recorded interviews with Kurth's widow, Marie-Louise Kurth (1891–1987), and with several of Kurth's students. Those materials, unpublished until now, added considerably to recounting Kurth's life and development as a scholar.

I devote the body of the book to a presentation of Kurth's theories as articulated in two of his four major publications, *Grundlagen des linearen Kontrapunkts* (1917) and *Romantische Harmonik und ihre Krise in Wagners "Tristan"* (1920).[1] The presentation is divided into chapters dealing with the linear aspects of Kurth's theories (chapters 2–4), and with their harmonic aspects (chapters 5–8). After the introduction I take up Kurth's ideas on *Fortspinnung,* melodic "spinning forth," and "endless melody" (chapter 2). I then discuss Kurth's theories of "developmental motives" (chapter 3) and polyphonic melody (chapter 4). Before turning to Kurth's analyses of Romantic harmony, I offer an orientation to his views on harmony in general, and then take up his treatment of harmony in *Grundlagen* (chapter 5) and in *Romantische Harmonik* (chapters 6–8). A discussion of form (chapter 9) brings the presentational sections of the book to a close. In order to set Kurth's work in historical perspective, in chapters 2–9 I often contrast his analyses with those of his contemporaries, as well as with my own views. A conclusion (chapter 10) discusses Kurth's influence on the writings of a few selected authors, and then reflects more generally on the impact of his work in Europe and the United States.

Regarding the order of my presentation, I do not follow Kurth's sequence of topics. Kurth tends to treat related subjects at different locations; for the sake of clarity and ease of reference, I gather similar materials in order to coordinate and summarize ideas where Kurth does not provide such summaries. By assembling and organizing various lines of analytical inquiry, I hope to initiate the reader into Kurth's musical world, and to provide a basis for evaluating his achievements.

The efforts and support of many people were involved in preparing this book. Before thanking those individuals who contributed directly to its content, I would like to acknowledge my wife, Anne, and children for their endless patience. They deserve first rather than a "last-but-not-least" mention for their unfailing support while I worked on this book. I owe a great debt to Professor David Lewin for his careful reading of the manuscript and for his numerous valuable suggestions, which helped shape both the style and substance of my work. His intellectual breadth significantly enriched and broadened this study. Dr. Robert Wason also deserves thanks for introducing me to the work of Ernst Kurth many years ago, when together we translated Kurth's first book, *Voraussetzungen der theoretischen Harmonik* (1913). His guidance in that project yielded many avenues of musical and music-historical research which I have pursued here.

Several other individuals and institutions contributed in important ways to this study. Frau Marie-Louise Kurth and several of Kurth's students gave generously of their time in order to help me with details of Kurth's life, as well as with those of the musical life of Bern, Switzerland during the 1920s and 1930s. I thank the staffs of the State Archives at Bern, the Archive of the University of Vienna, and the Vienna Magistrate's office for supplying me with many facts as well as documents containing biographical information that this book makes available for the first time. I am grateful to the Council on European Studies at Yale University for a grant (1981) that financed a trip to Switzerland. Thanks also go to Dean Michael Spence of the Faculty of the Arts and Sciences, Harvard University, for helping to finance the cost of producing the musical examples. Finally, I would like to thank Catherine Gjerdingen, who edited the manuscript, and the staff of the University of Pennsylvania Press, for their assistance in readying my work for publication.

NOTE TO PREFACE

1. Kurth published two other major works, a monograph entitled *Bruckner* (1925) and a final, summary work entitled *Musikpsychologie* (1931). While these two volumes are undeniably important for understanding Kurth's writings as a unified body of thought, dealing with them adequately would have greatly enlarged an already sizable book. Besides the consideration of size, there are other reasons for excluding these two works from our investigation. In *Bruckner,* there are difficulties with the symphonic scores Kurth used for analysis, making a discussion of his analyses problematic. I touch on the problems with *Bruckner* in chapters 1 and 9. *Musikpsychologie,* which deals with specialized issues and questions regarding the psychological dimensions of basic musical elements, as well as with the cognitive mechanisms for understanding those elements in musical contexts, lies outside the scope of a study which focuses mainly on Kurth's analytic procedures and their bases. For these reasons, *Bruckner* and *Musikpsychologie* will remain on the periphery of our discussion, and will be addressed primarily to corroborate ideas proposed in *Grundlagen* and *Romantische Harmonik.*

CHAPTER 1

Introduction

Ernst Kurth was born in Vienna, in 1886, at a crucial time in that city's history. By the late 1880s, Vienna, a longtime political, commercial, and cultural center, had undergone far-reaching changes which transformed it from an old-world seat of an absolutist monarchy into a pace-setting, metropolitan capital of a constitutional monarchy. Military defeat had ended the aristocratic rule of the Hapsburgs over Austria nearly forty years earlier, making possible the gradual ascent of the progressive liberals to power in the 1850s. Under their administration, the population of Vienna grew prodigiously from just under 500,000 in 1857 to 1,365,000 in 1890. By 1909 the city was under a socialist regime, and its population had swelled to over 2,000,000, a fourfold increase in a brief fifty-year period.

From 1890 to 1910, during Kurth's youth and teen-age years, Vienna was the center of activity for some of history's most revolutionary and influential figures, among them Sigmund Freud in psychology, Ernst Mach in physics and philosophy, Otto Wagner and Adolf Loos in architecture, Gustav Klimt in art, Hugo von Hoffmanstal in literature, and Gustav Mahler and Arnold Schoenberg in music. When Kurth entered the University of Vienna in 1904, the scandal over Klimt's controversial ceiling paintings *Philosophy* and *Medicine,* intended for the Great Hall of the university, was still in full swing.[1] Kurth spent his formative years in this extraordinary city at a truly unique time.

In addition to experiencing the dynamic cultural atmosphere of Vienna, Kurth witnessed the results of sweeping political and sociological changes, which had been under way for several years before his birth and continued throughout his adolescence. Beginning in the early 1880s, Austrian liberalism and the bourgeois society it had created began to crack under mounting pressures from lower working-class groups led by the anti-Semites Georg Ritter von Schönerer and Karl Lueger. Already weakened in the early 1870s by a faltering economy, the liberal regime gradually succumbed to the rising movements of Schönerer and Lueger. Watching its ideals and life style slipping away, bourgeois society turned inward, developing a preoccupation with the self and psychic life. The liberals' cultivation of art for art's sake and the resultant aestheticism, formerly a common haven from the hectic business world of the 1870s and 1880s, became in the 1890s an escape from the realities of their threatened life style and values. Kurth grew up in this waning culture of liberalism.[2]

Kurth's father, Lev (Leopold) Kohn (1834–1900), moved to Vienna from Prague in the late 1850s or early 1860s, during waves of immigration from the east into the Austro-Hungarian Empire when Austrian liberalism was on the rise. Under the lenient provision outlined in the Austro-Hungarian *Ausgleich* of 1867, Kohn built up a successful jewelry business during the so-called *Gründerzeit* of the mid-1860s and early 1870s. He was registered as a jeweler in 1867 at Spiegelgasse 10 in Vienna's first district, an address still surrounded by jewelry firms today. Kohn's business must have prospered, for Kurth, born on June 1, 1886, grew up in a desirable quarter of the city. The family lived at Piaristengasse 36, in Vienna's eighth district, not far from Parliament and other major government buildings, and within walking distance of the university.

Kurth rarely spoke about his early years, so that little is known of his life in Vienna. What information there is comes from various isolated statements recalled by those closest to Kurth in his adulthood, particularly his wife, Marie-Louise Kurth. Doctoral students who later worked with Kurth also remember fragments of information, making the record of his youth at best a composite of memories going back over fifty years.[3] Nevertheless, the reasonably clear picture that emerges is consistent with certain verifiable facts, with the cultural and sociological climate in Vienna at the turn of the century, and with Kurth's adult personality.

Kurth was the second of two children born to Lev Kohn's second wife, Ida Sorer (1853–1923), who had brought several daughters and at least one son with her into the marriage. Kurth, the youngest by far among the siblings, developed a close relationship only with his one full sister.

Kohn had been in the jewelry business for over twenty years by the time Kurth would have developed childhood memories. The father no doubt provided a comfortable home; in fact, the family was probably quite well off. Kohn was able to afford an annual three-month vacation at Bad Ischl, a resort southeast of Salzburg. Those vacations offered Kurth an escape from the tumult of city life, which he apparently disliked. It was during those vacations that Kurth developed a love for the outdoors and began his lifelong hobby of butterfly collecting.

In contrast to his siblings, Kurth showed musical talent and received cello and piano lessons during his primary and secondary schooling. He also regularly attended concerts and opera performances during his years at the Maximilliansgymnasium. These artistic pursuits and interests may have compensated for the lack of close familial relationships.

Later in life, Kurth spoke with great respect and a special fondness for his father. Kohn, in his sixties when Kurth was a youngster, must have seemed more like a grandfather than a father to Kurth. When Kohn died in 1900, Kurth, a sensitive adolescent of fourteen, must have felt a great loss. After Kohn's death, Kurth's thirty-three-year-old half brother, Albert, took over the business and assumed responsibility for the family.[4]

Kurth had a less than satisfying relationship with his mother. Her frustrating overprotectiveness inhibited the growth of Kurth's independence. Even during his high-school years, Kurth had to endure her constant worry and concern.

After graduating from the *Gymnasium,* Kurth enrolled at the University of Vienna in the fall of 1904. His major course of study, directed by Guido Adler, was musicology. Kurth took minors in philosophy, the required secondary field of concentration, and in history, which he chose as an elective field. During his university training, he studied piano privately with Robert Gund.

Kurth's enrollment schedules, filled out at the beginning of each semester, show that he studied a wide variety of subjects in his major and minor fields.[5] Musicology courses, offered chiefly by Adler, focus on the Classical and Romantic periods. Courses entitled "Explanation and Identification of Art Works" and "Exercises in the Music-Historical Institute" (Musikhistorisches Institut) probably refer to seminars in Baroque, Renaissance, and Medieval music.[6] Kurth also lists a few courses in harmony and counterpoint.

Kurth's studies in philosophy and other subjects are equally extensive. In each of seven semesters, he attended weekly three or four courses in fields outside of music, including lectures on particular philosophers as well as on schools and trends in philosophy from the Greek to the Romantic period. By the time Kurth graduated, he had accumulated fifty-five credit hours (*wöchentliche Stunden*) in philosophy, literature, and psychology, compared with forty-seven in musicology, so that in fact over half of his studies were in areas other than music.

Kurth's broad university curriculum strongly influenced his later music-theoretical outlook and scholarly activities, which are more characteristic of a polymathic humanist than of a technician. His approach to music theory and analysis attributes equal importance to intramusical and extramusical elements, such as philosophical influences, psychological dispositions, psycho-auditive effects, and dramatic criteria. This is especially true in his analyses of Wagner's vocal music, but it is also evident in those of Bach's instrumental works, music which, except in the writings of a few authors (Albert Schweitzer, Hermann Kretzschmar, Arnold Schering), generally received strictly "objective" treatment in the contemporary literature.

For a music student, Vienna was an ideal place to be in the first decade of the twentieth century for both music-academic training and music-cultural exposure. By 1904, Guido Adler was a celebrated and dominant figure in musicology, making the University of Vienna a prestigious center for musicological research. He had studied theory and composition with Anton Bruckner and had earned a Ph.D. degree in 1880 under Eduard Hanslick, whom Adler succeeded in 1898 as professor at the university. Adler co-founded the scholarly journal *Vierteljahresschrift für Musikwissenschaft* in 1884, and in 1885 he published therein a landmark essay outlining the principles of musicology as an academic discipline.[7] This essay helped to put musicology, a relatively new doctoral-level field of study at the time, on an equal footing with more traditional and recognized disciplines. Adler's efforts to define and systematize musicology as a *science,* and so to establish it as a bona fide academic discipline, surely inspired Kurth's later endeavors to initiate a formal musicology program at Bern, where, until 1920, music subjects were accessories or electives in other degree programs.

Besides being a center of academic activity, Vienna was the locale of groundbreaking events in music composition. During Kurth's years at the university, Arnold Schoenberg composed certain pivotal works that led to fundamental changes in his contemporaries' approach to composition as well as to the aesthetics of music. The years from 1905 to 1907 mark a turning point when Schoenberg began evolving new principles for creating musical structures.[8] Kurth no doubt was aware of these events, but being of a conservative mind and studying with a classical scholar, he had neither an interest in nor an appreciation for the avant-garde.[9]

Kurth did, though, have a deep appreciation for the music of Bruckner and Wagner. Guido Adler, who had studied with Bruckner and had co-founded the Academic Wagner Society (Akademisches Wagnerverein), surely influenced Kurth in this respect.[10] Nonacademic factors may also have helped to determine Kurth's musical tastes. During the concert seasons between 1904 and 1908, the Vienna Philharmonic orchestra and Vienna Concert Society programmed various Bruckner symphonies no less than fourteen times. From 1903 to 1906, Gustav Mahler, collaborating with the secessionist designer Alfred Roller, staged productions of *Tristan und Isolde* and other Wagner operas at the Court Opera in an unprecedented manner. Kurth, already a seasoned concert and opera enthusiast by the time he entered the university, no doubt took time from a busy academic schedule in order to experience Vienna's concert life.

In 1908, Kurth earned a Ph.D. degree with a thesis entitled "Der Stil der opera seria von Gluck bis zum Orfeo." While writing his thesis, Kurth served as librarian in Adler's Music-Historical Institute. Adler appointed Kurth to that post for the academic year 1907–8. Apparently, Adler had great confidence in Kurth's abilities, for he tried through various channels to help him initiate a career. As mentioned above, he introduced Kurth to Mahler, who suggested a career in conducting. Adler further assisted Kurth by publishing a revised version of his thesis in the first volume of the *Studien zur Musikwissenschaft,* a monograph series intended to supplement the *Denkmäler der Tonkunst in Oesterreich.*[11] Before leaving Vienna, Kurth arranged for a second publication, an article entitled "Critical Remarks on the Fifth Chapter of 'Ars cantus mensurabilis' of Franco of Cologne," probably a revised seminar paper.[12]

With degree in hand, Kurth left Vienna for Germany. He never returned to Austria. Following Mahler's advice, he tried conducting. For about two and a half years, from the fall of 1908 to February of 1911, Kurth worked as a rehearsal pianist (*Korrepetitor*) and conductor in Leipzig, Bamberg, and Barmen.[13] His stint as conductor ended unhappily for various reasons. The repertoire consisted of decidedly "lowbrow," primarily mediocre, singsong operettas, which Kurth disliked. Furthermore, Kurth lacked the self-assurance necessary for a conductor, since he had neither formal training nor practical experience to draw on. Finally, being an introvert by nature, he felt uncomfortable performing before audiences. An unsuccessful love affair with an actress brought Kurth's conducting career to an abrupt close.

Following a recuperative vacation at a resort in the Thuringer Forest, Kurth took a position teaching music in a private school at Wickersdorf, about seventy miles southwest of Leipzig, near Saalfeld, in what is now East Germany. His experiences at Wickersdorf, from February 1911 to March 1912, were crucial to his development as a teacher and thinker. There, he came in contact with the ideas of Gustav Wyneken, an outspoken pioneer in the educational reform sweeping over Germany around 1900, and with those of August Halm, a composer-theorist, aesthetician, and educator. The so-called Freie Schulgemeinde Wickersdorf was one of many experimental country boarding schools (*Landerziehungsheime*) founded during the first decade of our century, based on models established by the German educator Hermann Lietz.[14]

The moving force behind the school was its strong-minded leader, Wyneken, an aesthete who considered himself a prophet not only of educational reform but of a new culture. Indeed, Wyneken saw in Wickersdorf the "germ of a new collective culture."[15] Wickersdorf's entire program and atmosphere was geared toward developing fully the intellectual spirit (*Geist*) and instilling in its students the highest German cultural values and traditions. Together with Halm, Wyneken aimed at creating an ideal fusion of spiritual, social, and above all, cultural education in an uninhibited, "free" atmosphere. At the hub of this new collective culture stood music, "the purest expression" of the objective intellect. Wyneken thus considered music to be the primary educative medium.

When Kurth joined the faculty at Wickersdorf, the daily routine of music making and listening was firmly established. After morning exercises, the faculty and students assembled for a brief musical presentation, generally selected from the keyboard works of Bach. As part of the daily activities, students received instrumental instruction and participated in ensembles. After dinner, faculty and students gathered once again for a one-hour musical performance or, alternatively, for a lecture-demonstration dealing with some musical or aesthetic issue.[16] Halm, who led the evening discussions, demonstrated his ideas by playing the piano. He stimulated the imaginations of the youthful listeners by supplementing his performance with a running commentary on the music, relying chiefly on metaphor and imagery suited to the aural effect of the music. Halm assumed little or no technical knowledge from his audience and thus avoided specialized terminology and unfamiliar music-theoretical ideas. He focused instead on general musical and music-aesthetic concepts, explained in everyday language. Halm's lecture-demonstrations served as a model for Kurth's teaching style both at Wickersdorf and later at Bern.

For training in communal responsibility and cooperation (*Gemeinschaftsar-*

beiten) at Wickersdorf, Halm established a school orchestra and choir. He also maintained a good "reading quartet" for lecture-demonstrations. The repertoire consisted mainly of the works of Bach, Beethoven, and Bruckner, along with some Handel, Haydn, and Schubert. Mendelssohn, Schumann, Brahms, and other late Romantics were forbidden. Wyneken and, through his influence, the students, too, were proud of this one-sidedness.[17]

Under Halm, the focus in Wickersdorf was clearly on instrumental music, with the emphasis on "music," not on "instrumental." Playing an instrument was for Halm only a means to learn about and experience music, not an end in itself. He and Wyneken aimed at raising a generation of culturally mature, discriminating listeners with a solid music-aesthetic foundation, not instrumental athletes. Accordingly, performances were "rational," that is, musically competent but not necessarily technically flawless. Musical gatherings led by students were thus more like workshops than formal recitals.[18]

When Kurth took over Halm's post, he preserved the established musical activities and daily routine, except in one regard: the emphasis in ensemble training shifted from instrumental to vocal music. He formed a collegium musicum, which met weekly for two hours and sang primarily works of Schütz and Bach. Like Halm, Kurth was willing to forgo polished performances in evening programs, in favor of achieving musical comprehension and aesthetic awareness.[19] Kurth also preserved the weekly evening lecture-demonstrations, always minimizing technical vocabulary and ideas while maximizing the musical *experience*.[20]

The environment in Wickersdorf differed sharply from the one Kurth had known in Vienna, as well as from the concert-hall environment in Germany. Kurth's training as a research scholar did not prepare him for teaching music to primary- and secondary-school children. It was, however, precisely this experience at Wickersdorf that shaped his pedagogical approach to music and music theory. He borrowed and adapted to his own musical sensibilities Halm's lecture-demonstration style, which vivified music through imaginative interpretations. Further, he learned to do without the common music-theoretical systems of his day. In Wickersdorf, as well as later in Bern, Kurth's interpretive lectures went a long way toward "humanizing" an otherwise mechanical music theory. Furthermore, by relying on impressionistic explanatory devices as teaching aids and so encouraging the students to experience the music inwardly, Kurth's style of analysis took on the psychological tone that characterizes his published work.[21]

In February of 1912, after working at Wickersdorf for about one year, Kurth learned of a vacancy for a music instructor at the University of Bern, Switzerland. On February 27, he addressed a letter of inquiry to the Ministry of Education in Bern and requested a letter of reference from Guido Adler, who recommended Kurth highly.[22] One month later, now residing in Bern, Kurth formalized his candidacy with another letter to the Ministry of Education, this time referring to his nearly complete inaugural dissertation (*Habilitationsschrift*), an independently written monograph required of candidates seeking posts in European universities. In June

1912, Kurth submitted his inaugural dissertation, "The Methods of Theoretical Harmony and the Principles of Their Extension," to the humanities faculty for review.[23] After being recommended to the ministry by the faculty, Kurth was appointed lecturer (*Dozent*) in musicology and was invited in late July to give an inaugural lecture (*Antrittsvorlesung*).

Kurth's inaugural dissertation, published under the title *Die Voraussetzungen der theoretischen Harmonik und der tonalen Darstellungssysteme,* sets the tone and marks out the territory for all of his subsequent publications. In it, he articulates embryonically several of his basic theoretical attitudes and concepts. The very beginning of *Voraussetzungen* boldly questions the "scientificity" (*Wissenschaftlichkeit*) of music theory—implying the neo-Kantianism of Helmholtz and the positivism of Riemann—and asserts the inescapable, determinative role of psychology and intuition in any theory of music.

> More than in acoustical phenomena, the roots [of music theory] lie in psychological phenomena, whose explanations form precisely the fundamental ideas of theoretical systems. . . . As long as tone psychology provides no clearly decisive solution to the basic question [of the transition from acoustics to music] as a foundation for building all systems of music theory, it must be admitted at the outset that our entire music theory cannot do without a certain instinctive character alongside of an objective scientific one.[24]

From *Voraussetzungen* onward, Kurth's writings focus in one way or another primarily on psychological questions, be they questions of cognition and analysis or of the psychic activity involved in the compositional act.

Kurth's concern for psychological questions arises naturally from the anti-positivist current alluded to briefly in the preface to this volume.[25] Like other authors of the time, in musical and nonmusical fields, Kurth was rejecting the prevailing tendency to apply the then common methods of natural science to human behavior and activities, as if they were objects of the natural world rather than products of the mind. In this regard, Kurth follows the philosopher Wilhelm Dilthey, who taught that the investigatory methods of the natural sciences were inappropriate for the study of art, and thus distinguished between the natural sciences (*Naturwissenschaften*) and the "cultural sciences" (*Geisteswissenschaften*).

Kurth was not the only musician of the time to adopt a psychological approach to music theory. Reacting similarly to overrationalized theories, Hermann Kretzschmar and his student Arnold Schering attempted to revive the eighteenth-century doctrine of affections as the basis for what they called "hermeneutic" analysis. The goal of hermeneutic analysis was to reveal the mental content of music by interpreting descriptively its exterior forms (Kretzschmar), and so to establish a realtionship between musical processes and those of psychic life (Schering). Schering held that hermeneutic analysis would enable the listener to achieve maximum "psychic resonance" with the forces of tension and release, which, according to him, govern all music.[26]

Kurth's work is closer to August Halm's than to Kretzschmar's or Schering's. Both Halm and Kurth tend toward what we might call "experiential" analysis, but Kurth depends more on psychological explanations, while Halm does not. Halm did have a strong appreciation for the "drama of dynamics" in music. Indeed he declared that

> the dynamic activity [in music], the drama of dynamics, is quite sufficient for me; [it is] for me also the actual concrete part [of music].[27]

> Motion is the life of music.[28]

Halm's evaluation of dynamic processes as the essence of music finds its way into Kurth's discussion of melody in *Voraussetzungen*.

> The most essential aspect of melody [*Melodik*] is mobility. . . . The primary elements of melody are the tone and the sensation of motion.[29]

> As a most general and primal concept, melody represents a path of motion over which a tone, as an imaginary body, travels.[30]

But while Halm stops short of specifying the origin of such musical dynamism, Kurth points emphatically to psychic energies as the wellspring of dynamism.

> For the origin of melody, . . . a connection with dynamic phenomena arising from psychic activity comes into play, rather than an analogy to the rigid phenomena of harmonic materials.[31]

Both Halm and Kurth carry their ideas of dynamism into the technical details of their theories, and on this level there is quite a bit of agreement between them as well. For instance, Halm says that the major third contains "the driving force and germ of movement." Conceptually, it disturbs the ideal consonance of the triad.

> In reality, the repose of the triad is disturbed with the entrance of the third.[32]

Basing himself on Halm's view, Kurth takes the theory a step further and applies it to both major and minor triads. The major third embodies an inherent upward-striving energy, the minor third, by contrast, downward-striving energy. Kurth concludes that

> both forms of the triad are disturbances of absolute chordal repose.[33]

Both Halm and Kurth identify the basic dominant/tonic cadence as the origin of all harmonic phenomena and diversity. In the preface to *Harmonielehre,* Halm observes that

> all music is . . . nothing other than a greatly expanded variation of the primordial musical form, i.e., the cadence.[34]

Once again, Kurth modifies Halm's view slightly to include not only the cadential dominant/tonic progression, but also its energetic opposite, the tonic/dominant progression, which initiates harmonic motion.

> These two cadences [V–I and I–V] are . . . the primal forms of all harmonic activity.[35]

For both men, the upward-striving tendency of the leading tone engenders the falling-fifth progression.[36]

For all their similarities, Halm and Kurth differ in their basic theoretical orientations. Halm is a "harmonic" theorist, influenced by Riemann, whereas Kurth is a "melodic" theorist. Both men agree on the germinal energy of the major third, for example, but they disagree on the origin of that energy. Kurth traces it to the leading tone, conceived as a harmonically independent, melodic phenomenon arising from the scale. When linked to the fifth scale degree, the leading tone energizes the resultant major third and related major triad.[37] Halm explains leading-tone energy in precisely the opposite manner. For him, the leading tone first acquires its characteristic upward-striving tendency through its association with the major third, itself dependent on, and theoretically inseparable from, the "chord of Nature" (*Naturklang*).[38]

These contrasting interpretations of the leading tone yield differing interpretations of the primordial dominant/tonic cadence, discussed above. When Halm singles out the leading tone as "the undeniable expression of the natural connection of the [dominant/tonic] progression," he is assigning that progression a harmonic origin, since the leading tone has a harmonic origin.[39] Kurth's leading tone has the same harmonic ramifications but is melodic-genetic, making the cadence itself melodic-genetic as well.[40]

It is clear from the preceding paragraphs that, after Guido Adler, it was Halm that had the greatest influence on Kurth. Their informal relationship was a particularly fruitful one, even if some of Halm's ideas had the curious effect of leading Kurth to conclusions opposite to those of Halm. In any case, Halm's opinions helped Kurth to crystallize his own ideas as they are expressed in *Voraussetzungen*. This highly interesting and informative study, with its unique critical review and comparison of then popular theories and its original psychological interpretations of harmony and melody, is an important document in the history of music theory. It could not help but impress the humanities faculty at the University of Bern.

When Kurth joined the faculty at Bern, he received permission to lecture (*venia legendi*) in musicology, although no formal degree program in musicology existed at the time. Kurth's predecessor, Karl Hess-Ruetschi, had been a part-time faculty member who divided his time between serving locally as a church organist and teaching basic music theory courses in harmony and counterpoint at the university. Kurth's objective was to transform this essentially accessory music program into a full-fledged Ph.D. curriculum in musicology. One of his first tasks was to build up the library, which when he arrived consisted only of Riemann's *Musiklexikon*. Over the years, Kurth assembled an admirable research collection, including standard music histories of the time, monograph studies on theoretical topics, and numerous theory treatises from all periods, as well as writings in aesthetics and psychology. He also acquired the then available complete works of composers, for example, the first Bach-Gesellschaft edition. In the early years at Bern, Kurth himself oversaw and cataloged all library acquisitions.[41]

Following the custom of European universities, Kurth taught in both seminar and lecture-hall settings. Seminars, attended by a select group of students with the requisite background, were small in comparison to the lectures and were taught on an advanced level. Lectures were attended by the general university community, students and faculty alike, as well as by interested individuals from the Bern community. For a set fee, nonmatriculant music teachers, musical amateurs, and laymen, called *Auskultanten,* could attend open lectures.[42] Here, Kurth's engaging lecture-demonstration style, transplanted from Wickersdorf, proved valuable.

Wickersdorf provided yet another important model for Kurth at Bern. In the winter semester of 1913–14, Kurth's second year in Bern, he founded the university's first collegium musicum, devoted to the performance of masterpieces of early vocal literature. In a letter to the Ministry of Education requesting a small sum of money to defray operating costs of the collegium, Kurth stated that the objective of the repertory group was to give informal performances based on "a profound understanding of [the music's] characteristics," in order better to achieve an "enlightened grasp of music history."[43] Although Kurth did not originally intend the collegium to perform in public, he did eventually initiate a semiannual concert program.

The collegium scored a success on its first run and enjoyed sustained popularity throughout Kurth's career at the university. It attracted an average of fifty participants each semester, including matriculant and nonmatriculant members, and met once weekly. Although Kurth was not paid for leading the group during its first years, he did it eagerly because he loved the music they performed, which included works of Monteverdi, Schütz, Bach, Prätorius, Purcell, and Gabrieli. Furthermore, the pedagogical format of the rehearsals supplemented the work of Kurth's seminars and lectures by bringing the music to life for students participating in both academic studies and the collegium. In this way, Kurth was able to deepen the students' understanding of both the music itself and its historical significance.[44]

Little is known of Kurth's life over the next several years. Presumably, he worked to broaden and strengthen the musicology curriculum and to expand the library, since it was literally a one-man department, with Kurth as teacher, librarian, academic adviser, and administrator. The work must have been very taxing; Kurth's busy schedule finally took its toll during the spring of 1914, when he requested and received a leave of absence for one semester owing to nervous exhaustion.[45] He was apparently very successful as a university lecturer, for in January 1917 he was re-appointed to his post for three additional years.

Kurth was not only an effective pedagogue but also an industrious, articulate scholar and highly original thinker. The publication of *Grundlagen des linearen Kontrapunkts* in 1917 established his reputation throughout the German-speaking world as a uniquely imaginative interpreter of Bach's music.[46] With this volume, Kurth took a conscious and, for his image as a theorist, decisive step away from the standard treatment of Bach's polyphony. In *Grundlagen,* Kurth tried to liberate melodic and contrapuntal analysis from the routine conventions of his day. He rejected the prevalent nineteenth-century explanation of Bach's counterpoint as deriving primarily from a harmonic framework. Instead, he insisted on the primacy of melody in the belief that the essential characteristics of Bach's polyphony derived from linear autonomy and sculpted multilinear designs. Further, he minimized the importance of labeling familiar contrapuntal artifices such as inversion, augmentation, and stretto, and challenged well-worn formal notions such as exposition, episode, and sequence. Although Kurth did not deny the presence of such phenomena in Bach's music, he viewed them as surface byproducts of underlying, fundamental processes rather than as compositional objectives in themselves.

Kurth insisted that theorists up to his day had proceeded from what he called the "outer layers" of music, busying themselves with exploring technical externalities rather than concerning themselves with the real stuff of music. To his mind, "real" music, "real" in the Romantic-idealistic sense, remained unaccounted for. The moving forces beneath these outer layers lay deeper, according to Kurth, in the flow of the composer's psyche. There, he argued, lay the origin and essence of music, in the unconscious, pre-sonic realm. Music thus represents the psyche externalized. Here we encounter the two chief elements that inform Kurth's work, an idealist philosophical outlook and a concern with psychological criteria. The combination of these two elements determines to a large extent his basic analytic assumptions and objectives, and clearly distinguishes his work from that of other theorists active at the time.

Fundamental to idealist thought is the opposition of appearance and Reality. The German idealist philosopher Immanuel Kant expresses this opposition by distinguishing between the transitory "phenomenal" world of appearances and the unchanging "noumenal" world of ultimate Reality. In *Grundlagen,* as well as in later publications, Kurth translates this distinction between the phenomenal and noumenal worlds into the "outside" and "inside" of music. The inside of music constitutes the ultimate Reality, of which we hear only the last reverberations when it becomes phenomenal, that is, acoustical, music.

> The form in which we become aware of [psychic events] is nothing more than their final effect in perceivable impressions, their *surface.*

Music and its audible counterpart, the impressions of sound (the concrete outer layer), relate to one another as Will and its [phenomenal] expression, as force and its resultant effect, as abstract ideas and their concrete realization.[47]

Kurth's idealist outlook derives mainly from Arthur Schopenhauer (1788–1860), whose treatise *The World As Will and Idea* (1819) gained wide recognition and popularity in the second half of the nineteenth century.[48] Indeed, Kurth's reference to the Will in the quotation cited above is clearly indebted to Schopenhauer. The influence of Schopenhauer on Richard Wagner's thought and music is well known and documented.[49] Fifty years after the unsuccessful revolts of 1848 and faced once again with political turmoil, turn-of-the-century Viennese could no doubt appreciate Schopenhauer's thematic notion of a relentlessly striving world Will "objectifying" itself in man's individual will and leading continuously back and forth between fulfillment and frustration. Furthermore, in an age keenly attuned to art and aesthetic values, Schopenhauer's emphasis on the fine arts was a confirmation of personal sentiments.

Schopenhauer's ideas on the arts in general and on music in particular have been sufficiently discussed elsewhere, making a repetition of his opinions unnecessary.[50] Suffice it to say that Schopenhauer ranks music first among the arts, since it is an exact copy of the notorious dynamic Will, and that he evaluates melody as the most outstanding element in music. It directs the whole musical organism "in the unbroken significant connection of one thought from beginning to end, representing . . . the intellectual life and effort of man."[51] Kurth found fertile ground in Schopenhauer for theorizing about music, just as Wagner had for composing it. The idea of music being a full embodiment of the Will, coupled with that of melody representing the continuity of mental life, provided Kurth with a philosophical basis for a theory of music, and with an important psychological basis for that theory as well.

As pointed out above, Kurth stresses the importance of psychology to music theory as early as 1912 in *Voraussetzungen*. In *Grundlagen*, Kurth takes an even stronger psychological stance.

In order to establish a theory of music, it is not enough merely to "hear" and to inquire time and again about sonic phenomena, but rather [it is necessary] to plumb deeper into the primal processes within ourselves. All sonic activity lies on the uppermost surface of musical growth. The tremendous striving, the tensions of the infinitely rich interwoven play of forces which we call the musical substance in sound, . . . lies beneath the sounds . . . and springs out of the undercurrents of melodic growth, out of psychic energies and dynamic tensions. Musical events merely manifest themselves in tones, but they do not reside in them.[52]

Acoustical sounds, along with the technical-syntactical relationships they project, thus represent the motions of the psyche externalized. This pre-sonic psychic motion is for Kurth the essence of music, and we must look primarily to it and understand it if we want to understand its sonic manifestations: "The origin of music, in the psychological sense, is a will toward motions."[53]

The above phrase about the musical substance arising from the "undercurrents of melodic growth" makes clear that, in contrast to most of his contemporaries, as well as to most nineteenth-century theorists in general, Kurth considered music to be melodic-genetic rather than harmonic-genetic. His opinion here is both a reaction against the nineteenth-century overemphasis on harmony—that is, against the under-evaluation of melody and counterpoint—and an affirming response to a general revival of interest in melody from both musical and philosophical circles around 1900. The study of non-Western music began around this time and developed gradually into modern-day ethnomusicology. This ethnomusicological activity sought to revitalize the stylistic languor of late nineteenth-century European art music by infusing it with non-European elements.[54]

The proto-Gestalt psychologist Christian von Ehrenfels relied on melody to illustrate and confirm the existence of Gestalt qualities in aural perception and, by extension, in visual perception. Henri Bergson used melody to clarify his concept of intuited, nonspatial motion, which, to his mind, constituted the "uninterrupted humming of life's depths."[55] Finally, the psychologist-aesthetician Theodor Lipps called on melody to exemplify continuity in his idea of "line." Like Kurth, Lipps emphasized the dynamic qualities of melody. He described its essence as

> internal motion which, in a uniform flow, passes through the tones and even fills the rests; [it is] a motion which is our motion, but for us [it lies] in the tones and also in the empty spaces between them.[56]

Compare Lipps's description of melody with Kurth's.

> The fundamental content of melody is, in the psychological sense, not a succession of tones . . . but rather the element of *transition* between the tones and passing over the tones.[57]

Kurth believed that melody was the first and purest externalization of the germinal psychic motion. He expresses this clearly in the very first statement of *Grundlagen,* "Melody is motion," which is in fact the motto of the book. The word *is* deserves particular stress here; it is used in the sense of "is identical with." The *identity* between externalized psychic motion and melody is of utmost importance to Kurth, and it is crucial to our understanding of his ideas. When Kurth equates melody with motion, he does not mean melody in the ordinary sense of *tune,* but rather in the primal sense of *tonal stream.* We might therefore slightly emend Kurth's thematic motto to read, "Melody is where Will moves sounds."

The primary elements of melody are tone and the sensation of motion.

Melody, as a most general and primal concept, represents a path of motion over which a tone, as an imaginary body, travels.[58]

The German word *Melodik* perhaps expresses Kurth's notion of melody here better than *Melodie,* which commonly means "tune." Kurth generally uses the word *Melodik* or the expression "absolute melody" when he specifically means tonal stream.[59] Melodic "line," "linear" motion, and above all, "linear counterpoint" are all concepts that would have been better understood and less often misrepresented had they been taken in the sense of primitive tonal stream.[60]

The first seventy pages of *Grundlagen* characterize primitive melody and assert its genetic role in polyphonic music. Absolute melody traces the ebb and flow of psychic forces in an indivisible stream, called a "span" or "phase of motion" (*Bewegungszug, Bewegungsphase*). In the particular composition of melody, the individual tones possess meaning only as markers along the path of a *Bewegungszug.* The essence of melody, as explained above, resides in the transition between the tones, where the motion passes through and connects them.

Kurth's innovative approach to contrapuntal theory sent a wave of excitement as well as bewilderment throughout the world of music theory, where, Kurth held, theory had obscured rather than explained music. His psychological bent brought him immediate notoriety, both desirable and undesirable. In a review entitled "Kontrapunkt und Neuzeit," Paul Bekker hailed *Grundlagen* as "one of the most significant achievements in the domain of music-aesthetic research"; Hugo Riemann had less flattering things to say.[61] The difference between composers and academics in their approach to music at that time perhaps best characterizes this disagreement. Franz Schreker, for example, praised Kurth's work, while Jacques Handschin roundly criticized it.[62] The musicologist Ernst Bücken, however, credits Kurth with finally breaking through the prevailing rationalism that had dominated music theory since the eighteenth century.[63]

The widespread popularity of *Grundlagen* won Kurth the unanimous support of the university faculty in his successful bid for a raise in salary. The financial improvement could not have been more timely, for Kurth, who married in March of 1917, was experiencing considerable financial difficulties owing to the political turmoil of World War I.[64] His family inheritance became tied up in Austria, and the number of private students, who provided Kurth with needed supplemental income, diminished significantly as young men returned to their homelands for military duty. Even with the raise, which doubled Kurth's annual salary, he continued to seek private students, since a low-ranking lecturer did not earn an adequate living wage.

In 1920, Kurth petitioned the Ministry of Education to establish a Ph.D. program in musicology. In a letter to the ministry, Kurth pointed out that musicology was no longer an uncharted academic discipline and that many European universities had long since acknowledged it as a doctoral-level field of study. Many students attending his lectures and seminars, Kurth explained, were interested in devoting themselves to musicology. But with no bona fide degree to consummate their studies and enable them to compete for jobs, potentially qualified candidates for degrees in musicology were choosing other careers or leaving Bern to complete their music studies elsewhere. Kurth also petitioned for a promotion to the rank of *extraordinarius,* since a Ph.D. curriculum would need a ranking academician to head the new program.

After two months of bureaucratic maneuvering, the ministry approved Kurth's request to institute a Ph.D. program and also promoted him to *extraordinarius,* which of course entailed a sizable raise, this time quintupling his salary.[65] Kurth's continuing success as author and pedagogue no doubt influenced the ministerial authorities' decision. In his petition, Kurth enumerated six publications, as well as one in preparation, an edition of Bach's sonatas and suites for violin and cello solo.[66] Among the works listed, Kurth included his newest publication, *Die Romantische Harmonik und ihre Krise in Wagners "Tristan,"* a study that outlines the development of harmony from the Classical period through the Impressionistic period and relates this development to cultural-intellectual currents.[67] As explained above, Kurth took the first steps in *Grundlagen* toward a psychological interpretation of music and, consequently, toward a psycho-auditive style of analysis. In *Romantische Harmonik,* he expands and crystallizes many of the ideas proposed in the earlier study. As in *Grundlagen,* the very first sentence of *Romantische Harmonik* is thematic: "Harmonies are reflexes from the unconscious." On the first page, Kurth comes right to the point concerning the "inside" and "outside" of music: "What we generally designate as music is in reality only its fading away, better yet . . . its final quivering."[68] The idealist opposition of appearance and reality is also clearly stated: "[Psychic] energies pass over into sensually perceivable wonders of sound as does the Life-Will into worldly images."[69] Finally, melody, the primal kinesthetic element, lies at the root of the mysterious transformation of psychic energy into sound: "The *boundary* where the creative will and its reflection in sonorous *expression make contact* lies in the melodic line. . . . The melodic line is the first projection of the will onto 'matter.' "[70]

The inwardness of Romantic music, and the psychological quality of Wagner's music dramas in particular, provided Kurth in *Romantische Harmonik* with an ideal backdrop for his psycho-auditive, intuitionist style of analysis. He had learned from Schopenhauer and idealist aesthetics that fully comprehending an art work requires "losing" oneself in it, so that one "can no longer separate the perceiver from the perception."[71] For Kurth, understanding music meant vicariously experiencing the flow of psychic energies, which gave rise to the music in the first place. In *Romantische Harmonik,* Kurth declares that music theory, in order to be of any value, must assist listeners in this endeavor.

The central task of all music theory is to observe the *transformation* of certain *tension processes* into *sounds.* Only in this way is it possible to awaken, even in theoretical reflection, an empathy and internal sympathetic resonance with the animated *creative* forces, and so to restore once again the connection, long since torn asunder, between theory and art.[72]

In demanding "empathy and internal sympathetic resonance" with the germinal psychic forces as prerequisites for genuine theorizing about music, Kurth makes contact with important ideas expressed by Dilthey and Lipps, mentioned earlier. Dilthey held that in order to comprehend products of the mind, such as art works, we must know them *internally,* not *externally,* as scientists investigate their objects. Gaining such internal knowledge, called "understanding" (*Verständnis*) requires an act of "self-projection" (*Sichhineinversetzen*), that is, projecting one's own mind into that of another in order to achieve the sympathetic experience of "reliving" (*Nacherleben*) that person's creative activity.[73] Lipps, too, spoke of sympathetic experience, which he called "aesthetic empathy" (*ästhetisches Einfühlen*). He described such empathy as mental imitation through which we attain a "direct kinesthetic image" of perceived objects or of experienced events, emotions, and so on.[74]

Empathy is for Lipps the basis of aesthetic contemplation and true appreciation of art. In *Romantische Harmonik,* Kurth translates Dilthey's and Lipps's ideas into a manner of experiencing music. By means of empathy, we must "relive" the composer's creative-psychic stream and so gain an "understanding," in Dilthey's sense of these words, of the music.

The work of Dilthey (1833–1911), Lipps (1851–1914), and other thinkers of their generation grew out of a pan-European antipositivist sentiment, which from around 1890 onward brought a revival of interest in and appreciation for the unquantifiable irrational and spiritual dimensions of life and art, as well as for the unique powers of human intuition to make contact with and understand—or at least to describe adequately—these otherwise hidden dimensions. Other authors of an antipositivist persuasion include the scientist Wilhelm Ostwald (1853–1932), who proposed the antiatomic theory of "energetics" for explaining matter; the sociologist Max Weber (1864–1920), whose social theory rests on the ideas of a blind instinct and a manufactured, rationalized reality; the physician Sigmund Freud (1856–1939), who founded psychoanalysis; and the French philosopher Henri Bergson (1859–1914), who posited intuition as the one faculty capable of achieving "absolute" knowledge of the world, a knowledge gained from *within* its objects and events. To this list of thinkers we must add Ernst Kurth, whose ideas in *Grundlagen* and *Romantische Harmonik* take a sharp turn away from the then dominating positivistic theories of Hugo Riemann.

Like *Grundlagen, Romantische Harmonik* was an immediate success. Indeed, it was so successful that within three years two further editions appeared. Most commentators on the book have referred to the third, revised and enlarged edition ever since it appeared in 1923.[75] Alfred Lorenz, then emerging as an authority on Wagner's operas, praised Kurth for the "inestimable value" of his contribution to the "scholarly understanding of the development of music in the nineteenth century."[76] But in an age striving to liberate itself from nineteenth-century art forms and modes of thought, *Romantische Harmonik,* with its distinctive late Romantic language and psychological slant, also elicited criticism. The art historian and musician Hermann Wetzel (1879–1973) found its mystical tone and subjective psycho-auditive approach to analysis imprecise and too unorthodox. Occasionally lapsing into less than objective opinions himself, Wetzel accuses Kurth of remaining firmly "enmeshed in [Wagner's] fairy world" and of grossly overrating Anton Bruckner—"a man afflicted with intellectual insufficiency"—as a "master of form."[77]

Despite similar criticisms from some quarters of the musicological establishment, *Romantische Harmonik* maintained its popularity in German-speaking countries long after the audience of the 1920s, who knew its *Weltanschauung* firsthand, had faded. Indeed, one reason the book remained valuable was that it provided an authentic contemporary viewpoint from that bygone era. Another reason for its sustained popularity was its use in the classroom. Although Kurth did not intend *Romantische Harmonik* to be a textbook, it was adopted by many universities because, at the time, it was the only large-scale treatment of nineteenth- and early twentieth-century harmonic practices; moreover, it was fully documented with musical examples.

But it was not only because of Kurth's success as an author and a university professor that the Ministry of Education cooperated with Kurth. He had done much to elevate the musical appreciation and taste of the wider, nonacademic Bernese community through his voluntary work with the collegium musicum. In addition to university students and faculty, elementary-school teachers seeking certification as secondary-school teachers often attended Kurth's lectures and proseminars during their two- to three-year part-time studies at the university. Many of these teachers participated in *Lehrergesangvereine,* signing societies for teachers, and they took back to their groups the collegium repertoire of Schütz, Monteverdi, and Purcell, as well as creative ways to interpret and perform the music. For most, Kurth's collegium probably provided their first contact with Bruckner, whose music was not well known or understood in Bern before Kurth's arrival there.[78]

Between 1920 and 1923, Kurth widened his influence yet further in the Bern community, particularly through his dissemination of Bruckner's works. In these three years, he regularly scheduled informal lecture-demonstrations of Bruckner's music in the Bernese countryside. Using his well-developed, impromptu lecture style, Kurth introduced lay audiences to Bruckner and his symphonies, which he played in four-hand arrangements with Elsbeth Merz, daughter of the minister of education.[79] Rural teachers probably attended these evening talks and no doubt absorbed some of Kurth's ideas. Through his collegium musicum and countryside lectures, then, Kurth became a dominant figure in the musical life in and around Bern.

In 1922, his financial problems resolved and his position at the university secure, Kurth moved to Spiez, on Lake Thun, some twenty miles southeast of Bern. There, in the tranquil forested areas surrounding Spiez, Kurth found a haven much like the one he remembered from his annual childhood vacations in the Austrian Salzkammergut. After a short early-morning walk in the woods and an hour of playing from Bach's *Well-Tempered Clavier,* Kurth would set to work, reading and writing. In good weather he worked outdoors, where he had a panoramic view of the Bernese Alps. With butterfly net close at hand, Kurth sat before a plank supported by two tree stumps and wrote most of *Bruckner.*[80] In this idyllic setting, Kurth wrote effortlessly, creatively formulating his ideas in a prose style tinged with Romantic-religious mysticism befitting Bruckner and the spirit of his music.[81]

Kurth devotes over two hundred pages of *Bruckner,* or about a third of volume 1, to sketching the composer's biography and identifying the forces behind his creative process. He also takes care to put Bruckner in historical perspective and speculates on the reasons for Bruckner's lack of success as a composer. The remainder of volume 1 proposes and illustrates a concept of musical form unlike that in any previous study. Rather than relying on tonal or thematic criteria alone to delineate form, Kurth observes the totality of the musical organism in an effort to get beyond the already completed, static musical *shape* of a work, in order to get at the heart of musical form, the evolutionary, dynamic *shaping* of a work. He posits the notion of hierarchically organized "dynamic waves," which simultaneously engage all facets of the musical texture. By "dynamic" Kurth does not mean acoustical volume but rather pan-musical intensifications and de-intensifications effected by tonal, melodic, registral, rhythmic, metric, timbral, or textural means, or any of these in combination. Kurth's approach is keenly musicial, unencumbered by traditional theory. It is hinted at in other aesthetic writings of his time, but it remained for Kurth to expound thoroughly the notion of dynamic form and to demonstrate its analytical ramifications.[82]

Anyone who has read *Bruckner,* or anything about it, is aware of the problems of this monumental thirteen-hundred-page study. First, Kurth's formal analyses of the symphonies are based on heavily edited and, in certain cases, severely abbreviated orchestral scores published by Ferdinand Löwe.[83] Löwe, along with other students of Bruckner, urged the composer to make many cuts and reorchestrations. While Bruckner approved some changes, others were made by students entirely on their own initiative. Thus a confusing catalog of versions has come down to us today, some more authentic, some less so.[84] Kurth was aware of this problem but decided to publish his study anyway, in hopes of bringing the musical world to a better understanding both of Bruckner as a person and of his poorly understood music.[85] This he certainly did, in Bern and elsewhere. For example, after *Bruckner* appeared, Fritz Brun, conductor of the Bern symphony orchestra and an ardent Brahms admirer, began to program Bruckner's work more frequently.[86]

A second problem lies in the analytical style of *Bruckner.* Contemporary musicologists and theorists who are looking for scientific exactitude and, above all, reliable, documented scholarship, will no doubt find Kurth's historical and analytical approach somewhat unsystematic and personal. In *Bruckner,* as well as in *Romantische Harmonik,* Kurth relied primarily on intuition, and less on established methodology, for his analyses. A musicologist writing in 1920 about Romantic music, and about Bruckner in particular, had few universally recognized canons of scholarship on which to base his work. There simply was no detailed research showing the evolution of Romantic harmonic practices, nor was there any book explaining formal processes in Bruckner's mammoth symphonies.[87] But from one point of view, this lack of acknowledged precursors benefited Kurth. Depending on intuition and extensive listening experience, he relinquished the safety of familiar but often unenlightening analytical approaches and so originated one appropriate for Bruckner's music and revealing of its essential nature.

How exactly did Kurth's approach to analysis originate? It probably grew out of the extemporaneous lecture-demonstrations begun years earlier in Wickersdorf, and then became refined in university seminars, open lectures, the collegium, and in the talks given in rural areas around Bern. This is certainly true of *Bruckner* and, to some extent, of *Romantische Harmonik* as well. Kurth had to be an especially inventive and engaging speaker on Bruckner because this music was considered inaccessible even by most professional musicians of the time. As he had in Wickersdorf, Kurth avoided specialized terminology and where necessary invented his own terms in everyday language. Further, he emphasized the affective impact of musical events in order to enhance the musical experience during listening. Consequently, he was largely unconcerned about bibliographic references; he rarely cited sources, even in university classes. Experiencing the music *directly,* without overintellectualizing, was for Kurth as essential to musical comprehension as any variety of technical analysis.

Three major publications within eight years, each a pioneering effort in its field, brought Kurth considerable notoriety. By the end of the 1920s, his works were known throughout the central European musical community. The reaction to them was, as stated earlier, mixed. Musicology, still in its first decades of growth and consolidation, was not yet ready to deal open-mindedly with Kurth.[88] A fledgling discipline trying to gain acceptance usually adheres to approved lines of inquiry and recognized methodologies in order to secure its academic status and to ensure high scholastic standards. This poses no problems for those who remain within the accepted boundaries. Kurth, whose work straddled the fields of music theory, aesthetics, and psychology, necessarily breached those boundaries. The response to his psycho-auditive theories about music was thus predictably cool. Kurth, in rejecting the methods and accomplishments of conventional theory, invited criticism from the academic community, whose very premises he was questioning.

In the mid-1920s, this criticism forced Kurth into a defensive posture particularly ill-suited to his temperament. Despite his assertiveness and command over his students, he was a deeply insecure man, and even without published criticism, he tended to create imaginary enemies for himself. He was especially critical of Riemann's theories, which were the accepted norm, and "classical" musicologists were equally skeptical of Kurth's style of theory. Kurth reacted openly and strongly to what he considered unobjective criticism of his work, further aggravating the situation. His students were occasionally caught between their mentor and various of his "enemies."

Although certain musicological quarters were skeptical of Kurth's ideas, others were very interested in them. During the 1920s, four prestigious German universities tried to lure Kurth away from Bern to teach in or direct departments of music, or both. Although he refused each solicitation, Kurth used the opportunities to improve his professional and financial lot, as well as the quality of his own department at Bern. The first offer came in 1922 from the Hochschule für Musik in Berlin, headed by Franz Schreker. After some negotiations with the Bern Ministry of Education, Kurth finally declined the offer. For his loyalty to Bern, he received a sizable raise in salary.[89] Five years later, Kurth received an offer to direct the Hochschule at Frankfurt. The job carried a promotion to *ordinarius* and a raise that would have more than doubled Kurth's income. Just one day after refusing the bid, Kurth was promoted to *ordinarius* at Bern, and he received a raise matching the Frankfurt offer.

In 1928, opportunity knocked again, this time from Cologne. Kurth actually traveled to Cologne and met with the university administration, but he eventually decided against the move. Again, his loyalty to Bern did not go unrewarded. In addition to a personal financial settlement, Kurth bargained for and received a one-time grant of ten thousand francs for his seminar library, as well as a commitment for six thousand additional francs, to be paid over a three-year period, to enrich the library further. With this considerable sum of money, Kurth purchased two valuable collections of music books in 1929, one from an Italian rare-book dealer and another from Alfred Einstein's seminar library in Berlin.[90]

Between 1925 and 1930, Kurth was hard at work on yet another landmark publication, *Musikpsychologie,* a truly pioneering enterprise devoted to the foundations of cognition involved in hearing music and comprehending its processes.[91] Previous authors on aesthetics and psycho-acoustics had sought to illuminate these mental processes but had based their work more on philosophical or acoustical premises than on musical ones. Writers such as Carl Stumpf and, before him, Hermann von Helmholtz did incorporate musical experience and evidence into their research, but they did so in an extremely limited, rather unmusical and mechanical fashion. The work of these and other authors differed from Kurth's mode of inquiry and objectives. They had tried to explain the psychological effects of context-free, discrete tone events, such as melodic and harmonic intervals, and chords. In *Musikpsychologie,* Kurth aimed at interpreting their individual and interactive psychological meanings and effects within genuine musical contexts.[92]

Kurth had taken much time to reflect on psychological meanings of musical processes. Beginning with *Voraussetzungen* and continuing with *Grundlagen, Romantische Harmonik,* and *Bruckner,* Kurth had explored in turn the psychological foundations of counterpoint, harmony, and form. After dealing singly with these elements for over a decade, it was only natural that he should undertake a general study summarizing his findings. With ample funds to stock his seminar library, Kurth spent several years assembling, researching, and absorbing the available literature. Compared with his earlier publications, *Musikpsychologie* contains by far the most bibliographic references. Kurth gathered and coordinated numerous disparate lines of psychological inquiry, musical as well as nonmusical, interpreted and synthesized them in his own unique way, and so founded the field of music psychology.[93]

The reaction of the musical community to *Musikpsychologie* was favorable. Eloquently and sensitively written by a master of the "inner ear," the work appealed to musicians, whose similar musical sensibilities allowed them intuitively to feel but were unable to express what Kurth was describing. Alfred Lorenz, for example, writes, "Whoever has immersed himself in these energetic processes of music must without question become a follower of Kurth. Moreover, there are many new things with which one may unreservedly concur."[94]

At least one psychologist versed in music did not, however, concur unreservedly. Albert Wellek, who not only earned a Ph.D. in musicology under Guido Adler but studied psychology under Karl Büchler and Felix Krüger in Leipzig, while praising Kurth's effort to bridge two disciplines vigorously questioned certain of his basic premises. Clarifying the relationship between subject and object, for example, is fundamental to psychological discourse and theory. Wellek accuses Kurth of failing to distinguish sufficiently between them.[95] Kurth states plainly, and frequently, that music is a "mental activity" residing with the subject.[96] Instead of identifying and analyzing "objective" musical processes, Kurth tends to objectify his "subject," Wellek claims, by locating essential musical processes in the listener. The listener mentally re-creates the music by retracing the paths of psychic activity marked out by the composer. Subject and object become one, thus effectively suspending their relationships and leading to purely subjective analysis. Furthermore, Wellek points out that "mental activity" remains for Kurth idealized, that is, uniform in all subjects. This idealization denies the inevitable variability of subject/object relationships, which in music audition depend crucially on the experience, training, and cultural background of the subject. Wellek also criticizes Kurth for misusing standard psychological vocabulary and concepts, and for neglecting a few pivotal studies in psychology available in the late 1920s.[97]

In Kurth's defense, we must consider the following points. Regarding bibliographic references, Kurth was hardly neglectful. A casual glance through the 317 pages of *Musikpsychologie* will quickly and convincingly attest to Kurth's thoroughness. It is not surprising that a trained psychologist like Wellek should consider certain key sources indispensable to understanding psycho-auditive experience. But the flood of material being published in the then emerging field of psychology, representing diverse and conflicting viewpoints, precluded exhaustive research for a nonprofessional in that field. As for Kurth's misuse of psychological terminology and concepts, Kurth states explicitly that in order to reach nonmusicians and nonpsychologists alike he often departs from "strictly technical viewpoints."[98] Kurth tried to make his ideas accessible to audiences in both disciplines, including dilettantes, which naturally required certain adjustments and compromises in the technical languages of both music and psychology. Kurth's strategy may be fairly criticized; whether it was ill-advised or genial, it was in any case not a result of inadvertence or incompetence. Merging two fields burdened with sophisticated, discriminative terminologies demands, by the very nature of the task, redefinitions and adjustments in their respective conceptual and terminological apparatus.

The 1930s were successful years for Kurth at Bern. Much of the controversy over his work had subsided, the doctoral program ran well, regularly attracting qualified students, and Kurth's open music lectures were well attended. By this time, the program had produced several graduates, two of whom later achieved international recognition. Both Willi Schuh (Ph.D., 1927), the biographer of Richard Strauss, and Kurt von Fischer (Ph.D., 1938), editor of volumes BIV: 3–4 of *RISM* and author on numerous topics in various periods of music history, earned their degrees under Kurth.

Other graduates went on to teach with Kurth at Bern. For several years, Max Zulauf (Ph.D., 1924) and Lucie Balmer (Ph.D., 1933) assisted Kurth by teaching courses in instrumentation and Medieval music and notation, as well as various other seminars. With the help of his junior faculty, Kurth was able to offer students a balanced curriculum, including courses in the history of music from the Medieval period through the early twentieth century, and in some areas of applied music (harmony, counterpoint, figured bass).[99]

Kurth himself offered courses on a wide variety of topics. He lectured on the history of opera, nineteenth-century national schools, and Russian music up through Scriabin, as well as on the music of individual composers, such as Schütz, Bach, Beethoven, Schubert, Wagner, and Bruckner.[100] He rarely spoke on the music of Brahms or Mahler, whose symphonies he deemed ephemeral. For Kurth, the great masters of the late Romantic period were Bruckner, Wagner, and Hugo Wolf, although his esteem for these leading composers did not prevent him from enjoying the music of lesser masters, such as Peter Cornelius. As a teacher, Kurth stayed abreast of the latest classroom aids. During the 1930s, he assembled a large collection of phonograph records, which he used for lecture-demonstrations on symphonies and operas. The latest equipment enabled Kurth to bring the music to life more effectively than was possible with four-hand piano transcriptions. Besides the obvious advantages of recorded music, there was yet another reason, less happy, for using recordings.

Shortly after publishing *Musikpsychologie* in 1931, Kurth began to show signs of Parkinson's disease, which worsened steadily during the following fifteen years. A growing lack of control over his hands prevented him from playing and writing. There were to be no more books, though Kurth had planned and begun preliminary work on a history of opera, one of his favorite subjects. Lecturing became increasingly strenuous for him. Fortunately, with the help of his junior faculty the program continued uninterrupted. Kurth advised all dissertations and in fact lectured regularly until shortly before his death.

After teaching classes on July 2, 1946, Kurth suddenly collapsed. He was at first taken to the State and University Hospital in Bern, but at the suggestion of the attending physician he was later transferred to a special clinic for chronic nervous disorders in Münchenbuchsee, a few kilometers outside of Bern. In the aftermath of

Kurth's collapse, his wife suffered a heart attack. Elsbeth Merz, Kurth's former piano partner and close friend, cared for him during the next weeks. Although the diagnosis of his illness is uncertain, Kurth probably had encephalitis. Merz reports that during this period Kurth frequently hallucinated and lost touch with reality. On August 2, 1946, one month after the collapse, Kurth died at the age of sixty. A day later, the University of Bern sent throughout the community a special notice mourning the loss of a "most worthy colleague."

Kurth had built up such a strong following in his over thirty years at Bern, and had left such an indelible stamp on the study of musicology there, that finding a suitable replacement proved difficult. In the summer of 1947, the search committee, assisted by various outside advisers, still had not chosen a successor. The field had been narrowed down to three candidates, including Kurt von Fischer. Professor Wilibald Gurlitt and Kurth's student Lucie Balmer held the musicology department together during the next few years until finally, in 1949, Arnold Geering became Kurth's successor as *ordinarius*.

Now that we have completed our biographical study of Kurth, and have identified some important sources of his intellectual and music-theoretical attitudes, we can better approach his ideas and appreciate their significance for the history of music theory. The reader should bear in mind that the foregoing introduction summarily reviews the main ideological currents out of which Kurth's work arose and is by no means exhaustive. In fact, I have intentionally postponed mentioning certain influential ideas in favor of discussing them where they apply directly to specific music-theoretical notions or analytical practices. Throughout the following chapters, then, we will add to the historical context. In the final chapter of the book, we will examine the effect of Kurth's work on his contemporaries and on succeeding generations of music theorists.

Notes

1. The paintings, commissioned in 1894 and shown in 1900, 1901, and 1903, were withdrawn by Klimt in 1905.
2. Sarah Gainham's book, *The Hapsburg Twilight* (New York: Atheneum, 1979), gives an interesting view of Vienna at the turn of the twentieth century.
3. All of the biographical information in the following paragraphs comes from letters exchanged with Frau Marie-Louise Kurth, as well as with students of Kurth, between 1978 and 1981. Several articles written at Kurth's death also provided certain biographical facts and personal insights. These include published essays by Kurt von Fischer, "In Memoriam Ernst Kurth," *Der Musik-Almanach*, ed. Viktor Schwarz (Munich: K. Desch, 1948), 228–52; Walter Kreidler, "Ernst Kurth † am 2. April [*sic*] 1946," *Die Musikforschung* 2 (1949): 9–14; K. von Fischer, "Ernst Kurth †," *Schweizerische Musikzeitung* 86.10 (1946): 373–74. Most valuable of all, however, were personal interviews, carried out in 1981, with Frau Kurth and with most of Kurth's surviving students, Kurt von Fischer, Willi Schuh, Fritz de Quervain, Paul Dickemann, Georg Bieri, Rudolf von Tobel,

Max Favre, and Elsbeth Merz. Information provided by the Bern and Vienna National Archives was also helpful in piecing together many biographical details.

4. According to Kurth's birth record, listed in the registry of the Vienna Israelite Community, protocol number 2940, the family name Kohn was changed to Kurth on March 31, 1901, about one year after Lev Kohn's death on February 10, 1900.

5. The Vienna National Archive provided photocopies of Kurth's enrollment schedules, which list course titles and professors.

6. Later, as a professor at Bern, Kurth taught similarly named courses, such as "Exercises in Musicology: Stylistic Explanation of Early Art Works," which was offered in the winter term, 1920–21.

7. Guido Adler, "Umfang, Methode und Ziel der Musikwissenchaft," *Vierteljahresschrift für Musikwissenschaft* 1 (1885): 5–20.

8. Allen Forte gives a summary of Schoenberg's compositional development through analysis of pivotal works around 1905 in "Schoenberg's Creative Evolution: The Path to Atonality," *Musical Quarterly* 64.2 (1978): 133–76.

9. It would be difficult to prove that Kurth heard Schoenberg's works of this period, but the activity of two short-lived Viennese societies for the performance of new music, the Ansorge Verein (1904) and the Vereinigung Schaffender Tonkünstler (1904–5), both founded by Schoenberg and Alexander Zemlinsky, offered ample opportunities for Kurth to hear Schoenberg's music of that period. Mahler, who took a personal interest in Kurth after being introduced to him by Guido Adler, was honorary president of the Vereinigung.

10. In 1904, when Kurth entered the University of Vienna, Adler had just published a series of lectures, given in 1875–76, entitled *Wagner* (Leipzig: Breitkopf und Härtel, 1904).

11. Ernst Kurth, "Die Jugendopern Glucks bis zum Orfeo," *Studien zur Musikwissenschaft* 1 (1913): 193–227.

12. Ernst Kurth, "Kritische Bemerkungen zum V. Kapitel der 'ars cantus mensurabilis' des Franko von Köln," *Kirchenmusikalisches Jahrbuch* 21 (1908): 39–47.

13. Kurth tells of his activities in Germany between 1908 and 1911 in his handwritten curriculum vitae, now contained in his file at the Bern State Archives.

14. These experimental country boarding schools arose in a wave of educational reform known today as the "New Education." The movement began in England with Dr. Cecil Reddie's school at Abbotsholme, Derbyshire, in 1889, and spread to Germany, through Hermann Lietz, and to other European countries. Wyneken taught at Lietz's first *Landerziehungsheime*, at Haubinda, before founding the school at Wickersdorf. William Boyd and Wyatt Rawson sketch the history and objectives of this movement in *The Story of the New Education* (London: Heinemann, 1965). They discuss the Wickersdorf school on p. 10.

15. August Halm, *Form und Sinn der Musik*, ed. Siegfried Schmalzriedt (Wiesbaden: Breitkopf und Härtel, 1978), 50: "Keimzelle einer neuen Gesamtkultur." Schmalzriedt cites this quotation from an article by H. Claussen entitled "Gustav Wyneken," in *Lexikon der Pädagogik Neue Ausgabe*, 4 vols. (Frieburg: Herder, 1971).

16. Halm, *Form und Sinn*, 52.

17. Ibid., 53.

18. Ibid., 53–54, 235.

19. Ernst Kurth, "Die Schulmusik und ihre Reform," *Schweizerische Musikzeitung* 70.9 (1930): 342, 344; originally published in *Schulpraxis* 19 (1930). Kurth left the orchestral conducting to Martin Luserke, Wyneken's successor, perhaps because Kurth had had his fill of conducting before arriving at Wickersdorf.

20. Kurth, "Schulmusik," 346: "The performance itself is only one part; supported by the accompanying discussion, it serves the musical experience." Ibid., 343: "The elucidation of music is actually one of the most essential means of intellectual training." Kurth explains that while only one weekly workshop performance was officially scheduled, performances took place on two or even three evenings a week.

21. In relying chiefly on interpretive, narrative analyses, Halm and Kurth seem to be following the lead of Hermann Kretzschmar, who in 1902 and 1905 published essays recommending and illustrating a style of "hermeneutic" analysis based on the eighteenth-century doctrine of affections. See the references to Kretzschmar later in chapter 1, and at the beginning of chapter 10.

22. Adler's letter, dated February 29, 1912, speaks of Kurth as an "industrious, conscientious" worker and a "refined, ambitious man" ("emsig, gewissenhaft . . . vornehmer, strebender Mann"). Both Kurth's and Adler's letters are in Kurth's file at the Bern State Archives.

23. "Die theoretischen Darstellungsmethoden der Harmonik und die Prinzipe ihrer Erweiterung" (letter to the minister of education, June 20, 1912).

24. Ernst Kurth, *Die Voraussetzungen der theoretischen Harmonik und der tonalen Darstellungssysteme* (The premises of the theory of harmony and of tonal systems) (Bern: Drechsel, 1913), 6:

> mehr noch als in akustischen liegen die Wurzeln der Musiktheorie in psychologischen Erscheinungen, deren Erklärungsversuche überhaupt die Grundideen der theoretischen Systeme bilden. . . . solange die Tonpsychologie keine eindeutig bestimmte Lösung jener Grundfrage als Grundlage für den Bau aller Systeme der Musiktheorie an die Hand gibt, muss von vorneherein zugestanden werden, dass unsere gesamte Musiktheorie neben einem objektiv wissenschaftlichen auch eines gewissen instinktiven Charakters nicht entbehren kann.

For a thorough discussion of the contents and importance of *Voraussetzungen,* as well as of its relationship to Kurth's later writings, see my Master's thesis, "Ernst Kurth's *The Requirements for a Theory of Harmony:* An Annotated Translation with an Introductory Essay" (University of Hartford, Hartt School of Music, 1979).

25. H. Stuart Hughes discusses the changing intellectual trends around the turn of the twentieth century in his book *Consciousness and Society: The Reorientation of European Social Thought, 1890–1930* (New York: Octagon Books, 1976), 33–41, 44–45, 63–66, 105–60 (chapter 4, "The Recovery of the Unconscious").

26. Hermann Kretzschmar, "Anregungen zur Förderung musikalischer Hermeneutik," *Jahrbuch der Musikbibliothek Peters* 2 (1902): 45–66; idem, "Neue Anregungen zur Förderung der musikalischen Hermeneutik," *Jahrbuch der Musikbibliothek Peters* 5 (1905): 75–86; idem, "Allgemeines und Besonderes zur Affektenlehre," *Jahrbuch der Musikbibliothek Peters* 18 (1911): 63–78; Arnold Schering, "Zur Grundlegung der musikalsichen Hermeneutik," *Zeitschrift für Aesthetik und allgemeine Kunstwissenschaft* 9 (1914): 168–75; idem, *Musikalische Bildung und Erziehung zum musikalischen Hören* (Leipzig: Quelle und Meyer, 1911).

27. Halm, *Form und Sinn,* 26. Halm makes this statement in his book *Einführung in die Musik* (Berlin: Deutsche Buchgemeinschaft, 1926), 139.

28. August Halm, *Die Symphonie Anton Bruckners* (Munich: G. Müller, 1914), 37.

29. Kurth, *Voraussetzungen,* 60.

30. Ibid., 62.

31. Ibid.

32. Halm, *Harmonielehre* (Berlin: Göschen, 1905), 64: "In Wirklichkeit ist die Ruhe des Dreiklangs schon mit dem Eintritt der Terz gestört."

33. Kurth, *Voraussetzungen,* 122: "Beide Dreiklangsformen sind Störungen der absoluten Akkordruhe."

34. Halm, *Harmonielehre,* 5: "Die ganze Musik ist nichts . . . anderes als eine ungeheuer erweiterte Variation der musikalischen Urform, d.i. der Kadenz."

35. Ernst Kurth, *Die Romantische Harmonik und ihre Krise in Wagners Tristan,* 3d ed. (1923; reprint, Hildesheim: Olms, 1975), 111: "Diese beiden Kadenzschritte sind . . . Ursprungsformen alles harmonischen Geschehens."

36. Halm, *Harmonielehre,* 27; Kurth, *Voraussetzungen,* 120–21.

37. Kurth, *Voraussetzungen,* 70–71.

38. Halm, *Harmonielehre,* 6–7.

39. Ibid., 26–27: "der unverkennbare Ausdruck für die natürliche Verbindung der . . . Akkordfolge."

40. Kurth, *Voraussetzungen,* 71.

41. Kurth's experience in Adler's library of the Music-Historical Institute no doubt prepared him well for building his own library at Bern. All of the books acquired and catalogued by Kurth are still in the Bern University Seminar Library, including many books donated by Frau Kurth to the library from Kurth's private collection.

42. High attendance was important, because Kurth was still a low-ranking lecturer and his salary depended partly on the number of attendants.

43. Letter from Kurth to the director of education, dated December 15, 1913: "ein tiefergehendes Verständnis ihrer Eigenschaften . . . wissenschaftliche Erfassung der Musikgeschichte."

44. In 1930, after nearly twenty years of directing the collegium, Kurth declared that "the entire reform of music [education] in the school should be based on the idea of the collegium musicum" ("Schulmusik," 345).

45. Letter to the director of education, dated April 17, 1914, written from Wickersdorf.

46. Ernst Kurth, *Grundlagen des linearen Kontrapunkts: Bachs melodische Polyphonie* (Bern: Drechsel, 1917). Later editions include Berlin: Hesse, 1922, 1927. Two reprints (Bern: Krompholz, 1946, 1956) attest to the sustained interest in *Grundlagen.*

47. Kurth, *Grundlagen,* 4: "Die Form in der wir ihrer bewusst werden, ist nichts als ihre letzte Auswirkung in bereits wahrnehmbaren Eindrücken, ihre *Oberschicht.*" Ibid., 6: "Musik und das Gehörsmässige an ihr, die Klangeindrücke (die konkrete Oberschicht), verhalten sich wie Wille und seine Äusserung, wie Kraft und Wirkungsbild, Abstraktes und seine Konkretisierung."

48. Arthur Schopenhauer, *The World As Will and Idea,* 3 vols., trans. R. B. Haldane and J. Kemp (London: Routledge and Kegan Paul, 1883; orig. Dresden, 1819). Fredrick Copelston provides a clear, well-organized exposition of Schopenhauer's *World as Will* in *Arthur Schopenhauer, Philosopher of Pessimism* (London: Search Press, 1946).

49. Jack Stein, *Richard Wagner and the Synthesis of the Arts* (Detroit: Wayne State University Press, 1960); idem, "The Influence of Schopenhauer on Wagner's Concept of the *Gesamtkunstwerk,*" *Germanic Review* 22 (1947): 92–105.

50. Dunton Green and Victor Bennet summarize and evaluate Schopenhauer's views on music in, respectively, "Schopenhauer and Music," *The Musical Quarterly* 16 (1930): 199–206; and "Referring to Schopenhauer," *Music Review* 11 (1950): 195–200. For Schopenhauer's opinion on Wagner, see Henry T. Finck, *Wagner and His Works,* vol. 2 (New York: Scribner, 1893), 251–52.

51. Schopenhauer, *World as Will,* 334.

52. Kurth, *Grundlagen,* 7:

> Um die Musiktheorie zu begründen, gilt es nicht bloss zu "hören" und immer wieder nach den Erscheinungen des Erklingenden zu fragen, sondern tiefer zu den Urvorgängen in uns selbst hinabzutauchen. Alles Klangspiel liegt bereits an der letzten Oberschicht der Musikwerdung; das gewaltige Drängen, die Spannungen eines unendlich reich durchwirkten Kräftespiels, das was wir als das Musikalische im Klang bezeichnen . . . liegt unterhalb der Klänge . . . und erquillt aus den Unterströmungen des melodischen Werdens, den psychischen Energien von Bewegungsspannungen. Das musikalische Geschehen äussert sich nur in Tönen, aber es beruht nicht in ihnen.

53. Ibid., 14: "Ursprung der Musik ist im psychischen Sinne ein Wille zu Bewegungen."

54. One of the earliest ethnomusicological studies was done by Carl Stumpf, "Lieder der Bellakula Indianer," *Vierteljahresschrift für Musikwissenschaft* 2 (1886): 405–26. Other studies of melody in the early twentieth century include Max Meyer, "Elements of the Psychological Theory of Melody," *Psychological Review* 7 (1900): 241–73; Theodor Lipps, "Zur Theorie der Melodie," *Zeitschrift für Psychologie* 29 (1902): 225–63; Fritz Wienmann, "Zur Struktur der Melodie," *Zeitschrift für Psychologie* 35 (1904): 340–79, 401–53; and Stumpf's student Erich von Hornbostel, "Studien über das Tonsystem und die Musik der Japaner," *Sammelbände der Internationalen Musikgesellschaft* 4 (1902–3): 302–60. Robert Lach, a student of Guido Adler, wrote a landmark dissertation in 1902 on the development of ornamental melo-poetics (Prague, 1902), published as

Studien zur Entwicklungsgeschichte der ornamentalen Melopoäia (Leipzig: Kahnt Nachfolger, 1913). Georg Capellen wrote two essays aimed at introducing exotic elements into European music: "Exotische Rhythmik, Melodik und Tonalität als Wegweiser zu einer neuen Kunstentwicklung," *Die Musik* 6.3 (1906–7): 216–17; and "Vierteltöne als wesentliche Tonleiterstufen," *Die Musik* 42.11 (1911–12): 334–41.

55. Christian von Ehrenfels, "Über Gestaltqualitäten," *Vierteljahresschrift für wissenschaftliche Philosophie* 14 (1890): 258–59 (Kurth cites Ehrenfels several times in *Musikpsychologie* [Berlin: Hesse, 1931; 2d ed., Bern: Krompholz, 1947], 26, 54, 96, 120). Henri Bergson, "The Perception of Change," in his *The Creative Mind,* trans. M. L. Andison (New York: Philosophical Library, 1946), 174, 176. "The Perception of Change" is an essay based on two lectures given by Bergson in 1911 at Oxford University.

56. Theodor Lipps, *Ästhetik,* vol. 1 (Leipzig: Voss, 1903), 411: "innere Bewegung, die in einheitlichem Fluss durch die Töne hindurchgeht und auch die Pausen erfüllt, eine Bewegung, die unsere Bewegung ist, aber für uns in den Tönen und auch in den leeren Zwischenräumen zwischen ihnen liegt."

57. Kurth, *Grundlagen,* 2. A statement in his *Romantische Harmonik* (p. 7) comes still closer to Lipps's characterization of melody: "The actual and more significant content of melody by far, from the simple melodic line on, is *the inaudible part* of it, or, to describe it more graphically, . . . the undrawn line which is only indicated by its notes; the force flows over the empty spaces between the notes and over the notes themselves" ("schon von der einfachen melodischen Linie an der eigentliche und bedeutungsvollere Inhalt [ist] das Unhörbare an ihr, oder, um es äusserlicher zu kennzeichnen, . . . die nicht gezogene Linie, die sich nur in einzelnen Noten andeutet; über die leeren Räume zwischen den Noten und über diese hinweg flutet die Kraft").

58. Kurth, *Voraussetzungen,* 60: "Die primären Elemente der Melodik sind der Ton und die Bewegungsempfindung." Ibid., 62: "Die Melodie als allgemeinster und ursprünglichster Begriff stellt eine Bewegungsstrecke dar, die der Ton, als Körper vorgestellt, durchläuft." In a footnote to this last statement, Kurth explains that the word "tone" here means "that which sounds" (*das Tönende*), and not fixed pitches in the conventional sense of "tone."

59. Kurth, *Voraussetzungen,* 60–62; idem, *Grundlagen,* 2–22 passim; idem, *Romantische Harmonik,* 4–5.

60. Schoenberg, for instance, after admitting that he had not read *Grundlagen,* criticized and dismissed as self-contradictory the notion of linear counterpoint, based on his own ill-informed conception of it (*Style and Idea,* ed. Leonard Stein, trans. Leo Black [New York: St. Martins Press, 1975], 289–97).

61. Paul Bekker, "Kontrapunkt und Neuzeit," *Frankfurter Zeitung* 62 (March 27, 1918): 1. Hugo Riemann, "Die Phrasierung im Lichte einer Lehre von den Tonvorstellungen," *Zeitschrift für Musikwissenschaft* 1.1 (1918): 26–39. Riemann attacks Kurth's unorthodox interpretation of Baroque phrase structure, which generally conflicts with Riemann's own (rather rigid) interpretations of rhythm, meter, etc. In a response to Riemann's critique, Kurth points out several misunderstandings and outright misquotations in Riemann's argument. Kurth published his remarks in "Zur Stilistik und Theorie des Kontrapunkts," *Zeitschrift für Musikwissenschaft* 1.3 (1918): 176–82. These two articles make up an interesting debate on fundamental issues of phrase structure and rhythm as understood by two influential figures in the history of music theory.

62. Letters from Schreker to Kurth, dated August 27 and September 12, 1921. Jacques Handschin, "De différentes conceptions de Bach," *Schweizerisches Jahrbuch für Musikwissenschaft* 4 (1929): 7–35.

63. Ernst Bücken, "Kurth als Musiktheoretiker," *Melos* 4 (1924–25): 358.

64. The following paragraphs are based on information found in documents contained in Kurth's file at the Bern State Archives.

65. Around 1920, Kurth was still experiencing financial difficulties. He had lost the family inheritance because of the drastic devaluation of Austrian currency in the years following World War I. The

minister of education, the father of Kurth's partner in playing four-hand piano scores for lectures, supported Kurth's bid for the promotion and doctoral program.

66. Ernst Kurth, *J. S. Bachs sechs Sonaten und sechs Suiten für Violine und Violoncello* (Munich: Drei Masken Verlag, 1921). Kurth also listed the article on Franco (see n. 12), *Voraussetzungen,* his dissertation, *Grundlagen,* and an article extracted from *Grundlagen* entitled "Zur Motivbildung Bachs: Ein Beitrag zur Stilpsychologie," *Bach-Jahrbuch* 1917): 80–136. The last publication is discussed in chapter 3.

67. Kurth, *Romantische Harmonik* (Bern: Haupt, 1920); see n. 35 above. A preview of *Romantische Harmonik* appeared in *Anbruch* 2.16–17 (1920): 539–43, 568–71, under the title "Zum Wesen der Harmonik."

68. Kurth, *Romantische Harmonik,* 1: "Was man gemeinhin als Musik bezeichnet, ist in Wirklichkeit nur ihr Ausklingen, noch besser . . . ihr Auszittern."

69. Ibid.: "Die Energien gehen in die sinnlich wahrnehmbaren Klangwunder über wie der Lebenswille ins Weltbild."

70. Ibid., 5: "Die *Grenze,* wo *Gestaltungswille* und seine Spiegelung im klangsinnlichen *Ausdruck sich berühren* . . . liegt in der melodischen Linie. Die melodische Linie ist die erste Projektion des Willens auf 'Materie.'"

71. Schopenhauer, *World as Will,* 231.

72. Kurth, *Romantische Harmonik,* 2: "Die *Umsetzung* gewisser *Spannungsvorgänge* in *Klänge* zu beobachten ist die Kernaufgabe aller Musiktheorie. So allein ist es möglich, ein Einfühlen und Mitschwingen der lebendigen *schöpferischen* Kräfte auch im theoretischen Betrachten zu erwecken, und die längst losgerissene Verbindung zwischen Theorie und Kunst wieder herzustellen."

73. Herbert A. Hodges, *Wilhelm Dilthey: An Introduction* (New York: Oxford University Press, 1944), 14–15. See also idem, *The Philosophy of Wilhelm Dilthey* (London: Routledge and Kegan Paul, 1952; reprint, Westport, Conn.: Greenwood Press, 1974), 116–18. For Dilthey, true understanding comes only from a "rediscovery of the I in the Thou" ("ein Widerfinden des Ich im Du"; Wilhelm Dilthey, *Gesammelte Schriften,* vol. 7 [Leipzig: Teubner, 1927], 191).

74. Lipps, *Ästhetik,* 1:120, 125–26: "die Innenseite der Nachahmung."

75. Kurth, *Romantische Harmonik,* 2d ed., rev. enl. (Berlin: Hesse, 1922); 3d ed. (Berlin: Hesse, 1923); reprint, 3d ed. (Hildesheim: Olms, 1975). All references in this study are to the third edition.

76. Alfred Lorenz, "Ernst Kurth: *Romantische Harmonik,*" *Die Musik* 16.4 (1924): 262.

77. Hermann Wetzel, "Zur Stilforschung in der Musik," *Die Musik* 16.4 (1924): 269. Kurth calls Bruckner a "genius of form" ("Genie der Form") in *Romantische Harmonik,* 331.

78. Information on the influence of Kurth's collegium comes from taped interviews held with two of Kurth's students, Fritz de Quervain and Georg Bieri.

79. Elsbeth Merz, who met Kurth in 1920 when she joined the collegium, provided this information. She assisted him in his university lectures and seminars, as well as in his countryside lectures, until 1923, when she left Bern.

80. Kurth, *Bruckner,* 2 vols. (Berlin: Hesse, 1925; rep. Hildesheim: Olms, 1971). *Bruckner* was previewed in *Die Musik* 16.12 (1924): 861–69; in an article entitled "Bruckners Fernstand," in *Anbruch* 6 (1924): 351–57; and in *Melos* 4 (1924–25): 364–70.

81. Interview with Frau Kurth and her son, Hans Kurth (b. 1920). Much of the material for *Bruckner* probably grew out of lecture notes used for university presentations, as well as for the informal countryside talks.

82. Karl Grunsky, *Musikästhetik* (Berlin-Leipzig: Göschen, 1907); August Halm, *Die Symphonie Anton Bruckners* (see n. 28). Birgitte Moyer gives a short summary and evaluation of Kurth's ideas on form in "Concepts of Musical Form in the Nineteenth Century" (Ph.D. dissertation, Stanford University, 1969), 219–21.

83. Ferdinand Löwe was a student of Bruckner and co-editor of some of the four-hand piano arrangements of Bruckner's symphonies that Kurth used for study.

84. Hans Hubert Schönzeler discusses the versions of Bruckner's symphonies in *Bruckner* (New York: Grossman, 1970), 170–78, as well as Kurth's analyses (p. 179).

85. Kurth, *Bruckner,* 2:603 n.

86. Kurth not only disliked Brun but mistrusted his musical judgment and taste. Indeed, Kurth disliked public concerts and concert life altogether. He rarely attended concerts, preferring to hear music mentally and to play it at the piano rather than subject himself to crowds. This aversion may have come from Kurth's unsuccessful years as a conductor. Once, a well-known guest conductor leading the Bern orchestra invited Kurth to a performance of Bruckner's Seventh Symphony. Kurth refused to attend both a final rehearsal and the evening concert, even though he was assured no one would be present at the rehearsal.

87. Heinrich Rietsch's *Die Tonkunst in der zweiten Hälfte des 19. Jahrhunderts* does describe the development of harmony in the late nineteenth century, but it is too brief and falls far short of Kurth's accomplishment. In *Bruckner,* 2:1313–19, Kurth provides an annotated bibliography of works dealing with Bruckner, among them a few analytical works that Kurth found useful: Oskar Lang, *Anton Bruckner* (Vienna: Österreichischer Schulbuchhandlung, 1924); Halm, *Die Symphonie Anton Bruckners* (1914).

88. The leader in establishing university chairs of musicology was Germany. Even so, it still had only seven full professorships at the rank of *ordinarius,* three of which were instituted in the year 1920, when Bern inaugurated its program with Kurth. The University of Vienna was an exception in this regard. In 1864, it had instituted a chair of music history and aesthetics, held by Eduard Hanslick, who attained the rank of *ordinarius* in 1870. For a history of musicology in Europe, see the *New Grove Dictionary of Music and Musicians,* 6th ed., s.v. "Musicology," section III, 4, and "Education in Music," section IVb, 5–7.

89. The Berlin offer and succeeding ones are documented in the Bern State Archives.

90. Einstein visited Kurth in Switzerland after fleeing Nazi Germany. In 1929, Kurth received one last opportunity to leave Bern when the University at Munich offered him a post; he wisely declined. Two years earlier, when Guido Adler was retiring, he planned to recommend Kurth to head the Music-Historical Institute at the University of Vienna. Adler apparently knew of Kurth's refusals to leave Bern and so decided not to nominate him. Adler explains this in *Wollen und Wirken: Aus dem Leben eines Historikers* (Vienna: Universal, 1935), 118.

91. Kurth, *Musikpsychologie* (Berlin: Hesse, 1931; 2d ed., Bern: Krompholz, 1947).

92. Stumpf's experiments, based on responses of trained and untrained listeners to questions about isolated intervals and chords, are akin to Wilhelm Wundt's elementaristic approach to psychological research, carried out in Leipzig, in the mid-1870s. Kurth's holistic approach to the psychology of music derives, by contrast, from Gestalt psychology, which arose around 1910 in reaction to Wundt's elementarism.

93. von Fischer, "In Memoriam Ernst Kurth," 235. Fischer summarizes the main ideas in *Musikpsychologie* on pp. 235–45. Albert Wellek, one of Kurth's chief critics, admits that the field of music psychology "in the strict sense . . . of the word, distinguished from tone psychology and psycho-acoustics, exists only since [the publication of] Ernst Kurth's pioneering book." Wellek expresses this opinion in his article "Der gegenwärtige Stand der Musikpsychologie und ihre Bedeutung für die historische Musikforschung," *Report of the Eighth Congress of the I.M.S.,* vol. 1 (Kassel: Bärenreiter, 1961), 121: "Eine Musikpsychologie im strengsten Sinne . . . des Wortes, unterschieden von Ton- und Gehörpsychologie, gibt es erst seit Ernst Kurths wegweisendem Buch." Wellek had already noted Kurth's groundbreaking efforts in a review of *Musikpsychologie,* published in *Acta Musicologica* (1933–34): 72. Except for cursory, peripheral references, most recent literature on the psychology of music and music audition does not even mention Kurth's pioneering work. Passing references to Kurth may be found in Leonard Meyer's *Explaining Music* (Berkeley: University of California Press, 1973), 22; and idem, *Music, the Arts, and Ideas* (Chicago: University of Chicago Press, 1967), 305. Meyer's *Emotion and Meaning in Music* (Chicago: University of Chicago Press, 1956) does not mention Kurth. Other more recent publications dealing directly with the psychology of music ignore Kurth altogether, for example, John Booth Davis, *The Psychology of Music* (Stanford: Stanford University Press, 1978); and Diana Deutsch, ed., *The Psychology of Music* (New York: Academic Press, 1982).

94. Alfred Lorenz, "*Musikpsychologie,*" *Die Musik* 23 (1930): 185: "Wer sich in diese energetischen Vorgänge der Musik hineingedacht hat, muss unbedingt Anhänger Kurths werden. Daneben gibt es viel Neues, dem man rückhaltlos zustimmen darf."

95. Wellek, "*Musikpsychologie,*" 72.

96. Kurth, *Musikpsychologie,* x: "geistige Tätigkeit."

97. Wellek, "*Musikpsychologie,*" 78. Among a few other publications, Wellek cites Erich von Hornbostel's "Psychologie der Gehörerscheinungen," *Handbuch der normativen und pathologischen Physiologie,* ed. Bethe et al. (Berlin, 1926), 701–30. Kurth does refer to other of Hornbostel's publications, but not to this one in particular.

98. Kurth, *Musikpsychologie,* x. Kurth states that, except for the most familiar ideas, many concepts discussed in *Musikpsychologie* "often indicate something other than the strictly technical viewpoints" ("vielfach anders darstellen als nach bloss fachtechnischen Gesichtspunkten").

99. Fritz de Quervain and Kurt von Fischer provided me with listings of courses offered at Bern during the mid-1930s. The Bern Conservatory traditionally taught applied music skills, and university music students often supplemented their academic training with studies at the conservatory. This occasionally led to conflicts between Kurth and conservatory instructors, with the students caught in the middle.

100. The preferred repertoire at Wickersdorf apparently made a lasting impression on Kurth.

CHAPTER 2

Fortspinnung

Because melody is for Kurth the germinal element in music, as well as the controlling one in musical processes, we will begin our study of his theories by discussing various melodic techniques and types presented in *Grundlagen* and *Romantische Harmonik*. As explained in chapter 1, Kurth conceived of melody in a special way. When he speaks of melody, he is thinking of a primal, monolinear stream. This is particularly clear in his characterization of the essence of melody as a path of motion traversed by tone. Earlier, I described Kurth's idea of melody using the German word *Melodik,* which does imply the idea of melody in general (*melopoeia*) and thus does come close to Kurth's notion of melody. Even *Melodik,* however, lacks the necessary strong connotation of linear primacy, that is, the quintessential property of linearity in melody which Kurth had in mind, a linearity preceding any consciously stylized succession of tones. Underlying this linearity is a force Kurth calls "kinetic energy."[1]

Having posited kinetic-linear force as the essence of melody, Kurth goes on actually to equate melody with free-flowing kinetic energy. The purest melody is the one that, in sonic form, most completely conveys a sense of kinetic energy and dynamic continuum, awakening a corresponding mental kinesthetic continuum in the listener. Kurth feels that Baroque melody (Bach) best exemplifies these qualities. Classical melody (Haydn, Mozart), on the other hand, with its stylized periodicity, is to Kurth's ear contrary to, or at least significantly less exemplary of, ideal melody.

Theoretically, Kurth's idealized melody embodies the genetic psychic forces he postulates for music and applies clearly to much of Bach's music, but it remains nevertheless a sort of primordial phenomenon, a conceptual idealization abstracted from Bach's compositions for solo violin and cello. As such, it should not be elevated unconditionally to become a gauge of melodic purity, quality, or validity. As mentioned earlier, Kurth's enthusiasm for and idealization of melody is a reaction to previous harmonic oversimplifications of music. The very title of his counterpoint book, with its deliberate expression "*linear* counterpoint," is clearly a polemical response to theories of his predecessors.

Critics of Kurth's melodic approach to counterpoint have uniformly overlooked the implicit assumption of harmonic reference throughout his work, which on occasion explicitly identifies harmony as the basis of certain monophonic and polyphonic structures. Kurth explains his view in the preface to the third edition of *Grundlagen,* where he hoped to correct some misinterpretations of his ideas.

> Not . . . a weakening of harmonic effects is intended but rather a supplementary infiltration of them with the polyphonic-melodic element. . . . The contrapuntal conception is . . . only intended as one component, not as the entirety of Bach's [musical] structure; not an isolation of two elements is meant with the extreme formulation, but rather a better understanding for their relationship.[2]

Kurth affirms here that a clear understanding of the harmonic structure of polyphony is a prerequisite for isolating purely melodic elements. He assumes that the thoughtful reader of *Grundlagen* will balance the fundamentally linear approach to analysis with the appropriate measure of harmonic sensibility. In frustration, he wonders whether that stated assumption "should have been hammered home anew page for page."[3]

Over the next three chapters, we will take up several aspects of melody, from the macromelodic techniques of Baroque *Fortspinnung* and its late Romantic corollary, endless melody, to the micromelodic, cellular "developmental motives," and finally to Kurth's innovative ideas on polyphonic melody and its resultant "overriding lines." These are the most important topics that Kurth explores in the domain of melody, and the ones he treats most extensively.

Fortspinnung, "spinning forth," is a descriptive term usually applied, though with some vagueness, to late Baroque melodic and formal techniques. According to one reference work, the word appears for the first time in an essay by Wilhelm Fischer, who like Kurth was a student of Guido Adler.[4] Fischer employs the word *Fortspinnungstypus* to denote certain melodic and phraseological traits, which he contrasts with the *Liedtypus,* or "song type." After documenting both types in Baroque music, he shows their influence on Classical music.

Other musicologists of the early twentieth century described basic differences between the melodic styles of the Baroque and Classical eras, though they did not develop well-defined analytical terminology for these distinctions. Hugo Riemann, in fact, used the word *Fortspinnung* before Fischer. Riemann praises Bach's "unprecedented ability of logical *Fortspinnung* and of disposition across large developments."[5] Riemann's student, Carl Mennicke, comments briefly on the characteristics of older as opposed to newer melodic styles in his study of early Classical symphonies.[6]

Riemann and his followers do not use the term *Fortspinnung* with much analytical specificity. In general, Riemann had little influence on Kurth and Fischer in this respect. Much closer to both Kurth and Fischer is the work of Guido Adler, who in his book *Der Stil in der Musik* speaks of "spinning out and contrast of [musical] thoughts, the motives; [thus] one can also speak of a motivic development of the melodic material."[7] Fischer and Kurth both studied with Adler in the same period, Kurth in 1904–8, Fischer in 1908–12, so it is not surprising that both men should devote their first scholarly efforts to comparing traits peculiar to Baroque melody with those of Classical melody. It is certainly possible, even likely, that Kurth read Fischer's work, since it appeared in a publication that originated at the University of Vienna and was edited by his mentor. If so, Fischer's influence would be considerable since Kurth was writing *Grundlagen* at the very time when Fischer's essay appeared, 1915–16.

Fischer and Kurth differ in their understanding of *Fortspinnung*, particularly with regard to phraseology. The former derives his model primarily from Bach's suites for keyboard. The themes of these suites, according to Fischer, exhibit a regularized metric scheme coupled either with a parallel melodic structure, where antecedent and consequent complement each other in their near identity (*Liedtypus*), or with a nonparallel structure, where the consequent "spins out" the motives presented in the antecedent (*Fortspinnungstypus*). Both types exhibit periodicity in their metric schemes.

Kurth, by contrast, bases his notion of *Fortspinnung* on Bach's violin and cello suites. He does not find in these works the metric periodicity that Fischer finds in the keyboard music, and while Kurth, like Fischer, identifies two melodic types, Kurth's models do not agree with Fischer's. Kurth calls his types *Gruppierung,* governed by regular rhythmic-metric groupings, and *Fortspinnung,* controlled by kinetic-linear energy. The latter corresponds roughly to Fischer's *Fortspinnungstypus,* spinning out the head motive or theme, but Kurth denies any periodicity. For him the very essence of *Fortspinnung* lies in "continuous transition . . . constantly forming anew out of the melodic energy, a continued effect of motion."[8] Using these two categories, *Fortspinnung* and *Gruppierung,* Kurth distinguishes the primarily linear Baroque style from the homophonic Classical style and, further, the kinetic-linear continuity of Baroque melody from the periodic segmentation of Classical melody. To judge from Kurth's statements and his choice of musical examples, he considers his two categories mutually exclusive.

By choosing to work with Bach's solo violin and cello suites, and by judiciously selecting examples from them, Kurth leaves no room in his definition of *Fortspinnung* for rhythmic, metric, or melodic periodicity, which for Kurth are all manifestations of Classicism. This restriction excludes a sizable portion of Bach's works, even some movements of the solo suites themselves—for example, the menuets and bourrees, which better fit Fischer's model.[9] In such cases, Kurth points to the influence of the dance itself and denies metric or melodic symmetries a genetic role in Bach's style.

In the case of polyphony, it would be entirely wrong to take as a point of departure accentuation and grouping into two-measure units, which in no way lead back to the uniqueness of the old linear style, and are essentially foreign to it. It is of fundamental significance not to assess the periodlike balance, which occurs often in Bach, as the core of melodic feeling and the point of departure for melodic development.[10]

Beyond the particulars of analysis, both Fischer and Kurth have historical aims. Both seek the relationship between early and late eighteenth-century music, but where Fischer sees dissimilarities and detects historical continuity, Kurth perceives discontinuity.

Kurth introduces *Fortspinnung* to describe an immediate continuation of melodic energy generated by an initial motivic or thematic statement. His conception of prototypal melody as unbounded kinetic flow takes on concrete musical shape in a series of examples demonstrating the notion of "initial energy" (*Anfangsenergie*) and its subsequent *Fortspinnung*.[11]

Essential to *Fortspinnung*, according to Kurth, is its organic quality. *Fortspinnung* must develop characteristics of the initial melodic segment in both short- and long-range dimensions.[12] The theme in Example 2-1, by virtue of its upward thrust and chordal profile, gives rise to an ascending *Fortspinnung*, which carries forward both the directional energy and the motivic character of the theme. The music forms an arch, consisting of a foreceful rise with peak on b′ (m. 3) followed by a balancing descent. For Kurth this creates a dynamic unit (*Bewegungszug*), whose form is delineated by increasing and decreasing tension.[13]

EXAMPLE 2-1. Bach, Cello Suite in D Major, Courante, mm. 1–8

Using excerpts from the Prelude of Bach's Suite for Violin in E Major (Ex. 2-2), Kurth traces motivic transformations within the *Fortspinnung* at various stages of formal development.[14] The *Fortspinnung* begins in measure 3 of Example 2-2*a*, when the varied rhythms in measures 1–2 resolve into uninterrupted sixteenth notes. Kurth observes that it starts by developing a thematic component (Ex. 2-3).[15] Measures 29–30 (Ex. 2-2*b*; Kurth's Ex. 61) are derived from the downward arpeggiation of the theme by inversion and diminution. Kurth does not specifically mention the succession of neighbor-note embellishment and arpeggiation as a link between measure 29 and the theme, but it is clearly in the nature of a *Fortspinnung* to create such a bond. Example 2-2*c* (mm. 39–41; Kurth's Ex. 62) is derived similarly, now with

EXAMPLE 2-2. Bach, Violin Suite in E Major: (*a*) mm. 1–10; (*b*) mm. 29–30; (*c*) mm. 39–41; (*d*) mm. 85–88

EXAMPLE 2-3.

descending arpeggiations. Example 2-2*d*, a derivative of Example 2-2*b*, demonstrates the gradual transition from established material (m. 85) to less dependent linear motion (Ex. 2-4).

EXAMPLE 2-4.

Kurth's first discussion of Example 2-2a examines spatial and directional balance. According to Kurth, the first ten measures of the E-Major Prelude represent one coherent "phase of motion," which grows out of the bracketed theme by means of *Fortspinnung*.[16] The downward sweep from e''' to e' (mm. 1–2) leads to a broader ascent, beginning with preliminary rising gestures (mm. 3 and 4). Sudden octave leaps followed by rapid descents interrupt the ascent, and the line finally achieves e''' through a two-octave scalar rise, at once the climax and a return to the point of departure, thus creating spatial and dynamic balance.[17]

In an essay on the E-Major Prelude, Heinrich Schenker criticizes Kurth's commentary for its vagueness. Schenker begins his critique by accusing Kurth of neglecting to explain why the dynamic balance in measures 1–10 of the Prelude (Ex. 2-2a above) occurs between the particular high and low points, e''' and e', mentioned by Kurth as the boundaries. Aside from remarking briefly that the momentum of the theme (m. 1) engenders an extension over an additional octave, Kurth does not in fact discuss the octave as a theoretical phenomenon, its primacy among intervals, or its role in linking pitches registrally—in short, the octave as an element of formal coherence and long-range developments—all familiar Schenkerian themes. But Schenker's claim that Kurth overlooks the formal implications of octave identity is less an instance of objective criticism than one of polemical pedantry. Kurth does state clearly why the *Fortspinnung* courses from e''' to e' and back. It creates a balanced phase of motion, constituting a formal unit. In Kurth's words, the balance arises from a return "precisely up to the original apex note."[18]

Schenker blames Kurth for not drawing what are for Schenker the unmistakable conclusions from these specific movements, which define the key of E major. But interpreting Kurth's lack of comment on the octave as an unawareness of the tonal implication of the e'''–e' framework is surely an exaggeration. Kurth was certainly aware of the relationship between the e'''–e' outline and the key, and his failure to mention it in connection with this set of melodic motions does not necessarily indicate ignorance, though this seems to be Schenker's conclusion. Kurth's momentary interests simply lie elsewhere.

Schenker also takes issue with Kurth's casually describing Example 2-2a, measure 1, as a "monophonic beginning" (*einstimmiger Satzanfang*) instead of stressing its harmonic origin in arpeggiation. The arpeggiation, though obvious, is no more trivial to Kurth than to Schenker. Indeed, Kurth is well aware of it and its subsequent formal influence. In a passage from *Grundlagen* cited by Schenker himself, Kurth does refer to the "chordal contours" (*akkordliche Kontouren*) of the theme. He thus forges an organic link between the theme and measures 29–30 of the piece (Ex. 2-5).

EXAMPLE 2-5.

Kurth's interpretation of excerpts from the E-Major Prelude clearly shows the gradual dissolution of an initial thematic gesture into a motivically related but quasi-independent line; he thus successfully demonstrates a fundamental stylistic trait of Bach's solo string works, *Fortspinnung*. This achievement deserves better than Schenker's sharp rebuke for "constant diligent evasion of all exactitude in concept and word."[20]

Kurth no doubt appeared vague to Schenker because, among other reasons, Kurth does not approach the music with the same analytical criteria or vocabulary in order to describe what he hears. Two points must be stated in Kurth's defense. First, recall that *Grundlagen* (1917) preceded those essays of Schenker in which his ideas and terminology first begin to crystallize. The early volumes of *Der Tonwille* (1921–22) come to mind in this regard. There, Schenker defines and illustrates the concept of the *Urlinie* with several close analyses. By the time he published the first volume of *Das Meisterwerk in der Musik* (1925), he had greatly refined his ideas and analytic technique. Compare, for example, the breadth and detail of the multi-level *Ursatz* analysis of the *Largo* from Bach's third violin sonata, or of Chopin's *Etude* Op. 10, No. 5 (*Das Meisterwerk* 1), with the single-level analysis of Bach's E♭-Minor prelude from volume 1 of the *Well-Tempered Clavier* (*Der Tonwille* 1). The *Urlinie* of the prelude is a middleground progression, and there is no *Ursatz,* at least not in the sense of those we see in the voice-leading sketches of only a few years later.

Schenker made his greatest strides in the early 1920s, several years after *Grundlagen* appeared. It is hard to say whether his criticisms of Kurth would have been as pointed had they been written before that time. Kurth's approach to the music may in fact have helped Schenker to crystallize his ideas in the early 1920s, allowing him then to attack Kurth with newly developed analytical resources.[21]

Second, and more importantly, Kurth's discussion of the examples in question is in fact very clear on the main points of Schenker's critique: the nature and content of the *Fortspinnung*. That Schenker fails to acknowledge Kurth's findings is indeed curious since Schenker quotes liberally from *Grundlagen,* notably, however, without including Kurth's examples.

Organic connections between a theme and its continuation extend ultimately to the structural development across an entire work. Kurth briefly suggests this process when, before discussing the E-Major Prelude, he states, "In the *motive* of the smallest unitary linear phase lies the fundamental Will, the primal shape of a span of motion, which controls an extensive passage, often the entire piece, . . . and unfolds in the larger formal process."[22] He cites the Prelude from Bach's Cello Suite in C Major as an instance of large-scale formal development deriving from the initial motives (Ex. 2-6). The division between scalar and chordal elements in measure 1 engenders the overall melodic course, which concentrates first on conjunct motion, shifts gradually to arpeggiations of various design (mm. 16ff.), and finally returns to scalar passages in measure 71. Kurth's characterizations of a theme as a "primal image of form," or a "primal image of motion," and of its compositional development as an "enlarged reflection and effect" of a theme's nature are most appropriate here.[23]

EXAMPLE 2-6. Bach, Cello Suite in C Major, Prelude (continued on pages 39 and 40)

While the previous examples support Kurth's thesis of short- and long-range genetic powers embodied in opening motives, his observations do not lend themselves to establishing predictive norms for *Fortspinnung*. Kurth's view that an upward-striving Will in the leap from B♯ to e in the subject of Bach's C♯-Minor Fugue (*Well-Tempered Clavier* I) is the origin of successively higher entrances in the remaining four voices is certainly insightful and convincing. The fugues in A major and B major from *WTC* II also bear out Kurth's thesis. But other fugues behave quite differently. The subject of the F♯-Minor fugue, *WTC* I, is a model of upward-striving Will, but the subsequent *Fortspinnung* does not bring ever-higher entrances.

Kurth's notion of a thematic *Urbild* and its *Fortspinnung* accounts well for evolving motivic transformations and, selectively, for larger musical spans. Kurth would not have wanted to formalize the idea of organic *Fortspinnung* into anything resembling a schematic analysis or a rigorous predictive mechanism. It is just such an approach to analysis that Kurth wanted to avoid. Accordingly, his notion of *Fortspinnung* must be applied flexibly, as must any analytical tool, in order to account for the myriad possibilities of melodic development in various formal dimensions. Thoughtfully tracing the *Fortspinnung* through a piece of music will explain the details of organic transition and growth from motive to theme, theme to phrase, and so on, and will yield a successive, cumulative unity in the formal overview.

ENDLESS MELODY

Kurth's historical views concerning the evolution of musical style and the forces guiding that evolution lead him to make a connection between Bach's linear polyphony and Wagner's "endless melody," the notorious *unendliche Melodie*. This link not only highlights the most important element in his philosophy of music—the flow of melodic motion as a sonic embodiment of psychic energy—but also organizes the evolution of musical style into clear, logical stages. Kurth confirms his historical outlook by identifying and demonstrating through examples a bond between melodic styles of such remote eras and artistic motivations as those of Bach and Wagner.

Richard Wagner's own writings are the basis of Kurth's idea of endless melody. In the first of two documents cited by Kurth, Wagner alludes to free-flowing melody as an outgrowth of textual expressiveness, requiring suitable musical form.

> In all cases where the expression of the poetic discourse so dominated me that I could justify the melody to my emotions only in light of the discourse, this melody, if it were not to stand in a forced relationship to the verse, had to lose nearly all rhythmic character; and with this technique I was immensely more conscientious and fulfilled in my task than if, conversely, I had sought to enliven the melody by means of arbitrary rhythms.[24]

For Kurth, purging expressive melody of "almost all rhythmic character" and thus avoiding a "forced relationship with the verse" signify Wagner's effort to break the mold of regular rhythmic groupings, which Kurth associates primarily with Classicism. Wagner's stated ideals led Kurth to a notion of endless melody as "continuity of motion" and "absence of pauses for relaxation."[25]

Wagner expands on the above remarks with the following thoughts.

> I recognize now that the special texture of my music . . . , which my friends now view as so new and significant, owes its integrated structure to the extremely sensitive feeling which directed me toward mediation and intimate connection of all instants of transition between the most diverse moods. I would call my finest and most profound art the art of transition, for my entire artistic fabric is made up of such transitions. . . . That is therefore also the secret of my musical form.[26]

Kurth seized on the references to "die Kunst des Übergangs," the art of transition, and on the allusions to rhythmic, harmonic, and melodic development in order to characterize endless melody still further.

> Thus, also in the technical sense, "endlessness" means something other, more substantial, than endless length; even in smaller proportions, the essence lines in the *"endlessness of transitions,"* i.e., in the principle of continuous spinning forth.[27]

"Continuous spinning forth" is the key phrase here, the link between the melodic idioms of Bach and Wagner. According to Kurth, Wagner's endless melody represents a "regaining of an ancient principle, but in new, unique forms." While Kurth realizes that he has found an important stylistic connection between Bach and Wagner, he acknowledges the dissimilarities between the two composers; he knows that the two realizations of the "ancient principle" are very different. In fact, he suspects that the shared stylistic traits may go unnoticed. The similarities, he points out, are not obvious: "In order to understand Wagner's endless melody, it is . . . necessary to understand the concealed *similarities* with Bach's linear art, as well as the great differences which distinguish Wagner's melody from that of Bach."[28]

For Kurth, Bach's music is the finest linear art, consummating all previous polyphonic composition. It is unaffected by the melodic periodicity that earmarks music of the later eighteenth century. Romantic music, on the other hand, had to struggle to overcome the firmly established conventions of melodic periodicity. To Kurth's ear, this struggle characterizes the music of the first half of the nineteenth century. Wagner's music achieves a synthesis that recaptures the essential kinetic-linear quality of Bach's polyphony, a synthesis arising from the harmonic-melodic struggle of the earlier Romantic style.

This view of music history derives, in part, from Kurth's conception of Classical style. Although his view may seem outdated to us, it was common in his time. It is not hard to imagine how musicians and authors whose ears were full of Wagner's music, as well as that of other late Romantics, might arrive at such an opinion of Classical music. The regular, binary phraseology suppresses the true essence of melody, kinetic energy. The roots of Classical style lie in "the feeling for rhythmic accent [which] penetrated to the surface of musical sensibility to the extent that it asserted itself as the governing foundation of all melodic composition."[29] This feeling for rhythmic accent infiltrates all formal levels, producing the arsis-thesis within each measure, heavy and light measures, and so on up to antecedent-consequent phrases. Further, rhythmic regularity extends its influence to Classical harmony, which Kurth perceives as a series of chords, linked according to voice-leading conventions but lacking any genuine linear dimension. Classical harmony, then, is properly homophonic, based on periodically organized themes with harmonic accompaniment, and enriched by figuration, motivic imitations, and so on.

The achievement of the Romantics, especially Wagner, was the gradual suppression of rhythmic periodicity and the reestablishment of kinetic-linear energy as the basis of melody.[30] Nevertheless, remnants of classicism, as Kurth understood it, linger in Wagner's melodic practices. Kurth's own exposition of endless melody thus begins with harmonic devices. Of the eight basic techniques discussed by Kurth, the following paragraphs describe three that are featured in Wagner's music.

Deceptive Cadence

The category of deceptive cadence embraces the numerous instances of regular phrasings or expected caesuras commonly evaded by means of deceptive progressions—a hallmark of the *Tristan* style—in order to help sustain forward motion. Of the countless examples Kurth might have chosen, he selects the excerpt from *Tristan* given in Example 2-7.[31] Wagner negotiates tempo and meter changes, shifts in or-

EXAMPLE 2-7. *Tristan*, I, 1

chestration, texture, and mood by means of a deceptive cadence (penultimate measure). Although Kurth does not mention the opposition between the vocal cadence by descending fifth and the deceptive progression, it is precisely this sort of artistic refinement that interests Kurth most with regard to endless melody.[32] The orchestral ascending fifth (violins) in the quicker tempo immediately reverses the effect of Brangäne's cadential gesture and contributes further to thwarting her would-be formal articulation. Isolde, who sings to an agitated accompaniment, obviously does not agree with her handmaiden's tacit acceptance (descending fifth) of their lot.

The passage in Example 2-8 appears in discussions of both endless melody and the deceptive cadence in general.[33] In keeping with his hypothesis of the third as the primal building block of harmony, Kurth derives the deceptive cadence by "supposition"; that is, a tonic (or quasi-tonic) root, expected as the bass note in a cadence, is replaced by an under-third (*Unterterz*), a tone a third lower.[34] Stylistically, the music in question may support this thesis. Sonorities in late Romantic music, and in Bruckner's music in particular, often do evolve out of accumulations of thirds. But Kurth tends to treat deceptive cadences in general as deriving from under-third cadences, even where the style may not support such a derivation.[35]

EXAMPLE 2-8. *Siegfried*, I, 1

Kurth also associates the deceptive cadence with modal progressions.[36] Such a contrapuntal explanation disagrees with the harmonic one suggested above. Kurth resolves the disagreement by observing that the Romantics' use of this modal progression reflects their "general preference for tertian effects in progressions," indicating that he understood the usage to be a characteristically Romantic adaptation of a modal device.[37] In any case, Wagner employed the deceptive cadence as one means of sustaining harmonic-melodic and, consequently, dramatic momentum in order to disguise what otherwise would have been clear, formal articulations. Kurth notes that, in this way, Wagner breaks down the conventional pattern of "number operas."

Melodic Tension

A conflict between two melodically motivated tones of the same pitch class but of contrasting linear tendencies produces a moment of ambiguity, of tension, and promotes momentum. If strategically deployed at a phrase ending, such instants of tension can effect transitions that camouflage structural junctures. To demonstrate this, Kurth offers the interesting passage from *Das Rheingold* in Example 2-9.[38]

EXAMPLE 2-9. *Rheingold*, 3

The progression in measures 16–18, V–I, arrives at a chord with added seventh, an element of shading that weakens the otherwise strong articulative power of the authentic cadence.[39] Kurth remarks that Wotan's g♭ (m. 18), reached through the cadentially definitive descending fifth, plays a dual role. As goal of the descending fifth, Wotan's g♭ effects a momentarily consonant, melodic closure, which quickly yields to the orchestral treatment of G♭ as neighbor to F in the bass. Just when the action slackens, Wotan seating himself with a descending melodic fifth to wait for Alberich's return, the drama suddenly presses onward as Alberich enters, driving the Nibelungs before him. At this point, the Forge-Motive reappears, accompanied by the bass's alternation between G♭ and F. Wotan's cadential gesture, coupled with its harmonic support, makes the bass G♭ sound like a root, thus confirming the vocal line and making the bass F sound like a neighbor to G♭. The rhythm of the bass seems to bear out such a hearing (Ex. 2-10).

EXAMPLE 2-10.

But the higher g♭ disappears immediately, as does the inner-voice b♭; both were crucial in establishing the sound of a G♭-major seventh chord in measure 18. According to Kurth, the orchestra picks up the vocal g♭ and transforms it into an accessory note in a new register. This frustrates Wotan's recent melodic closure, for his g♭ root now appears as an appoggiatura to F in the bass. It is just this dual function of the pitch class G♭, as cadential tone in the highest voice and appoggiatura in the lowest, that disguises the juncture and propels the music forward, an example of "continuous transition" at work on the most detailed level.

Kurth does not state exactly how the orchestra converts Wotan's cadential note into an appoggiatura in the bass, but the context of the note, as well as events leading to the measures in question, supports Kurth's argument. As the g♭ and b♭ in the upper parts vanish, the bass ascends in an apparent arpeggiation of a G♭-major triad (Ex. 2-11). After abandoning G♭ (m. 1), the bass outlines a fourth, F–B♭, which in conjunction with the Forge-Motive begins to project the sound of B♭-minor harmony. The bass continues to D♭, further strengthening this hearing and clarifying the meaning of the eighth notes. As accessories to a B♭-minor arpeggiation, the eighths function variously as incomplete lower neighbor notes or as chord tones. This arrangement yields the progression sketched in Example 2-12. The Forge-Motive appears repeatedly in similar harmonic settings—for example, the motive circling about the fifth and third of a chord—further confirming this reading.[40] Kurth, acutely sensitive to such details, correctly explains the technical basis and dramatic effect of Wagner's subtle melodic-harmonic ambiguity.

EXAMPLE 2-11. (above)   EXAMPLE 2-12. (below)

Kurth presents several other techniques of endless melody. These include skewed harmonic and melodic phrasing (*Romantische Harmonik,* 457); wide, dissonant melodic intervals (p. 458); changing meter (p. 459); metric shifting of a single repeated motive (p. 461); and finally, interlocking motives (p. 462). Of all these devices, Kurth underscores the musical and dramatic significance of the last one and devotes several examples to it. Besides the fact that interlocking motives are particularly important to Kurth, there is another reason that the technique deserves our attention. It is closely related to the technique of *Fortspinnung;* this strengthens Kurth's thesis about the link between Bach's and Wagner's melodic procedures.

Interlocking Motives

The technique of interlocking motives touches on the essence of melodic formation. It belongs to the internal workings of melody, as opposed to the externally applied harmonic devices affecting the linear dimension, and thus lies at the heart of endless melody. Here phrase endings are not disguised by harmonic means, as in the preceding examples; rather, one motive slips imperceptively into another, enriching and varying the melodic content. Because the motives used are the familiar leitmotifs in *Tristan,* the ongoing psychological drama finds appropriate and often striking musical expression.

In Example 2-13, Kurth recognizes a delicate transition from the sad strains of the English horn, which recall the hopeless desolation of Tristan's banishment, to the Torment-Motive.[41] Specifically, in measure 15, where Tristan takes up the ascending fourth (a♭ to d♭′), the orchestra (m. 16, upper voices) interweaves the gesture symbolizing Tristan's torment. This motive appears just as the mortally wounded Tristan awakens and begins to recall the events leading to his present plight. The vocal line hovers on d♭′, permitting the torment motive to emerge clearly.

EXAMPLE 2-13. *Tristan,* III, 1

Following the emotional outburst occasioned by the remembrance of the fateful love potion (*Tristan,* III, 1), Tristan envisions Isolde approaching the castle by ship. This hallucination is accompanied by an oboe solo, ascending chromatically in reference to the Love-Motive, which then yields to the Curse-Motive, highlighted by a timbral shift to the clarinet (Ex. 2-14).[42] Of utmost importance for Kurth are the psychological implications (Zug ins Psychologische) of such motivic transitions. The bitter curse of Tristan and Isolde's love, the futility of Tristan's predicament, and the harsh reality of the vision that briefly uplifts his waning spirit are the cumulative dramatic background on which the orchestra comments.

EXAMPLE 2-14. *Tristan,* III, 1

An even subtler instance of interlocking motives occurs in Example 2-15.[43] Here, the Daylight-Motive passes into the Love-Motive by melodic overlapping. Transposed to the present pitch level, the Daylight-Motive, which first appears at the opening of act II, would sound as shown in Example 2-16. But Wagner modifies it chromatically so that C$\sharp$ becomes C$\natural$, the link which allows a smooth transition into the chromatic ascent of the Love-Motive. Like Examples 2-13 and 2-14, this motivic association has psychological implications, though Kurth does not take time to elaborate on them. The entire section leading to Example 2-15, as well as the subsequent vocal duet, focuses on light, symbolizing Tristan's first encounter with Isolde, his later awakening to love, and the looming threat of daybreak. We could therefore hear Example 2-15 as a musical compression of these dramatic undercurrents. In Example 2-17, the Curse-Motive combines with that of Torment, yielding a reference to the "terrible draught," as Tristan recalls the fateful potion.[44]

EXAMPLE 2-15. *Tristan,* II, 2

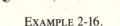

EXAMPLE 2-16.

EXAMPLE 2-17. *Tristan*, III, 1

These examples of interlocking motives, together with all of the other examples of endless melody presented so far, are isolated instances illustrating just one dimension of endless melody. Wagner's, and Kurth's, idea of "continuous transitions" is inadequately, indeed falsely, described if it is reduced to cleverly disguised phrase junctures or to a motivic patchwork. The techniques presented up to now, though important, are but outgrowths of more comprehensive and profound musical processes.

Kurth does not restrict endless melody to the linear mosaic described above. He penetrates to its essential motivation—continuous transitions—and expands the notion of endless melody to engage the "*totality of homophony.*" It is Kurth's belief, then, that "in its resolution into the polyphonic network of orchestral voices, [Romantic homophony] embodies as its chief characteristic the flow of *continuous Fortspinnung.*"[45] In the broadest musical sense, Kurth sees this generalized concept of endless melody in the continuous "sweep of overlapping dynamic waves over one another [Übereinanderstreichen der Wellen]": "One glance at the score shows that in all instances where one part is in active development, oftentimes before reaching its apex, the beginnings of new subsidiary lines arise, some of which disappear, while others appear in their places."[46] He calls these symphonic undulations the "endless melody of form," while the polyphonic texture represents the "endless melody of harmony."[47] For Kurth, endless melody in this comprehensive sense leads back to the very genesis of music, psychic energies. The Romantics, attuned to spiritual, natural, and cosmic forces, made these energies the ideal basis of melody, harmony, and form, and tried to express them sonically.

If we compare the various facets of endless melody with those of *Fortspinnung*, noteworthy differences emerge. Some traits of endless melody, such as changing meter, melodic syncopation, and unusual intervals, are absent in Baroque *Fortspinnung*. Harmony in particular exerts considerable influence in Wagner's idiom, while Baroque *Fortspinnung* depends primarily on melodic processes. Kurth acknowledges these distinctions but goes on to emphasize Wagner's "power of *regeneration*" (*Regenerationskraft*), his ability to renew inherited materials by reaching down to their deepest roots and tapping their hidden powers—the powers of kinetic energy.[48] Wagner wrested himself from Classical ideals and arrived at a melodic style featuring continuity of motion, thus providing a glimpse of the unbroken stream of psychic forces beneath the outer shell of music.

Kurth's idea of endless melody as a reincarnation of Bach's *Fortspinnung* and, furthermore, as a liberation from the ostensible rigidity of Classical melody did not escape criticism. Hermann Wetzel chides Kurth for attempting to explain endless melody without first defining "ending" melody.[49] He takes Kurth to task for overlooking nonsymmetrical, free-flowing melodic structures in Bach and Beethoven, whose music Wetzel claims established admirable models of endless melody long before Wagner.

Kurth would naturally concur with Wetzel's opinion of Bach's music. Perhaps Wetzel had not read *Grundlagen*. Furthermore, Kurth does acknowledge Beethoven and the Classical masters, Haydn and Mozart, for their Adagio movements. Some of these, Kurth observes, exhibit a "certain intrinsic power and an impulse toward unfoldment of the purely linear expression . . . even within metric uniformity."[50] Undeniably, a certain prejudice regarding Classical music colors Kurth's understanding of that era. As noted earlier, such prejudices were typical in his day. But Wetzel's remarks, colored by a strong conservative bent and dislike of Wagner's music, are themselves not entirely objective.[51] Wetzel accuses Kurth of failing to hear the irregular melodic structure of many great masters. Once again, Wetzel seems to have read Kurth incompletely, for Kurth had written in *Romantische Harmonik,* "Who then wished to assert that with the Classicists the sense of the unrestrained shaping forces of motion was completely dead!"[52]

Wetzel's main criticism is that Kurth oversimplified the evolution of musical style by establishing and maintaining too rigid an opposition between the kinetic and rhythmic styles of melody explained at the beginning of this chapter (*Fortspinnung* versus *Gruppierung*). Kurth does tend to favor what he hears as a kinetic-melodic style, as a reflection of the creative-psychic stream. Consequently, he makes the kinetic-melodic type his model of ideal melody against which other melodic types are gauged for their musical "depth," in the psycho-genetic sense. Wetzel objects to such speculation and to Kurth's implication that Baroque melody and its nineteenth-century counterpart, endless melody, are more ideal and deeper than, say, Classical melody.

We could take issue with Kurth's historical views here, but I do not think it would serve any useful purpose. What influential theorist has not held fast to some views that today seem suspect? Hugo Riemann and Heinrich Schenker come to mind in this regard.[53] Music theory would be considerably poorer were we to ignore the important contributions of Kurth and other men because of certain dated opinions. As with most theorists, so too with Kurth, we must glean that which is useful for understanding music; and although we should be aware of their ideological motivations, we need not necessarily agree with them.

In *Grundlagen* and *Romantische Harmonik,* Kurth goes beyong the nontechnical and oftentimes vague discussions of *Fortspinnung* and endless melody by pinpointing and classifying some technical bases for these procedures. He broadens the idea of *Fortspinnung* from a technique of continuous motivic transformation to a principle of organic form. Further, in studying endless melody he reveals important psycho-dramatic details that are crucial to Wagner's music. Both of these achievements extend and refine the work of his precedessors. In the next chapter, on developmental motives, we will see how Kurth probes yet deeper into melodic processes and uncovers the bases of large-scale dynamic-formal organization.

NOTES

1. Kurth borrowed terms such as *kinetic energy* and *potential energy* from the field of physics, though he did not use them according to their strict scientific meanings. He used them "in analogy to the corresponding physical-mechanical concepts" ("in Analogie zu den entsprechenden physikalisch-mechanischen Begriffen"; *Grundlagen,* 12), and "in free imitation of the mode of designation in physics" ("in freier Anlehnung der Bezeichnungsweise der Physik;" *Romantische Harmonik,* 10). For Kurth, kinetic and potential energy signify, respectively, the flow of melody and its momentary restraint in harmony. Kurth's adoption of these scientific terms reflects the important research and discoveries in the field of physics (energy, matter, and their relationship) made at the beginning of the twentieth century. He uses them throughout his writings, starting with *Voraussetzungen* (65, 71: kinetic; 69, 71: potential), and continuing with *Grundlagen* (9: kinetic; 68: potential) and *Romantische Harmonik* (5: kinetic; 9–10: potential).
2. Kurth, *Grundlagen,* xiv: "Nicht . . . eine Abschwächung der harmonischen Wirkungen ist gemeint, sondern ihre ergänzende Durchsetzung mit dem mehrstimmig-melodischen Element. Die kontrapunktische Durchdringung ist . . . nur als eine Komponente gedacht, nicht als Gesamtheit der Bachschen Struktur; mit der geschärften Ausprägung ist kein Isolierung zweier Elemente gemeint, sondern besseres Verständnis für ihren Zusammenhang."
3. Ibid., xiv: "Seite für Seite neu hätte eingehämmert werden müssen."
4. William Drabkin, *New Grove Dictionary of Music and Musicians,* 6th ed., s.v. "Fortspinnung," 6:725. Wilhelm Fischer, "Zur Entwicklung des Wiener klassischen Stils," *Studien zur Musikwissenschaft* 3 (1915): 24–84.
5. Hugo Riemann, *Handbuch der Musikgeschichte,* vol. 2/3, 2d ed. (Leipzig: Breitkopf and Härtel, 1922; 1st ed., 1913), 104: "beispiellose Fähigkeit der logischen Fortspinnung und der Disposition über grössere Entwicklungen." See also the section entitled "Neue Keime," 119, as well as 132–33, 165. Earlier, in the *Grosse Kompositionslehre,* vol. 1 (Berlin and Stuttgart: Spemann,

1902), 39–87, Riemann had already spoken of the "spinning out of motives into movements" ("Ausspinnung von Motiven zu Sätzen").

6. Carl Mennicke, *Hasse und die Brüder Graun als Symphoniker* (Leipzig: Breitkopf and Härtel, 1906), 18–19.

7. Guido Adler, *Der Stil in der Musik*, 2d ed. (Leipzig: Breitkopf und Härtel, 1929; 1st ed., 1911), 119: "Ausspinnung und Gegenüberstellung der Gedanken, der Motive, man kann auch von einer motivischen Bearbeitung des melodischen Stiles sprechen." See also sections entitled "Melodische Kompositionstechnik," 24–27, and "Stilarten der Mehrstimmigkeit," 240–71, especially 241 and 246–49, where in the second edition Adler refers to Kurth's concept of linearity.

8. Kurth, *Grundlagen*, 225: "fliessender Übergang . . . stetige Neuerformung aus der melodischen Energie, eine Weiterwirkung der Bewegung."

9. See, for example, Cello Suite No. 2 in D Minor, Menuet I; No. 3 in C Major, Bourree I; Violin Partita No. 3 in E Major, Gavotte en Rondeau.

10. Kurth, *Grundlagen*, 152–53: "doch wäre es ganz verfehlt von der zweitaktigen Akzentuierung und Gruppierung bei der Polyphonie auszugehen, die keineswegs zur Eigenart des alten Linienstiles zurückführen und ihm ursprünglich fremd sind. Es ist von grundlegender Bedeutung, die periodenartigen Ebenmasse, die sich öfters bei Bach finden, nicht als Kern melodischen Empfindens und Ausgang melodischer Entwicklung einzuschätzen."

11. Ibid., 226.

12. Friedrich Blume stresses this organic quality in his essay "Fortspinnung und Entwicklung," *Jahrbuch der Musikbibliothek Peters* 36 (1929): 51–70. He contrasts organic *Fortspinnung* (p. 59) with mechanical *Fortspinnung* (p. 58), the latter being a spinning out of melodic material unrelated to the theme or head motive in a free-flowing, independent development. Like Fischer, Blume builds a concept of *Fortspinnung* with the underlying assumption of periodic phraseology.

13. Kurth, *Grundlagen*, 226–27.

14. Ibid., 229, 243–44.

15. Ibid., 243.

16. Cf. Example 2-1 and the discussion there. Kurth distinguishes between *Phrase*, which he associates with melodic structures segmented according to rhythmic-metric regularities, and *Phase*, which denotes an indivisible linear whole, a "unified span of tension" ("einheitlicher Zug einer Spannung"). The phase may include moments of greater or lesser tension, but the uninterrupted flow is primary (*Grundlagen*, 20–23).

17. Kurth, *Grundlagen*, 230.

18. Ibid., "genau bis zum ursprünglichen Gipfelton." Schenker's critique is in *Das Meisterwerk in der Musik*, vol. 1 (Vienna: Drei Masken Verlag, 1925; reprint Hildesheim: Olms, 1974), 93–98.

19. Schenker, *Meisterwerk*, 1:94; Kurth, *Grundlagen*, 234.

20. Schenker, *Meisterwerk*, 1:95: "ständige geflissentliche Ausweichen vor jeglicher Bestimmtheit in Begriff und Wort."

21. Schenker, *Das Meisterwerk* 1:63–73 (*Largo* from Bach's third violin sonata; translated by John Rothgeb in *The Music Forum* 4 [1976], 141–59); Schenker, *Das Meisterwerk* 1:163–73 (Chopin's *Etude* Op. 10, No. 5); idem, *Der Tonwille* 1 (Vienna: A. Gutmann, 1921): 38–45 (Bach's E♭-Minor prelude). Other of Schenker's pre-1917 publications include an edition of Bach's chromatic fantasy and fugue (Vienna: Universal, 1909; ed. Oswald Jonas [Vienna: Universal, 1970]; trans., ed. Hedi Siegel [New York: Longman, 1984]), and editions of Beethoven's piano sonatas, Opp. 109, 110, and 111 (Vienna: Universal, 1913, 1914, 1915; ed. Oswald Jonas [Vienna: Universal, 1971–72]). Schenker does uncover what he later would call middleground progressions in the chromatic fantasy (pp. 27–28; trans. pp. 37–38), and in the fugue (p. 32; trans. pp. 44–45), but they are presented rather informally in comparison to the analyses of the early 1920s. Out of all of the pre-1917 works, the edition of Beethoven's Op. 110 stands out. Here Schenker analyzes in detail a passage from the second movement (mm. 41–72) and provides a middleground voice-leading sketch whose foreground interpretation is clarified in the commentary (pp. 53–57). The sketch is not nearly as developed as those in the later volumes of *Tonwille* or in volume 1 of *Das Meisterwerk*, but the line

of thought is comparable. We might also mention Schenker's interpretation of a passage from the first movement of Op. 110 (mm. 38–56), in which he shows a "descending line" (*sich senkende Linie*) spanning the development section and the beginning of the recapitulation (Op. 110 ed., p. 34).

22. Kurth, *Grundlagen*, 208: "Im *Motiv* der kleinsten als Einheit geschlossenen Linienphase liegt der Grundwille, das Urbild eines Bewegungszuges, welcher eine längere Entwicklung und Durchführung, oft den ganzen Satz beherrscht . . . und der in der fernen Formenentwicklung seine Entfaltung findet."

23. Kurth, *Grundlagen*, 211. The theme is a "Form-Urbild" or a "Bewegungsurbild"; its development is a "vergrössertes Abbild und Auswirkung."

24. Kurth, *Romantische Harmonik*, 445, taken from Wagner's *Gesammelte Schriften,* vol. 4 (Leipzig: Breitkopf und Härtel/Siegel, 1907), 327: "Überall, wo mich wiederum der Ausdruck der poetischen Rede so vorwiegend bestimmte, dass ich die Melodie vor meinem Gefühle nur aus ihr rechtfertigen konnte, musste diese Melodie, sobald sie in keinem gewaltsamen Verhältnisse zum Vers stehen sollte, fast allen rhythmischen Charakter verlieren; und bei diesem Verfahren war ich unendlich gewissenhafter und von meiner Aufgabe erfüllter, als wenn ich umgekehrt die Melodie durch willkürliche Rhythmik zu beleben suchte." The quotation is from Wagner's, "Mittheilung an meine Freunde."

25. Kurth, *Romantische Harmonik,* 453: "Kontinuität der Bewegung," "kein volles Absetzen zur Entspannung."

26. Ibid., 454, from a letter to Mathilde Wesendonck, October 29, 1859: "Ich erkenne nun, dass das besondere Gewebe meiner Musik . . . , was meine Freunde jetzt als so neu und bedeutend betrachten, seine Fügung namentlich dem äusserst empfindlichen Gefühle verdankt, welches mich auf Vermittelung und innige Verbindung aller Momente des Übergangs der äussersten Stimmungen ineinander hinweist. Meine feinste und tiefste Kunst möchte ich jetzt die Kunst des Übergangs nennen, denn mein ganzes Kunstgewebe besteht aus solchen Übergängen . . . Das ist denn nun auch das Geheimnis meiner musikalischen Form."

27. Ibid., 453: "Daher bedeutet 'Unendlichkeit' auch im technischen Sinne noch etwas anderes, noch Wesentlicheres als unendliche Längen; der Kern liegt schon im Kleinen in der '*Unendlichkeit der Übergänge,*' d.h. im Prinzip fortfliessender Weiterspinnungen."

28. Ibid., 449: "Um das Wesen von Wagners unendlicher Melodie zu verstehen, ist es daher notwendig, sowohl die verborgenen *Gemeinsamkeiten* mit Bachs Linienkunst zu begreifen, als andererseits die grossen Gegensätze, die sie durchgreifend von ihr unterscheiden."

29. Ibid., 444: "das rhythmische Betonungsgefühl dermassen an die Oberfläche des Musikempfindens vorgebrochen, dass es sich zum herrschenden Untergrund aller Melodiebildung durchsetzte."

30. Ibid., 446–47.

31. Schirmer piano-vocal edition, 7:18–22. The numbers after the colon indicate the measure numbers on the given page of the piano-vocal score. My text will refer to these measure numbers. Acts will be indicated by roman numerals and scenes by arabic numerals, separated by a comma, e.g., I, 1.

32. See the following section, "Melodic Tension."

33. Kurth, *Romantische Harmonik,* 252–62, 455–66. Schirmer, 27:30–32.

34. Kurth's idea of the *Unterterz* first appears in his *Voraussetzungen,* 38–46.

35. In *Voraussetzungen,* 36–37, Kurth speaks of the universality of tertian structures and gives several examples of under-third cadences taken from the music of Bach and Wagner.

36. Kurth, *Romantische Harmonik,* 253: "The Romantics in particular revitalized this old device, which has come down from modal progressions" ("gerade die Romantiker [griffen] diese alte, noch von kirchentonartlichen Wendungen her überkommene Erscheinung lebhaft wieder [auf]").

37. Ibid., 253: "Vorliebe für Terzwirkungen in Klangfolgen überhaupt."

38. Ibid., 456. Schirmer, 130:14–20.

39. Shading is discussed in chapter 8.

40. See the end of scene 2, Schirmer, 113–14; Alberich's exit in scene 3, p. 121; and Mimi's complaint, pp. 124–25.

41. Kurth, *Romantische Harmonik,* 373–74. *Tristan,* III, 1; Schirmer, 249:13–17.

42. Kurth, *Romantische Harmonik*, 463. Schirmer, 260:17–18; 261:1–7.

43. Kurth, *Romantische Harmonik*, 463. *Tristan*, II, 2; Schirmer, 148:25–27.

44. Kurth, *Romantische Harmonik*, 84. *Tristan*, III, 1; Schirmer, 253:7–11.

45. Kurth, *Romantische Harmonik*, 563: "*Gesamtheit der Homophonie,* die bei ihrer polyphonischen Auflösung in das ganze orchestrale Stimmengeäder den Fluss *stetiger Fortspinnung* als ihr Hauptmerkmal in sich trägt." Chapter 5 explains Kurth's notion of what I call "Romantic homophony."

46. Ibid., 563–64: "ein Blick auf die Partitur zeigt, wie allenthalben an den Stellen, wo noch eine Stimme in Entwicklung ist, oft noch nicht über den Höhepunkt hinaus, schon die Anfänge neuer, zunächst oft untergeordneter Linien entstehen, von denen einige auch wieder verschwinden, andere aber die früheren Stimmen ablösen."

47. Ibid., 568, 566.

48. Ibid., 450: "die starke *Regenerationskraft,* mit welcher das Genie die Erscheinungen bei ihren letzten Wurzeln aufgreift, der Sinn für das Ursprünglichste, das Allereinfachste und seine geheime Gewalt."

49. Wetzel, "Zur Stilforschung," 262–69.

50. Kurth, *Romantische Harmonik*, 448: "eine gewisse Eigenkraft und ein Entfaltungsdrang des rein linearen Ausdrucks . . . auch schon innerhalb der Takteinheit."

51. Of Wagner's melodic style, Wetzel says, "in allowing his melodies to run wild in this way, Wagner was, fatefully, a model of negligence" ("Zu solchem Verwildernlassen der Tonfolge gehört eine Rücksichtslosigkeit, in der Wagner verhängnisvoll vorbildlich war"; "Zur Stilforschung," 267).

52. Kurth, *Romantische Harmonik*, 448: "Wer wollte auch behaupten, dass bei den Klassikern der Sinn für die frei gestaltende Bewegungsenergie völlig erstorben sei!"

53. In a review of *Romantische Harmonik*, published in *Die Musikforschung* (1972), 225, Carl Dahlhaus remarks that, judging from the work of three leading early twentieth-century thinkers, Riemann, Schenker, and Kurth, an "obstinate, self-assured one-sidedness" appears to go hand in hand with being an important theorist.

CHAPTER 3

Developmental Motives

By examining closely what are generally labeled transitions or "episodes" in Bach's instrumental works, Kurth discovers certain recurrent motivic types to which he attaches great significance not only for local musical contexts but also for broader formal processes and, ultimately, for the entire (late) Baroque style. Primarily, these recurrent types represent tiny units of motion—in Kurth's words, absolute motion—whose shapes are outlined in tones. They are a "distillation of melody down to pure symbols of motion."[1]

In contrast to stylized themes and thematic fragments, these "developmental motives" (*Entwicklungsmotive*) are generic in character owing to their undistinguished melodic profiles. This indistinctiveness, unsuitable for themes or head motives, is in fact highly suitable for developmental motives, since it is precisely the generic character of these motives that lends them great musical flexibility and, consequently, stylistic universality.

For Kurth, simplicity of form signals closeness to primal origins, psychic energies. Generalized, recurrent motives thus point toward trans-stylistic creative impulses. To discover their occurrence in various periods is, for Kurth, to penetrate the stylistically individualized surface of art works and lay bare their very foundations, thereby getting at the essence of musical art.[2] One may dispute Kurth's genetic argument or reject his equation of "simplicity" with "primacy" and psychic depth. These are points of contention to be sure. But we need not accept such theories in order to appreciate the utility of developmental motives as effective analytical tools and interpretive historical references.

Because of the commonplace nature of developmental motives, we tend either to treat them as musically self-evident or to overlook them altogether. Instead, we focus attention more readily on distinctive features, the unique surface details, which overshadow the underlying roots of melody. Kurth observes, "The usual tendency to overlook [these developmental motives] lies thus in their concealment, not in their emptiness, nor in their lesser intensity of effect."[3]

Our preoccupation with the stylized thematic surface and our resultant inattentiveness to directional impulses beneath it characterize not only our usual mode of listening but also the composer's creative activity. There, too, developmental motives operate at an "unconscious" level.[4] Nevertheless, they are the first and most primitive musical embodiment of a composer's creative-psychic stream. Themes themselves, the main objects of a composer's conscious activity, are elaborated crystallizations of these fundamental melodic motions, and as such they represent secondary manifestations of the creative will.[5]

Kurth's idea of the unconscious psyche giving rise to developmental motives, as opposed to the conscious psyche producing stylized themes, resembles ideas on the structure of the psyche proposed in the early years of the twentieth century by Carl Gustav Jung. Jung, like Kurth, worked and lived most of his life in Switzerland. In 1912, the year Kurth moved to Bern, Jung published his *Wandlungen und Symbole der Libido,* later translated as *Psychology of the Unconscious* (1916).[6], Kurth, who from 1912 on lived within fifty miles of Jung, was probably familiar with the psychologist's work.[7]

According to Jung, the psyche consists of two components, consciousness and unconsciousness, with the ego mediating between the two. Consciousness, containing highly differentiated data, is only a small part of the psyche. It controls and adapts our deep-lying, instinctive psychic dispositions to the social environment through four basic "psychological functions": thinking, feeling, sensation, and intuition.[8] The instinctive psychic dispositions, as I have called them, belong to the unconscious realm, which divides into the personal and the collective unconscious. Our interest here lies chiefly in the collective unconscious, which contains undifferentiated data, "humanity's typical forms of reaction since the earliest beginnings [of man]."[9]

Jung hypothesizes organizing forces amid the undifferentiated data in the collective unconscious. These forces, called *archetypes,* act as centers of gravity imposing order on the experiences sinking through the personal unconscious into the collective unconscious. Primal emotions and images such as Fear, Anger, and Mother are examples of archetypes, which are limited in number because they represent the most primitive human experiences.[10]

Just as Jung's archetypal images impinge upon conscious activities, so Kurth's prototypal melodic gestures and developmental motives impinge upon deliberate compositional acts. Both Jung's and Kurth's primal forms, as unconscious stimuli, engender results whose sources are unknowable to the conscious psyche. In the case of Jung's archetypes, for example, an unconscious image of Mother produces a certain conscious behavior toward mother; in the case of Kurth's developmental motives, an unconscious psychic urge to rise produces a consciously stylized thematic profile, which gives a corresponding sonic form to that urge. Through objective, psychologically oriented analysis, we can discover the germinal archetypes or motives.

DEVELOPMENTAL MOTIVES IN BACH'S MUSIC

Kurth discusses developmental motives in *Grundlagen* and in the article "Zur Motivbildung Bachs: Ein Beitrag zur Stilpsychologie" ("On Bach's Motivic Formation: A Contribution to the Psychology of Style"), which expands on the ideas presented in *Grundlagen*. The following paragraphs describe Kurth's developmental motives and their role in Bach's music. Each is presented initially as an idealized melodic shape. It is important to remember that the motives are extracted, or "distilled" as Kurth puts it, from the surface of the music—the themes and their offshoots. The motives themselves have no independent existence, except as source elements of the unconscious. The distillation process is an analytic act similar to the process of psychoanalysis. Kurth "psychoanalyzes" the music in search of developmental motives just as Jung might psychoanalyze a patient, searching for, among other things, archetypes that cause certain patterns of behavior. The results of such analysis illuminate the process of individuation in the case of the patient, and the creative process in the case of music.

Developmental motives fall into three categories, based on the three possible courses musical motion can take: ascending (*ansteigend*), descending (*absteigend*), and oscillating (*schwebend*). In the dynamic-formal development of a piece, these terms correspond respectively to upward and downward arches, and to preservation of musical tension at some given level.[11] Each category possesses its own musical shape, though Kurth stresses that hybrid forms are more common; in fact, they are the rule since developmental motives, as distillations of melody, represent ideal forms. The three basic shapes are thus "limiting cases" (*Grenzfälle*), ideal boundaries within which countless intermediate forms arise, each uniting elements of the ideal forms. This characteristic reflects the very essence of polyphony itself, which by nature, according to Kurth, is an art of fluent transitions. By categorizing the motives into fundamental types, we merely obtain convenient references. Such references must not be applied too inflexibly or the result will be analytic schematicism, which trivializes developmental motives and obliterates their complex definition.

It is important to realize that Kurth did not discover developmental motives by searching for and then mechanically classifying distilled melodic gestures. Quite the contrary, while charting the overall dynamic-formal shape of musical works, he observed a tendency of the music to develop local, generic motivic shapes which matched and thus promoted the momentarily prevailing dynamic-formal curve. These curves, arching slowly upward or downward, or oscillating, engender appropriate developmental motives, and not vice versa.[12] Kurth thus integrates the local and global dimensions of dynamic form into an organic whole.

Ascending Motives

The model for the ascending motive is the upper tetrachord of a scale (Ex. 3-1). Its

EXAMPLE 3-1.

defining characteristics include the ascending movement across a fourth, crowned by the leading-tone effect, which Kurth considers its most poignant feature. The motive moves toward a point of extreme tension, as though magnetically attracted, and then resolves resolutely. Kurth offers several variations of the ascending motive, all of which "approximate the model" (*Annäherungsformen*) (Ex. 3-2). The last of these approximations (Ex. 3-2*c*) does not fit the prototype as closely as do the other two. Here, the fourth has become a fifth, which in this rhythmic setting impresses an arpeggiation on our ears and thus de-emphasizes the characteristic leading-tone effect. Kurth includes the example nevertheless, probably because of the striking b♮, which acts like a leading tone within the F–C fifth.

(a)   (b)

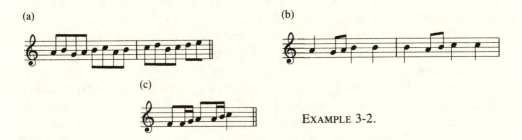

(c)

EXAMPLE 3-2.

In addition to the more or less closely related variations of Example 3-2, Kurth includes the melodic shapes in Example 3-3, "climbing formations," in this category. We can see this variation of the motive in Examples 3-4*a* and *b*.[13] Kurth refers to the climbing formation, with its leap to a leading tone and subsequent resolution, when introducing yet another form of the ascending developmental motive, the upward leap of a fourth, which he identifies as an intensification of the model. Example 3-5 illustrates this motive. Kurth notes the gradually ascending imitations (right hand), which further enhance the ascending-fourth leap. A step downward after each ascending fourth in the descant balances the previous leap and effectively draws out the overall dynamic rise to its apex. Further, the compensatory downward steps prevent the line from overshooting its goal, b″, exactly one octave away from its starting point. The bass, by leaping up a fourth across each bar line, counteracts the slackening in the descant each time it steps downward, thus sustaining the overall momentum. The C-Major Fugue, *WTC* I, not mentioned by Kurth in this context, provides an excellent example of ascending fourths (Ex. 3-6). Here, the scalar and disjunct fourths in close proximity complement each other. Kurth might have included the last melodic gesture (bracketed) preceding the second entrance as a descending scalar fourth. It might be viewed as relief from tension generated by the two foregoing disjunct fourths, which together form a descending pattern and so help prepare for the final release.[14]

EXAMPLE 3-3.

(a)

(b)

EXAMPLE 3-4. Bach, B-Minor Fugue, *WTC* I: (*a*) mm. 7–9; (*b*) mm. 24–26

EXAMPLE 3-5. Bach, B-Major Fugue, *WTC* II, mm. 68–71

EXAMPLE 3-6. Bach, C-Major Fugue, *WTC* I, mm. 1–3

Kurth actually interprets Example 3-7 similarly. His bracket indicates that he views the ascending fourth a♯–d♯′ as an entity.[15] In an analysis that coordinates melodic and harmonic dimensions, the a♯ is a neighbor note between two b's in a B-major harmony (Ex. 3-8). Kurth's overall analysis of this theme as a broad structural descent from f♯′ to d♯′, contrasted dynamically with three local ascents, e♯′–f♯′, c♯′–e♮′ and b–d♯′, indicates that he understood the ascending a♯–d♯′ as an embedded motivic detail. Occasionally, however, Kurth's analyses do go against the harmonic grain. In such cases, it is a matter of fundamental analytic premise—linear, harmonic, or linear-harmonic. Results from one approach may conflict with those of another. For instance, let us return in Example 3-9 to the excerpt from

EXAMPLE 3-7. Bach, F♯-Major Fugue, *WTC* II, mm. 1–5

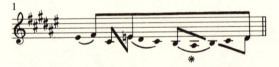

EXAMPLE 3-8.

Bach's C-Major Fugue, *WTC* I, quoted earlier in Example 3-6. The descending scalar fourth, a'–e', is a motivic entity that reverses the direction of the previous ascending fourths, including the initial scalar one, c'–f'. The a'–e' descent thus provides directional balance at the conclusion of the subject. Of course, as a linear-motivic unit, a'–e' conflicts with the harmonic progression, which assigns the a' a neighbor-note function. Kurth's tacit acceptance of harmonic factors does not exclude this view, and the a'–e' could remain intact as a melodic motive, harmony notwithstanding.[16] In Kurth's analysis, linear elements take precedence. Had he referred to this fugue subject, and further to the role of harmony in it, motivic unity would have guided his ear.[17]

EXAMPLE 3-9.

Descending Motives

Compared with the ascending developmental motive, and with the oscillating types to be discussed shortly, the descending motive is less common. According to Kurth, the relative infrequency of descending developmental motives is a natural outcome of the infrequency of the uninterrupted descending dynamic-formal curves ("curvilinear developments") that would engender corresponding developmental motives.[18] Kurth lists a few forms of the descending developmental motive, whose prototype is shown in Example 3-10a. Examples 3-10b, c, and d are common hybrid or transitional forms (*Übergangsformen*), which illustrate the interdependence of the descending and oscillating types. Because Kurth finds that the descending type is most often associated with the oscillating type, or passes readily into it, he devotes only a few explanatory paragraphs to descending motives and cites no musical examples of them.[19] Kurth's main source of examples of other developmental motives, Bach's keyboard works, do contain some striking instances of the descending type. Example 3-11 offers three of many possible illustrations; that such examples are so plentiful indicates that the descending motive perhaps deserves more autonomy than Kurth was willing to grant it. Observe how the descending fourth in Example 3-11a participates first in an overall descending curve (mm. 32–36), then in an ascending curve (mm. 36–39). In Example 3-11c, the motive incorporates a neighbor note; in this it is similar to Example 3-9. As noted above, Kurth does not always feel obliged to account for vertical influences on what he considers horizontal phenomena. De-

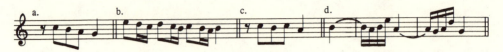

EXAMPLE 3-10. (above)

(a)

(b)

(c)

EXAMPLE 3-11. (below) (*a*) Bach, Little Fugue in E Minor, BWV 900, mm. 31–40; (*b*) Bach, Two-Part Invention No. 3, mm. 1–4; (*c*) Bach, Two-Part Invention No. 8, mm. 1–4

velopmental motives are *melodic* fragments, which maintain linear autonomy regardless of the harmonic overlay.

Oscillating Motives

The neighbor-note figures shown in Example 3-12 are the models of the oscillating or "circling" motive (*Schwebemotiv*). Oscillating motives are single tones embellished by "a slight flickering of motion," the primary function of which is to preserve a given pitch level.[20] Examples range from simple extensions, such as the double neighbor note, to the more commonly encountered hybrid forms shown in Example 3-13. Ascending or descending sequential patterns, seen in Examples 3-13*c* and *e,* lead to what Kurth labels descending or ascending oscillations (Examples 3-14*a* and *b* respectively).[21]

EXAMPLE 3-12.

EXAMPLE 3-13.

EXAMPLE 3-14.

Each melodic shape in the preceding two examples exhibits qualities of the oscillating motive, qualities modified by either descending or ascending motives. Compared with these oscillating types, the unmodified rising and falling types communicate more immediately their directional impulses; consequently, they have a heightened dramatic effect. Compare Examples 3-15*a* and *b* with Example 3-14*b*. The oscillating element acts as a retardant, preventing too rapid an ascent. Depending on the momentary stage of formal development in a piece—for example, preparation for, or immediate approach to, a primary or secondary apex; departure from an apex; or transition—the music may exhibit motivic forms closer to the ideal models, or it may feature one of the hybrid forms.

EXAMPLE 3-15.

Let us study Examples 3-16 and 3-17 to see how developmental motives behave over the course of a piece. In Example 3-16a, observe how the descending oscillation, interrupted by quarter notes, proceeds downward a measure at a time. Compare this with Example 3-16b, where the oscillation descends one step with each dotted quarter. Example 3-16a, the first transitional section in the piece, leads to a renewed presentation of the theme (m. 20), now inverted. Example 3-16b, with its steadier descent, contains the final statement of the inverted subject in what has, by this time, developed into a re-exposition of the theme in inversion (mm. 20–31).

Measures 34–39 (Ex. 3-16c) exhibit increased agitation as the music, now tonally unsettled, moves toward a thematic exposition in minor (mm. 38ff.). Here, the motion alternates between unrelieved descent, distributed over both hands

(a)

EXAMPLE 3-16. Bach, G-Major
Fugue, *WTC* I:
(*a*) mm. 17–21;
(*b*) mm. 29–32

(b)

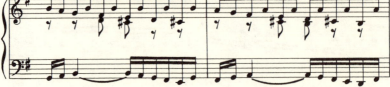

(c)

EXAMPLE 3-16c. mm. 34–39

(mm. 34–35 of Ex. 3-16*c*), and uninterrupted ascents (mm. 36–37), occasioning the thematic section in E minor. Note also how these uninterrupted scalar motions interact with the slower ascent of the complementary part. This polyphonic opposition creates internal tensions, which lead to the dynamic-textural resolution of measure 38. A different kind of tension/resolution event occurs in measures 54–56 of the same fugue (Ex. 3-17), where the voices coordinate their motions and, with two sudden, rhythmically agitated allusions to the fugue subject, cooperate in bringing the piece to a powerful climax. As the preceding examples show, developmental motives follow the dynamic-formal curve of a piece, reflecting its current stage of evolution. This is what Kurth means when he says developmental motives are "architectonic."[22]

EXAMPLE 3-17.

Kurth shows a keen awareness of coordination among strands of a musical texture. He observes balances between contrasting developmental motives, even within a single voice, as, for example, in the appearance of the second theme in Bach's C♯-Minor Fugue, *WTC* I, measures 35–38 (Ex. 3-18).[23] The gradually descending

EXAMPLE 3-18. Bach C♯-Minor Fugue, *WTC*, mm. 35–38

oscillation over a third (g♯″–e″) balances the previous, relatively quick ascent of a fourth (d♯″–g♯″). In Example 3-19, Kurth observes the interaction of the "stretching" or "reaching" motive (*Ausbreitungsmotiv*) with the oscillating motive, which balances the preceding rise.

EXAMPLE 3-19. Bach, French Suite No. 1, Allemande, mm. 8–10

Themes may exhibit such equilibrium, as in the subject of the G-Major Fugue, *WTC* I, in Example 3-20. Of course, the three-note ascent in this example is not the same as the four-note rising developmental motive. Nevertheless, Kurth accepts this variation, even though it omits the leading-tone effect.[24] Such flexibility can create problems for the theory of developmental motives by causing an analysis to lapse into observations of general directional tendencies.

EXAMPLE 3-20.

Themes may also feature a single type of developmental motive, as in the Prelude and Fugue in A♭, *WTC* I.[25] In order to understand themes fully, we must comprehend their tonal profile as an "expression of processes of motion" (*Ausdruck von Bewegungsvorgängen*). Kurth views themes as elaborations and concentrations of underlying basic motions, often identifiable as developmental motives in various guises: "As seen from this point of view, linear movement in the most general sense represents the primary phenomenon, [and] the characteristic stamp of themes [represents] a progressive individualization based on this movement."[26] When analyzing a theme, then, we must examine its constituent directional impulses, its developmental motives. But Kurth warns against the danger of routine, mechanical dissection of a theme into particles. That approach obscures the main issue, the *transition* between motives, and the meaning of the motives within the whole: "a theme is just as little a sum of component motives as the melodic line is a sum of tones."[27]

Kurth broadens the sphere of developmental motives from polyphonic strands and themes to embrace tonal motions of larger proportions. By associating successive, nonadjacent melodic goals, Kurth derives what he calls "curvilinear developments." He calls the constituent melodic goals "curvilinear apexes" and the resulting large-scale melodic continuity an "overriding line."[28] The most common curvilinear development associates apexes a second apart, since our ear readily follows their stepwise connection. Example 3-21 illustrates an overriding line that traverses a third, from a″ to f♯″. Example 3-22 is similar.[29]

EXAMPLE 3-21. Bach, C♯-Minor Prelude, *WTC* I, mm. 5–7

EXAMPLE 3-22. Bach, B-Major Fugue, *WTC* II, mm. 29–33

Example 3-23, not cited by Kurth though based on the same principle as Examples 3-21 and 3-22, points up two important and far-reaching ramifications of curvilinear developments. First, although the overriding line descends, each apex represents the goal of an *ascending* developmental motive. This internal opposition between individual rising components in the local context and an overall descent in the larger dimension heightens the level of tension produced by the broader formal development.[30] Furthermore, the curvilinear descent itself, c″–f♯′, is a kind of large-scale inversion of the ascending developmental motive covering a fifth, although the descent is modified so that the leading-tone effect occurs at the bottom of the fifth rather than at the top. Kurth's ideas here clearly indicate a notion of hierarchically organized dynamic-formal levels.

EXAMPLE 3-23. Bach, Little Fugue in C Major, BWV 952, mm. 5–8

Developmental Motives in Wagner's Music

According to Kurth, Baroque and Romantic styles share characteristics belonging to a primitive stage of musical formation, the subconscious realm of developmental motives. Just as the developmental motive, at the pre-sonic stage, represents a flickering of motion within the borad contours outlined by the *Fortspinnung,* it plays an analogous, though less precise, role in the domain of endless melody. Kurth's initial remarks on endless melody deal with elements of harmony, meter, melodic phraseology, and leitmotifs.[31] Developmental motives, as discussed so far, resemble leitmotifs, though the former operate at a more fundamental level of melodic composition.

Kurth differentiates between leitmotifs and developmental motives. Leitmotifs, with their dramatic and psychological associations, are extrinsic to the musical process itself and amount to surface manifestations reflecting the drama. Developmental motives, on the other hand, are intrinsic to the musical structure and do not rely on extramusical meanings. As Kurth observes "In delving down to the most general absolute processes of motion, the [developmental] motives detach themselves from conceptual meaning."[32] They are symbols of psychic activity, not of concepts, emotions, or the like.[33] Furthermore, while leitmotifs project consciously sculpted and strategically deployed motivic profiles, developmental motives remain in the background. They generally do not participate directly in the stylized musical surface. Instead, they are absorbed into the cumulative dynamic flow; "indeed, certain rudimentary linear developmental motives do not disappear entirely, but they remain rare and less significant, [and they] appear swept away by the overall [musical] undulations." Additionally, Kurth declares that in Romantic music the "small, linear developmental motives . . . do not cooperate as independent, single lines [as they do in Baroque polyphony], but rather, on the contrary, strive to wrest themselves from the harmonic totality to achieve independence."[34]

This "invisibility" of developmental motives is as much a historical as a musical phenomenon. In an attempt to liberate themselves from Classical conventions, the Romantics recover the more potent energies of free-flowing melodic motion, modified by the evolutionary process of recovery itself. They create intricate, supple linear complexes, which are absorbed by homophonic remnants, now in an intensified harmonic environment. The smaller constituent motions embedded in this linear fabric melt into the comprehensive harmonic-rhythmic stream.

Kurth does not pursue a systematic treatment of each motivic prototype in *Romantische Harmonik,* as he had done earlier in *Grundlagen* and "Motivbildung." Instead, he reviews the prototypes with reference to Bach, because in Bach's music "the developmental motives . . . [are] more clearly . . . recognizable than in the Romantic period, where to a large extent . . . they must first be extracted from entanglement within other phenomena, if one wishes to perceive them clearly."[35] After a summary presentation of the models, Kurth abandons viewing them as "ideal boundaries." Instead, he characterizes them as an "average of countless and illimitable related forms," whose chief trait is illimitability of transition from one form to another.[36] The idea of developmental motives as "averages" is different than that of developmental motives as "ideal boundaries." Kurth has redefined theoretically the motivic prototypes in Romantic music, but he does not offer any referential models. Lacking such models, we can no longer speak of such ambivalent motivic forms as hybrids among *Grenzfälle* and therefore must accept any directional impulse outlined in tones as a developmental motive. Previously a clear-cut gauge of dynamic-formal progress in various musical strata, developmental motives in this context lose their distinct identities and become gestures of "going up," "going down," and so on. But how else is music to move?

Kurth understands that it is the *unique forms* of musical motion, rather than motion per se, that are important for analysis. Even though specific melodic shapes may be lacking, developmental motives may still convey directional impulses and thus give insight into dynamic-formal or dramatic events. Greater or lesser melodic individuality, and more or less harmonic influence, measure stylistic differentiation. Indeed, it is precisely with these guidelines in mind that Kurth views the relationship between Bach's reserved, objective art and the Romantics' unrestrained, subjective art.

For Kurth, developmental motives have a peculiar significance because, as "pure symbols of motion," they are the particles constituting the larger stream of psychic forces. They are sonic manifestations of the composer's mental life and belong to the essence of the musical fabric. Uncovering and defining the dynamic function of developmental motives is thus equivalent to apprehending that essence.

Kurth cites the last movement of Beethoven's Piano Sonata Op. 31, No. 2 ("Tempest"), to show how motivic elements, in the right hand, may yield to the overall harmonic momentum: "It would be highly inappropriate here to label this motive with the minor sixth as melody, the rest as accompaniment. . . . The relationship of melody and accompaniment, a cardinal trait of homophony, is completely overturned."[37] Kurth also refers to the beginning of the first and last movements of Beethoven's Op. 27, No. 2 ("Moonlight"), in this regard. Both of these works sufficiently integrate melody and accompaniment so that Kurth detects in them the emergence of endless melody.

Harmonic currents transform the Baroque oscillating motive, for example, into swaying or billowing figures (*Wellenfiguren*), illustrated in Example 3-24 by an excerpt from Wagner's *Wesendonck-Lieder*. Nothing remains of the Baroque neighbor-

EXAMPLE 3-24. Wagner, "Der Engel"

note embellishment except a feeling of registral-textural suspension. Example 3-25 draws a closer relation between the Baroque and Romantic forms of the oscillating motive than does Example 3-24. Right- and left-hand parts, both executing "ascending oscillations," join to create a sense of upward swaying. The overall effect is paramount. It represents the "totality" out of which the individually crafted lines seek autonomy. Kurth observes, "This is not a 'combination' but rather a primal totality which frays into fibers." [38] In Example 3-25, the neighbor-note embellishment is clearly visible. The relationship between Baroque and Romantic developmental motives is less clear when, as in Example 3-24, specific melodic shapes fade.

EXAMPLE 3-25. *Walküre*, II, 5

Example 3-26, from the second movement of Bruckner's First Symphony, includes a wave figure that, according to Kurth, recalls Bach's oscillating motives. It appears that various motivic profiles that hover in a narrow pitch range or gradually ascend or descend in sequence qualify as wave figures, whether or not they feature neighbor-note embellishment. Given the differences between Romantic and Baroque melodic conventions, and given Kurth's emphasis on the primal role of harmony in Romantic music, wave figures are a reasonable extension of the oscillating motive. By contrast, Romantic modifications of ascending and descending developmental motives bear less resemblance to Bach's practices.

EXAMPLE 3-26. Bruckner, Symphony No. 1, II, mm. 96–97

Romantic "vaulting" and "plunging" wave figures (*Anstiegswellen* and *Absturzwellen*) sweep dramatically upward or downward in one continuous gesture. Tonally, they are often less well defined and intervallically much less constrained than their Baroque forerunners. Example 3-27 demonstrates both ascending and descending waves, which frame a powerful climax. [39] Kurth finds precedents for such dramatic sweeps in early Romantic music, as in Example 3-28, which he compares with Example 3-29.[40] In contrasting these two passages, Kurth asserts stronger "linear independence" (*lineare Selbständigkeit*) for the Wagner excerpt. Though he does not support this claim analytically, perhaps he reasoned along the following lines. Against the two sustained chords in the lower parts, the upper voice in Example 3-29 passes chromatically over chord members, beginning with a strident accented upper neighbor note, A. The neighbors do promote a feeling of linearity in Example 3-29. In general, though, the plunging figure relies as much on underlying harmonies for definition of its constituents as do the descending arpeggiations in Example 3-28. What Kurth is hearing is the difference between a descending gesture based on pure arpeggiation (Ex. 3-28) and one based on the melodic procedure of (chromatic) passing notes (Ex. 3-29). Kurth's contrast of the two passages draws our attention to the overall effect, the aural character of the two plunging figures, rather than to the note-to-note detail.

EXAMPLE 3-27. *Tristan,* I, 4

EXAMPLE 3-28. Heinrich Marschner, *Der Vampyr,* II (Finale)

EXAMPLE 3-29. *Tristan,* I, 3

Had Kurth widened the context slightly, his point in Example 3-29 would have been even better supported (see Ex. 3-30). The harmonic progression in Example 3-30 introduces scene 3 of *Tristan*. It is largely contrapuntal. There is a hint of an augmented sixth chord at the end of measure 6, which resolves to a C♯-minor six-four chord in measure 7 (clouded by the accented upper neighbor note, A), and a hint of a four-two chord moving to a sixth chord between measures 7 and 8. But these sonorities are exceptional in that they have clear contrapuntal functions. In any case, measures 5–6 are harmonically uncertain and definitely transitory. The entire segment up to measure 8 lends itself well to a primarily linear analysis, and Kurth's intuition of "linear independence" in Example 3-29 seems all the more convincing in light of the expanded context shown in Example 3-30.[41]

EXAMPLE 3-30.

In addition to considering passages in which overall harmonic forces serve as a background for developmental motives, Kurth includes one interesting example in which the overall linear impulse is primary (Ex. 3-31). A descending developmental motive (the first five tones) inspires an ascending vaulting wave, which spins out sequentially a series of interlocking, descending steps derived from the last fragment of the motive. Kurth, however, maintains that the compositional process follows a different path: first comes the impulse to rise, then the details that implement that rise. Given the descending developmental motive at the head of this passage, the consequent is clear. But Kurth does not comment on exactly why an upward surge should originate from a descending motive in the first place.[42]

EXAMPLE 3-31. *Walküre*, I, 3

Developmental motives interact with leitmotifs and so promote the organic flow of endless melody. For Kurth, observing transitions between surface melodic elements, such as leitmotifs, and the more fundamental motions embodied in developmental motives is essential to analysis. It is precisely the elusive passage from generic motives to consciously shaped themes, from subconscious impulses to "phenomenal" music and vice versa, that marks the evolutionary path of musical creation.[43]

The passages in Examples 3-32 and 3-33 demonstrate this process. Example 3-32 represents Isolde's discontent (Anger-Motive), stated at the beginning of act I. Later, in scene 4, Isolde refuses Tristan's offer to escort her from the ship. At that point, the motive returns in the turbulent form shown in Example 3-33.[44] Observe how the original motive of Example 3-32 maintains its contour at the beginning of Example 3-33 but then loses its distinctive intervallic series (Ex. 3-34). Subsequently, the leitmotif dissolves into a falling developmental motive, which in its registral climb is part of an overall ascending wave.[45] The transition from leitmotif to developmental motive progresses gradually from a melodic variation to a directional tendency.

EXAMPLE 3-32. *Tristan*, I, 1

EXAMPLE 3-33. *Tristan*, I, 4

EXAMPLE 3-34.

The preceding examples of ascending and descending developmental motives indicate that Romantic melodic techniques realize more fundamentally their essential nature as sonic motion than do those of the Baroque. The directional impulse is primary; the specific melodic expressions depend on style. Bach's developmental motives are more contained. They generally traverse only a fourth or fifth, and they ascend or descend gradually, through sequential repetition, to create curvilinear developments. Wagner's idiom significantly expands the dramatic as well as registral latitude of developmental motives and greatly accelerates their movements. This should accelerate correspondingly the curvilinear developments. Unfortunately, in *Romantische Harmonik* Kurth does not deal with such large-scale linear processes in Romantic music.[46] A demonstration of broad melodic control in Wagner's operas would have helped neutralize criticisms like those of Hermann Wetzel.

Kurth concludes his discussion of developmental motives by reminding us of their elusiveness in nineteenth-century music. They lead a precarious existence, in constant danger of being "drowned out by the harmonic flow, mostly suppressed into the musical underground, sometimes forcing their way to the surface, only to sink back quickly once again."[47]

Several questions arise. Can we believe in musical phenomena that, because of their ostensible "deep" native realm, have limited sonic reality? Perhaps they exist only in theory after all, in some artificial form such as Kurth's prototypes. They may in fact be no more subconscious manifestations than are many other possible melodic fragments manipulated consciously by composers. Furthermore, if directed movements and not their specific sonic embodiments are primary, is it fair to apply the term "motive" to them at all? Of course from the viewpoint of directionality alone, it is reasonable to assert a pervasive, concealed existence for a few motivic types. Music without direction, including stabilization, is impossible. But is directionality a motive?

Kurth answers these questions only partially and indirectly. Assuming the genesis of music to be psychic energies manifested sonically as linear forces, Kurth takes linear simplicity as a sign of primitiveness and thus as a direct expression of psychic forces. These crystallize into certain musical shapes, the developmental motives. If we accept Kurth's psychological premises, we can further accept the idea of a limited number of universal motives. If our music-analytic views are less oriented toward psychology, a developmental motive may seem like just one among many possible melodic figures, simple to be sure, but no more primitive than its derivatives.

Kurth sees no conflict between melodic specificity on the one hand and directional generality on the other. If sonic phenomena are merely exterior, only the impulses beneath are consequential. This attitude comes through most clearly in *Romantische Harmonik,* where Kurth applies the term "developmental motive" to rapidly ascending scales, as well as to general ascents and descents. In *Bruckner,* Kurth further modifies the notion of developmental motives. Because Bruckner's symphonies lack the comparatively pristine, recurrent melodic shapes of the high Baroque, Kurth widens the scope of his definition of developmental motives to include coloristic and orchestral effects, such as tremolos and undulating accompanimental figures.[48]

Perhaps "developmental motive" in Kurth's sense ought more properly to be "motivation"—directional, psychological, or programmatic motivation—rather than "motive," which has unavoidable analytical connotations. Depending on the circumstances, a composer may be motivated to write ascents or descents, or to choose stabilization. A composer may adopt trills or tremolos to set a mood, establish sonic motives of various sorts to symbolize thoughts or ideas, employ scales or arpeggios to reflect a stage of formal development. These are artistic motivations; they guide the dramatic unfolding of a work and are classifiable within a given piece, composer's output, or historical style. Their analytical potency lies chiefly in the domain of form. Indeed, Kurth studies developmental motives as keys to formal processes. From this standpoint, developmental motives are most valuable because they focus attention on routine musical events, which for Kurth are indispensable guides for discerning the local and global shape of a composition.[49]

NOTES

1. Kurth, *Grundlagen,* 436: "Abklärung der Melodik zu reinen Bewegungssymbolen."

2. Kurth, "Motivbildung" (see chap. 1, n. 66), 80.

3. Ibid., 81: "Das gewöhnliche Übersehen liegt dann an ihrer Verborgenheit, nicht an ihrer Leere, auch nicht an ihrer geringerer Wirkungsintensität."

4. Ibid., 87: "unbewusst."

5. Ibid.

6. Jung elaborated and further refined his ideas in subsequent publications, for instance in *The Structure and Dynamics of the Psyche,* vol. 8 of *Collected Works,* ed. Sir Herbert Read, et al., trans. R. F. C. Hull, Bollingen Series 20 (New York: Bollingen Foundation, 1960); and in *Two Essays on Analytical Psychology,* vol. 7 of *Collected Works* (New York: Bollingen Foundation, 1953; orig. Zurich: Rascher, 1928).

7. It is interesting to note that Kurth was still studying in Vienna when Jung began studying there with Freud in 1907. Remember, too, that Kurth was writing *Grundlagen,* where he first discusses developmental motives, sometime between 1912 and 1916. It is uncanny that Kurth never cites Jung's writings, even in *Musikpsychologie,* where he refers to numerous authors outside of music.

8. Jolande Jacobi, *The Psychology of C. G. Jung,* trans. K. W. Bash (London: Kegan Paul, 1942), 9–11. Jung calls thinking and feeling "rational," sensation and intuition "irrational."

9. Ibid., 8. The personal unconscious is a repository of items once held in the conscious psyche but at some point suppressed into the personal unconscious. Items suppressed into the personal unconscious may be recalled at any time into consciousness. Items held in the collective unconscious are irretrievable. See Frieda Fordham, *An Introduction to Jung's Psychology,* 3d ed. (Middlesex, Eng.: Penguin Books, 1966), 22–23.

10. Jacobi, *Psychology,* 41–42, 46.

11. Kurth, "Motivbildung," 88.

12. Ibid., 87, 115–16; Kurth, *Grundlagen,* 417–18, 436.

13. Kurth, "Motivbildung," 90: "rankende Bildungen." Kurth cites Example 3-4a in *Grundlagen,* 421, as an example of the climbing formation.

14. The descending fourth is the second motivic prototype; it is discussed in the next section. Hermann Kretzschmar characterizes this fugue subject as a "most resolute affirmation of the Will . . . the

expression of a sense of energy" ("entscheidende Bejahung des Willens . . . der Ausdruck eines Kraftgefühls"; "Anregungen" [see chap. 1, n. 26], 62). See also Kretzschmar's "Neue Anregungen," 76. Wilhelm Werker notes the motivic prominence of ascending and descending fourths in the C-Major Fugue subject and relates them to the Prelude. He deals with the pieces in his *Studien über die Symmetrie im Bau der Fugen und die motivische Zusammengehörigkeit der Präludien und Fugen des 'Wohltemperierten Klaviers' von Johann Sebastian Bach,* Abhandlungen der Sächsischen Staatlichen Forschungsinstitut zu Leipzig, Forschungsinstitut für Musikwissenschaft, vol. 3 (Leipzig: Breitkopf und Härtel, 1922), 3–4.

15. Kurth, "Motivbildung," 124.

16. In measure 8 of the fugue, the a″ in an a″–e″ descending fourth is harmonic.

17. As the second voice enters, the fugue subject spins itself out with a final descending fourth, f′–c′ (Ex. 3-9). This concluding gesture confirms the motivic significance of the immediately preceding fourth.

18. "Curvilinear developments" are discussed in the next section.

19. Kurth, "Motivbildung," 96.

20. Ibid., 92–93: "ein leichtes Flackern von Bewegung."

21. Ibid., 94: "Aufwärtsschwebungen," "Abwärtsschwebungen." These elaborations of the neighbor-note figures in Example 3-12 increase the number of developmental motives from three to four.

22. Kurth, "Motivbildung," 87.

23. Ibid., 117.

24. Ibid., 119. August Halm offers an interesting analysis of balance in the G-Major Fugue subject, in *Von zwei Kulturen der Musik,* 3d ed. (Stuttgart: Klett, 1947; 1st ed., Munich: G. Müller, 1913), 228–32.

25. Kurth, "Motivbildung," 120–21.

26. Ibid., 116–17: "Aus diesem Gesichtspunkt besehen, stellt sich demnach die allgemeinste Linien-bewegung als Primärerscheinung dar, die charakteristische Eigenprägung von Themen als eine von ihr ausgehende fortschreitende Individualisierung."

27. Ibid., 124: "ein Thema ist ebensowenig eine Summe von Teilmotiven als die melodische Linie eine Summe von Tönen ist."

28. Ibid., 98–99. Kurth's terms are *Kurvenentwicklung, Kurvenhöhepunkte,* and *übergreifende Linie.*

29. Kurth cites Examples 3-21 and 3-22 in "Motivbildung" on pp. 105 and 100 respectively.

30. Kurth calls the broader formal development "übergreifende Steigerungsentwicklung" ("Motiv-bildung," 99).

31. These aspects of endless melody were discussed in chapter 2.

32. Kurth, *Romantische Harmonik,* 536: "im Hinabdrängen zu den allgemeinsten absoluten Be-wegungsvorgängen, die Motive [lösen sich] von Begriffsbedeutung."

33. Ibid., 536: "they symbolize . . . fundamental processes of music," and we must understand them as "tonal symbols of certain dynamic forms of motion, thus as purely energetic processes" ("sie symbolisieren . . . psychische Grundvorgänge der Musik"; they are "Tonsymbole gewisser dyna-mischer Bewegungsformen, also rein energetischer Vorgänge").

34. Ibid., 540: "Zwar verschwinden gewisse rudimentäre lineare Entwicklungsmotive nicht vollständig, aber sie bleiben selten und bedeutungsloser, erscheinen weggespült von den Gesamtwellen." Ibid., 548: "[die] kleinen linearen Entwicklungsmotive . . . nicht als selbständige Einzellinien zusam-menwirken, sondern umgekehrt aus einer Gesamtheit harmonischen Charakters zur Selbststän-digkeit herausstreben."

35. Ibid., 547–38: "die Entwicklungsmotive . . . [sind] klarer . . . erkennbarer als in der Romantik, wo sie . . . zum grossen Teil erst aus einer Verstrickung anderer Erscheinungen herauszuschälen sind, wenn man sie klar erkennen will."

36. Ibid., 539: "die angerührte Form [gilt] als ein Durchschnitt durch zahllose und unabgrenzbare Annäherungsformen . . . , für die Übergänge zwischen den einzelnen Formen das Unabgrenzbare [ist] als das Wesentliche zu verstehen."

37. Ibid., 544: "Es wäre hier längst unzutreffend, dieses Motiv mit der kleinen Sext als Melodie, das übrige als Begleitung zu bezeichnen. . . . Das Verhältnis von Melodie und Begleitung, ein Hauptzug der Homophonie, ist hier vollständig umgestülpt." Hugo Riemann, in his *Grosse Kompositionslehre* 2:227–39, discusses the "suspension of differentiation between melody and accompaniment" ("Aufhebung der Unterscheidung von Melodie und Begleitung"). Riemann cites Beethoven's *An Elise* as well as the last movement of Op. 31, No. 2, as examples of such suspension.

38. Kurth, *Romantische Harmonik,* 558: "das ist keine 'Kombination,' sondern ursprüngliche Gesamtheit, die sich zerfasert." The passage from *Walküre* is in Schirmer, 176:8–9.

39. Kurth, *Romantische Harmonik,* 551. Schirmer, 61:7–8.

40. Kurth, *Romantische Harmonik,* 555. Schirmer, 27:7. Example 3-28 can be found in the Peters piano-vocal score of *Der Vampyr,* p. 236 (mm. 12–13), at Davenaut's words "Ha! wagst du's dich zu widersetzen?"

41. Perhaps Kurth assumed the context cited in Example 3-32, which led him to cite the passage as chiefly "linear" in the first place.

42. Kurth, *Romantische Harmonik,* 557. Example 3-31 is in Schirmer, 48:7–8.

43. Kurth discusses this process at length in *Grundlagen,* part 4, chapter 4, "Verdichtung und Auflösung der thematischen Bewegung," 408–38.

44. Kurth, *Romantische Harmonik,* 472, 551. Schirmer, 6:26–28; 61:5–8. Isolde's indignation at Tristan's suggestion is heightened by the drama of the moment. This puts the Anger-Motive (*Zorn-Motiv*) in sixteenths rather than the eighths of Example 3-34. Can Isolde, determined to drink a death potion with Tristan, allow the man who killed her lover to escort her into the arms of the king?

45. This demonstrates well the "striving and counterstriving" ("Strebung und Gegenstrebung") expressed by developmental motives on the one hand and the cumulative motion to which they contribute on the other (Kurth, *Romantische Harmonik,* 540). The result is a state of formal tension produced by these conflicting directional impulses.

46. In *Romantische Harmonik,* Kurth does hint once at higher-order melodic continuities, in connection with the third movement of Beethoven's Piano Sonata Op. 31, No. 2. The melody there, he suggests, comprises the "wave crests" (*Wellenkämmen*), which are "linked from measure to measure, and are drawn across the whole as a thin veil" ("durch die Takte gekettet und über das Ganze als dünnen Schleier gezogen"; *Romantische Harmonik,* 544).

47. Ibid., 562: "von den grossen Klangflutungen übertönt, meist in den Untergrund der Musik hinabgedrängt, bisweilen an die Oberfläche emportreibend, um rasch wieder zu versinken."

48. Kurth, *Bruckner,* 333, 345. A tremolo, for example, is a stylized modification of an enduring tone. Kurt von Fischer follows Kurth's expanded view of developmental motives. In his inaugural dissertation, *Die Beziehung von Form und Motiv in Beethovens Instrumentalwerken* (Zurich: Heitz, 1948), 1–76, Fischer establishes a large body of developmental motives, melodic and rhythmic—for example, the sighing motive (*Seufzermotiv,* or unprepared appoggiatura), scales, arpeggios, sequences, tone repetitions, trills, tremolos, and turns—with which he examines form in Beethoven's music.

49. Presenting developmental motives apart from their main function distorts their significance somewhat in Kurth's writings. I have included this chapter on developmental motives here since they are technically linear elements. Functionally, however, they are agents of form. Chapter 3 therefore provides background for chapter 9, on form.

CHAPTER 4

Polyphonic Melody

In chapter 3, we saw how developmental motives in Bach's instrumental works participate in "curvilinear developments." By examining characteristics of linear contour in general, such as the use of register, leading tones, and melodic leaps, Kurth discovers other broad, linear continuities. Using these insights, he reveals implicit polyphonic substructures that enrich monophonic pieces. In these polyphonic substructures, he identifies linear refinements such as motivic exchanges among "apparent voices" (*Scheinstimmen*), the subtle emergence and dissipation of apparent voices, and the interaction of apparent voices with the "actual voice" (*Realstimme*), the note-to-note development of the monophonic line itself.[1]

Kurth was not the first theorist to recognize polyphonic networks implied in a single-line melody. Several eighteenth-century writers, among them Johann Mattheson and Johann Phillip Kirnberger, discuss melodies that project two or more constituent strands.[2] Both authors assert a harmonic basis, arpeggiation, for this phenomenon. A given two-, three-, or four-voice progression may be transformed into a single melodic line that, with registral adjustments, projects the sound of the original harmonic succession. Compare Mattheson's and Kirnberger's conclusions:

> The practice has been introduced that often, in a single voice of this type, three or four pitches in the full yet broken chord are heard successively.

> When a single-line melody is composed in such a way that its harmony is implied and sounds like a two- or three-part piece, the forbidden [melodic] progressions no longer sound bad.[3]

By contrast, Kurth generally concentrates on linear details apart from harmony. By dealing mainly with the horizontal dimension, Kurth produces linear analyses that differ from those aimed at coordinating harmony and melody. It is important to remember that this latter approach, associated today primarily with Heinrich Schenker, was unknown to Kurth in 1915–16.[4]

Kurth worked largely without the benefit of precedent in his investigation of broad linear continuities. While he was surely familiar with the above-mentioned eighteenth-century treatises, the writings of his contemporaries probably influenced Kurth more directly. Hugo Riemann's volumes on Bach's *Well-Tempered Clavier,* for example, reduce many of the Preludes to what Riemann calls their "elementary harmonic form," or "harmonic basis." Each of these analytical sketches consists of a bass line coupled with a skeletal soprano line made up of the "melodic peaks."[5] As will become clear shortly, Riemann's melodic peaks are particularly significant for Kurth's analyses of polyphonic melody. But the disjunct melodic progressions found in most of Riemann's skeletal reductions differ from Kurth's overriding lines, which generally follow a stepwise course. Guido Adler's brief, nontechnical discussion of composite melodic structures and broad linear unity may also have inspired Kurth to go beyond the surface of Bach's polyphony.[6] A theorist as resourceful as Kurth finds a dearth of forerunners no obstacle. Where analytical models and terminology are wanting, he establishes his own. Kurth's analytical insightfulness more than compensates for a scarcity of historical precedent.

Chordal outlines—arpeggiations—are the simplest and most direct form of monophonic enrichment. Melodic contours based predominantly on arpeggiation convey the sound of individual chords and their voice-leading connections. According to Kurth, these implied harmonies counteract the "poverty of a single line." Kurth acknowledges a harmonic element in all melody but denies any pre-existent harmonic basis. In his words, "The line did not emerge from primary, latent harmonic formation, but rather, conversely, embodies in its form the harmonic factors out of which grows harmonic meaning in developed musical consciousness."[7] We could argue that it is precisely this "developed musical consciousness" that furnishes the very harmonic background against which melody arises, but such a discussion would take us too far afield, leading to the familiar question of whether melody issues from harmony, or vice versa.[8] We will not take time here trying to resolve that question, since the discussion would be unlikely to advance our understanding of Kurth's views. His position is clear. He does recognize the importance of harmony, despite his characteristic melodic-genetic outlook, but he refers to harmony as a resultant, nongenerative element of music.

Kurth takes an interesting view of the harmonic arpeggiation in his discussion of Example 4-1. He gives two reasons, one general, one context-specific, for maintaining a linear, melodic-genetic approach to this example. First, he does not believe that such arpeggiations are merely cyclings through chord tones. In reference to the Prelude from Bach's Cello Suite in G major, Kurth distinguishes between a rounding out of a line over chordal contours and pure arpeggiation.

Contrary to the usual theoretical explanation, here we see something essentially different than a mere rolling off, an "arpeggiating," of chords. In such passages we have, rather, in a reverse developmental process, a broadening out of the line over chordal contours and, concomitantly, an influx of rich harmonic fullness, but always a process of approximating and advancing toward chordal effects, not a fundamental chordal feeling. . . . Even where Bach's line is fully rounded out over chordal contours, it never founders in dull outlining of harmonies.[9]

EXAMPLE 4-1. Bach, Cello Suite in E♭ Major, Prelude, mm. 1–15

Kurth conceives of such passages linearly; that is, he believes an otherwise conjunct line has widened its stepwise course to form arpeggiations. It is a question of theoretical perspective, he insists, whether we understand such arpeggiations melodically or harmonically.

> One and the same phenomenon in a musical piece presents itself differently according to the theoretical premise. . . . Something which from the harmonic viewpoint must be merely *transitional tones* between chord tones, a *figuration* of a framework, something "nonessential," [i.e.,] the *motion* which enters into a repose of a chord as rhythmic animation, is from the opposite perspective the formative, propulsive element.[10]

The second, context-specific reason Kurth asserts a linear basis for Example 4-1 has to do with the melodic connections between nonadjacent tones, or what we call polyphonic melody.[11] Kurth selects these nonadjacent pitches based on registral prominence. In Example 4-1, he derives two upper parts by associating the second and fifth eighth-notes, the melodic apexes (*Gipfeltöne*), of each beamed group. He further identifies a melodic bass composed of the first pitches in each of measures 9–13 as a sequel to a long E♭ pedal. Example 4-2 sketches Kurth's analysis. The apex notes in Example 4-2 are offset from one another in order to preserve the image of linear autonomy for each polyphonic strand. This is important since later, in what Kurth understands to be purely linear contexts, he disregards what we might consider harmonic influences over longer-range melodic progressions.[12] Two basic ideas are implicit in Kurth's analysis of Example 4-1. First, melodic continuities broader than those of immediate melodic succession exist, and second, registral prominence is the key to locating the nonadjacent tones creating those continuities. The second idea is decisive in analyzing passages in which linear features predominate.

EXAMPLE 4-2.

Suspensions are common melodic devices in polyphonic melody. They often resolve after several pitches have intervened, extending the effect of the dissonance: "with such suggestions of chordally dissonant tones, Bach often achieves increased tension by delaying the tone of resolution [and so] extending their effect." [13] Example 4-3 illustrates a suspended g' on the second sixteenth of measure 14, prepared by the seventh of an implied dominant seventh chord on A at the end of measure 13. [14] Unfortunately, Kurth does not specify which f♯' resolves the g', the third or the fifth sixteenth of measure 14. From a purely linear standpoint, the first f♯' would be the resolution, the second one a reinforcement. Kurth probably intends this reading, but he makes no analytical markings which would answer that question. Kurth finds another suspension later in the same work (mm. 24–26), shown in Example 4-4. Following an implied dominant harmony, a tonic chord (G major) arrives on the downbeat of measure 25. Then, for two sixteenths of beat two, f♯ is suspended (Ex. 4-5). Here the resolution is unequivocal, and Kurth's interpretation points toward a notion of aural prolongation.

EXAMPLE 4-3. Bach, Cello Suite in G Major, Allemande, mm. 13–14

EXAMPLE 4-4.

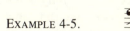

EXAMPLE 4-5.

The examples presented so far illustrate dissonant linear prolongations based on psycho-auditive criteria. The ear grasps dissonances touched on in the melodic

flow and retains them in aural memory until they resolve. In other words, the dissonances "hang" until we hear their continuation. According to Kurth, their "effect is
prolonged owing to the delayed arrival of the resolution." [15]

After explaining the elementary multilinear techniques presented so far, Kurth
takes up more sophisticated procedures involving still broader melodic connections.
As will become clear, Kurth's preference for linear interpretations occasionally disagrees with contemporary attitudes, which attempt to coordinate vertical and horizontal dimensions. Where such disagreements are interesting, I will supplement
Kurth's interpretations with alternate analyses.

To the criteria of registral prominence, harmonic dissonance, and melodic dissonance, Kurth adds another criterion for determining the course of larger-scale melodic motions: directional interruption.

> In audition, the tone with which the linear progression was first broken off
> is retained and then associated with the subsequent tones. . . . In this way
> continuities outside of the whole linear complex are formed between the
> individual tones. [16]

Pitches associated in this manner produce a "higher-order linear phase" (*übergeordnete Linienphase*) similar to the overriding curvilinear motions described earlier in
connection with developmental motives. In the outer voices, a higher-order line
"reaches across several phases of the monophonic unfoldment itself, . . . [creating]
a sensation of unity across large stretches [of music]." [17]

A higher-order line whose unfoldment was interrupted may resume its motion
after a few intervening notes, or sometimes after an entire measure or more. Example 4-6 shows a line ascending gradually over an octave, with brief directional
reversals interrupting the higher-order line. [18] Kurth does not highlight the rising
scale by extending the stems as is done in the example, but his description implies
this reading. In Example 4-7, ascending and descending scalar tritones underlie the
excerpt. Following a rapid ascent from c♯' to g', a more broadly paced higher-order
line descends gradually back to c♯'. Observe how the pitches composing the descending line are registrally highlighted, and how the arrival of each one is followed
by a directional reversal leading away from and back to the register of the higher-
order line.

Dramatic leaps mark the path of a higher-order line in Example 4-8. Kurth refers to a descending line from d' to f♯ but does not specify which notes belong to this
overriding linear phase. [19] The line marked by extended stems is the one Kurth probably had in mind, each pitch being projected registrally into the aural foreground and
highlighted further by directional interruptions. Such an interpretation assigns higher-
order status to pitches highlighted linearly. An analysis that accounts for harmonic
influences might follow the sketch shown in Example 4-9, in which a chain of 7–6
suspensions produces a descending line traversing a sixth, over a pedal D. This reading derives not only from the intervallic progression but also from the rhythmic fig-

EXAMPLE 4-6. Bach, E-Minor Fugue, *WTC* II, mm. 1–6

EXAMPLE 4-7. Bach, Cello Suite in D Minor, Prelude, mm. 43–48

ure that initiates the descent. By applying that figure (eighth plus two sixteenths) to subsequent, analogous leaps (in the first and third quarters of the following measures), we can establish the remaining notes of the descent. According to Example 4-9, the abrupt return to c′ in beat three of measure 29 (Ex. 4-8) is a lower-order reference to the higher-order c′ at the beginning of that measure. In my counter-interpretation, it is the b on the third sixteenth of beat three, not the b in beat one of the following bar, which now continues that c′. The remainder of the line descends analogously.

EXAMPLE 4-8. Bach, Cello Suite in G Major, Prelude, mm. 28–31

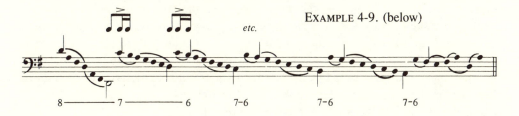

EXAMPLE 4-9. (below)

Kurth does not select higher-order pitches based on successions of vertical intervals (intervallic progressions) or on rhythmic motives. Instead, he determines the makeup of higher-order lines by observing certain distinctive melodic features. In Example 4-8, the b in beat one of measure 30, because of its registral placement and interruptive power, continues the previous c' (m. 29, beat three), which for Kurth is equivalent to the c' of beat one, measure 29. Kurth's higher-order line, unlike that shown in Example 4-9, is not based on a fixed intervallic progression. In fact, he rejects intervallic progressions as a basis for counterpoint, and traces all attempts to explain contrapuntal phenomena through these progressions back to Fux's species counterpoint. Kurth argues at length against the notion of *punctus contra punctum* as a way of viewing counterpoint.

> With this [method] the tendency toward a horizontal musical structure is destroyed at the very roots. . . . "Note against note" means connecting tones in specific intervals; however, two-voice composition in which each vertical tone pair ("note against note") underlies the structure, is a series of individual harmonic phenomena.
>
> First "species" is in actuality a harmonic structure.[20]

To Kurth's mind, analyzing polyphonic melody based on intervallic progressions conflicts with that melody's ideal genesis.[21]

Kurth's ideas on polyphonic melody may reflect performance practices of the time, as well as his own experiences playing Bach's cello suites. Pablo Casals, for instance, in a recording of the suites, frequently lengthens or dynamically stresses pitches distinguished by register and directional shifts. Kurth, however, cautions against unduly stressing the notes of higher-order lines.[22]

Stressing linear contour alone, without some harmonic checks, can occasionally produce analyses that disagree with aural intuition. Example 4-10 is a case in point. Kurth interprets measures 1–6 convincingly as an octave descent from eb', passing over db' (m. 3), c' and bb (m. 4), ab, g, and f, and ending on eb (m. 6).[23] In measures 6–11 Kurth traces a linear phase that ascends from eb to g', balancing the previous octave descent. The rise of over a tenth, however, is less satisfying than the initial octave descent. Beats one and four of measure 7 introduce f and g respectively, initiating the ascent. But then, in an attempt to connect the g with c' (m. 9), Kurth chooses as continuations a♮ and bb, two successive sixteenths in measure 8, the latter of which is "touched upon fleetingly." The bb in measure 8, following so closely after a♮ and lacking the reiteration accorded the preceding pitches of the ascent, seems an unlikely link to c' in measure 9. True, bb is the highest pitch of the bar, but it is a♮ that receives a motivic embellishment analogous to that of the previous g. According to motivic criteria, then, a♮ seems to dominate the end of measure 8 rather than being superseded by bb. But Kurth does not take motivic considerations into account here; instead, he hears the line ascending to bb, the peak of the preceding scalar ascent and the final pitch prior to a directional shift.

EXAMPLE 4-10. Bach, Cello Suite in E♭ Major, Allemande, mm. 1–12

One cannot help wondering why Kurth did not hear the line in measure 8, which ascends gradually from g to a♮ on the third and fourth beats, as analogous to the line in measure 7, where f ascends to g. Reading measures 7–8 in that way would, of course, leave a gap between the a♮ and the c in measure 9. Conversely, it is curious that Kurth heard a–b♭ in measure 8 without considering the same interpretation in measure 7, that is, g–a♭ within beat three.[24] He must have heard the dominant seventh quality of a♭, which signaled a return to g. In measure 8, by contrast, the a♮ must have signaled a rise to b♭. Further, without b♭ the stepwise continuity between g and c′ is broken, jeopardizing the otherwise complete line of a tenth from e♭ up to g′.

The notes constituting the higher-order lines in Examples 4-8, 4-9, and 4-10 occur with some rhythmic regularity. Kurth cites Example 4-11 to show that this is not always the case. The passage contains a descending "apex line" (*Höhepunktslinie*) from g″ down to d″.[25] Though each note stands out registrally, preceding or initiating a directional shift, Kurth's linear analysis differs from one that takes intervallic progression into account (Ex. 4-12). So long as Kurth's "projected notes"

EXAMPLE 4-11. Bach, Violin Suite in B Minor, Double 2, mm. 6–9

(*vorspringende Punkte*) match those guiding the upper voice in the intervallic progression suggested in Example 4-12, the analyses agree. But the higher-order status Kurth assigns d″ (m. 8) conflicts with the local, neighbor-note status assigned to that pitch in the voice-leading sketch. In addition to conceptual differences, Kurth's musical context—the first three of the four measures shown in Example 4-11—prevented Kurth from locating the d″ in the next bar. Apparently, the contents of measure 9 did not affect his opinion. Perhaps he heard the two d‴'s occurring there as aural reinforcements of a d″ already established in measure 8. This would be particularly clear to him since that d″ is registrally and linearly highlighted.

EXAMPLE 4-12.

The preceding examples point up the main problem in Kurth's analyses of higher-order linear continuities. They lack the comprehensiveness necessary to account for musical structures that integrate linear elements with elements of intervallic progression and harmony. Although some readers have dismissed Kurth's work because of this shortcoming, his insights into Bach's intricate polyphonic art are genuinely valuable because they call attention to many melodic elegancies which are otherwise easily and routinely absorbed into higher strata of rigorously hierarchical analyses. Among the many linear refinements illuminated in Kurth's study of Bach's polyphonic melody, three stand out: (1) the presence of motivic formations in apparent voices; (2) the emergence and dissipation of apparent voices; and (3) the interaction of the actual voice and its embedded apparent voices. The following paragraphs discuss each of these techniques.

MOTIVIC FORMATIONS IN APPARENT VOICES

Apparent voices not only execute continuous ascending or descending motions but also create motivic contours in one or more polyphonic strands, depending on the complexity of the *Realstimme*. Kurth demonstrates this technique with the passage in Example 4-13, which contains, he believes, the apparent voice shown in Example 4-14. Kurth calls the given rhythmic values "approximate" (*Annäherungswerte*).[26] By expressing those pitches occurring on the first sixteenths of each beat as eighth notes, he implies a sense of aural prolongation and, hence, greater structural meaning for certain notes. The b′ on beat one, measure 1, for instance, remains in effect for three sixteenths before b″ dislodges it. Did Kurth hear the b′ extended through beat one and, similarly, hear the remaining pitches notated as eighths extended over three sixteenths as a result of arpeggiations attached to most of those notes? If, as explained earlier, Kurth interprets the arpeggiations linearly, as a "rounding out" of a line over "chordal contours," the tones cannot be considered harmonically generated, or "prolonged" in the modern-day sense of that word. It must have been the rhythmic stress or motivic parallelisms motivated him to single out the two b's. Registral distinction and directional reversals also seem to have guided Kurth's ear. Finally, performance practice may have had some influence, as was suggested in connection with Example 4-8.

EXAMPLE 4-13. Bach, Violin Suite in B Minor, Double 1, mm. 1–3.

EXAMPLE 4-14.

The passage in Example 4-15 contains a more elaborate motivic structure along with an implied pedal point, which subsequently acts as a harmonic bass.[27] Over a six-measure pedal on g, an apparent voice beginning in measure 21 outlines the motivic contours shown in Example 4-16. As the implied harmonic bass rises by step to a in measure 27 and then skips to d′ in measure 29, the apparent voice presents a sequential repetition of its motives (Ex. 4-17). Again, the apparent voices are "metric approximations." Criteria of performance practice no doubt come into play here, too. Each rhythmically enlarged note occurs either directly on the beat (mm. 22, 24), or following a large leap from the pedal bass (mm. 21, 23), that is, at spots where performers tend to lean on notes, however slightly. Kurth's reading implies that each of these pitches is aurally prolonged, usually for the duration of a quarter note. Several are head-notes of descending thirds or are attached to thirds, which brings Kurth's criteria for higher-order melodic continuities in line with harmonic factors.

EXAMPLE 4-15. Bach, Violin Sonata in C Major, Allegro, mm. 21–30

EXAMPLE 4-16.

EXAMPLE 4-17.

Apparent voices may even execute motivic imitations (see Ex. 4-18). In three-voice polyphony a cadential bass supports registrally distinct, imitative upper parts.[28] In Example 4-19, there are five apparent voices, two of which participate in an imitative dialogue. Kurth indicates the imitative voices with asterisks and plus signs.[29] The other parts include a cadential bass, composed of the first pitches in each bar; a suggestion of a descending inner voice, including the first sixteenths of beat two in measures 8, 10, and 12; and a higher-order descending line in the soprano, e'–d'–c'. Kurth concludes the unit on G since it is the end of the motivic imitation under study. He surely also sensed a tonal conclusion there. But he needed one additional measure so that the higher-order c' in the uppermost apparent voice could resolve to b. This would yield descending parallel tenths expressed in the bass and soprano, creating a linear-harmonic unit modulating to the dominant.

EXAMPLE 4-18. Bach, Violin Sonata in G Minor, Presto, mm. 12–17

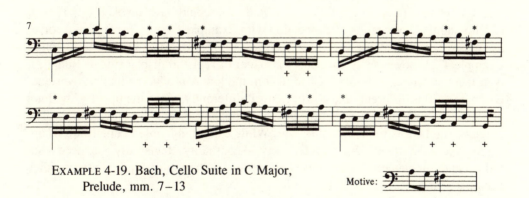

EXAMPLE 4-19. Bach, Cello Suite in C Major,
Prelude, mm. 7–13

EMERGENCE AND DISSIPATION OF APPARENT VOICES

According to Kurth, the emergence and dissipation of apparent voices is one of Bach's most elegant linear techniques. Having established the phenomenon of apparent voices, Kurth shifts his emphasis from their content and interactions with one another to the delicate manner in which they evolve out of and recede back into the *Realstimme*. He identifies four means by which apparent voices fade in and out: harmonic implication, retardation of the apparent voice, syncopated continuation, and pedal-like effects.

Harmonic Implication

An apparent voice that ascends or descends toward a specific pitch may stop short of that goal and so interrupt the linear continuity. In such instances, arpeggiating a chord containing the anticipated melodic goal, out of register, implies the missing note.[30] In Example 4-20, an ascending line beginning in measure 121 reaches from a to f♯' (m. 126), which as leading tone in G minor demands resolution to g'. The next measure frustrates this expectation by avoiding the awaited g'. By arpeggiating a G-minor triad in measure 127, Bach implies the melodic resolution to g' and thus temporarily satisfies our desire for that pitch. Then, in measure 128, g' appears as part of a newly introduced pattern of descending thirds (Ex. 4-21). The conclusion of the ascent that had begun in measure 121 is therefore veiled not only by the one-measure delay of g', but also by the incorporation of that pitch in a fresh intervallic sequence. Observe, too, that the resolution of f♯', the lower note of the final third shown in Example 4-21, is delayed until the g' arrives in the next measure. In the meantime, the thirds have become sixths.

Kurth might have referred to an example he had presented earlier in *Grundlagen,* which demonstrated nonadjacent pitch relationships between a leading tone and its in-register resolution. In the example given in that context, a leading tone, g♯, resolves provisionally to A an octave lower, followed shortly thereafter by the in-register resolution (Ex. 4-22). Kurth states that "the ear provides itself with the actual tone of resolution in the higher octave."[31] He could have invoked this idea of psycho-auditive completion in connection with Example 4-20; there, f♯' can resolve, by registral displacement, to g" in measure 127. The psycho-auditive completion in Example 4-22, however, is not simply a matter of registral displacement. Rather, it is in fact a potential acoustical phenomenon, the low A producing its first overtone. Example 4-20 is different, and Kurth treats it differently, since the upper g" will not produce an "undertone" an octave lower, Riemann's theory notwithstanding. The crucial issue here is registral continuity. While examining veiled conclusion of apparent voices, Kurth appears to prefer registral continuity. Registrally displaced resolutions may supplement literal linear completions by harmonic implication, but they apparently may not substitute for them.

So far, our discussion of Example 4-20 has dealt with the disguised completion of an apparent voice. Kurth also notices the inconspicuous beginning of that same voice. If we examine measures 119 and 120, we will not find a starting point for the higher-order line from a to g". Kurth states that the hypothetical starting point, g, is implied by the G-minor tonic harmony in measure 120, itself clarified by the preceding dominant arpeggiation. Without the initial pitch, the ensuing apparent voice seems to develop from nowhere: "Its beginning is to be understood as [the] tone g, which, without being touched upon itself, emerges from out of the sound of the G-minor contour."[32]

EXAMPLE 4-20. Bach, Violin Sonata in G Minor, Presto, mm. 119–29

EXAMPLE 4-21.

EXAMPLE 4-22. Bach, Cello
Suite in D Minor,
Allemande, mm. 11–12

Retardation of the Apparent Voice

An apparent voice moving at an established rate of speed may be made to recede slowly back into the actual voice through a gradual deceleration of that rate. The excerpt in Example 4-23 illustrates this phenomenon. Kurth observes how the upper apparent voice descends from e♭′ to g (mm. 49–54), each downward step approximately twelve sixteenths apart.[33] At measure 55, a change in motivic pattern signals a slowing of the descent as the apparent voice passes over g♭ and then f (the last eighth in m. 56). The g♭ arrives fourteen sixteenths after g, and f follows a little more than fourteen sixteenths later. The ultimate goal, e♭, does not arrive until measure 61, and the intervening material further conceals the resumption and completion of the linear progression. One interesting detail that Kurth does not mention in con-

EXAMPLE 4-23. Bach, Cello Suite in E♭ Major, Courante, mm. 49–61

nection with this example is the rapid descent, in hemiola, from g to e♭ in measures 60–61. This quicker descent replicates in microcosm the preceding gradual deceleration, which in fact began with g.

Syncopated Continuation

An apparent voice embedded in an unvaried rhythmic stream—for example, in continuous eighths or sixteenths—may abruptly shift its rhythmic distribution from an established pattern to an unpredictable one. The "projected notes" often do not follow a set rhythmic disposition, Kurth warns. "These projected points are not . . . always to be sought at rhythmically corresponding positions, but rather very often are to be followed only by reference to the curvilinear development."[34] He makes this statement in connection with Example 4-11, which illustrates the irregular rhythmic distribution of projected notes. In examining the syncopated dissipation of apparent voices, Kurth cites a passage from the same violin suite (Ex. 4-24). His analysis, indicated by his plus signs (+), shows how the cómponents of the linear descent occur regularly, from e″ to g′, on the first sixteenth of each group, but are syncopated thereafter.[35] Consequently, the final pitches of the *Scheinstimme* seem to fade into the *Realstimme*. Kurth bases this view on registral prominence and directional interruption, particularly with regard to the movement from f♯′ to e′, the syncopated portion of the line (Ex. 4-25). He chooses the f♯′ stemmed in Example 4-25 as the continuation of the initial g′, because this f♯′ follows immediately on the heels of a second g′ (short stem), which marks a sudden directional interruption and a registral reference to the first g′. A directional interruption also signals the arrival of e′, which, like the f♯′, is syncopated.

EXAMPLE 4-24. Bach, Violin Suite in B Minor, Double 2, mm. 44–48

EXAMPLE 4-25.

The voice-leading sketches in Example 4-26 offer a different view. Here, inter-vallic and linear progressions combine to produce a cadential formula, shown in Ex-ample 4-26*b*. Kurth's asterisked f♯' is no longer the sequel to the two g''s, which function similarly in his analysis. Instead, f♯' is a local passing tone between g' and e'. Example 4-26*a* thus reduces the status of f♯' in Kurth's analysis from a higher-order event to a local one.[36] For Kurth, it is the first f♯' of measure 47 (Ex. 4-24) that stands out, for reasons stated above. According to his hearing, the second f♯', on beat three, reaffirms the first one, just as the g' one sixteenth before, on beat two, reaffirms the g' on beat one. This melodic parallelism, together with the rhythmic parallelism that syncopates both f♯' and e', supports Kurth's reading. Of course, designating the second f♯' as the continuation of g' would not only preserve the syn-copating but also maintain it on the analogous sixteenth note for both f♯' and e'. Such an analysis would also accord with the harmonic implication of beat three in measure 47.[37]

EXAMPLE 4-26.

Pedals

In the solo string works, Bach frequently creates the impression of pedal tones by reiterating a particular pitch at regular time intervals. Often, these reiterations do not form true pedals but rather "pedal-like effects" (*orgelpunktartige Wirkungen*), as Kurth refers to them. He observes how Bach subtly introduces an apparent voice when the melodic strand containing such a quasi pedal begins to ascend or descend; Example 4-27 illustrates this technique.[38] The pedal-like c in measure 9 initiates a descending apparent voice, which reaches down to E in measure 11. Kurth's example ends there. The remainder of measure 11 continues the apparent voice to D and then, as a harmonic bass, to G, thus concluding the first section of the Allemande on dominant harmony.

EXAMPLE 4-27. Bach, Cello
Suite in C Major,
Allemande, mm. 9–11

In Example 4-28, Kurth detects five apparent voices, all of which grow out of pedal-like effects. The uppermost apparent voice begins as a quasi pedal on c″, first encountered on beat four of measure 43 (*). From a harmonic standpoint, the c″ in measure 43 is a passing note, and the c‴'s in measure 44 form a suspension and its resolution. Kurth focuses attention on c″ from the standpoint of linear contour. He assigns importance to c″ in measure 44 because of its registral isolation, and he associates that pitch with the first occurrence of c″ at the end of measure 43. There, it does not stand out registrally, nor is it reached by directional interruption. Nevertheless, as the first hint at what evolves into a pedal-like effect, c″ in measure 43 initiates what becomes an apparent voice. This voice continues with c♯″ and d″ in measure 45, and rises further to d♯″ and e″ in measure 46. The g in measure 43 (+) initiates another pedal, which continues through measure 44 before ascending stepwise to c′. Kurth associates these pitches, forming a second apparent voice, on the basis of registral prominence.

EXAMPLE 4-28. Bach, Violin Sonata in A Minor, Allegro, mm. 43–47

The remaining three melodic strands are embedded in the polyphonic texture as inner voices. The first of these begins with a pedal in measure 43, beat two, on f′. After a fourfold repetition, extending up to the first beat of measure 44, it descends to e′ and further to d′. Kurth indicates in a reduction, to be presented shortly, that the d′ in beat two, *not* in beat one, concludes this line. The final two apparent voices form a canon. The *dux* begins on g′, the third sixteenth of beat three in measure 44; g′ is then repeated up through beat two of measure 45, after which there is a scalar descent to b, the first note in measure 46. The *comes*—up-stemmed notes in the example—enters just after the *dux* begins its descent. The imitative descent of the *comes* is likewise prefaced by a pedal-like effect on the a′.

Kurth provides a reductive sketch of the three inner voices (Ex. 4-29).[39] This sketch implies that the three long notes (f′, g′, a′) are prolonged. Reiterating those pitches prolongs them in a very real sense. They remain active in our hearing right up until their respective descents. The first apparent voice shown in Example 4-29, beginning on f′, is particularly interesting since the goal of its descent (d′), unlike that of the subsequent imitative voices, is anticipated four notes earlier (see Ex. 4-30).

Kurth says nothing about the d′ that is marked with an asterisk in Example 4-30, but his reduction shows clearly that it is not the final note in the descent. Perhaps he thought of the first d′ as a neighbor note, distinguished solely by its linear function and lacking reference to harmonic dissonance. Kurth does not define "linear" neighbors. In general, he avoids conventional terminology, such as "neighbor note," because of its narrow connotations. Nevertheless, that d′ is such a linear neighbor is a reasonable explanation for prolonging e′ in Kurth's reduction of Example 4-28.

EXAMPLE 4-29.

EXAMPLE 4-30.

INTERACTION OF APPARENT AND ACTUAL VOICES

An apparent voice whose direction has been established may transfer its progression into the *Realstimme*. When the transfer occurs, the pace of the linear unfoldment, as initiated in the apparent voice, accelerates considerably. Example 4-31 illustrates this process. A gradually descending apex line (+) abruptly passes from the *Schein-stimme* into the *Realstimme* (m. 30), which according to Kurth's bracket carries the motion down to d′.[40] By extending the line to d′, Kurth leaves what we might call a neighbor note unresolved. The E♭-major arpeggiation, which continues for two additional beats after Kurth's example ends, did not deter Kurth from allowing the d′ to "hang." His chief interest here, though, is not harmonic-melodic syntax but rather the linear drive. Once this line is transferred from the apparent to the "real" voice, the linear drive continues unabated until the d′. Example 4-32 illustrates the opposite process, the transfer of a linear progression from the *Realstimme* to the *Schein-stimme*. Plus signs mark the descent in the apparent voice.

EXAMPLE 4-31. Bach, Violin Suite
in D Minor, Allemande,
mm. 28–31

EXAMPLE 4-32. Bach, Cello Suite in C Major, Gigue, mm. 105–8

Motivic exchanges between real and apparent voices further integrate these two dimensions of polyphonic melody. The apparent voice marked by plus signs in measure 8 of Example 4-33 presents an augmentation of the bracketed motive in measures 4–5. That a linear motion may shift rapidly between apparent and real voices is shown in Example 4-34.[41]

EXAMPLE 4-33. Bach, Violin Sonata in C Major, Allegro, mm. 3–9

EXAMPLE 4-34. Bach, Violin Sonata
in G Minor, Fugue, mm. 64–70

Tracing the interactive movements of real and apparent voices can sometimes be a tricky affair, especially without intervallic progressions as guides. In Kurth's analysis of Example 4-35, plus signs mark a descending line that begins in the *Realstimme* on a, halts suddenly on d, and then after a brief interruption continues its downward course as a *Scheinstimme*. Interwoven with this voice is a separate descending line, indicated by asterisks. The voice-leading graph in Example 4-36 sketches Kurth's analysis. Kurth says very little about Example 4-35 so that much is

EXAMPLE 4-35. Bach, Cello Suite in D Minor, Allemande, mm. 14–15

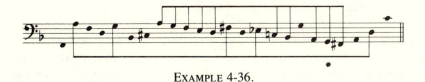

EXAMPLE 4-36.

left for us to decide. One interesting question is whether the progression from a to d in the asterisked line is related to the initial five notes of the *Realstimme,* which span that same interval. Such an association would clearly indicate interdimensional unity of an even more sophisticated nature than the motivic exchanges among apparent voices illustrated in Examples 4-18 and 4-19. Another interesting question is whether the two lines influence each other in any way. Kurth implies that they are independent of one another when, after pointing out the line identified by plus signs, he states, "Besides this [line, there is a] descending apparent voice: a–g–f♯–e♭–d (designated by asterisks)."[42]

Kurth's analysis (Ex. 4-36) shows that the two lines unfold overlapping intervals, one a tenth from a to F♯, the other a fifth from a to d. These linear intervals outline D-major harmony and so motivate an overall progression toward G minor in beats three and four of measure 15. These two beats, which Kurth omits from his excerpt (Ex. 4-35), are given in Example 4-37. The D-minor triad on beat one, measure 14, is inflected chromatically on beat four to become a secondary dominant on D. Before the two lines reach their respective conclusions, an initial resolution to G minor occurs on beat one, measure 15, followed by a final resolution on beat three. Embedded within this harmonic context, the linear continuities identified by Kurth unify the passage as a whole. Example 4-38 summarizes the events just described.

EXAMPLE 4-37. (above)   EXAMPLE 4-38. (below)

According to this sketch, both Kurth's actual and apparent voices (indicated by asterisks and plus signs) contain notes that do not belong to the same structural levels. His plus-mark line begins in the upper voice and ends in the lower voice in the two-part framework sketched in Example 4-38. Similarly, his asterisk line starts in an upper voice and finishes in an inner voice. Besides these differences, Kurth's analysis does not point out the c♯–g tritone outlined in measure 14, beat two, of his Example 4-35, which resolves to the d–f minor third in the following beat (Ex. 4-39). Instead, his reading links g with f♯ (* in Ex. 4-38). Kurth probably chose f♯ as the continuation of g because it interrupts the preceding sixteenth-note descent from a to d. Kurth finds a different continuation not only for g but also for the f♯. He shows the f♯ descending to e♭ and further to d, concluding the line. This reading is peculiar for Kurth in light of his usual alertness to nondiatonic leading tones and their resolutions. With f♯ descending to e♭, the g in measure 15 lacks a melodic connection with either the apparent or the actual voice. Further, leading f♯ to e♭ is curious because directional interruptions surrounding the g highlight it even more than the f♯.

EXAMPLE 4-39.

Perhaps some other priority guided Kurth in analyzing Example 4-35. The overall harmonic motion from D-minor harmony to an applied dominant may have led him to connect f♯ with e♭, which then resolves to d, the root of the applied dominant. In this way Kurth coordinates the overriding linear unfoldment with the harmonic progression. An ascent to g would have left that note suspended. While conjectural, this reading does explain why Kurth uncharacteristically disregards a leading tone, and in a more positive sense, it shows that he recognizes broad linear-harmonic unity.

The questions raised in connection with Example 4-35, as well as the uncertainty surrounding the "linear" neighbor suggested in Example 4-30, point to the need in Kurth's analyses for a more clearly defined relationship between the *Realstimme* and the *Scheinstimme* as two dimensions of melodic structure. Can the *Realstimme* act as a prolongational agent, and if so, when and in what sense? In his bidimensional melodic structures, Kurth addresses "prolongation" primarily with respect to psycho-auditive association of nonadjacent pitches. Such psycho-auditive prolongation plays a role in our perception of melody when there is (1) delayed resolution of dissonances; (2) stepwise connection of linearly prominent notes forming *Scheinstimmen;* or (3) literal pitch reiteration in the *Realstimme.* In the first case, one or more notes of the *Realstimme* extend the effect of a dissonance (suspension) by delaying its resolution. The second case involves the notes of the *Scheinstimme,* which "join together in creating overriding linear progressions since each of [the 'rim notes'] distinguishes itself sufficiently to be retained unconsciously by our hearing and [to be] united with the next ones." [43] Here, the intervening notes of the actual voice are not prolongational at all; rather, the notes of the apparent voice, by virtue of their linear distinction, in a sense "prolong" themselves. In the third case, notes of the actual voice contribute directly to prolonging one or more notes of the apparent voice. By repeating a sufficient number of times the note most recently achieved in the apparent voice, the actual voice sustains that note in our hearing.

Kurth's analyses depend primarily on the second type of prolongation, where the actual voice *does not* act as a prolongational agent. The notes of the actual voice that fall between successive notes of the apparent voice sustain elements of the apparent voice neither in a structural nor in a psycho-auditive sense. Rather, the actual voice pursues an independent linear unfoldment. The actual and apparent voices represent, then, two simultaneously unfolding melodic strata; this is a bi-dimensional organization primarily in the sense that one stratum transcends the note-to-note succession although it lacks the underpinnings of harmonic-contrapuntal prolongations. Once the *Scheinstimme* is established, we feel the continued influence of each successive pitch as we anticipate the arrival of the next one. Kurth himself intimates such a notion of psycho-auditive prolongation when he says that the notes of the apparent voice are "retained unconsciously by our hearing and [are] united with the next ones." [44]

In *Musikpsychologie* (1931), Kurth speculates on the psycho-auditive apparatus underlying our awareness of apparent voices and the overriding lines they create. [45] The apexes of each melodic curve, which contribute to an overriding line, contain, Kurth says, a significant measure of tension owing to their local registral and linear dynamic qualities. Each tension-laden apex, charged with linear energy, remains psychologically active beyond its brief sonic existence. As listeners, we sense these forward-striving concentrations of energy and thus experience what Kurth calls "anticipatory audition" (*Voraushören*), which psycho-auditively links the apexes into an overriding line.

Having identified two levels of melodic activity, the actual and apparent voices, Kurth postulates a "dual-track auditory process" for comprehending the resultant bi-dimensional melodic structure. [46] The actual voice requires one auditory track, primary audition, and for the apparent voice Kurth proposes a second track, "accessory" or "collateral audition." [47] In order to account for our ability to comprehend overriding lines that change direction and thus reverse their dynamic profile, Kurth proposes yet another psycho-auditive faculty, "retroactive audition," for storing in tonal memory the paths of recent curvilinear developments. Through retroactive audition, we can compare immediately past curvilinear developments with current ones and so gain a better mental image of the overall linear flow. In 1931, with his notions of anticipatory, collateral, and retroactive audition, Kurth pioneered efforts to analyze and understand our ability to recognize broad linear continuities.

Kurth's ideas on the perception of curvilinear developments anticipate the work of several modern-day authors who, like Kurth, have tried to explain similar phenomena from a psycho-auditive viewpoint. Recent publications by Diana Deutsch, the team of Fred Lerdahl and Ray Jackendoff, and the experimental psychologists A. S. Bregman and W. J. Dowling have explored various aspects of musical perception, among them the perception of polyphonic melody.[48] While some of this work may strike the musician as naive or even musically irrelevant, the findings often bear out musical intuition. Dowling, for example, who uses the expression "melodic fission" to describe polyphonic melody, pairs up familiar tunes such as "Frère Jacques" and "Happy Birthday."[49] In testing the awareness of simultaneous melodic streams, he alternates, or as he puts it, "interleaves," pitches of two melodies at various fractions of a second. In some tests, he differentiates two pitch streams in other ways, for example, by volume or timbre. Although the experiments are generally improbable and artificial from a musician's standpoint, Dowling's conclusions do agree with musical experience. His findings concerning our ability to trace aurally simultaneous musical streams rely chiefly on registral and temporal distinctions among interleaved pitches rather than on any sort of harmonic-contrapuntal prolongation.[50]

The musical materials used by both Deutsch and the Lerdahl-Jackendoff team are of more interest to musicians than those used by Dowling. Deutsch's experiments with "channeling," which include distinguishing two melodies in a monophonic line, are clearly relevant for polyphonic melody. In a recent article, she discusses "pseudo-polyphony," using principles developed by Gestalt psychologists. She cites, for example, the law of contiguity or proximity, and the law of good continuation.[51] The first of these laws, contiguity, asserts that things near each other spatially or temporally are perceived as belonging together; the second asserts that viewers will impose upon a collection of visual stimuli the most meaningful interpretation. I use the words "viewers" and "visual stimuli" because Gestaltist principles are derived from the results of visual experiments. Whether those principles are transferable into the domain of sound, where time and a kind of metaphorical "registral space" substitute for actual space, remains an open question.[52] Christian von Ehrenfels, in his eassy of 1890, "Über Gestaltqualitäten," used music effectively to demonstrate Gestalt qualities, but few music theorists have followed up on these ideas, and those who have, have done so in an interpretive manner.[53]

Kurth's ideas of psycho-auditive perception of curvilinear developments are clearly related to Gestalt-psychological notions of perception. When Kurth aurally associates tones of an overriding line based on registral prominence (*Gipfeltöne*), it is much the same as when Deutsch relates similarly isolated pitches by the Gestalt law of proximity, "frequency proximity" substituting for spatial proximity.[54] Where Kurth speaks of the extended life of tension-laden melodic apexes engendering "anticipatory hearing," and to the resultant psycho-auditive linkage of apexes into overriding lines, Deutsch speaks of the Gestalt law of good continuation, or to the so-called Phi-Phenomenon. Lerdahl and Jackendoff might refer here to the cumulative effect of their Grouping Preference Rule (GPR) 3a, which establishes boundaries for tone groups based on register.[55]

One of the most interesting ideas developed by Gestalt psychologists, that of "figure-ground" perception, has remained largely unnoticed by music theorists. The notion of figure-ground in the visual-spatial domain does seem to have a clear analog in Kurth's idea of bi-dimensional melodic structure in the aural-temporal domain. According to the Gestalt psychologist Wolfgang Köhler, two complementary shapes can be presented in such a way that, in segregating them visually, a viewer will perceive one as protruding out in space from the other, which then appears as a sort of background.[56] The analogy to Kurth's bi-dimensional melody is plain: his actual voice corresponds to the ground, from which emerges the distinct profile of the apparent voice, corresponding to the figure. Of course, the unique spatial properties of images exhibiting the figure-ground illusion are different from the registral properties of pitches illustrating the apparent-actual voice relationship. But where "real" space is wanting, music substitutes temporal order and the melodic-dynamic qualities of apex pitches constituting the apparent voice. It is precisely these interactive dynamic qualities, fundamental to Kurth's conception of bi-dimensional melody, that allow the apparent voice to "protrude" from the actual voice. Another difference between figure-ground relationships and Kurth's bi-dimensional melody concerns the nature of the real voice. The purposive contour of the real voice, often rising toward and falling away from the apexes, and thus guiding our ear to them, contrasts with the looseness and indefinite character of Köhler's ground.

Despite the differences just described, the figure-ground model of visual perception is a good framework for understanding Kurth's concept of bi-dimensional melody; it is better, in any case, than familiar hierarchic-prolongational models, which rely on techniques of harmonic-contrapuntal prolongation less related to Kurth's bi-dimensional melody. For this reason, any comparison of the two models based on criteria laid down by only one must necessarily fail. The figure-ground model, on the other hand, gives us an opportunity to approach Kurth's ideas positively, without distortive biases.

It is evident that Kurth's notions of actual and apparent voices, and their bi-dimensional structure, differ fundamentally from Heinrich Schenker's notions of foreground and middleground. Schenker, working independently of Kurth, developed ideas on higher-order linear continuities at about the same time that Kurth did. But while Kurth bases his views on manifest characteristics of linear contour and their psycho-auditive ramifications, Schenker bases his views on historical voice-leading models derived from strict counterpoint according to Fux, combined with eighteenth-century figured-bass practice according to C. P. E. Bach. One important similarity between Kurth's and Schenker's higher-order linear progressions is that they both feature stepwise motion. They are very different in other respects, however.[57]

In addition to their contrasting theoretical premises, Kurth and Schenker differ in their evaluation of musical detail, the "foreground." Schenker interprets foreground events as a means for uncovering deeper levels of musical structure. For Kurth, "foreground" events are an end in themselves. This is not to say that Schenkerian analysis can ignore the foreground or permit misinterpretations at that level in order to satisfy middleground voice-leading requirements. Schenker does gain vast analytical scope, though sometimes at the expense of flexibility, by systematically incorporating local events into a fixed global scheme. Kurth, on the other hand, feels no obligation to pursue such a systematic course. His higher-order structures trace linear connections which have psychological, not fixed syntactic, underpinnings. Kurth thus places intuitive, psycho-auditive logic ahead of syntactic logic. Schenker, on the other hand, places syntactic logic first and then, from there, finds the way to what he considers the correct aural logic. These divergent methodological approaches and dissimilar analytical criteria often lead to disagreements between the conclusions of the two men. Comparing their interpretations raises the question of which is "right." But the issue is not one of right or wrong; rather it is one of analytical objective, as regards the two theorists, and of historical perspective, as regards the evolution of analytical practices. In order to understand fully the emerging recognition of large-scale musical unity in the years around 1920, we must familiarize ourselves with Kurth's work no less than with the work of those authors recently acknowledged as part of theoretical traditions that prepared the way for Schenker. The establishment of terminology in Kurth's writings is particularly significant in this respect, since Kurth, in *Grundlagen,* is the first to apply consistently the terms *Zug* and *übergeordnete Linie* to phenomena like those described in Schenker's works from around 1920 on.[58]

Kurth's exploration of polyphonic melody is a milestone in the study of large-scale linear unity. The numerous analyses presented above, along with those discussed earlier in connection with curvilinear developments, show clearly that Kurth helped lay the groundwork for multilevel analysis of complex melodic structures. In formulating his ideas, Kurth intentionally refrains from systematization. Nineteenth-century ideas on morphology, so important for Schenker's work, had no appreciable effect on Kurth.[59] He is not interested in reducing all details to increasingly higher-level structures, ending in a primitive kernel. And while he does experiment with reductive analyses, he does not develop them in any systematic way, nor does he take them beyond one reductive stage. His investigations move from an examination of broader linear motion, aural prolongation, and so on, to the finer points of Bach's melodic style, though he does not always integrate initial analytical findings with later ones.

As mentioned at various points in the foregoing presentation of Kurth's ideas, this lack of integration can lead to inconsistencies. These are not difficult to point out. The work of any pioneer leaves certain issues unresolved, as well as room for expansion and refinement, and Kurth's work is no exception in this regard. Nevertheless, nowhere in musical literature on Bach is an analytical effort of such breadth, insight, and sensitivity to be found prior to the appearance of *Grundlagen.* For his valuable contribution toward a deeper understanding of large-scale melodic structures in Bach's polyphony, Kurth deserves more acknowledgement than some critics have granted him.[60]

NOTES

1. "Apparent voices" are the individual melodic strands, made up of nonadjacent pitches that are embedded in the single-line melody. The "actual voice" is the composite line, the note-to-note melodic unfoldment out of which evolve one or more apparent voices. Kurth coins the word *Scheinstimme* to describe such a strand, but he uses the term only after ample illustration of polyphonic melody. Before the first occurrences of the word *Scheinstimme* (*Grundlagen*, 279, 282), Kurth simply describes the constituent voices and resultant polyphonic complex as "implied" (*angedeutet*) (*Grundlagen*, 263, 267).

2. Johann Mattheson, *Der vollkommene Capellmeister* (1739), ed. M. Reimann, Documenta Musicologica, vol. 5 (Kassel-Basel: Bärenreiter, 1954), 352–56; Ernest C. Harriss, trans., *Johann Mattheson's Der vollkommene Capellmeister: A Revised Translation With Critical Commentary* (Ann Arbor, Mich.: UMI Research Press, 1981), 670–77. Johann P. Kirnberger, *Die Kunst des reinen Satzes*, vol. 1 (1771), 139, 205 ff.; idem, *The Art of Strict Musical Composition*, trans. David Beach and Jurgen Thym, Yale Translation Series, vol. 4 (New Haven: Yale University Press, 1982), 156, 218–20. The nineteenth-century author Adolf Bernhard Marx discusses polyphonic melody in his *Compositionslehre*, vol. 1, 2d ed., rev., enl. (Leipzig: Breitkopf und Härtel, 1841), 351–60, "Die harmonische Figuration," and particularly 359–60, "Der melodische Gesichtspunkt."

3. Harriss, *Johann Mattheson's Der vollkommene Capellmeister*, 670 (Mattheson, *Capellmeister*, 352: "[es] ist eingeführt worden, dass man offt in einer einzigen solchen Stimme drey bis vier Klänge im völligen doch gebrochenen Accord, nach einander hören lässt"). Kirnberger, *The Art of Strict Musical Composition*, 156 (Kirnberger, *Die Kunst des reinen Satzes,* 139): "Wenn ein einstimmiger Gesang so gesetzt ist, dass er einigermassen seine Harmonie mit sich führet, und wie ein zwey oder dreystimmiger Satz klinget, so sind die verbothenen Fortschreitungen darin nicht mehr widrig"). Before Mattheson and Kirnberger, Johann David Heinichen, in his discussion of "theatrical dissonances," acknowledges implied voices as a means of explaining unconventional leaps to dissonances as well as delayed resolution of dissonances (*Der Generalbass in der Komposition* [Dresden, 1728], 588–99, 601).

4. Schenker's work in this area came chiefly after *Grundlagen* appeared in 1917. See the discussion of Schenker at the end of this chapter, as well as in chapter 3.

5. Hugo Riemann, *Katechismus der Fugenkomposition*, vol. 1 (Leipzig: Hesse, 1890), 1, 10, 18. For more details on Riemann's work, see Robert Morgan's article, "Schenker and the Theoretical Tradition," *College Music Symposium* 18 (1978): 92–95, and note 58 of the present chapter.

6. Guido Adler, *Der Stil in der Musik*, 100. In a section entitled "Melodie," Adler declares that certain rhythmically prominent tones are the "supports," the "bearers," of the melody (*Stützen*, *Träger*). The intervening tones are "subordinate groups" (*Untergruppen*). Arnold Schering's essay on "coloration" in thirteenth-century organ madrigals may also have contributed to early twentieth-century concern with fundamental melodic structures underlying surface embellishments. See his "Das kolorierte Orgelmadrigal des Trecento," *Sammelbände der Internationalen Musikgesellschaft* 13 (1911), 1911–12): 172–204.

7. Kurth, *Grundlagen*, 263: "Armut der Einstimmigkeit." Ibid., 17: "*die Linie ist nicht aus primärem, latentem harmonischen Gestalten hervorgegangen, sondern enthält umgekehrt in ihrer Erscheinungsform die klanglichen Momente, aus denen im entwickelten Musikbewusstsein harmonische Volldeutung wird.*" The beginning of my chapter 5 explains Kurth's basic attitude toward harmony in *Grundlagen*.

8. Eighteenth-century musicians tended to champion either the melodic-genetic or the harmonic-genetic view of music. See, for example, J. P. Rameau, *Treatise on Harmony*, trans. P. Gossett (New York: Dover, 1952; orig., Paris, 1722), 152; Mattheson, *Capellmeister*, 133–34, 138–39; Friedrich W. Marpurg, *Handbuch bey dem Generalbass* (Berlin, 1755–60), 22–23.

9. Kurth, *Grundlagen,* 258–60:

> im Gegensatz zur üblichen Darstellungsweise der Theorie erblicken wir hier etwas wesentlich anderes als eine blosse Aufrollung, "Zerlegung," von Akkorden. Was an solchen Stellen vorliegt, ist vielmehr im umgekehrten Entwicklungsvorgang eine Ausbreitung des Linienzuges über akkordliche Konturen und damit zwar zugleich das Hereinströmen reicher harmonischer Klangfülle, aber immer der Vorgang eines Annäherns und Entgegentreibens zu akkordlichen Wirkungen, kein akkordliches Grundempfinden. . . . Niemals versandet aber Bachs Linie, auch bei aller Rundung über akkordliche Konturen, in matter Umspielung von Harmonien.

10. Ibid., 499–500:

> ein und dieselbe Erscheinungsform im musikalischen Satz stellt sich je nach der theoretischen Grundeinstellung verschieden dar. . . . was von der harmonischen Betrachtungsweise aus bloss *Zwischennoten* zwischen Akkordtönen, *Figurierung* eines Akkordgerüstes, etwas "unwesentliches" darstellen muss, die *Bewegung,* welche in die Ruhe des Akkords als rhythmische Belebung eintritt, ist hier, bei der umgekehrten Perspektive, als das gestaltende, treibende Element.

11. Ibid., 264–65.

12. See, for instance, Kurth's Example 217 (*Grundlagen,* 343), a reductive analysis that interprets a series of parallel thirds literally as a chain of 2–3 suspensions offsetting the thirds by a sixteenth note. It should be noted that Kurth offers no graphic reduction like the one in Example 4-2, at least not in the initial discussion of polyphonic melody. He does provide some reductive sketches for other examples, to be discussed later.

13. Kurth, *Grundlagen,* 268: "Bach erzielt oft mit solchen Andeutungen akkordlich-dissonanter Töne dadurch eine erhöhte Spannkraft, dass er den Auflösungston verzögert eintreten lässt, ihre Wirkung verlängert." Note Kurth's use of the verb *verlängern* here, meaning extending or prolonging the effect of the dissonance.

14. Ibid., 268.

15. Ibid., 269: "diese unaufgelöste Töne *hängen* solange, bis wir ihre Weiterführung hören." Ibid., 268: "Ihre Wirkung [ist] verlängert."

16. Ibid., 272: "im Hören der Ton, mit welchem der Linienzug zuerst abgerissen wurde, erhält sich und dann mit den späteren Tönen in Verbindung gebracht wird. . . . So bilden sich zwischen den einzelnen Tönen wieder Zusammenhänge ausserhalb des ganzen Linienbildes." Kurth calls this process "interruption of a defined directional motion" ("Unterbrechung einer bestimmten Bewegungsrichtung").

17. Ibid., 272–73: "greift über mehrere Phasen der einstimmigen Ausspinnung selbst, . . . Einheitsempfindung über grössere Strecken."

18. Ibid., 272.

19. Ibid., 273.

20. Ibid., 100: "Damit ist eine Tendenz zu einer horizontalen Satzstruktur schon an den Wurzeln zerstört. . . . 'Note gegen Note' heisst Aneinanderbindung von Tönen in bestimmten Intervallen; ein zweistimmiger Satz aber, in welchem je zwei Tönen als ein gleichzeitiger Zusammenklang ('Note gegen Note') der Struktur zugrundegelegt werden, ist eine Folge einzelner akkordlicher Erscheinungen." Ibid., 112: "Die erste 'Gattung' ist in Wirklichkeit ein harmonischer Satz."

21. Kurth's negative attitude concerning intervallic progression conflicts with the historical development of polyphony. From the earliest documentation of multivoice composition, controlled intervallic progression and polyphony were inseparable. Carl Dahlhaus discusses the evolution of intervallic progression as a structural basis for counterpoint in chapter 2 of his *Untersuchungen über die Entstehung der harmonischen Tonalität,* Saarbrückener Studien zur Musikwissenschaft, vol. 2 (Kassel: Bärenreiter, 1968).

22. Remember that Kurth published an edition of the violin and cello suites and sonatas. Kurth, *Grundlagen,* 283: "the proper measure in the emphasis of such projected notes will come about on its own" ("das richtige Mass in der Betonung solcher vorspringender Punkte ergibt sich von selbst").

Kurth recommends giving the notes of higher-order lines an agogic accent by lengthening them slightly. He warns against arbitrarily creating higher-order linear continuities according to the "external features of notation" (*Grundlagen*, 283). In forming such continuities based on registrally highlighted pitches, though, Kurth naturally associates pitches that stand out notationally.

23. Ibid., 275–76.

24. Kurth does occasionally leave such gaps in higher-order lines. Such gaps result, he says, from harmonic influences (ibid., 286–89, Exx. 131–33).

25. Ibid., 275.

26. Ibid., 293.

27. Ibid., 303–4.

28. Ibid., 304.

29. Ibid., 305.

30. Ibid., 328.

31. Ibid., 270–71: "Das Ohr ergänzt sich dann den eigentlichen Auflösungston in der höheren Oktave selbst."

32. Ibid., 329: "als ihr Anfang ist [der] Ton g zu verstehen, welcher ohne selbst berührt zu sein aus der g-moll Kontour . . . heraustönt."

33. Ibid., 329–30.

34. Ibid., 274: "Nicht immer sind . . . diese vorspringenden Punkte an rhythmisch einander entsprechenden Stellen zu suchen, sehr oft vielmehr bloss an der Kurvenentwicklung der Linie zu verfolgen."

35. Ibid., 330. Kurth does not comment on the gap between d♯″ and b′ in measure 3, except to say that such gaps result from harmonic influence (see n. 24).

36. Compare the analysis in Example 4-26 with the one in Example 4-12, which also interprets one of Kurth's projected notes as a local passing tone.

37. In light of Kurth's unique conception of arpeggiation as linear unfolding over chordal contours, measure 47 of Example 4-24 is no less harmonic than measure 119 of Example 4-20, where Kurth acknowledges harmony. Kurth's selective references to harmony as a means of explaining certain linear techniques occasionally lead to inconsistencies in his analyses.

38. Kurth discusses pedal-like effects in *Grundlagen*, 330–33.

39. Ibid., 333.

40. Ibid., 334.

41. Examples 4-33 and 4-34 are discussed in *Grundlagen*, 334–35.

42. Ibid., 345: "Überdies eine fallende Scheinstimme: a–g–fis–es–d (bezeichnet mit *)."

43. Ibid., 277: "sich untereinander zu weiter ausgreifenden Linienzügen zusammenschliessen, da jeder von ihnen genugsam hervortritt, um vom Gehör unbewusst festgehalten und mit den nächsten zusammengeschlossen zu werden." Kurth uses the expression "rim line" (*Randlinie*) as a generic description for higher-order lines occurring in both the highest and lowest voices (*obere Randlinie* and *untere Randlinie; Grundlagen*, 289). He refers to the tones belonging to such a line as "rim points" (*Randpunkten; ibid.*, 277).

44. See note 43 above. Dissipation of an apparent voice, for example, constitutes such a psychoauditive prolongation. By retarding the progress of a *Scheinstimme* nearing its conclusion, the *Realstimme*, interpolating ever more notes between pitches of the apparent voice, focuses our attention on, and heightens our anticipation of, each newly arriving *Scheinstimme* pitch. In this way the *Realstimme* does contribute to prolonging the notes of the *Scheinstimme*.

45. Kurth, *Musikpsychologie*, 256–59.

46. Ibid., 258: "doppelspuriger Hörverlauf."

47. Ibid., 258: "Nebenher-Hören."

48. Diana Deutsch, "Music Perception," *Musical Quarterly* 66 (1980), 165–79; idem, *The Psychology of Music* (see chap. 1, n. 93), 118–23; idem, "Two Channel Listening to Musical Scales,"

Journal of the Acoustical Society of America 57.2 (1975): 1156–60; Fred Lerdahl and Ray Jackendoff, "Generative Music Theory and its Relation to Psychology," *Journal of Music Theory* 25.1 (1981): 45–90; W. J. Dowling, "The Perception of Interleaved Melodies," *Cognitive Psychology* 5 (1973): 322–37; A. S. Bregman and J. Campbell, "Primary Auditory Stream Segregation and Perception of Order in Rapid Sequences of Tones," *Journal of Experimental Psychology* 89 (1971): 244–49.

49. Before Dowling, G. A. Miller and G. A. Heise used the term *fission* to describe polyphonic melody, in "An Experimental Study of Auditory Patterns," *American Journal of Psychology* 64 (1951): 68–77; cited by Deutsch, *Psychology,* 118.

50. Dowling, "Interleaved Melodies," 325. Although Dowling uses simple folk tunes, and only fragments of these, he does refer to the traditional literature as illustrating melodic fission. Significantly, he cites the opening of the Gigue from Bach's Cello Suite No. 3, which he diagrams according to frequency (p. 323).

51. Deutsch, "Music Perception," 168–70. It should be noted that by "channeling" Deutsch also means distinguishing different sound stimuli present simultaneously to both ears.

52. Kurth devotes an entire chapter of *Musikpsychologie* (chapter 4, 116–41), to "The Phenomenon of Musical Space" ("Das musikalische Raumphänomen").

53. See note 55, chapter 1. The foremost representative of this style of music theory is Leonard Meyer. Ideas in chapters 3–5 of *Emotion and Meaning in Music* derive from Gestaltist principles.

54. Deutsch, "Music Perception," 170. "Frequency proximity" is a key factor in Deutsch's pseudopolyphony.

55. Lerdahl and Jackendoff, "Generative Music Theory," 62. In their new book, *A Generative Theory of Tonal Music* (Cambridge: MIT Press, 1983), 153–55, Lerdahl and Jackendoff discuss a passage from a Bach cello suite that exhibits polyphonic melody. The passage illustrates what they call "fusion" of two events into one: the "head," or main event of a musical time span, fuses with other events in the same time span to produce a single event (cf. Dowling's fission). Fusion, they continue, "corresponds to the perceptual phenomenon of 'auditory stream segregation,' where one hears two voices instead of a single, oscillating one" (cf. Bregman and Campbell in note 48 above).

56. Wolfgang Köhler, *Gestalt Psychology* (New York: Liveright Publishing Co., 1947), 202–3. Köhler points out that, depending on how we look at the shapes, the relationship of the two may change back and forth, first the one appearing to protrude from the other, and then vice versa. Following Edgar Rubin, Köhler calls the protruding shape, which has the illusion of solidity, "figure," and he calls the environment against which this figure appears superimposed "ground" (Edgar Rubin, *Visuell wahrgenommene Figuren,* trans. Peter Collett. Copenhagen/Berlin, 1921. Rubin's study was originally published as *Synsoplevede Figurer.* Copenhagen, 1915). Ian Bent, in his article "Analysis," *New Grove Dictionary of Music and Musicians,* 6th ed., 1:354, notes the inverse relationship between the Gestaltist idea of figure-ground and reductive analysis, where a musical foreground is hierarchically reduced to various middleground strata and, ultimately, to a background structure.

57. As mentioned in notes 24 and 35, Kurth does allow skips of a third in his overriding lines. Such skips illustrate the effects of harmony on linear procedures (*Grundlagen,* 286–89, "Movement of Apparent Voices over Chordal Contours" ["Rundung von Scheinstimmen über akkordliche Umrisse"]). Schenker's early *Urlinie,* as presented in the volumes of *Tonwille* (1921–24), follows a stepwise course throughout. In Schenker's early publications, higher-order lines both ascend and descend; in later publications, the *Urlinie* is limited to descending motion.

58. Robert Morgan gives the background for Schenker's analytical approach in "Schenker and the Thoretical Tradition," 72–96. See also Floyd Grave's article, "Abbé Vogler's Theory of Reduction," *Current Musicology* 29 (1980): 41–69. Morgan gives the impression that Hugo Riemann, in his reductive analysis of Bach's E♭-minor prelude *WTC* 1 (*Katechismus der Fugenkomposition* [Leipzig: Hesse, 1890–91], 58–60), had something like Schenker's linear progressions (*Züge*) in mind. Riemann says his analysis illustrates "the structure of the piece in its *Grundzüge*" (ibid., 58). In the context of the analysis, as well as of the book as a whole, *Grundzüge* ought to be

translated neutrally as "basic characteristics" or "main features," rather than as Morgan's "fundamental spans" (Morgan, 93). With "fundamental spans" Morgan gives Riemann's language an unwarranted Schenkerian ring and, further, implies that Riemann was using *Grundzüge* in some technical sense when in fact he is using the word generically. The broad linear continuities formed by Riemann's "melodic peaks" (*Melodiespitzen;* see note 5 of the present chapter) do at times resemble Schenker's linear progressions but, like Kurth's overriding lines, they are based on entirely different criteria (among others, registral prominence, metric and hypermetric disposition). Schenker vigorously denies any similarity between Riemann's ideas and his own in an article on the Eb-minor prelude (*Der Tonwille* 1 [1921]: 45). Schenker's warning about the highest notes of a melody not necessarily belonging to the *Urlinie* may have been motivated by Riemann's melodic peaks and Kurth's rim lines (see my chapter 10, note 19).

59. William A. Pastille studies the origins of Schenker's ideas in intellectual trends of the nineteenth century in his Ph.D. dissertation "*Ursatz:* The Musical Philosophy of Heinrich Schenker" (Cornell University, 1985).

60. Among Kurth's harshest critics are Oswald Jonas, *Das Wesen des musikalischen Kunstwerkes, eine Einführung in die Lehre Heinrich Schenkers* (Vienna: Saturn Verlag, 1934), 31, 47, 69, 105 (implied); John Rothgeb, trans. and ed., *Introduction to the Theory of Heinrich Schenker: The Nature of the Musical Work of Art* (New York: Longman, 1982), 35, 55, 62, 83, 128; Friedrich Neumann, "Das Verhältnis von Melodie und Harmonie im dur-molltonalen Tonsatz, insbesondere bei J. S. Bach," *Die Musikforschung* 16 (1963): 30–31; and Helmut Federhofer, *Akkord und Stimmführung in den musiktheoretischen Systemen von Hugo Riemann, Ernst Kurth und Heinrich Schenker* (Veröffentlichungen der Kommission für Musikforschung, ed. Franz Grasberger, vol. 21. Vienna: Verlag der Österreichischen Akademie der Wissenschaften, 1981), 33–54. In a review of Federhofer's book, Rothgeb has little praise for Kurth. See *Music Theory Spectrum* 4 (1982): 132–33.

CHAPTER 5

Kurth's Historical View of Harmony

Present-day musicians who are unfamiliar with Kurth's thinking may find his ideas on harmony very different from their own; indeed, they are sometimes even contrary to what are now commonly held views. Basic theoretical and methodological issues such as the reality of "dualism," the relevance of psycho-acoustics, and the relative merits of "step" theory and "function" theory were the mainstays of theoretical discourse in the late nineteenth and early twentieth centuries. Anyone writing about music theory was expected to address those issues and to take a stand on them. Such matters no longer command the attention of theorists as they once did. Many basic notions about harmony tacitly accepted during the first decades of the twentieth century have since yielded to new ideas. Nowhere is this more apparent than in the area of chromatic harmony, the proving ground for many theorists active between 1900 and 1930. In that period, the residue of nineteenth-century harmonic theory gradually began to disappear as authors sought new solutions to old problems. Kurth published *Romantische Harmonik* (1920) in the midst of that unsettled era, an era that in retrospect proved to be a turning point in the history of music theory as well as of compositional style.[1]

The vast changes that music and music theory have undergone since that age have given rise to many issues left unexplored by early twentieth-century authors. Nevertheless, the fundamental materials of tonal harmony—tertian structure, chord progression, voice leading, and large-scale tonal organization (harmonic form)—remain the chief areas of study. Kurth examines these topics in both *Grundlagen* and *Romantische Harmonik*. In order to understand his ideas, we must first understand his mode of expression. This is particularly crucial in Kurth's case because his writing style is as personal as it is complex. Additionally, although Kurth's writings and current theoretical works often use the same terminology, this correspondence does not necessarily indicate conceptual agreement between them. Indeed, such correspondence lulls the reader into a false sense of comprehension of Kurth's ideas or, more often, spawns criticism of them. Furthermore, while we may accept Kurth's hypotheses concerning the existence of certain harmonic qualities and properties, we may reject his theoretical explanations of them, as well as his speculation regarding their origins. Regardless of whether we accept or reject his theories, we must nevertheless understand his general philosophy of music—his music-theoretical ideology—as well as his music-historical outlook. Kurth's analytical observations derive as much from these factors as they do from his musical instincts.[2]

The difficulties just described, along with the formidable linguistic and stylistic barriers, are major obstacles for those interested in learning about Kurth. Difficult though it may be to read his works, a broad overview of them is essential, especially in matters of harmony. Throughout *Grundlagen* and *Romantische Harmonik,* Kurth develops and refines notions of harmony as it is used in various musical circumstances and style periods, so that an extensive knowledge of both works is necessary for getting a clear picture of his thought. Unfortunately, the sheer size of these two volumes turns most readers away from such a time-consuming task. Differences between *Grundlagen* and *Romantische Harmonik* further complicate matters. The following paragraphs outline the ideological tenets of both studies and will thus serve as an orientation to chapters 5–8 of this book, which concern the harmonic elements of Kurth's theories.

As explained in chapter 1, Kurth's psychological approach to music leads him to a melodic-genetic conception of its basis. He therefore considers harmony a nongenerative element in the evolution of musical structures, at least prior to the Classical era. While most of Kurth's contemporaries—for example, Hugo Riemann, Georg Capellen, August Halm, and Heinrich Schenker—take a harmonic-genetic view of music, Kurth, by contrast, treats harmony as a result, a "secondary consequent" arising from the intersection of several melodic lines.

> The incursion of vertical aspects of [musical] structure first sets in where the lines come into contact, so that this contact and the harmonic relationships always represent a consequent, something secondary, which results only from the simultaneity of linearly directed designs.[3]

The strength with which kinetic-melodic energy asserts itself in a given musical style determines Kurth's perception and analytical interpretation of harmony in that style. Bach's music, representing the culmination of a long evolution, best exemplifies pure "linear" polyphony. Kurth does not deny the presence of harmony in Baroque counterpoint, but in *Grundlagen* he does reject it as the motive force behind the confluence of voices. Instead, harmony is the outcome of a multilinear texture, whose discrete linear forces create harmony as they balance one another to produce an equilibrium of tensions.

> The harmonic repose of chords represents the image of an *equalization of forces,* a *result.* . . . *Harmony is a play of forces aimed at this equilibrium.*
>
> Counterpoint does not *proceed from the chord* but rather *reaches consummation in the chord.*[4]

In the third edition of *Grundlagen,* Kurth responds to criticisms of what was for his time a radically new approach to Bach's music. Kurth clarifies his conception of harmony in Bach's counterpoint by explaining that "secondary" does *not* mean secondary in artistic importance, nor does it mean subsidiary. The same lines, so ardently defended as "primary," can also be explained from the harmonic-tonal standpoint. "In a musical mind," he observes, "the harmonic and linear conception can never be separated completely."[5] He goes on to say that the linear-analytic view pursued in *Grundlagen* does not free us from harmonic analysis, and he points out that the "fundamental significance" of harmony is substantiated throughout his book.[6] Kurth assumes that the reader will balance his linear analyses by keeping in mind the influences of harmony, whose workings Kurth considers self-evident.

A tone of self-defense rather than conviction emerges in these qualifying statements, probably in response to criticism of *Grundlagen.* While it is true that in *Grundlagen* Kurth does clarify linear characteristics as well as peculiarities by referring to harmony, such references are somewhat unsystematic. His harmonic explanations are often appropriate, but they are occasionally questionable, as will become apparent in our discussions of Kurth's analyses. Generally, his acknowledgement of harmony in *Grundlagen* is of the self-evident, unstated variety.

Because Kurth consciously adopts an attitude toward counterpoint and harmony unlike that of his predecessors, he readily contrasts his own views with traditional ones. For example, in an oblique reference to Kirnberger and figured-bass theory in general, he declares that so-called coincidental (*zufällige*) chord formations are in reality "*not yet chords*" (*noch nicht Akkorde*), that is, they have not yet attained full equilibrium. He contrasts his view with that of traditional harmonists, who according to Kurth believe that such "coincidental" formations are "*no longer chords*" (*nicht mehr Akkorde*).[7] While Kurth's interpretation of Kirnberger and his followers is not completely accurate, his meaning is clear. Rather than taking tertian harmony as a point of departure and observing occasional disturbances arising from the external influx of melodic forces, Kurth takes melody as his point of departure and observes relative degrees of equilibrium arising from the imposition of tertian norms.

Harmony in the Baroque contrapuntal style is thus not inherently reposeful; rather, it symbolizes an equilibrium among forces and counterforces operating in a fundamentally linear texture. Genetically, the linear progressions "*get caught* in chords." When listening to music, we tend to hear the equilibrium.

> The process of equalization in harmonies cannot always be consciously separated [from the linear origins of harmonies], especially in the case of advanced musical training, [where] the integration into chords and tonal coherencies occurs, for the most part, simultaneously with the conception of linear polyphony.[8]

Kurth thus formulates a theoretical basis for integrating horizontal and vertical dimensions in Baroque polyphonic structures. But he does not consistently put the theory to use, as was shown earlier in the discussion of polyphonic melody. He often refers to an interpenetration (*Ineinanderwirken* or *Ineinandergreifen*) of melody and harmony, but because harmony in Baroque polyphony is, conceptually, a result, it remains musically passive and, except in certain cases, does not govern the course of musical events. Kurth's resistance to a balanced evaluation of melody and harmony in *Grundlagen* is no doubt a polemical response to the exaggerated emphasis on harmony typical of music theory in Kurth's day. Most counterpoint manuals of that time—for example, those of Hugo Riemann, Ernst Friedrich Richter, and Felix Draeseke—are explicitly based on harmony.[9]

In *Grundlagen,* Kurth insists that melody and harmony are "heterogeneous phenomena"—phenomena that are "fundamentally different"—not "homogeneous," as maintained by harmonically oriented theorists.[10] It is unclear why the two should be any less homogeneous according to Kurth's melodic-genetic view of music than according to a harmonic-genetic view. Melody and harmony are no less homogeneous if, as Kurth claims, melodies consolidate to produce harmony. To be truly heterogeneous, they would have to consist of dissimilar parts or originate dissimilarly. But the "parts" of harmony are the melodies themselves, according to Kurth the very origins of harmony.

In order to understand Kurth here, we must realize that he is really talking about two kinds of harmony. On the one hand there is "polyphonic harmony," that is, harmony as a cumulative, dependent result, and on the other there is a notion of "homophonic harmony," independent tertian harmony based on intervallic "fusion" (Stumpf). With this distinction in mind, we can better understand what Kurth means when he says that melody and harmony are heterogeneous. He is contrasting *homophonic* harmony with melody, the one inherently vertical, the other horizontal. But this distinction does not justify Kurth's strict separation of melody and harmony, since he claims the two are heterogeneous *within* the Baroque style, where the polyphonic type of harmony predominates. Between the two extremes of homophonic and polyphonic harmony lies a third form of harmony, "polyphonic homophony," a synthesis of melodic and harmonic forces brought about by a stylistic evolution during which music is transformed from a fundamentally linear art to a harmonic one, and finally to a linear-harmonic one. By distinguishing among these three types of harmony we can understand Kurth's analytical as well as historical observations about music.[11]

In the last half of the eighteenth century, the codification of figured-bass technique and the dissemination of Rameau's ideas, along with a stylistic shift toward periodic rhythmic-metric structures, brought on a form of harmonic thinking that fragmented previously contrapuntal textures into discrete vertical events, chords, whose voice-leading connections Kurth viewed as meager remnants of earlier, free-flowing polyphony. The ever-increasing tension between linear and harmonic forces, which according to Kurth characterizes Renaissance music, reached a pinnacle in the mid-eighteenth century. At this crucial stage of music's development, the effect of "harmonic cohesion" between tones—the intrinsic property of tones to attract one another and so to form chords—prevailed over linearly directed forces, and Baroque

contrapuntal art began to degenerate.[12] Kurth traces the beginnings of this degenera-
tion back to the birth of figured bass at the turn of the seventeenth century. The gradual proliferation of harmonic forces led to Classicism. With the deaths of Bach in
1750 and Handel in 1759, Kurth observes, "linear counterpoint, prepared over many
centuries, suddenly collapses, to be engulfed by the new stylistic elements of the
harmonic-homophonic compositional technique of Classicism."[13]

Promoted by figured bass and "harmonic cohesion," the increased harmonic
consciousness had its immediate source in the melodic style of Classical music,
which features periodic, hierarchical binary phrasing. The regularization of melodic
cadences—and these cadences may be complete or incomplete, as in antecedent-
consequent phrases—brings out their harmonic implications.

> Along with the divisions of the melodic course itself, the grouped accents
> also cause a periodic convergence of the melodic line into such partial
> closures, at which an especially clear chordal effect establishes itself.[14]

The cumulative effect of these periodic, harmonically prominent phrase endings is
an aural impression of an overriding harmonic framework; this impression affects
our perception of the melody as a whole. From the compositional standpoint, Kurth
believes that the strong effect of these clear harmonic cadences "dominates the
whole linear technique."[15]

Kurth contrasts the relative strength of harmonic elements in Baroque and
Classical melody, and states that Baroque melody does not possess "in so pronounced a measure the character of a mere melodic configuration about a chordal
framework."[16] Does Kurth mean to imply that Classical melody does possess such a
character? His tone in *Grundlagen* suggests that he interprets Classical melody in
precisely that way, as melodic elaboration of harmonic successions.[17]

During the Classical period, harmonic elements thus supplant the primacy of
melodic ones, which are now monitored in composition only to assure that they do
not hinder smooth chord connection.[18] In this capacity, the melodic dimension takes
on a "*negative* meaning" (that of not hindering chord connection), rather than a
positive one (that of wending melodic ways through chords). Kurth characterizes
harmony and counterpoint as either positive or negative, depending on the generative basis of the music. In polyphony, for example, melody is positive while harmony is negative. The music of the Viennese Classicists reverses this relationship.
In harmonic music "the melodic aspect . . . takes on a *negative* meaning."[19]

The suppression of linear forces and resultant dominance of harmonic ones
produce homophonic harmony. Melodic development becomes stifled in the Classical era. Melody is restricted to the uppermost part, "melodic" inner voices being
essentially animated chordal connectors. Even the principal melody is for Kurth controlled primarily by harmonic succession and periodic rhythmic accent, both of
which circumscribe and thus weaken the overall linear thrust of the melody. Under
these stylistically determined constraints, genuine, linearly conceived melody lies
dormant.

Kurth maintains that a gradual shift from Classical to Romantic aesthetic ideals—from clarity, objectivity, and emotional reserve, to ambiguity, subjectivity, and emotional abandon—inspired a turn inward by Romantic artists, who sought individual rather than universal expression. Kurth envisions the Romantic composer psychically harnessing the primordial force of the Will, which achieves sonic expression in his music.[20] The most immediate musical expression of the composer's Will-driven psychic forces, kinetic-linear energy, emerges from dormancy and gradually infiltrates the musical fabric. Melodic forces begin to break down the rigid harmonic texture of Classical homophony from within.

> From beneath, the Classical harmonic forms are set into undulating motion and are resolved to complete fluidity, so that all structural characteristics are destroyed and the potentiality arises for new conditions of chord formation. Precisely the *drive* of these tensions against the resistance of Classical tonality, which they strive to breach and disintegrate, causes far more forms of potential than kinetic energy to appear in the most diverse ways, and a musical style had to arise which was entirely different from the dynamic effects of linear polyphony *before* Classicism.[21]

Note that Kurth contrasts Baroque and Romantic styles based on their relationship to Classical style. He stresses that the "dynamic effects of linear polyphony" developed "*before* Classicism," that is, *before* homophonic harmony. Thus linear polyphony (polyphonic harmony) differs from Romantic harmony, whose very origin is the influx of kinetic-melodic energy into Classical harmony. Romantic harmony is neither wholly linear nor completely "harmonic," but rather a synthesis of these two extremes. In analyzing Wagner's music, Kurth tries to determine the nature of a given chord, and the sense of the progression to which it belongs, by assessing the relative strength of two competing qualities of harmony: the "sensuous" qualities (*klangsinnlich*) and the "energetic" qualities (*energetisch*).[22]

Klangsinnlich connotes two harmonic traits, which derive from the German word *Sinnlichkeit:* the "sensuousness" of tertian chords on the one hand and their "materiality" on the other. The sensuousness of tertian chords, particularly those beyond the triad, refers to their delightful appeal as full-sounding, harmonious structures. Materiality refers to their harmonic stability, to the unified mass of tertian chords as seamlessly fused interval collections, which according to Kurth "weigh" on a fundamental.[23] Kurth interprets sensuous chords as representing material "resistance" to the flow of melodic forces, which try to wedge apart chords at their intervallic seams.

> Chords are a hindrance to the effect of [melodic] energies . . . the artistic effect rests precisely on the intensity of this conflict between surging energies and material resistance, and its strength [i.e., of the conflict] is the first characteristic of artistic creativity and inner tension.[24]

Chordal sensuousness and materiality are thus harmonically "self-preservational" in that they help to preserve tertian integrity by counteracting the stress of linear-energetic forces.

Kurth refers to energetic qualities of harmony when explaining nontonal tertian and nontertian sonorities composed of multiple leading tones "on their way," as it were, to a tertian chord. Additionally, Kurth explains, familiar diatonic, tonal-tertian sonorities that behave in an unconventional manner are energetic. He shows that all such harmonies arise from "neighbor-note interpolations" (*Nebentonein-stellungen*), that is, from single or multiple neighbor notes substituted for some, or occasionally even all, of the notes of a chord to which the neighbors eventually resolve.[25] In the most general sense, Kurth understands virtually all harmony, from the simplest triad to the most complex, as latently energetic.[26] In contrast to the self-preservational role of sensuousness/materiality, Kurth interprets the energetic qualities in chords as harmonically self-destructive.

Kurth's purpose in formulating these two facets of harmony transcends all music-technical interests. Ultimately, it grows out of his belief that all music, and Romantic music in particular because of its aesthetic premises, is a reflection of psychic energy. Recall the motto of *Romantische Harmonik,* "Harmonies are reflexes from the unconscious." Similarly, Kurth says that "every chord carries within itself traces of the silent depths from which it is uprooted."[27] Chords, their connections, and the broad harmonic-tonal flow symbolize a drama in the artist's psyche. His every disposition is transformed into a sonority characterized by harmonic energy and volatility, or sensuousness and stability. In modern-day terms, Kurth is contrasting *klangsinnlich* and *energetisch* to distinguish between those tertian chords which convey a strong root sense, resulting in harmonic inertia, and voice-leading chords, tertian and otherwise, which convey a sense of melodically inspired harmonic momentum. The former exemplify Kurth's notion of chordal "weight," the latter "potential energy."[28] These two contending facets of harmony interact to produce what I have called polyphonic homophony.

Theoretical precedents for distinguishing between *klangsinnlich* and *energetisch* harmonies exist in various writings from the late eighteenth century onward. Kurth's distinction is roughly equivalent to what are sometimes called "essential" and "nonessential" chords (*wesentlich* and *zufällig*) after Kirnberger's *Die Kunst des reinen Satzes.* J. A. P. Schulz, Kirnberger's student, coined the term "intermediate" or "passing chord" (*Zwischenakkord*) to describe sonorities consisting of multiple accessory tones.[29] Abbé Vogler and Gottfried Weber, generally viewed as "harmonic" theorists, also acknowledged passing harmonies.[30] In the mid and late nineteenth century, Simon Sechter, his disciple Karl Mayrberger, and Josef Schalk all spoke of passing chords. Schalk in particular dealt with chromatic passing chords, albeit briefly and in a limited way. His work may have influenced the team of Rudolf Louis and Ludwig Thuille, who dealt at some length with contrapuntal chords, as well as with chromatic voice leading.[31] Kurth was familiar with all of these works. Using his keen musical sensibilities, he adapts and enlarges on their ideas, and recasts them in a distinctive vocabulary of dynamism. Further, he uses his analytical findings to show a coherent evolution of harmonic techniques in the nineteenth century that reflects an evolution in the psychological motivations behind musical art works.[32] A union of the three elements suggested here, intuitive sensibilities, creative use of language, and psychological interests, distinguishes Kurth as a theorist from his contemporaries. This is especially true in his treatment of late Romantic harmony. No other writer before 1920 had dealt so extensively and eloquently with this subject, nor had anyone offered such appealing and effective solutions to the enigma of Wagner's harmonic practices.

In summary, according to Kurth harmony exhibits two properties, sensuousness and energy. Their mixture, in various proportions, determines the finished musical product. Although in theory he allows for both properties, in practice, because of his melodic-genetic views, he devotes more time to energetic than to sensuous aspects of harmony. By closely examining harmonic practices over time, we can measure the relative strength of its two properties. From Kurth's standpoint, the resultant historical overview exhibits three stages, compared above to Hegel's dialectical interpretation of change. During the first stage, linear energy dominates; it is gradually refined until it reaches a zenith in Bach's polyphonic harmony. In the second stage, rhythmic-metric forces emerge and eventually grow to dominate musical structure. Linear continuity is disrupted, causing harmonies to be severed from their linear embedment and thus producing homophonic harmony. Finally, kinetic-linear energy reasserts itself, destablizing some tertian aggregates while intensifying others, resulting in polyphonic homophony.

Kurth divides the sections of *Grundlagen* devoted to analysis almost equally between discussions of monophonic and polyphonic compositions. In his remarks on polyphony, where he might focus on harmony, he chooses instead to focus on linear dynamics, motivic-thematic considerations, and other melodic issues. In part 4 of *Grundlagen,* on polyphony, one relatively brief section deals with how harmony and linear dynamics are coordinated. In part 5, on "linear coupling," Kurth discusses harmony more frequently, but even there his discussion bears directly on "coupling" in relatively few cases.[33] In the remainder of the present chapter, we will review those sections of *Grundlagen* that specifically address harmony. Our review will be somewhat selective and will not exhaust Kurth's attention to harmony. Elsewhere in *Grundlagen* Kurth explains various monophonic techniques by referring to harmony. Furthermore, as pointed out in the beginning of this chapter, Kurth assumes there is harmonic activity in all of the examples discussed in *Grundlagen,* even when he does not specifically mention it.[34]

In polyphonic textures, a melodic high point and subsequent directional reversal are often accompanied by a dissonant harmonic event that enhances the two linear events. Kurth calls this phenomenon "highlighting of pivotal apexes."[35] He illustrates this technique with the passages in Example 5-1. Kurth points to the melodic apex on f′ in Example 5-1*a,* the pivot at which the linear phase reverses direction. An implied diminished seventh chord in the polyphonic setting of Example 5-1*b* enhances the linear-dynamic tension of the pivotal apex. Bach coordinates the harmonic with the linear dimension and thus achieves maximum dynamic effect.[36] Kurth uses the excerpts from Bach's Two-Part Invention in D Major in Example 5-2 to demonstrate how harmonic treatment of pivotal apexes reflects the overall dynamic flow of a piece. When the left hand presents the subject in measures 2–4 (Ex. 5-2*a*), the two pivotal apexes, on g and a, form consonances with the companion voice.[37] Later, when the piece reaches the dominant key area, representing a higher level of tension in the overall dynamic form, the pivotal apexes clash with the companion voice, enhancing the apexes and inducing a sharp rebound in the opposite direction (Ex. 5-2*b*). Kurth's plus signs call attention to notes analogous to the apex in measure 1, Example 5-2*a.*

It is important to note that Kurth does not speak here of harmony per se but rather of "intervallic relationships," "intervallic dissonances," "dissonant clashes," or "friction."[38] He consciously uses such expressions, I believe, not just as a way of avoiding the word "harmony," but instead as a way of avoiding its connotations, which are foreign to his idea of polyphonic harmony. For example, by saying "intervallic dissonances" instead of harmonic dissonances, Kurth need not define what is harmonic and what is nonharmonic. In this context he understands *Zusammenklingen* in the very literal sense of notes "sounding together." An intervallic dissonance is dissonant not because one of the notes of the interval is dissonant against the other but because, as an entity, the interval is *collectively* dissonant. An intervallic dissonance is an autonomous vertical event, which may not be broken down into a dependent tone and a reference tone.

Example 5-3 reinterprets Example 5-2*b.* According to this sketch, measures 12 and 13 of Example 5-2*b* project A-major harmony, measures 14 and 15 E-minor. In Example 5-3, Kurth's pivotal apexes (+) are neighbor notes; the dissonances result from a clash between these neighbors and notes of the underlying harmonies. Example 5-3 tends to neutralize the very features that interest Kurth, the pivotal apexes of d′ and a″ (mm. 13 and 15), intensified by the strategic deployment of the companion voice.[39] The analysis in Example 5-3 does not deny the existence of Kurth's intervallic dissonances. But by "normalizing" the deployment of the voices it draws attention away from those unique traits of linear-harmonic interplay that are affectively and stylistically, if not always "structurally" definitive.

Intervallic dissonances may also enhance melodic low points, as in the opening measures from the Bach fugue in Example 5-4. The first *X* marks the low point of the melody, which at the second *X* rebounds upward from a dissonant clash.[40] Observe that Kurth's reading focuses attention on the linear rebound of the ascending sixteenth notes rather than on the chordal seventh in the bass, which would be the focus of a conventional analysis. In the customary view, the dissonance on beat one of measure 3 is created by the left-hand c♯, which as the bass of a four-two chord re-

EXAMPLE 5-1. Bach, *Art of the Fugue*, No. 3: (*a*) mm. 1–5; (*b*) mm. 9–11

EXAMPLE 5-2. Bach, Two-Part Invention No. 3: (*a*) mm. 1–4; (*b*) mm. 12–18

EXAMPLE 5-3.

quires a stepwise descending resolution. Kurth, also interested in the linear consequences of dissonance, maintains that in measure 3 the upper voice "strikes against a dissonance," which motivates the ascending rebound in that upper voice. He states that the fugue subject is often woven into the polyphony such that "the lowest tone strikes against a dissonance, from which the motion undergoes a deflection."[41] Kurth's wording here, "strikes against *a* dissonance," suggests that he may be thinking of the bass c♯ as the dissonant tone, against which d♯' strikes. The difference between Kurth's analysis of Example 5-4 and one based on a four-two chord lies in his attention to the upper voice rather than to the lower voice. If by "a dissonance," however, Kurth means the collective intervallic dissonance of c♯/d♯', as suggested earlier, then his linear reading leads to conclusions opposite to those of the harmonic, four-two reading. In the harmonic reading, it is the d♯' that causes the c♯ to *descend,* not the c♯/d♯' that causes the d♯' to *ascend.* Here, as is often the case with Kurth's analyses, structural and psycho-auditive explanations contrast with one another. The bass seventh and its resolution may be structurally central, but what stand out psycho-auditively are the dissonant clash and the soprano rebound, which are under way *before* the bass descends.

In an article that examines Kurth's notion of linear counterpoint, Carl Dahlhaus discusses Kurth's analysis of Example 5-4. He remarks that without the mediation of familiar contrapuntal devices, such as syncopated and passing dissonances, Kurth's notion of linear primacy leads to a "neglect of historical premises, to which some phenomena owe not only their origin but also their content, and without which they would not be what they are."[42] By "historical premises" and "some phenomena" Dahlhaus means the evolution of the syncope. Kurth does recognize the basis and traditional practice of syncopated dissonances. Nevertheless, he maintains that "contrapuntal intuition" points to a different origin for such devices.

> As a consequence of the usual theory, the dissonant interval had to appear the primary factor in all such cases, and the linear development would merely be deduced from the dissonant interval. . . . [T]he relationship is, however, the other way around, as every correct contrapuntal intuition must certainly teach. As everywhere in a genuine linear-contrapuntal structure, the *primary* factor and the essential point lies in the linear motion, which in such cases affects harmonic phenomena; [it lies] in the melodic tensions, not in dissonant chords. *The dynamics of the harmonic activity are influenced by the linear dynamics.*[43]

As in monophony, so too in polyphony, Kurth *feels* "primarily" the force of linear progressions. His statements indicate that linear primacy constitutes the *structural* basis of music, but careful study of Kurth's text suggests another interpretation of linear primacy.

Kurth says at one point that careful "observation" (*Beobachtung*) is the chief "guide to sympathetic projection of oneself [*Einfühlung*] into Bach's instrumental

EXAMPLE 5-4. Bach, C♯-Minor Fugue, *WTC* II, mm. 1–3

counterpoint," and further that the essential goal of observing compositional procedures is "the awakening and stimulation of that art of instinctive sympathetic projection."[44] These statements suggest that by linear primacy Kurth does not mean logically or syntactically primary, but rather *empathetically* or psycho-auditively primary. His analytical approach implies a specific mode of listening, a listening strategy.[45]

For those wishing to define, delimit, and balance the structural roles of harmony and melody rather than to experience the dynamics of Bach's counterpoint by "sympathetic projection," Kurth's psycho-auditive basis for analysis may seem vague and inadequate. Remember that Kurth is trying to show us what is auditively distinctive in multilinear textures, not necessarily what is theoretically normative. He points out that *there is* a dissonant event and discusses its consequences, without specifying *which* tones are dependent on which. The dissonances are evaluated as reflections of or accessories to linear events. Kurth examines polyphony in order to highlight certain interlinear techniques, largely without referring to harmony.

In part 4 of *Grundlagen,* "The Technique of Linear Coupling," Kurth proposes to explain some interlinear details where harmony does come into play. Much of the discussion deals with what he calls "intervallic irregularities." Taking exceptional rather than normal events as a methodological basis goes back to the fundamental opposition Kurth hypothesizes between harmony and counterpoint.[46] In contrapuntal music, where melody is "positive" and harmony "negative," negative means not only the material resistance of chords but also the *"avoidance of disturbing intervallic results"* between melodic lines. Those intervals that to Kurth's ear disturb the linear flow include dissonances approached in parallel or similar motion, as well as fifths and fourths approached in parallel, similar, or contrary motion.[47] Fifths and fourths approached by oblique motion, and dissonances approached by either oblique or contrary motion are all unproblematic.

Kurth argues against fifths and fourths in two-part counterpoint because of their "emptiness," and claims that

> every thirdless fifth has in actuality the same characteristic effect which arises with forbidden parallels in the voice leading of the harmonic structures. In two-voiced structures the empty effect of the *fourth* is hardly less than that of the fifth.[48]

Kurth makes an analogy here between a voice-leading phenomenon in harmony, parallel fifths, and an aesthetic phenomenon in counterpoint, the empty *sound* of a fifth. It is clear that Kurth's critical attitude toward fifths in two-part counterpoint is based on aesthetic rather than on structural grounds because he dislikes them even under traditionally acceptable circumstances. Kurth's cautious attitude toward fifths leads him to question Fux's acceptance of them when they are approached by contrary motion in first species. Whether approached by contrary motion or not, the fifth, to Kurth's ear, still lacks "the massiveness [of sound] which the contrapuntal texture requires."[49]

Kurth's discussion of linear coupling takes up various techniques that temper the undesirable sonic effect of fifths and fourths in a variety of musical circumstances. Not all of these techniques depend on harmony; in fact, only one is strictly harmonic. Nevertheless, even in those instances where Kurth relies on means other than harmonic ones to temper the effect of disturbing intervals, his awareness of harmonic procedures in Bach's counterpoint, as well as his understanding of the interaction between harmonic and melodic procedures, is made clear.

Harmonic influences can temper the objectionable effect of fifths and fourths in two-voice counterpoint. In Example 5-5, arpeggiation cancels the sense of emptiness at the intervals marked by Kurth. This arpeggiation absorbs the fourths and fifths approached in similar motion into the momentary harmony, and the intervallic irregularities are thereby "overcome."[50]

EXAMPLE 5-5. Bach, Two-Part Invention No. 13, mm. 22–23

Kurth explains the fifth in measure 4 of the excerpt in Example 5-6 similarly. He claims that measure 4 cumulatively projects the harmonic effect of a B♭ dominant seventh chord, which mitigates the hollowness of the fifth.[51] This hearing seems unlikely because, in reducing measure 4 to a single harmony, a second-inversion seventh chord, it denies the clear falling-fifth progression between roots F and B♭. Furthermore, this hearing implies an analogous interpretation of measure 3, which yields an unusual harmonic progression between measures 3 and 4, a succession of two second-inversion seventh chords. Though Kurth reminds us that even here the two-part linear structure is primary, the harmony secondary, his harmonic reading of measure 4 and its implications for progression in Example 5-6 are peculiar.

Arpeggiation can also temper the harshness of dissonances approached in similar or contrary motion. A dissonant interval, for example, a seventh, becomes contrapuntally understandable and aurally acceptable when it is the second in a pair of

EXAMPLE 5-6. Bach, Organ Sonata, BWV 526, Allegro, mm. 3–5

intervals adding up to a dissonant chord. Example 5-7 illustrates this concept. Kurth marks the seventh, c′–b♭′, on beat two, which follows a fourth, g′–c″, on the preceding sixteenth, and before that a sixth, g′–e″. The intervals add up to a dominant seventh chord on C, which cushions the impact of c′–b♭′. Kurth does not mention the diminished fifth, e′–b♭″, on beat one, nor the ninth, b♭–c″, on the fourth eighth. Presumably he would reason that the latter follows a fifth, c′–g′, on the preceding sixteenth.[52]

EXAMPLE 5-7. Bach, Partita No. 1 in B♭ Major, Allemande, m. 16

Kurth's method of justifying intervallic irregularities by means of harmony has clear precedents in popular counterpoint manuals of his day, for example, those of Hugo Riemann and Stephan Krehl. While these two authors do not reject fifths by contrary motion in two voices, they do state that the emptiness of the fifth is less offensive when the interval results from arpeggiation, or when a nonharmonic tone (passing or neighboring) coincides with an arpeggiated tone. Like Kurth, both authors explain unprepared dissonances in soprano voices by means of arpeggiation.[53] Examples from both works illustrate their ideas (Ex. 5-8). Riemann and Krehl explain the fifths and fourths as "afterbeat" (*nachgeschlagene*) intervals within the implied harmony. Kurth generally avoids harmonic explanations of contrapuntal phenomena, but he follows the "harmonic" contrapuntists in dealing with certain intervallic irregularities.[54]

EXAMPLE 5-8. (*a*) Riemann, p. 12, Exx. 15–16; (*b*) Krehl, p. 12, Ex. 3

In order to explain fourths and fifths that are not absorbed into an arpeggiation of a single harmony, Kurth extends the influence of harmony to include chord pairs. He specifies two chord pairs, one whose roots are related by third (major and relative minor), the other by fifth (dominant and tonic or an analogous relationship). He probably singles out third-related chords because of their close tonal-functional relationship; as frequent substitutes for one another, in a sense they represent an extension of a single harmony. Fifth-related chords, on the other hand, represent contrasting tonal functions. Kurth justifies his second chord pair by pointing out the traditional acceptance of "horn fifths." The following paragraphs discuss each chord pair separately.

Kurth finds that fifths and fourths in two-part counterpoint are tempered by chord pairs "when the fifth or fourth stands in the relationship of a *relative* [major or minor] chord with the preceding interval."[55] He illustrates his idea with the intervallic progressions in Examples 5-9*a* and *b,* which show how fourths and fifths may be satisfactorily approached in contrary and similar motion. In Example 5-9*b,* Kurth even goes so far as to allow bald parallel fifths when they arise coincidentally in such arpeggiations. He does not say that each interval represents a chord, nor does he say that their succession implies a harmonic progression between the two third-related chords. He simply declares that the distance between the two questionable intervals must correspond to the one between the "relative" chords.

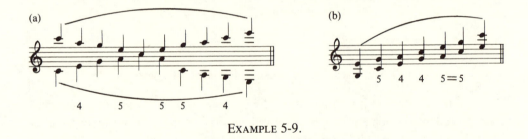

EXAMPLE 5-9.

Kurth cites Example 5-10 in support of his thesis. By examining it, we can tell that this technique need *not* entail a harmonic progression. The fourth d′–g′, as if part of a G-major harmony, is moderated because it follows a doubled e′. The e′ is clearly part of an E-minor harmony, but surely Kurth does not mean that the last three sixteenths of the measure project a G-major chord.[56] To judge from Kurth's statement on the effect of third-related chords, the intervallic progression is permitted, not because a harmonic *progression* takes place, but because of the harmonic *similarity* of the chords containing those pitches. Examples 5-11*a* and *b* further illustrate vertical intervallic series justified by chords a third apart. Following f–c″, associated with F-major harmony, the a–d″ fourth on beat two of Example 5-11*a* loses some of its harshness because it suggests D-minor harmony, the relative of F major. Similarly, Kurth explains the two fourths in Example 5-11*b,* on beats one and two, as belonging to C-major and A-minor harmonies, respectively.[57]

Kurth's explanation of the fourths in Examples 5-11*a* and *b* is not entirely satisfactory. By reading the intervals so literally, he weakens his concept of Bach's polyphony as a tension equilibrium of melodic and harmonic forces. Over F-major
harmony in measure 1 of Example 5-11*a*, the soprano traverses a melodic fourth
from c″ to f″, crossing over the passing notes d″ and e″ in the process, while the bass
makes a chordal skip from the root to the third of the chord. These events are rhythmically disposed such that the bass note, a, coincides with the soprano (accented)
passing tone d″, coincidentally producing the fourth. Kurth reads the fourth too literally and so attributes quasi-harmonic meaning to a melodic element, the accented
passing tone. Thus, for Kurth, the a–d″ fourth becomes part of an inferred, quasi-D-
minor chord, relative of F major. To his ear, the aural allusion to this harmonic relationship mitigates the stridency of the fourth. We accept the fourth, however, not
because of a closely related chord pair, but rather because of the unity of the melodic
fourth in the soprano and, accordingly, the coincidental origin of the vertical fourth.

EXAMPLE 5-10. Bach, Clavier Fugue in A Minor, BWV 944, mm. 49–50

EXAMPLE 5-11. Bach, *Für Anna Magdalena Bach,* Menuet in F Major: (*a*) mm.
1–2; (*b*) mm. 10–11

Kurth misreads Example 5-11*b* for similar reasons. In measure 10, the first and third eighth notes, c″ and a′, are accented passing tones leading to b′ and g′. The passing tones cause an oblique intervallic succession from g–b′ to e–g′. Implied is a progression from G-major to E-minor harmony, not one from C major to A minor, as Kurth would have it (Ex. 5-12). Here, when Kurth specifies harmonies and is thus able to make conventional distinctions between melodic and harmonic elements, he misreads the harmonic process by misjudging the melodic one. It seems that Kurth has succumbed to the very sort of overly vertical analysis criticized in *Grundlagen*.

A pair of chords related by fifth may also help to counteract the empty sound of fifths and fourths. As mentioned earlier, Kurth invokes horn fifths to explain intervallic progressions involving an open fifth. He extends the idea of the chord pair to explain not only fifths but also fourths, for which he suggests the expression "horn fourths."[58] Fifth-related chords and, by extension, intervallic successions derived from those chords convey an even stronger sense of root progression than do third-related chords, so that harmonic activity is more pronounced. But Example 5-13 shows clearly that Kurth is not thinking of actual harmonic progressions. He marks the fifth f′–c″, which follows d′–bb′. The sixteenth-note rhythm surely rules out any meaningful progression between Bb- and F-major harmonies. The membership alone of the intervals in those chords is sufficient, for Kurth's ear, to reduce the hollowness of the f′–c″ fifth.[59] In his interpretation of Example 5-14, Kurth takes a less literal view of intervallic succession. He says that the sixth c♯–a′ leads in *similar* motion to the fifth e–b′, implying harmonies on A and E. In analyzing Example 5-14, Kurth has broadened his perspective from the most literal reading of c♯/c♯″–e/b′ to form the succession c♯/a′–e/b′, that is, in the second reading the e–b′ fifth is approached in similar rather than in contrary motion. In connection with this example, Kurth explains that it is not always possible to uphold a strict distinction between parallel and contrary motion.

> Taken out of context, [the fifth] exhibits an entrance in contrary motion.
> . . . In actuality . . . one hears the continuity of the upper voice such that
> one senses the ascending motion from the second half of the measure
> onward.[60]

By attributing greater weight to some melodic notes over others in order to determine the intervallic succession in Example 5-14, Kurth has taken an important step away from the literal, note-to-note readings of Examples 5-11*a* and *b*.

If Kurth was able to understand Example 5-14 as he did, why then did he interpret others, such as Examples 5-11*a* and *b*, as he did? Remember that it is the empty, thin *sound* of fourths and fifths in two-part counterpoint that motivates him to isolate and attempt to justify them in the first place. The sonic impact of two voices meeting on a fourth or fifth only exaggerates their thinness; this is why, to Kurth's ear, they disturb the contrapuntal flow.[61] Oblique motion, lacking such an impact, tempers the effect of fourths and fifths and renders them acceptable. Clearly, Kurth's concern

EXAMPLE 5-12.

EXAMPLE 5-13. Bach, "Sei gegrüsset, Jesu gütig," BWV 768, var. 1, mm. 8–9

EXAMPLE 5-14. Bach, Italian Concerto, I, mm. 81–82

with intervallic irregularities hinges on psycho-auditive rather than on structural cri-
tera. Nevertheless, in explaining certain irregularities, for example, unprepared dissonances, Kurth calls on the structural relationship between the voices, which requires
a clear-cut distinction between melodic and harmonic elements.

Herein lies the main problem with Kurth's analyses: Without a sufficiently
comprehensive structural basis for coordinating melody and harmony, given the diverse ways in which the two interact, Kurth occasionally interprets melodic elements
harmonically, as he does in Examples 5-11a and b, or vice versa.[62] In one analysis he
stresses melody to justify an irregularity, in another harmony, thus carrying over into
analysis his concept of a negative-positive opposition between melody and harmony.

Kurth does emphasize that polyphony is an organic union of harmony and
counterpoint, and that a fully mature polyphony conveys the sound of mature tonal
harmony. But in his discussion of intervallic irregularities, where harmony plays a
prominent role in his thinking, he tends to highlight either harmony *or* melody, leading him occasionally to undervalue or misinterpret the other.[63]

NOTES

1. Older theories of harmony include such works as Ernst Friedrich Richter's *Lehrbuch der Harmonie* (Leipzig, 1853; 25th ed., 1907); Karl Mayrberger's *Lehrbuch der musikalischen Harmonik* (Pressburg, 1878), discussed in Robert Wason's book *Viennese Harmonic Theory from Albrechtsberger to Schenker and Schoenberg* (Ann Arbor: UMI Research Press, 1985), 85–95; and Salamon Jadassohn's *Lehrbuch der Harmonie* (Leipzig, 1883; 23d ed., 1923). "Newer" theories include Rudolf Louis's and Ludwig Thuille's *Harmonielehre* (Stuttgart, 1907), Heinrich Schenker's *Harmonielehre* (Vienna, 1906), Arnold Schoenberg's *Harmonielehre* (Vienna, 1911), and Hermann Erpf's *Studien zur Harmonie- und Klangtechnik der neueren Musik* (Leipzig, 1927).

2. The need for a sound philosophical basis to undergird a theory of music has traditionally been important to European writers but has been less of a concern for their American counterparts.

3. Kurth, *Grundlagen,* 442: "*wo sich die Linien berühren,* setzt erst das Eingreifen der vertikalen Satzelemente ein, so dass diese *Berührung* und die *Zusammenklangsverhältnisse* stets eine *Folgeerscheinung, das Sekundäre,* darstellen, das sich erst aus der Gleichzeitigkeit der linear gerichteten Entwürfe ergibt."

4. Ibid., 62: "die klangliche Akkordruhe stellt . . . die Form eines *Kräfteausgleichs,* ein *Ergebnis* dar. . . . Die Harmonik ist ein Kräftespiel um diesen Gleichgewichtszustand." Ibid., 444: "Der Kontrapunkt *geht nicht vom Akkord aus,* sondern *gelangt zum Akkord.*"

5. Ibid., xvi: "this 'secondary' does not refer to artistic importance, which lies precisely in the powerful interaction of the two elements. . . . Less yet does 'secondary' mean anything such as subsidiary" ("das 'sekundär' bezieht sich nicht auf die künstlerische Bedeutung, die ja gerade im kraftvollen Ineinanderwirken der beiden Elemente beruht. . . . Noch weniger bedeutet 'sekundär' soviel wie nebensächlich"). Ibid.: "in einem musikalischen Kopf lassen sich harmonische und lineare Vorstellung auch nie ganz trennen."

6. Ibid., xvi: "The harmonic developments and their . . . constitutive significance are substantiated throughout the present volume" ("Die harmonischen Entwicklungen und ihre . . . konstitutive Bedeutung sind überall im vorliegenden Buche nachgewiesen").

7. Ibid., 445. Kurth, *Voraussetzungen,* 67. Suspension chords that appear to be consonant triads are one class of "coincidental" sonorities. They are in fact "not yet chords," just as Kurth suggests. Such suspension chords achieve equilibrium when the suspended note, or notes, resolves. Passing chords, for example, Kirnberger's passing seventh chord, better fit Kurth's interpretation of such coincidental harmonies. See Kirnberger, *Die Kunst des reinen Satzes,* 1:86; and idem, "The True Art for the Practice of Harmony," trans. David Beach and Jurgen Thym, *Journal of Music Theory* 23.2 (1979): 192–95.

8. Kurth, *Grundlagen,* 61: "die Linienzüge . . . *fangen sich* in Akkorden." Ibid., "der Vorgang des Ausgleichs in den Harmonien ist nicht immer bewusst zu sondern, besonders bei vorgeschrittener musikalischer Schulung . . . erfolgt die Einfügung in Akkorde und tonale Akkordzusammenhänge im wesentlichen schon zugleich mit der Konzeption der linearen Mehrstimmigkeit."

9. Hugo Riemann, *Lehrbuch des einfachen, doppelten und imitierenden Kontrapunkts* (Leipzig: Breitkopf und Härtel, 1888), 1; Ernst Friedrich Richter, *Lehrbuch des einfachen und doppelten Kontrapunkts* (Leipzig: Breitkopf und Härtel, 1872), 13–14; Felix Draeseke, *Der gebundene Stil,* vol. 1 (Hanover: Örtel, 1902), 7. Carl Dahlhaus remarks that Kurth's expression "linear counterpoint" is essentially a polemical response to harmonic counterpoint. See his article "Bach und der 'lineare Kontrapunkt,'" *Bach-Jahrbuch* 49 (1962): 58.

10. Kurth, *Grundlagen,* 60: "heterogene Erscheinungen, von Grund auf zweierlei."

11. The three types of harmony correspond roughly to the styles of Bach, Haydn-Mozart, and Wagner. Kurth's evolutionary view of harmony suggests a Hegelian dialectical interpretation, with the polyphonic-harmonic stage as thesis, the homophonic-harmonic stage as antithesis, and the polyphonic-homophonic one as synthesis.

12. Kurth postulates a natural gravitational pull between tones sounded together: "Between simultane-

ously sounding tones exists an attraction, a gravitational force which strives toward coalescence in a definite chordal image, the consonant triad" ("Zwischen gleichzeitigen Tönen herrscht eine Anziehung, eine gravitierende Kraft, die nach Verfestigung in einem bestimmten Akkordbild, dem konsonanten Dreiklang, hindrängt"; *Grundlagen,* 62).

13. Kurth, *Grundlagen,* 127: "Mit ihrem Tode (Bach stirbt 1750, Händel 1759) bricht die jahrhundertelang vorbereitete lineare Kontrapunktik jäh zusammen, um von den neuen Stilelementen der harmonisch-homophonen Setzweise des Klassizismus überflutet zu werden." Note how Kurth describes the texture of Classical music as "harmonic-homophonic," along the lines of the second type of harmony I described above.

14. Ibid., 166: "die Gruppenakzente bewirken auf diese Weise zugleich mit den Einkerbungen des Melodieverlaufs selbst auch ein periodisches Einmünden der melodischen Linienentwicklung in solche Teilabschlüsse, an welchen eine besonders deutliche akkordliche Wirkung sich festsetzt."

15. Ibid., 167: "beherrscht die ganze Linientechnik."

16. Ibid., 168: "gewinnt die Tonartlichkeit der Linie nicht in so ausgeprägtem Masse den Charakter einer blossen melodischen Umspielung eines Akkordgerüsts."

17. Ibid., 166–69.

18. Ibid., 129: "nur . . . soweit berücksichtigt wird, als es [das melodische Moment] einer guten und reibungslosen Akkordverbindung nicht entgegenwirkt."

19. Ibid., 129: "das melodische Moment . . . gewinnt . . . eine *negative* Bedeutung." See also ibid., 441: "Therefore, linear counterpoint, in its whole theoretical elaboration and in all of its [musical] manifestations, represents the negative aspect of chordal frameworks" ("Daher stellt sich die lineare Kontrapunktik in ihrer ganzen theoretischen Durchführung und in allen ihren Erscheinungen als das Negative der akkordlichen Anlagen dar"). Moritz Hauptmann's description of the nature of melody and harmony may have inspired Kurth to oppose them as negative and positive. In connection with the major scale, Hauptmann states that "we can at first think of the *melodic* principle abstractly as the *moving principle*. In opposition to this, [we can think of] the *harmonic* [principle]] as the *fixing one*. [We can imagine] the former as the tendency to emerge out of something established, without further conditions in themselves. It [the melodic principle] acquires these conditions only in the harmonic elements" ("Wir können das *melodische* Prinzip zuerst abstrakt uns denken als das *bewegende*. Ihm entgegengesetzt das *harmonische* als das *fixierende*. Jenes als die Tendenz aus einem Bestehenden herauszugehen, ohne weitere Bestimmungen an sich; diese Bestimmungen erhält es erst in den harmonischen Momenten"; *Die Natur der Harmonik und Metrik* [Leipzig: Breitkopf und Härtel, 1853], 52). Kurth's contrast of these two elements has been discussed most recently by Helmut Federhofer, who criticizes Kurth for overlooking the role of voice leading as a motivation for harmonic progressions: "Kurth did not consider the possibility . . . that even chords explainable by tonal means might owe their existence to voice leading" (*Akkord und Stimmführung,* 40: "Die Möglichkeit . . . , dass auch tonal erklärbare Akkorde sich der Stimmführung verdanken, wird von Kurth nicht erwogen").

20. Chapter 1 explains the influence of Schopenhauer's idea of the Will on Kurth. Kurth's view of the Romantic artists goes back to early nineteenth-century writers, such as E. T. A. Hoffmann. See, for example, the excerpts from his works in Oliver Strunk's *Source Readings in Music History* (New York: Norton, 1950), 775–97, particularly 775–81, 788–89, 790, 795–7.

21. Kurth, *Romantische Harmonik,* 31:

> von unten herauf werden die klassischen Harmonieformen aufgewellt und bis zu vollem Zerfliessen gelöst, so dass die ganzen Strukturgrundzüge zerstört werden und für neue Bedingungen der Klangbildung die Voraussetzungen entstehen. . . . Gerade das *Andrängen* dieser Spannungen gegen den Widerstandsdruck der klassischen Tonalität, die sie zu zersprengen und zu zersetzen streben, bewirkt es, dass weitaus mehr die potentiellen als die kinetischen Energieformen in mannigfachste Erscheinung treten und ein ganz anderer Musikstil entstehen musste als *vor* dem Klassizismus in den Bewegungsauswirkungen der linearen Polyphonie.

22. Ibid., 33, 312, 318–83.

23. Kurth, *Voraussetzungen*, 28–29. Kurth speaks of the "sensation of weight" (*Schwerkraftempfin-dung*) that chords possess. Carl Stumpf postulates the idea of interval "fusion" (*Verschmelzung*) in his *Tonpsychologie*, vol. 2 (Leipzig: Hirzel, 1890), 128.

24. Kurth, *Romantische Harmonik*, 382–83: "Für die Auswirkung der Energien haben . . . die Klänge eine hemmende Bedeutung . . . die künstlerische Wirkung . . . beruht gerade in der Intensität dieses Kampfes zwischen drängenden Energien und Widerstand der Materie, und seine Stärke ist das erste Merkmal künstlerischer Gestaltungskraft und innerer Spannung." From this passage it is clear that for Kurth the competition between energetic and sensuous traits in harmony is not just a feature of Romantic music; rather, more generally, it symbolizes the very essence of the creative process. During the nineteenth century, the two traits confront each other directly in the domain of harmony; in Classical music they exist side by side as melody and accompaniment.

25. Hugo Leichtentritt follows this method but takes it to extremes in his article "Arnold Schoenberg's Op. 19," *Die Musik* 25.1 (1932–33): 405–13. Leichtentritt refers to Op. 19 as exemplifying the new style of "linear" counterpoint (p. 413). See also Leichtentritt's comments on Schoenberg's Op. 11 in *Musikalische Formenlehre*, 3d ed., rev., enl. (Leipzig: Breitkopf und Härtel, 1927), 436–57.

26. As explained in chapter 1, Kurth hears leading-tone tendencies in the thirds of both major and minor triads. Thus, energetic forces are latently present in the most basic harmonic formations.

27. See the discussion of *Romantische Harmonik* in chapter 1. Kurth, *Romantische Harmonik*, 11: "Jeder Klang trägt die Spuren der unklanglichen Tiefe in sich, aus der er emporgerissen."

28. Kurth, *Voraussetzungen*, 20; idem, *Romantische Harmonik*, 9–10. Kurth discusses these same distinctions in *Grundlagen*, 68–70.

29. Kirnberger, *Die Kunst des reinen Satzes*, 1:30; idem, *The Art of Strict Musical Composition*, 42–43, 90ff. Schulz, *Die wahren Grundsätze zum Gebrauch der Harmonie* (Berlin, 1773), trans. David Beach and Jurgen Thym "*The True Principles for the Use of Harmony*," *Journal of Music Theory* 23.1 (1979): 192, Exx. 42–43.

30. See Floyd Grave's "Abbé Vogler's Theory of Reduction," 56. Grave points out that Vogler uses the expression "melodic harmony" to explain chords in exceptional progressions that arise from the melodic flow of voices. Weber also shows an awareness of passing and neighboring harmonies, which he calls "apparent chords" (see *Versuch einer geordneten Theorie der Tonsetzkunst*, vol. 3 [1821], 226–28, 242–43, where Weber illustrates *Scheinakkorde* in Exx. 151, 281–82, 310).

31. Simon Sechter, *Die Grundsätze der musikalischen Komposition*, vol. 1 (Leipzig: Breitkopf und Härtel, 1853); Mayrberger, *Lehrbuch der musikalischen Harmonie* (1878); Josef Schalk, "Das Gesetz der Tonalität," *Bayreuther Blätter* 11 (1888): 65–70; Louis and Thuille, *Harmonielehre* (1907), 226ff. Wason discusses Sechter and Louis-Thuille in *Viennese Harmonic Theory*, 31–64 and 116–19, 121–32, respectively.

32. Kurth gives a psychological interpretation of the evolution of musical style from the Classical period through the late nineteenth century in *Romantische Harmonik*, 14–43. His analyses throughout the book assume that the reader knows that psychological background.

33. In part 4 of *Grundlagen*, "The Polyphonic Structural Design," Kurth investigates topics such as interlinear dynamics (complementary rhythm, linear contrast among voices, staggered climaxes), formal dynamics (surge and ebb through melodic and rhythmic means), and motivic-thematic techniques (thematic concentration and dissolution, developmental motives), all essentially melodic topics. Part 5 deals with the "Technique of Linear Coupling," ("Technik der Linienverknüpfung"), 439–52; see especially chapter 2, "Harmonic Effects on Structural Irregularities," 459–70.

34. As mentioned at the beginning of chapter 2 (see chapter 2, note 2), Kurth is not deaf to the harmonic dimension of Bach's music. Indeed, he observes that "an essential requirement of any contrapuntal piece is that the coincidence of voices achieves the most compact, autonomous harmonic effects." He goes on to say that "the ultimate goal [of polyphony] is a work of the most perfect harmonic structure in the intervallic relationships" (*Grundlagen*, 439–40: "eine wesentliche Forderung eines kontrapunktischen Satzes liegt darin, dass die Zusammenklänge möglichst zu

kompakten harmonischen Eigenwirkungen gesteigert sind"; ibid., 441: "das letzte Ziel ist ein Satz von vollendetster harmonischer Durchbildung in den Zusammenklangsverhältnissen"). Kurth insists further that "tone for tone . . . the lines must also be harmonically and tonally explainable in analysis" ("die Linien analytische Ton für Ton auch harmonischtonal erklärbar sein . . . müssen"; ibid., xvi).

35. Ibid., 374: "Schärfung der Höhepunktswendungen."
36. Examples 5-1*a* and *b* are on pp. 375–76. In measures 7–13 of Fugue No. 4, the analogous pivotal apexes are not set with harmonic dissonances. Kurth also refers to Fugue No. 9, measures 16 and 19, to illustrate his point, but measures 46, 89, and 99 do not bear out his thesis. It would perhaps have been prudent had Kurth claimed that pivotal apexes are particularly susceptible to such harmonic enhancement, which may be applied in one setting or withheld in another, with pronounced musical effect in either case.
37. Ibid., 382.
38. Ibid., 374, 384, 386 (*Zusammenklangsverhältnisse*); 377, 379, 387 (*Zusammenklangsdissonanzen*); 375, 384 (*dissonanter Zusammenstoss*); 384, 385 (*dissonante Reibung*). In *Voraussetzungen*, 112, Kurth mentions the phenomenon of linear "clashes," where two tones forming a second rebound away from each other. He says such dissonances and consequent directional rebounds constitute a "clashing sensation" (*Stossempfindung*).
39. Kurth might also have mentioned that in Example 5-2*b* the melodic apexes on a″ (m. 13, right hand), e′ (left hand), and b′ (m. 17, right hand) clash with the companion voice. Two of these apexes, a″ and b′, are further intensified by the tonal coincidences on the first sixteenths of measures 14 and 18.
40. Kurth, *Grundlagen,* 383.
41. Ibid., 382–83: "der tiefste Ton schlägt gegen eine Dissonanz, von der die Bewegung wieder einen Rückstoss erleidet."
42. Dahlhaus, "Linearer Kontrapunkt," 61–62: "Vernachlässigung geschichtlicher Voraussetzungen, denen manche Phänomene nicht nur ihren Ursprung, sondern auch ihren Gehalt verdanken und ohne die sie nicht wären, was sie sind."
43. Kurth, *Grundlagen,* 387:

> Bei allen derartigen Fällen musste sich der gewohnten Theorie zufolge der dissonante Zusammenklang als das Primäre darstellen und die Linienentwicklung wäre aus diesem abgeleitet . . . das Verhältnis ist aber . . . ein umgekehrtes, wie jedes richtige kontrapunktische Fühlen ohne weiters lehren muss; das *Primäre* und die Hauptsache liegt, wie überall bei einer echten linear-kontrapunktischen Satzanlage im linearen Bewegungszug, der in solchen Fällen auf die Zusammenklangserscheinungen hinwirkt, in den melodischen Spannungen, nicht in den dissonanten Akkorden. *Aus der linearen Dynamik ist die Dynamik des Klangspiels beeinflusst.*

This is a good example of what Kurth calls an "extreme formulation" (*geschärfte Ausprägung*) of linear counterpoint, as an antidote to the harmonic extremism found in most counterpoint manuals of his day (*Grundlagen*, xiv).
44. Ibid., 349–50: "Anleitung zu einer Einfühlung in Bachs instrumentale Kontrapunktik"; "Erweckung und Anregung jener Kunst des instinktiven Einfühlens."
45. Dahlhaus concludes similarly that Kurth's linear primacy amounts to "a demand directed at musical hearing," a demand on the listener rather than on the structural characteristics of the music ("Linearer Kontrapunkt," 59).
46. This opposition was explained at the beginning of this chapter.
47. Kurth, *Grundlagen,* 440: "in counterpoint . . . the vertical intervals which come into play from the simplest union of two lines onward are at first to be regarded as *negative,* i.e., the first and basic task in achieving two simultaneously unfolding lines is . . . the *avoidance of disturbing intervallic results*" ("im Kontrapunkt sind . . . die Zusammenklangsverhältnisse, welche von der einfachsten Verknüpfung zweier Linien an in Betracht kommen, zunächst in *negativem* Sinne zu berücksichtigen; d.h. die primäre und primitive Aufgabe, zwei gleichzeitige Linienentwicklungen zu er-

möglichen, wird . . . *die Meidung störender Zusammenklangsergebnisse"*).

48. Ibid., 449: "jede terzlose Quint hat an sich die gleiche charakteristische Wirkung, die in der Stimm-führung des harmonischen Satzes bei verpönten Parallelen hervortritt. . . . Die leere Wirkung der *Quart* ist im zweistimmigen Satz kaum geringer als diejenige der Quint."

49. Ibid., 450n: "Solchen leeren Quinten fehlt die Massivität, die der kontrapunktische Satz beansprucht."

50. Ibid., 459: "überwunden."

51. Ibid., 461.

52. Ibid., 468.

53. Riemann, *Lehrbuch des Kontrapunkts,* 11–12; Stephan Krehl, *Kontrapunkt* (Leipzig: Göschen, 1908), 12–14. Kurth cites Riemann and Krehl in *Grundlagen,* 103, 136, 473, and 479. See also Richter, *Lehrbuch des Kontrapunkts,* 48–51, where in a brief four-page discussion of counterpoint in two voices Richter asks that students avoid fifths and octaves if possible, and to choose intervals whose harmonic meaning is clearly perceivable. He dislikes fourths by arpeggiation, which Kurth allows. It is this kind of harmonicized counterpoint to which Kurth objects. Harmonic approaches to counterpoint extend back at least to Kirnberger (*Die Kunst des reinen Satzes,* 142; *Art of Strict Musical Composition,* 159) and continue with Johann G. Albrechtsberger (*Gründliche Anweisung zur Komposition* [Leipzig: J. G. I. Breitkopf, 1790], 24–27); J. C. Lobe (*Lehrbuch der musikal-ischen Komposition* [Leipzig: Breitkopf und Härtel, 1860], 3:99, 103, 122) and Sechter (*Grund-sätze,* 3:3) are nineteenth-century representatives of this harmonic outlook.

54. Dahlhaus asks how harmony, the "negative" element in counterpoint, can cancel the effect of fifths and fourths, themselves "negative" ("Linearer Kontrapunkt," 61). Kurth's method of overcoming structural irregularities then amounts to overcoming a negation by means of a negation.

55. Kurth, *Grundlagen,* 463: "wenn die Quint oder Quart mit dem vorausgehenden Zusammenklang im Verhältnis eines *Parellel*klanges steht."

56. Ibid., 464.

57. Ibid.

58. Ibid., 465.

59. Ibid., 466.

60. Ibid., 451: "aus dem Zusammenhang gerissen, zeigt [die Quint] Eintritt in Gegenbewegung . . . in Wahrheit aber hört man die Oberstimme in der Weise zusammenhängend, dass man von der zweiten Takthälfte an die Aufwärtsbewegung empfindet." Kurth might have invoked the *Schein-stimme* theory in order to clarify his ideas on Example 5-14.

61. Kurth also explores dissonances in two-part counterpoint. These, too, represent "wrinkles" in the linear unfoldment. He explains them with the same techniques as those applied to fourths and fifths, and with a few additional melodic procedures (ibid., 468–501, on !eading-tone tension, motivic energy, implicit oblique motion, and apparent voices).

62. In *Grundlagen,* 513, where Kurth discusses a passage from a piece in the *Notebook for Wilhelm Friedemann Bach* (Menuet III, mm. 27–29), he mistakes a note belonging to the harmony for an unresolved neighbor note and comments on its exceptional, disjunct continuation. Helmut Feder-hofer refers to Kurth's analysis in *Akkord und Stimmführung,* 49–51.

63. Kurth does insist that the "linear polyphony can sustain tonally mature and vigorous, sonorous harmony without being sustained by it" ("lineare Mehrstimmigkeit kann tonal durchgebildete und kraftvolle, prangende Harmonik tragen, ohne von ihr getragen zu sein"; *Grundlagen,* 145).

CHAPTER 6

Kurth's View of Romantic Harmony

BASIC CONCEPTS

Psycho-auditive and aesthetic considerations, already important in Kurth's understanding of Bach's polyphonic harmony, are even more important to his analyses of Wagner's polyphonic homophony. In Bach's genetically linear style, harmony is both a result and, as Kurth puts it, negative. It is a hindrance and material resistance to the linear unfoldment.[1] By contrast, Wagner's polyphonic homophony, an outgrowth of Classical homophony, exploits harmonic effects for their own sake. Harmony is no longer a byproduct of linear interaction, as described in *Grundlagen*. Indeed, in *Romantische Harmonik*, Kurth says that "every tone of a melody contains a latent chord."[2] But polyphonic homophony is not just a rehash of Classical homophony, with sharper dissonances and novel chord connections. It transforms Classical homophony by reviving fluent linearity. Polyphonic homophony synthesizes Classical and Baroque stylistic tendencies, intensifying both up to the limits of the tonal system. The expanded activity of psychic forces makes this dynamic evolution possible.

In the first section of *Romantische Harmonik*, "Foundations," Kurth explores and elaborates on the meaning of his motto that harmonies are "reflexes from the unconscious," the motto's implications for music theory, and its significance for the psychology of the Romantic era.[3] Although harmony is properly the subject of *Romantische Harmonik*, the work is more than a purely technical study. Rather, it takes up the psychological and resultant music-technical evolution of the late Romantic idiom and its bequest to impressionism and the early twentieth century. We might describe the book, then, as a psycho-historical study of the Romantic style, illustrated by means of various harmonic procedures. These serve as palpable evidence of the Romantic creative psyche and as guideposts on the evolutionary path.

For Kurth, harmony is not an end in itself but rather a means for expressing mental states.

> Considered in themselves, harmonies represent empty matter. . . . The vital activity of harmonies resides in their ability to allow us always to feel the surging forces which pass from the unconscious foundations of [artistic] creation into palpable shape as sensuously perceivable harmonic forms.

> *Every chord is only an acoustically conceived image of certain energetic impulses.*[4]

Music is a "symphony of energetic currents," and harmony is the "transformation of [these] energetic tensions into sound stimuli." The goal of theory, then, is clear. It must begin at the very genesis of music, the "*outbreak* and *growth toward sound*," and must proceed to "observe the *transformation* of certain tension *processes* into *sounds.*"[5] As explained in chapter 1 of the present study, by starting from the "inside" of music Kurth hoped to rectify the failed attempts of his nineteenth-century predecessors to establish a connection between theory and art.[6] Illuminating this presonic realm of music does not, of course, cancel the obligation to explain the material forms of harmony. Kurth is not content to discuss intangible psychic qualities only; after an introductory chapter, he gets down to the practical business of analysis. But in contrast to conventional methods, Kurth, working from the inside of music outward, treats each tone of polyphonic homophony as a psycho-energetic unit of force, striving in one direction or another.[7] Each sonority is then an energetic composite of its constituent units. Kurth's approach to analysis provides insights into the drama, as well as into the mental states of its characters.

In making his psycho-auditive analyses, Kurth employs a minimum of technical-analytical apparatus. He limits himself to roman numerals and to standard terminology for nonharmonic tones. Those who study his work today may find his use of roman numerals somewhat awkward and too narrow in scope. Workaday, mechanical analyses of late nineteenth-century vintage brought out the worst in roman-numeral analyses and have tinged our attitude toward their utility in general. For the study of highly chromatic music, the pitfalls are all too familiar. Local chord identifications, often limited to a series of chord pairs in various keys for apparent lack of any broader harmonic relationships, seem to dominate. Kurth himself is not without fault in certain cases, as we shall see. Nevertheless, we must remember that he uses roman numerals only as a convenient "common denominator" in order to make his ideas clear to the widest audience. They are not an end in themselves.[8] The rudimentary notation is only a springboard for the substance of Kurth's analyses. If we are to learn anything about late Romantic harmony through Kurth's mind and ear, we will have to look beyond the notational apparatus, noting some debatable interpretations, and focus instead on his rich insights into the dynamic vitality of Wagner's harmonic idiom.

As explained in chapter 5, Kurth distinguishes two qualities of harmony, energy and sensuousness. Music may at any point feature one or the other quality.

Kurth listens to each sonority in an effort to hear greater or lesser degrees of energetic tension. We have already seen that he adopts the terms kinetic and potential
energy from physical science to describe energetic processes in music. Kinetic-
linear forces energize the texture of polyphonic homophony. Potential energy measures the force of chords that momentarily arrests the motion of their variously
directed notes, each charged with a share of the kinetic-linear flow. Just as a dam
builds up potential energy in restraining the flow of water, so do certain sonorities
build up potential energy in restraining the active flow of linear impulses.

Two categories of sonorities emerge from Kurth's analysis of Romantic harmony. Diatonic tertian sonorities that have been altered chromatically exemplify one
form of potential energy. One or more alterations heighten the tension level of the
chord and impel it onward to the next sonority. Examples of such chords are those
with diminished or augmented fifths, diminished thirds and augmented sixths, and
so on. They are products of *chordal* alteration. Sonorities in the second category are
products of *melodic* alterations. These include appoggiatura formations, which contain multiple nonharmonic tones ("neighbor-note insertions") whose coalescent kinetic impulses are restrained and so transformed into potential energy. Appoggiatura
formations may or may not exhibit a uniform tertian structure. If they do not, their
meaning is generally clear. If they do, some confusion may arise, for then they often
look like tonal chords although they do not, in fact, function as such. At any point,
enharmonic redefinition may convert a tertian-structured appoggiatura formation
that is potentially native to the prevailing tonality, or even one foreign to it, into a
decidedly tonal chord. Tertian appoggiatura chords thus represent a link between energetic and sensuous harmony.

Kurth uses Wagner's *Tristan* as the centerpiece in his study of Romantic harmony. This is not surprising, for that opera has long been considered a turning point
in the evolution of musical style. Its pervasive chromatic voice leading and seemingly wayward harmonic-tonal idiom refine and extend techniques pioneered by
Wagner's predecessors. Wagner's stylistic heirs then used the procedures worked out
in *Tristan* as resources for their own creative inspiration and technical instruction.[9]
Music theorists, too, were quick to recognize the significance of *Tristan* and the
problems it posed for analysis. With outmoded analytical tools inherited from generations of authors from Vogler up through Sechter, theorists of the 1870s and 1880s set
to work on *Tristan*'s slippery chromatic harmonies. Beginning with Cyrill Kistler in
1879, several theorists, including Karl Mayrberger, Salamon Jadassohn, Cyrill
Hynais, and Georg Capellen, tried their hands at explaining the enigmatic opening
of the Prelude to act I. Not until Max Arend's brief study of 1901 did anyone attempt
to analyze the entire piece.[10] With a forty-year accumulation of analytical initiatives
and a substantial historical legacy behind it, *Tristan* was, by 1920, the touchstone for
any theorist. It is no wonder that, given this inheritance of relatively short, largely
fragmentary analyses, Kurth should undertake a comprehensive study of harmonic
practices in the opera.

Out of the perpetual flow of harmonic currents and countercurrents in *Tristan*,

Kurth extracts the so-called *Tristan* chord as a microcosmic expression of the striv-
ings of the Will. For Kurth, the sonority is at once a symbol of the late Romantic
psyche and an analytical paradigm.

> The symbolic meaning of the unique introductory sonority . . . indicates
> very generally the *unfulfillable,* the *unredeemability* of love's desire. . . .
> [O]ne can designate it as the *fundamental tension of the entire drama,* as
> its "urgency." . . . [T]he agonizingly conflictive mood of the work finds
> in it, with a single sonorous reflex, an initial and most direct outbreak.

> The very first harmonic event . . . is a chord which seems to focus all the
> rays [of the *Tristan* style] in one point. . . . [I]t contains essential tech-
> nical characteristics. . . . [T]he entire style is also reflected in it.[11]

Just as Kurth treats the initial cadence of the Prelude as a synoptic paradigm for the
chromatic language of *Tristan,* so we can take his interpretation of this passage as a
paradigm of his analytical habits. Having discussed this and a few more representative analyses by way of introduction, we can then proceed to review other analyses
illustrating the various harmonic procedures that make up the *Tristan* style.

ANALYSIS

Kurth speaks of the *Tristan* style as the "alteration style," and of its compositional
basis as the "alteration technique."[12] For Kurth, alteration means chromatic inflection of diatonic pitches. It may affect harmonic as well as melodic elements, either
separately or simultaneously. Example 6-1 illustrates both types. According to Kurth
the basic harmonies of measures 2–3 are two dominant seventh chords, the first one
rooted on B, the second on E. Together, they form a "simple *cadential gesture,*"
whose components are "distorted by chromaticism."[13] The f♮ in the bass, originally
the chordal fifth, f♯, is a "chordal alteration." Kurth points out that the alteration
enhances the melodic connection in the bass from measure 2 to measure 3, but that
the altered note itself is harmonic, that is, it is part of a previously ordinary tertian
structure. Dynamically, the f strives *out of* its native chordal habitat into the following sonority.[14] The g♯' in the upper voice is an example of melodic alteration. In
contrast to the bass f♮, g♯' is nonchordal. It is a "free neighbor-note insertion" (*freie
Nebentoneinstellung*), an appoggiatura directed at a resolution tone, the seventh,
which belongs to the dominant seventh on B. Dynamically, the kinetic force of g♯'
flows *into* the governing harmony. The energetic release into a' leaves sufficient residual energy, built up over the first five beats of the bar, to overcome the otherwise
obligatory downward resolution of the seventh.[15] This residual energy propels the a'
upward into a♯', which, coinciding with a harmonic change, gains additional linear
momentum before coming to rest on the fifth of the new chord. Meanwhile, the f♮
spends its energy an eighth earlier in resolving to e.[16]

EXAMPLE 6-1. *Tristan,* Prelude to act I, mm. 1–3

Both alterations thus possess a specific dynamic function, and Kurth warns against considering them "arbitrary shifts in color"; they are "always linked to *melodic*-chromatic continuation." [17] The f♮ striving out of the B[7] chord toward e, and the g♯' striving into B[7] toward a' and beyond impart their collective kinetic energies to the overall sonority, now a highly unstable chord suffused with potential energy.

> The chromatic modifications indicate . . . a permeation of the chords with dynamic tensions. . . . Their energies are absorbed into the chord, and a charged force field envelops it as a whole. . . . [K]inetic energy transforms itself into potential energy.[18]

We might well stop and ask exactly what Kurth offers that is analytically different from, say, Mayrberger's interpretation, which is similar to Kurth's. Aside from dealing with technical-analytical matters—identifying the basic chords with their harmonic and melodic alterations—Kurth's analysis pinpoints the salient melodic and harmonic moments symbolizing the psychic currents that drive the music. Such a psycho-auditive interpretation evokes a vivid mental picture of the elemental forces in the music, a picture that comes to life as we "hear" the strain of the sonority and respond with our own inner stress. This is what Kurth means when he says that music transforms tension processes into sounds, and that harmonies are reflexes from the unconscious. Kurth's psycho-auditive approach to analysis is in itself a noteworthy change from the matter-of-fact and at times mechanical approach of other writers, even if he does not always reach different conclusions. But Kurth's findings differ from those of his predecessors in certain technical respects as well. For example, while Mayrberger reads a D root in measure 1 (Ex. 6-1), Kurth reads an A root. Additionally, Kurth does not call on Sechter's hybrid chord, as Mayrberger does, to explain the *Tristan* chord. Mayrberger must invoke the resources of two keys, A minor and E minor, in order to unite f♮ and d♯' into one chord. Kurth, allowing both notes as altered, argues that Mayrberger, "with anxious distortion, wants to hold together that which by nature flows apart." [19]

Concerning root and chord type, Kurth's view differs sharply from that of Cyrill Kistler, whose *Harmonielehre* appeared a few years before Mayrberger's. According to Kistler, g♯' is not a melodic delay but rather the root of a VII[7] in A minor, whose structure has been modified from a diminished to a minor triad on G♯. Thus, g♯' is chordal, not incidental, and d♯', not f, is the altered tone.[20] With Kistler's reading of measure 2 as a VII[7], the progression to measure 3 becomes a comparatively weak one, a dominant-like VII "progressing" to V. Kurth's applied-dominant cadence, with its dual alteration, comes closer to our musical experience of the progressions than does Kistler's static VII[7]–V.

Kurth's analysis is still further removed from those of Max Arend and Hugo Riemann, who read the *Tristan* chord as an altered subdominant projected downward from A, A–F–D♯–B, according to the "dualistic" conception of the subdominant.[21] Here again, d♯', not f, is the altered tone. In contrast to Kistler's chordal view of g♯', Riemann, Arend, and Kurth all agree on the g♯' appoggiatura. Unlike the dualists, however, Kurth rejects outright any subdominant quality in the *Tristan* chord. More than anything else, this disagreement has divided theorists into two camps, one defending a subdominant function for the chord, the other defending a dominant function.[22]

Kurth insists that the most distinctive feature of the *Tristan* chord is its dominant character; he thus maintains that the cadence is "dominantic." By dominantic, Kurth means that the first chord of the pair is major and thus contains leading-tone energy, and that the root movement is by falling fifth, imitating in all respects a progression from dominant to tonic. He singles out what he feels are mistaken analyses which interpret the *Tristan* chord as an altered II in A minor, probably because for him II, in whatever form, suggests subdominant qualities.[23] By asserting that the characteristic subdominant pitch, f♮, is an altered form of an otherwise expected f♯, Kurth has denied any relation to the subdominant at the very outset. Apparently, he wants to keep the chord on the dominant "side" of the tonic and thus prefers to consider it a dominant of the dominant. To call it a subdominant, or to derive it from a subdominant-like chord, would be to give it the wrong tonal disposition. According to Kurth, then, the chord is an applied dominant and cannot be equated with an altered subdominant.[24]

So far, we have concentrated on the pitch content and tonal disposition of the *Tristan* chord. Little has been said about its successor, the resolution chord. As a dominant seventh chord, it is not the reposeful consonance we would expect of a genuine resolution. Kurth takes note of this peculiarity and informs us that "partial resolutions" (*Teilauflösungen*) are a feature of chromatic music. Compared to altered harmonies charged with potential energy, seventh and even ninth chords seem relatively reposeful. Wagner often exploits the tension differential between dynamically dissonant, altered chords and comparatively consonant, if not entirely tension-free, chords by using seventh chords in place of triads at cadences. The sense of resolution is a relative matter, as Kurth points out, by which he seems to mean that it differs according to changing historical styles or local contexts. A seventh or ninth chord, dissonant in one style or local context, may appear frequently as a pseudo-consonant sonority of resolution in another historical or musical setting. Most would agree with Kurth's findings here. The problem is, he does not explicitly distinguish between local and global contexts. For example, the E[7] in measure 3 of the Prelude may be sufficiently consonant to act as a local resolution, but it remains globally, that is, tonally, dissonant. Kurth says the seventh chord "approaches the impression of a consonant chord." He might have gone on to say that a momentary reduction of local *harmonic* tension does not necessarily imply a reduction of *tonal* tension.[25]

Let us summarize the main features of Kurth's analysis of Example 6-1, since they will help us to pinpoint certain analytical habits as we proceed to other examples. Regarding melody, the analysis asserts a five-beat appoggiatura in measure 2 and a brief chromatic passing note, a♯', at the head of measure 3. The g♯' is by far the more important of the two for Kurth's subsequent analyses. Having established this reading, Kurth nearly always treats the first and third pitches of the four-note chromatic ascent (Love-Motive) as non–chord tones. If applied analogically to similar melodic gestures, this fixed interpretation may yield questionable results. So long as neighbor-note insertions occur singly and resolve within the duration of their harmonic reference, they are unproblematic. But when several occur simultaneously, or when they resolve after the harmony changes, their status as non–chord tones becomes ambiguous.

Even with a single neighbor-note insertion, as in Kurth's analysis of the *Tristan* chord, ambiguity may still persist. Why not label both f and d♯' (= e♭') as neighbor-note displacements of e and d' respectively? Then there would be no progression between the *Tristan* chord and its resolution. The two would be, in Kurth's words, "identical."[26] What is *non*harmonic depends, of course, on what is *harmonic*. In order to evaluate Kurth's work, we must try to understand his decisions in such matters.

Three harmonic issues raised in connection with Example 6-1 are consequential for Kurth's analytical procedures. First, there is the technique of harmonic alteration. While melodically motivated, the chromatically inflected note has a diatonic chordal counterpart and is thus integral to the harmony. Second, there is the diatonic cadential model (V–I), which influenced Kurth's thinking, just as it had directed that of most nineteenth-century theorists. The augmented sixth f–d♯', the a', however fleeting, and the stationary b created too familiar a pattern for Kurth to ignore. Finally, there is the conflict between the resolution character of the dominant seventh chord at the local level and the tonal tension that the chord creates at the global level. This conflict points up a general consideration regarding musical context in Kurth's analyses. Kurth concerns himself with harmonic events in passages from two to six measures long, the average size of his examples, but he does not always interpret those events within a larger contextual framework. Consequently, while his analyses are revealing for short musical segments, they may be superseded in more comprehensive overviews.

Much has been written by theorists attempting to explain the third and most enigmatic chord pair of the Prelude (mm. 10–11; see Ex. 6-2). The chords are particularly significant because they prepare the structural dominant of the Prelude, which ensues five measures later. Compared with the previous chord pairs, this one does not conform so readily to a cadential model. By 1920, it had already generated a formidable literature.[27] Like Capellen, Kurth suggests an E root for the sonority in measure 10. The lower voices, c′ and f′, are both free neighbor-note insertions substituting for b and e′ respectively. Kurth contrasts the initial two chord pairs of the Prelude, derived from dominant cadences, with this final pair, which derives from a subdominant cadence, a *rising* fifth progression from an E[7] to a B[7] harmony.[28] In addition to reversing the root movement and altering the cadential type, Kurth's explanation of Example 6-2 also alters the function of the first note in the Love-Motive. It is no longer an appoggiatura delaying a chordal seventh, as it is in Example 6-1, but rather is a chordal seventh itself. Like the seventh in Example 6-1, the one in Example 6-2 does not, and in fact cannot, resolve. But while Kurth has a ready explanation for the earlier anomaly—residual kinetic energy—the behavior of the present seventh cannot be similarly explained. No extended upward-striving appoggiatura precedes this seventh. The subsequent d♯″ propels the line upward to be sure, but what sends d″ to d♯″?[29]

EXAMPLE 6-2.

Another question raised by Kurth's analysis is the neighbor-note insertion c′. While the f′ above it resolves within the duration of the asserted E[7] harmony, c′ remains fixed until the harmony changes. Now it is not so unusual in Romantic music to find appoggiaturas resolving over a change of harmony. But here, with only an imaginary root to provide harmonic reference, the very function of c′ as a free neighbor-note insertion becomes problematic.

Other theorists have had no less trouble deciphering the music in Example 6-2. Mayrberger reads an A root with f′, d″, and g♯′ as appoggiaturas, resolving over a change of harmony. Reading c′ as harmonic and g♯′ as nonharmonic produces an analysis exactly opposite to Kurth's. Lorenz hears a B root with a fourfold neighbor-note insertion, c′ to b, f″ (= e♯″) to f♯″, g♯′ to a′, and d″ (c×) to d♯″. The entire first configuration becomes an appoggiatura chord, making the two sonorities "identical." Jadassohn avoids all neighbor-note insertions and claims that measure 10 amounts to a half-diminished seventh chord on D. With this last view we have run the gamut from complete neighbor-note displacement to no displacement at all. Any chord admitting of such contradictory explanations must be extraordinarily troublesome indeed! Rather than arguing the merits of these interpretations, let us concentrate instead on what Kurth's reading of Example 6-2 tells us about him as analyst and about his ability to balance analytical consistency with musical sensitivity.

Kurth earns good marks in both categories. He abandons the appoggiatura interpretation of the initial note in the Love-Motive, a decisive element in his analysis of Example 6-1, and designates d″ as chordal in Example 6-2. This indicates a musical sensitivity that overrides any compulsion for absolute uniformity. It is clear to Kurth that d″ does not strive toward d♯″ in Example 6-2 the way g♯′ strives toward a′ in Example 6-1. Inferring an E⁷ chord in Example 6-2 allows a logical (subdominant) connection with the second measure of the example. Even within the most ambiguous of circumstances, Kurth tries to maintain a diatonic cadential model. In analyzing Example 6-2, he shows sensitivity to changing local context without sacrificing analytical consistency.

Analytical consistency among various transformations of referential musical gestures, such as leitmotifs, is not an abstract, theoretical idea for Kurth. The analyses of Examples 6-1 and 6-2 demonstrate his readiness to accommodate changing musical circumstances. We must not lose sight of the psychological point of view informing all of his work. A transformation of musical functions from one context to another, similar one (Ex. 6-1 compared with Ex. 6-2) is a logical consequence of the variable psychological states and drives that attach to those contexts. Occasionally, though, Kurth does not rely heavily enough on psychologically motivated transformations of musical gestures in making an analysis. For instance, he tries to impose his initial reading of the Love-Motive on the changed psychological and musical circumstances of Example 6-3, which he contrasts with Example 6-1. He points out that the diatonic character of Example 6-3 reflects decreased tension, symbolizing Tristan's life-weariness and despair. The urgency of the chromatic ascent, so vivid in Example 6-1, changes to whole-step motion at the end of the motive. Compared with Example 6-1, Example 6-3 is a languid melodic gesture that conveys the gloomy psychological mood and physical circumstances of Tristan's isolation and exile.

EXAMPLE 6-3. *Tristan,* Prelude to act III, mm. 1–2

Kurth sets roman numerals F: IV⁷–I under measures 1 and 2 respectively, making a subdominant, and thus appropriately less energetic, cadence.[30] By analogy to the g♯′ in the Prelude to act I, Kurth considers the g♮ at the opening of act III nonchordal, a neighbor-note insertion to a♭, which is the seventh of a B♭-minor harmony. Analogic interpretations, while helpful in some cases, may be misleading in others, owing to changing contexts. Having acknowledged the different dramatic circumstances, Kurth still rejects interpreting g as harmonic in a II^7 chord.

> It would be wrong . . . to interpret the first chord as g–b♭–d♭–f (II^7); for once the motive is correctly understood, the musical tension makes the tone g appear not as a chord tone but rather, in analogy to the harmonizations of the opening, as a nonchordal, inserted neighbor note.[31]

He seems to have overlooked the fact that the orchestral and piano scores treat g as chordal. While the first violins abandon g on the last eighth of measure 1, the second violins sustain it up until the first violins reach c′ in measure 2. Only then do the second violins ascend from g to a♭. If g were a neighbor-note insertion, would not the second violins follow the first violins? Calling g chordal and a♭ nonchordal would mean a progression from II^7 to I, which Kurth apparently rejects in light of other, clear root movements by fifth harmonizing the Love-Motive. While the analysis of Example 6-3 is consistent with the Love-Motive appoggiatura in Example 6-1 and with the harmonic progressions in both Example 6-1 and 6-2, it is based more on analogy than on musical fact and is less convincing.[32] Wagner's style demands that we remain alert to varying contextual details and to the unexpected. Although we must keep the big picture in mind, we must define motives, harmonies, and their relationships on a case-by-case basis, allowing for intentional ambiguities and for new possibilities that Wagner may be exploring.

Kurth's analysis of the music in Example 6-4 brings together several of the issues touched on in the foregoing paragraphs: analogy, ambiguity, and local versus global contexts. The music in Example 6-4 comes at one of the most dramatic moments of the opera, just after Tristan and Isolde have drunk the love potion and begin to feel its effect. Appropriately, from the musical as well as the psycho-dramatic point of view, measure 16 refers back to the *Tristan* chord. Now, however, instead of resolving directly to an E^7 harmony, the chord undergoes a gradual transformation in measures 17–19 before finally reaching E^7 in measure 20 (Ex. 6-5).[33] Kurth's analysis shows that measures 16–19 elaborate a secondary dominant, starting with a V/V in measures 16–17, a B-major chord with altered fifth (F♯ to F♮), and continuing with an altered diminished seventh chord, VII^7/V (D♯–F–A–C), in measures 18–19. The persistent alteration of F♯ to F♮ intensifies the movement toward E in measure 20, just as the *Tristan* chord strives toward E^7 in measure 3 of the Prelude to act I.

By analogy to his reading of the Love-Motive in Example 6-1, Kurth interprets the upper-voice d♯ in Example 6-4, measure 16, as a free neighbor-note insertion, an appoggiatura that resolves up by whole step to f. This reading is confirmed, he states, by Wagner's score, which specifies e♭, rather than the d♯ of Buelow's piano transcription. For Kurth, Wagner's notation is "clear *evidence* that he [Wagner] once again understands the *first tone* of the motive as a dissonant neighbor-note insertion."[34] Nevertheless, e♭ as a free neighbor note would seem to point more toward d♮ than toward f, which is notated here as e♯. But why read d♯ (e♭) as a neighbor at all? Given Kurth's harmonic reading of measure 16, it is possible, even logical, to read d♯ as chordal and e♯ as a passing note. Indeed, d♯ is the crucial leading tone for Kurth's V/V. Although his analysis and the counteranalysis offered here agree on the chord in measures 16–17, B–D♯–F, Kurth's reading, with its appoggiatura e♭, allows only a single brief harmonic note in the melody, the f (e♯) in measure 16.[35] Kurth's analogically derived analysis disagrees with the context. Reading d♯ and e♯ instead of Kurth's proposed e♭ and f does not solve all problems. No matter which melodic pitch in measure 16 is chordal, f♯ and g♯ in measure 17 are nonchordal.

Both of the readings suggested above assume the altered chord B–D♯–F as the harmonic foundation. Example 6-6 offers another, quite different, interpretation, in which enharmonic spelling reveals a sonic reference to a motivically significant enharmonic version of the *Tristan* chord, the one stated repeatedly at the climax of the Prelude to act I, measures 81 ff. There, Wagner treats the sonority as II[7] in the key of E♭ minor. The enharmonic respelling in Example 6-6 hints at what Kurth would call the sensuous form of the *Tristan* chord, the tertian configuration F–A♭–C♭–E♭.

EXAMPLE 6-4. *Tristan*, I, 5

EXAMPLE 6-5.

EXAMPLE 6-6.

This transformation points toward an entirely different chord of resolution, V^7 in E♭ minor, as opposed to V^7 in A minor. The harmony of Example 6-6 alludes to but ultimately avoids the key of E♭ minor, just as it did at the climax of the Prelude (mm. 83–84). Avoiding E♭ minor symbolizes the frustration that plagues Tristan and Isolde's love. At the very moment when they drink the potion, the music makes a clear pass at the key of E♭ minor, both harmonically and melodically. But just as the melody is about to complete a rising fifth from e♭ to b♭, clinching E♭ minor, it abruptly changes course, substituting the foil, a♮ (b♭♭), for the "fulfilling" b♭.[36] Wagner undermines the key of E♭ minor with an a in the melody and begins to direct the harmony back toward the key of A minor (unfulfillment). At the a, Wagner takes the opportunity to introduce the pitches of an A-major chord along with the motivic contour associated with Isolde's curse, "Todgeweihtes Haupt! Todgeweihtes Herz!"[37] Indeed, for all the rapture it produces, the potion turns out to be a curse. The musico-dramatic references described above are extremely important in Wagner's music and require comment. Kurth does often point out musical "flashbacks" and "previews" to past and future dramatic events. But in Example 6-4, the Love-Motive, with its characteristic appoggiatura, seems to have guided his ear, and consequently he overlooks other possible musico-dramatic references.[38]

Although Kurth does seem to have overlooked the interpretation shown in Example 6-6, his analysis of Example 6-4 is still valuable in itself. Given the context he presents, his reading is insightful. He identifies a referential sonority and shows, in a difficult passage, how this sonority is extended and transformed by chromatic voice leading before reaching a cadence. His reading of the chromatic voice leading is satisfactorily context-sensitive for the span of music he examines; it suits the music surrounding Example 6-4, though only to a certain extent. The *Tristan* chord with B–D♯ (energetic) follows logically from the six measures preceding Example 6-4, but in the seventh through ninth measures before Example 6-4, the sensuous *Tristan* chord, with C♭ and E♭, prevails. Kurth seems to have chosen certain passages to illustrate specific points, and he tends, then, to focus on the details of those passages alone, necessarily simplifying matters somewhat, perhaps in order to achieve didactic clarity. Consequently, he sometimes excludes from consideration certain informative musical or extramusical details that lie outside the boundaries of his examples.

It is apparent from the examples discussed so far that Kurth favors energetic over sensuous interpretations of chords. Where the context is ambiguous and either analysis might hold, Kurth usually adopts the dynamic view. This reflects his hypothesis about the aesthetics and harmonic foundations of Romantic music in general. Of course theoretically, and practically, too, as we shall see later, Kurth does devote considerable space to sensuous interpretations of chords.[39]

Occasionally, Kurth confuses energetic and sensuous elements of the music, as in his analysis of Example 6-7. Here, Kurth speaks of e♭′ (d♯′) and f′ as neighbor-note insertions to e♮′ and g♭′ in measures 8 and 9. The underlying progression is C^7 to F^9, the first chord having an altered fifth (g to g♭).[40] The first chord is a transposition of the *Tristan* chord. Occurring just as Brangäne suggests that she mix a love

EXAMPLE 6-7. *Tristan*, I, 3

potion so that Mark will love Isolde, the sonority achieves maximum psychological effect.

Kurth observes that Wagner resolved the *Tristan*-like chord in Example 6-7 differently than he did in its original version. Instead of resolving it to a C♭ seventh chord, imitating Example 6-1, Wagner brings in F♭⁹.[41] As F♭⁹ arrives, the Love-Motive has reached its third note, f′, according to Kurth an appoggiatura and, simultaneously, the chordal root. Kurth claims that the subsequent g♭′, the minor ninth, possesses a "resolution character" owing to the "intensive appoggiatura character" of the f′.[42] To speak of the resolution character of the minor ninth resulting from the appoggiatura character of f′ is to confuse harmonic with melodic factors. The F♭⁹ is no more, and probably less, satisfying in itself as a harmonic close than the E⁷ in Example 6-1, measure 3. The g♭′ in Example 6-7 is a *motivic,* not a harmonic, resolution. Kurth ought to distinguish between these two kinds of resolution. Of course, he does say "resolution *character,*" implying less than a full-fledged resolution. Furthermore, in connection with a similar example featuring "resolution" on a minor ninth, Kurth does in fact attribute the resolution character of the melody note to "motivic continuity," which causes the minor ninth to sound like a resolution.[43]

The problem is a verbal as well as a conceptual one. Kurth pinpoints the reason for the resolution character of the ninth—motivic continuity—but goes on to emphasize the harmonic phenomenon rather than its melodic origin. He ought to spell out the difference, conceptually and terminologically, between harmonic and melodic resolutions. That the final note of the Love-Motive is coincidentally a minor ninth in the supporting harmony does not mean that the minor ninth is a harmonic resolution. Harmonic tension lingers, while motivic tension has subsided. Kurth's affirmation, "*we hear dynamically, not acoustically,*" is on the mark; clearly, he hears Example 6-7 "dynamically." But the details of his verbal analysis do not fully reflect his aural instincts.[44] In blurring the distinction between harmonic and melodic elements, Kurth weakens his general distinction between homophonic harmony and polyphonic homophony. Example 6-7 exemplifies clearly the melodic forces that often infiltrate and distort a resolution chord; it thus illustrates well a definitive characteristic of Wagner's polyphonic homophony. Accordingly, this passage offers Kurth a good opportunity to remind us of how polyphonic homophony works. Instead, however, he focuses on the sensuous aspect of harmony, rather than on the designed blending of sensuous with energetic harmony that characterizes the *Tristan* style. Kurth's analysis of Example 6-7 contrasts with others presented earlier. Examples 6-3 and 6-4 in particular stress the active, energetic qualities of the music. In

Example 6-7 and others like it, Kurth would have done better to point out latent ambiguities that obscure the boundary between energetic and sensuous qualities of the music, for it is the interplay of these components that makes polyphonic homophony such a remarkable artistic achievement.[45]

After surveying a number of examples illustrating the energetic qualities of harmony, Kurth turns his attention to the sensuous aspects. Once again, he presses the *Tristan* chord into service. He focuses on the version at the climax of the Prelude to act I, F–A♭–C♭–E♭ (mm. 81–84), and on the internal dynamic transformation, symbolized by enharmonic redefinition, that produces the chord. Example 6-8 shows the passage in question. Appearing both at the very beginning of the Prelude and at the *fortissimo* climax of the piece, the *Tristan* chord is for Kurth the "focal point of the architectonic disposition of the Prelude."[46] Its dual nature is adequately expressed, he says, by the orthography of the first half of measure 83, where Wagner intermingles D♯, G♯, and B with E♭, A♭ and C♭ respectively in the orchestral score.[47] In the last half of measure 83, the sensuous version of the chord, symbolizing near fulfillment, yields to the energetic one. Kurth explains the dramatic meaning of this switch by paraphrasing Wagner's own statements: "The unfulfilled, sorrowful longing of love grows from the most tender impulse to a tempestuous fury, and *sinks back, unfulfillable, in itself* to endless longing."[48]

EXAMPLE 6-8. *Tristan,* Prelude to act I, mm. 81–84

The enharmonic procedure that transforms the energetic into the sensuous *Tristan* chord and vice versa is, for Kurth, concrete evidence of his ideas about the genesis of music, a clear indication that "a chord is merely an image of psychic tensions captured in tones," and that perceiving music is a dynamic, not an acoustical, activity. The enharmonic notation is only a sign of "processes of the internal harmonic dynamics, as [are] ultimately all other processes in the external harmonic image."[49]

Kurth cites various occurrences of the sensuous *Tristan* chord in order to show some possible tonal interpretations.[50] Example 6-9*a* shows the chord with e♭″ as a suspension, resolving to a second-inversion V[7] in the key of G♭ major. The version shown in Example 6-9*b* follows immediately after the energetic spelling (with D♯, etc.) and symbolizes the change from Kurvenal's fear that Tristan is dead to his hope on discovering that Tristan is alive.[51] A deceptive cadence in Example 6-9*c* results in a transposition of the chord at the double bar, where it serves as VI[7] in E♭ major/minor.

EXAMPLE 6-9.

> (*a*) *Tristan*, I, 3;
> (*b*) *Tristan*, III, 1;
> (*c*) *Tristan*, I, 2

Kurth finds it particularly significant, from the psycho-dramatic point of view, that the *Nachtgesang* in act II, scene 2, features the sensuous version of the *Tristan* chord. The "gravity" of tertian structures expresses the heaviness of the muggy, still night, which temporarily shuts out ("restrains") the danger threatening Tristan and Isolde's love. A certain calm spreads over the music, which in the surrounding scenes and acts is necessarily more agitated owing to their dramatic content. This is not to say that only sensuous structures appear in the *Nachtgesang,* but rather that they dominate the music, along with relatively steady, broad tonal lines.[52]

Kurth explains how Wagner uses the *Tristan* chord in both its energetic and its sensuous forms to express musically various psychological circumstances that arise during the opera. As examples, Kurth cites Tristan's remembrance of the magic potion in act III, scene 1, at "Der Trank! der furchtbare Trank!"; "ich selbst, ich hab' ihn gebraut"; at his curse, "Verflucht, wer dich gebraut"; and at numerous other passages. He goes on to point out additional sonic motives in Wagner's works and then, referring to other composers, speaks of the motivic value of opening and closing chords in general.[53] In a study such as the present one, which aims at a general exposition of Kurth's ideas on Romantic harmony, it is impossible to dwell at length on any single aspect of his work. Instead, having familiarized ourselves with Kurth's basic analytic methods, we will continue by examining how he applies these methods to various harmonic phenomena that for him are historically important in the evolution of the *Tristan* style.[54]

In sections 3 and 4 of *Romantische Harmonik,* Kurth investigates energetic and sensuous aspects of harmony in greater detail than he does in section 2, which is largely introductory. The presentation is evolutionary in outlook; the treatment of energetic and sensuous qualities in harmony evolves gradually over the nineteenth century. Kurth generally introduces several examples, taken from the music of Schubert and Schumann, with a few from Berlioz and Liszt, and then shows how Wagner adapted and extended earlier practices.[55] He goes on to explain how Wagner's techniques led to the main developments in late nineteenth- and early twentieth-century style, impressionism (sensuous) and expressionism (energetic). In the next chapter, we will take up various practices that highlight the sensuous qualities of harmony.

NOTES

1. Viewing harmony in Bach's music as a result of the multilinear unfoldment on the one hand and as "negative" on the other hand appears to raise a logical contradiction. How can tonal harmony be negative and, at the same time, the consummation of polyphony? One way to resolve this contradiction would be to consider negative harmony as referring to homophonic harmony; that is, a homophonic style of harmony would be "negative" in polyphonic music, where melody is positive and harmony a "result." The contradiction, noted by Dahlhaus ("linearer Kontrapunkt," 58), derives from Kurth's neglect to specify which type of harmony he means when he calls Bach's harmony negative.

2. Kurth, *Romantische Harmonik,* 135: "jeder Ton einer Melodie enthält einen Akkord latent." Kurth

says this in connection with a few basic ideas about chord progression. Secondary chords (ii, iii, vi) can relate to one another as quasi dominants and subdominants, just as I, IV, and V do. He concludes that "just as every tone of a melody contains a latent chord, so every chord in a progression contains a latent key," that is, as a tonic to its pseudo-dominant or subdominant, as a pseudo-dominant to its tonic, and so on.

3. Ibid., 1–43, "Disposition Toward Theory" (chapter 1, "Einstellung zur Theorie"), and "The Psychological Premises of Romantic Harmony" (chapter 2, "Die psychologischen Grundlagen der romantischen Harmonik").

4. Ibid., 1–2: "Für sich betrachtet, stellen die Harmonien leere Materie dar. . . . Das lebendige Grundgeschehen der Harmonien . . . beruht darin, dass sie immer die heraufwirkenden Kräfte empfinden lassen, die sich aus den Untergründen des Gestaltens zu greifbarer Gestalt in den sinnlich wahrnehmbaren Klangformen umsetzen." Ibid., 11: "*Jeder Klang ist nur ein gehörsmässig gefasstes Bild von gewissen energetischen Strebungen.*"

5. Ibid.: "Symphonie energetischer Strömungen" (p. 2); "Umsetzen von Spannungsenergien in Klangreize" (p. 10); "*Ausbrechen* und *Werden zum Klang*" (p. 3); "Die *Umsetzung* gewisser *Spannungsvorgänge* in *Klänge* zu beobachten ist die Kernaufgabe aller Musiktheorie" (p. 2).

6. Dahlhaus discusses the discrepancy between theory and art in his recent book, *Die Musiktheorie im 18. und 19. Jahrhundert, Erster Teil: Grundzüge einer Systematik,* Geschichte der Musiktheorie, vol. 10 (Darmstadt: Wissenschaftliche Buchgesellschaft, 1984), 5–9.

7. Kurth criticizes conventional theory for being distracted completely by the material forms of harmony: "From the moment theory lapsed into taking the external harmonic images as a point of departure, it was condemned to run aground" ("Von dem Augenblick an, da die Theorie darauf verfallen war, am äusseren Klangbild anzusetzen, war sie verurteilt, im Trockenen zu versanden"; ibid., 12).

8. *Romantische Harmonik,* 45 n: "I have endeavored generally to retain customary terms and symbols as far as possible; with the great variety exhibited by methods and textbooks today, whoever is accustomed to other symbols will not find it hard to adapt to those used here" ("Ich [war] durchgängig bemüht, gebräuchliche Ausdrücke und Zeichen soweit als möglich beizubehalten; wer etwa bei der grossen Verschiedenheit, die heute Methoden und Lehrbücher aufweisen, andere Bezeichnungen gewohnt ist, dem wird es kaum schwer fallen, sich auf die hier benützten einzustellen").

9. Elliot Zuckerman offers a history of *Tristan* in *The First Hundred Years of Wagner's "Tristan"* (New York and London: Columbia University Press, 1964); see pp. 149–87, particularly 154–55, 168–70. In standard references of the late nineteenth century, *Tristan* was soon recognized as highly original and a true embodiment of the "music of the future." This attitude is evident in Eduard Bernsdorf's *Neues Universal-Lexikon der Tonkunst,* supplement (Offenbach: Andre, 1865), 348–49; and in Grove, *A Dictionary of Music and Musicians,* s.v. Wagner, 1st ed. (1889), 4:368.

10. Cyrill Kistler, *Harmonielehre für Lehrer und Lernende* (Munich, 1879), 33–34; Karl Mayrberger, "Die Harmonik Richard Wagners," *Bayreuther Blätter* 4 (1881): 169–80; Salamon Jadassohn, *Melodik und Harmonik bei Richard Wagner* (Berlin, 1899); Cyrill Hynais, "Die Harmonik Richard Wagners in Bezug auf die Fundamenttheorie Sechters," *Neue musikalische Presse* 10.4 (1901): 50–52, 10.6:80–81, 10.7:97–100; Georg Capellen, "Harmonik und Melodik bei Richard Wagner," *Bayreuther Blätter* 25 (1902): 3–23; Max Arend, "Harmonische Analyse des Tristanvorspiels," *Bayreuther Blätter* 24 (1901): 160–69. Alfred Lorenz summarizes the attempts to analyze the opening of the Prelude in *Der musikalische Aufbau von Richard Wagners "Tristan und Isolde"* (Berlin: Hesse, 1926), 194–96. The most comprehensive and detailed, modern survey is Martin Vogel's *Der Tristan-Akkord und die Krise der modernen Harmonielehre,* Orpheus Schriftenreihe zu Grundfragen der Musik, vol. 2 (Düsseldorf: Verlag der Gesellschaft zur Förderung der systematischen Musikwissenschaft, 1962). Robert Wason reviews several important *Tristan*-chord analyses in *Viennese Harmonic Theory,* 90–96.

11. Kurth, *Romantische Harmonik,* 82: "der symbolische Sinn des einzigartigen Einleitungsklanges . . . bedeutet ganz allgemein das *Unerfüllbare,* die *Unerlöstheit* des Liebessehnens . . . man

kann ihn als die *Grundspannung des ganzen Dramas* bezeichnen, als seine 'Not'. . . . die qualvoll zerrissene Grundstimmung des Werkes findet in ihm mit einem einzigen Klangreflex ersten und unmittelbarsten Ausbruch." Ibid., 44: "der allererste Klang . . . ist ein Akkord, der selbst wieder alle Strahlen in einem Brennpunkt aufzufangen scheint. . . . er enthält auch wesentliche technische Züge zusammengefasst. . . . auch in ihm spiegelt sich der ganze Stil."

12. Ibid., 97, 46.

13. Ibid., 45–46: "einfache *Kadenzierung,* . . . durch Chromatik entstellt." At various points in the opening analytical sections of *Romantische Harmonik,* Kurth expresses this notion that chromaticism derives from "simple" diatonic structures. Referring to the first three cadential gestures of the Prelude, Kurth says that "in their origins, they are very simple cadential progressions" ("sind in ihren Wurzeln sehr einfache Kadenzfortschreitungen"; ibid., 51). He emphasizes the necessity to reduce complicated chromatic passages down to "simplified fundamental progressions" ("vereinfachte Grundfortschreitungen") in order to grasp larger tonal unity in Wagner's music (p. 53). Kurth inherited his idea of chromatic alteration from the nineteenth century. It is one that remains strong up through the early twentieth century. Robert Wason discusses these matters in *Viennese Harmonic Theory,* 23, 33, 53.

14. Kurth, *Romantische Harmonik,* 184: "akkordliche Alteration." Kurth does not relate the motivic f'–e' of measure 1 to the bass f–e in measures 2–3. He is generally sensitive to such motivic details; in this case, however, he does not make the connection. A possible reason for this is given below in note 24.

15. Ibid., 49. Kurth observes that the rhythmic brevity and extremely weak metric placement of a', unusual for a seventh, are characteristic of an intensely chromaticized style. The force of conventional dissonances is often superseded by that of more powerful alteration dissonances.

16. Karl Mayrberger, "Die Harmonik," 170–71, was the first to read measure 2 as a dominant seventh chord with a G♯ appoggiatura. See Vogel, *Tristan-Akkord,* 18–19. Unlike Kurth, who uses the idea of "alteration," Mayrberger explains the f♮ by means of Sechter's "hybrid chord" (*Zwitterakkord;* Sechter, *Grundsätze,* 1:147). "Altered chord," Mayrberger remarks, "is the older term for hybrid chord." Kurth refers to Mayrberger's analysis in *Romantische Harmonik,* 49n, and expresses surprise at his terminological preferences. As a technical term, "alteration," in the sense of chromatic inflection, has a long history dating back at least to the eighteenth century. J. G. Walther registered the term in his *Musikalisches Lexikon* of 1732 (facs. ed., ed. Richard Schaal [Kassel: Bärenreiter, 1953]). Witnesses to its endurance as a theoretical term in the nineteenth century include various texts and lexicons, for example, J. C. Lobe's *Lehrbuch* (1866), vol. 1, chapter 19; and Hermann Mendel's *Conversations-Lexikon* (Berlin: Heiman, 1870), vol. 1, s.v. "Alteration."

17. Kurth, *Romantische Harmonik,* 46: "willkürliche Umfärbungen"; "ketten sich immer an *melodisch*-chromatische Weiterleitung."

18. Ibid., 47: "Die chromatischen Veränderungen bedeuten . . . die Durchdringung der Klänge mit Bewegungsspannungen. . . . Indem deren Energie in den Klang aufgenommen wird, ergiesst sich ein gespannter Kraftzustand über diesen als Ganzes. . . . kinetische Energie setzt sich zu potentieller Energie um."

19. Ibid., 49 n: "mit ängstlicher Gewaltsamkeit zusammenhalten will, was seiner Natur nach auseinanderflutet."

20. Kistler, *Harmonielehre* (Munich, 1879), 81–82. William Mitchell takes a similar view in his essay "The Tristan Prelude: Techniques and Structure," *The Music Forum* 1 (New York: Columbia University Press, 1967): 176.

21. Hugo Riemann, *Musik-Lexikon,* 7th ed., s.v. "Klangschlüssel"; Arend, "Tristanvorspiel," 162.

22. Vogel discusses these two camps in *Tristan-Akkord,* 31–34, 36.

23. Kurth stresses the "dominantic character [of the Tristan chord] in relation to its resolution chord" (*Romantische Harmonik,* 49). Mitchell warns against excessive "mothering of the theory of harmonic function," subdominant and applied dominant alike. He denies a functional progression in measures 2–3 and stresses instead a voice exchange between the soprano and tenor parts (oboe and

bassoon) ("Tristan Prelude," 176). Such a view goes beyond the purview of nineteenth-century writers, who focus primarily on chord-to-chord progressions, and is irrelevant as a criticism of those writers, whatever its merits as an observation about the music.

24. Kurth probably passed over the melodic echo between measure 1 and the bass of measures 2–3 because he viewed the f in the bass of measure 2 as an altered f♯. A diatonic f would invest the *Tristan* chord with a subdominant quality, which Kurth rejects. However, the f'–e' in measure 1 motivates nicely the chordal alteration in measure 2. Alfred Lorenz, Kurth's chief opponent on the dominant/subdominant issue, remarks that "since . . . the relationship of subdominant and secondary dominant is universally recognized, the difference of opinions is really not so great" ("Da . . . die Verwandtschaft von Sub- und Wechseldominant allseitig anerkannt ist, ist ja der Unterschied der Ansichten gar nicht so gross"; *Tristan,* 196). See also Vogel, *Tristan-Akkord,* 38–39. Lorenz's statement shows a disregard for the dominant-subdominant polarity about a tonic. True, both applied dominants and subdominants can prepare a dominant, but the similarity ends there. While a subdominant may relate directly to a tonic, an applied dominant does not; it relates directly to the dominant.

25. Kurth, *Romantische Harmonik,* 50. Kurth makes this distinction much later, in section 4, entitled "Paths of Harmonic Development" ("Klangliche Entwicklungslinien"; 230–31). During the analysis of the *Tristan* cadence, he alludes to this later discussion.

26. Kurth calls two chords identical (*identisch*) when a single harmony is unfolded over two sonorities, the first being a neighbor-note displacement of the second. For Kurth, the relationship between a given chord and its predecessor or successor is a dominant, subdominant, or tonic one (*Romantische Harmonik,* 61). The tonic relationship applies to chords that Kurth calls identical. "Functionally equivalent" perhaps describes such a relationship better than "identical." The latter term implies that one thing is *exactly* the same as something else, which is not true in this case.

27. Mayrberger, "Die Harmonik," 172; Jadassohn, *Melodik und Harmonik,* 27; Capellen, "Harmonik und Melodik," 10; Arend, "Tristanvorspiel," 163.

28. This cadential contrast prefigures the juxtaposition of subdominant and dominant key areas; these areas, according to Kurth's analysis of the Prelude, organize measures 17–36. We shall study this analysis in chapter 9.

29. We might speculate that the "clash" between the bass c' and the soprano d" forces d" upward.

30. Kurth, *Romantische Harmonik,* 53–54. In contrast, dominant-tonic cadences are energetic because of the leading tone striving upward toward the key note.

31. Ibid., 54: "Falsch wäre es . . . den ersten Akkord als g–b–des–f (II⁷) aufzufassen, denn die musikalische Spannung lässt, sobald das Motiv einmal richtig erfasst ist, den Ton g nicht als Akkordton, sondern in Analogie zu den Harmonisierungen des Anfangs als einen akkordfremden, eingestellten Nebenton erscheinen." Martin Vogel warns of the dangers of applying "analogic thinking" to musical analysis (*Tristan-Akkord,* 69–70).

32. Kurth does not comment on the ascending seventh, a♭. He might have pointed out its brevity and metric weakness as ways of explaining its unexpected ascent. Edward Aldwell and Carl Schachter claim that the concurrence of f and g is due to a rhythmic displacement of f, which ideally occupies beat one of measure 1. Both g and a♭ are passing notes in their analysis, and b♭ is an accented passing note. The dissonant g in measure 2 would then be a suspension, prepared in measure 1 by a passing note. They discuss the passage in *Harmony and Voice Leading,* vol. 2 (New York: Harcourt, Brace and Jovanovich, 1979), 79.

33. Kurth, *Romantische Harmonik,* 55. Schirmer, 90:16–21. The surprise of both characters is combined with their sudden, overpowering attraction for each other. Isolde thinks Brangäne prepared a death potion, which will avenge Morold's murder and end her agonizing secret love for Tristan. Tristan goes along with Isolde's offer of a drink to a truce but knows all the while that the drink is a death potion, which will free him from his perfidious love for Mark's bride-to-be (see Schirmer, 153–54, where Tristan sings "In deiner Hand den süssen Tod, als ich ihn erkannt, als den sie mir bot; als mir die Ahnung hehr und gewiss zeigte, was mir die Sühne verhiess").

34. Kurth, *Romantische Harmonik,* 55: "ein deutlicher *Beweis,* dass er den *ersten Motivton* abermals als *dissonierende Nebentoneinstellung* auffasst." Kurth complains about some changes made by Buelow in the piano transcription but admits that Wagner's notation is not always exact. In connection with our Example 6-4, Kurth says, "even with Wagner himself the orthography is not always exact" ("auch bei Wagner ist die Orthographie nicht immer genau"; ibid., 55 n).

35. The counteranalysis allows a longer harmonic note in measure 16, d♯, which agrees with the d♯ in the left hand of the piano transcription. Still, only one note (d♯) is harmonic.

36. Two instances of rising melodic fifths occur shortly before the music in Example 6-4. In both cases, the melody traverses a perfect fifth, b′–f♯″ and a′–e″, over pedal tones (Schirmer, 86:1–4 and 5–7). Note that Example 6-6, featuring a diminished fifth in the melody, also incorporates a pedal tone.

37. Schirmer, 16:5–11.

38. In a section of *Romantische Harmonik* entitled "Der Klang als Symbol," 81–90, Kurth points out several harmonic flashbacks and previews.

39. Chapter 7 deals with sensuous harmony.

40. Kurth, *Romantische Harmonik,* 60. Schirmer, 52:8–9. In the first edition of *Romantische Harmonik* (1920), 58, Kurth claimed that the two chords were identical, F^9. He called the b♭ in the first sonority a neighbor-note insertion displacing a of the second sonority. Martin Vogel criticizes this reading (*Tristan-Akkord,* 70–71). Vogel surely knew the third edition of *Romantische Harmonik* when preparing his book, published in 1962, but he fails to mention that Kurth later changed his analysis from the original interpretation to the one given above.

41. A fateful threefold repetition of this cadence, each time a step higher, leads to the music of "Todgeweihtes Haupt!" where Isolde, considering Brangäne's advice about a magic spell, hints at her intention to mix a death potion instead of a love potion.

42. Ibid., 60: "Auflösungscharakter," due to "intensiver Vorhaltscharakter." Cf. p. 231: "Like no other technical characteristic, the resolution effect of the minor ninth, as compared with the preceding octave, . . . brings out the natural feeling for tertian structure as a harmonically fused unit" ("die Lösungswirkung der kleinen Non gegenüber dem vorangehenden Oktavton . . . bringt wie keine andere technische Eigentümlichkeit die Normempfindung für die Terzstruktur als eine klangliche Einheitsverschmelzung zum Ausdruck").

43. Ibid., 59: "motivischer Zusammenhang." Kurth's remark applies to his Example 9 (p. 58), which, like our Example 6-7, closes on a minor ninth chord. In a review of *Romantische Harmonik,* Alfred Lorenz doubts the resolution character of the ninth (*Die Musik* 16.4 [1924]: 258).

44. Kurth, *Romantische Harmonik,* 59: "*wir hören dynamisch, nicht akustisch.*"

45. Similar problems beset a few of Kurth's analyses in *Grundlagen.* See Examples 5-11 and 5-12 and the accompanying discussion.

46. Kurth, *Romantische Harmonik,* 63: "Kernpunkt der architektonischen Anlage vom Vorspiel."

47. Dover orchestral score, p. 18, m. 3. Violas, bassoons, and horns play B–D♯, oboes G♯, and flutes B, while the trombones, trumpets, and remaining strings play A♭, C♭, and E♭.

48. Kurth, *Romantische Harmonik,* 66: "das unerfüllte, leidvolle Liebessehnen schwillt aus zartester Regung zu stürmischer Gewalt an, und *sinkt unerfüllbar wieder in sich selbst* zu endlosem Sehnen *zurück.*" Wagner's own characterization of the Prelude, written as an explanatory program at the time of the Paris concerts in 1860, appears in his *Gesammelte Schriften,* 12:344. William A. Ellis translates Wagner's program in *Richard Wagner's Prose Works,* vol. 8 (London: Routledge and Kegan Paul, 1899), 387.

49. Kurth, *Romantische Harmonik,* 62: "ein Klang [ist] nur ein in Tönen aufgefangenes Bild von Spannungen"; ibid., 68: "Vorgänge der inneren Klangdynamik, wie letzten Endes auch sämtliche Vorgänge im äusseren Klangbild."

50. Ibid., 77 (Ex. 6-9a; Schirmer, 49:25–28); 78 (Ex. 6-9b; Schirmer, 259:23–24, 260:1); 101 (Ex. 6-9c; Schirmer, 7:18–21).

51. A similar switch from the energetic to sensuous spelling occurs in act II, scene 2 (Schirmer, 161: 3–5), where Tristan speaks of his love for the glorious night and mistrust of the deceptive day.

52. Noteworthy examples of sensuous harmony occur at "O sink' hernieder" (Schirmer, 163), "Liebe-heiligstes Leben" (Schirmer, 168), "ew'ge Nacht" (Schirmer, 183), and many other passages. Lorenz outlines the main tonalities of the Love Duet in *Tristan,* 111–23. Note the juxtaposition of A♭ major with A major, derived from the Death-Motive, during Isolde's song "Dies süsse Wörtlein 'und'" (Schirmer, 176–78). After the shift to A major at the word "Tod," the music lingers on V, avoiding A-major harmony, as Tristan sings "Was stürbe dem Tod . . . Isolde immer zu lieben, ewig zu *leben*" (italics mine). Earlier in the opera, the jarring effect of A-major harmony following A♭ major signified death. Here, the absence of that chord signifies a temporary overcoming of death through love. There is, of course, a good deal of A/A♭-major contrast in the section leading up to "Dies süsse Wörtlein," starting at "O sink' hernieder" (Schirmer, 163–73).

53. Kurth, *Romantische Harmonik,* 81–87. Schirmer, 253:7–9; 256:4–6; 258:3–4. In Wagner's music, Kurth singles out the A-major chord and key in *Lohengrin* (Grail), the so-called Siren-chord in *Tannhäuser,* and the open fifth, D–A, in *Der fliegende Holländer* (*Romantische Harmonik,* 89–96). Louis and Thuille note the special effect of this last sonic motive in their *Harmonielehre,* 9.

54. Kurth understands all sonorities as symbols: "not only in a single style period but in music generally, the sonority is only a symbol, a reflex of the Will" ("nicht nur im einzelnen Zeitstil, sondern in der Musik an sich ist der Klang nur Symbol, Willensreflex'" *Romantische Harmonik,* 96). Cross-referential treatment of chords and keys has been studied by Robert Bailey in "The Structure of the *Ring* and Its Evolution," *Nineteenth-Century Music* 1.1 (1977): 48–61, particularly 50 ff.; and in "Visual and Musical Symbolism in German Romantic Opera," *Papers of the Congress of the International Musicological Society* (Berkeley, 1977), 436–44, especially 440–43. See also Patrick McCreless, *Wagner's "Siegfried": Its Drama, History and Music* (Ann Arbor, Mich.: UMI Research Press, 1982), in the index, s.v. "Tonality." For a psycho-motivic analysis of *Tristan,* see Karl Grunsky, "Das Vorspiel und der I. Akt von 'Tristan und Isolde,'" *Richard Wagner-Jahrbuch* 2 (Berlin: Paetel, 1907): 207–84.

55. Section 3 is entitled "From the Cadence to the Alteration Style of *Tristan,*" and 4, "Paths of Harmonic Development." Although from their titles it would seem that each section treats only one aspect of harmony, the two overlap somewhat. For example, chapter 2 of section 4 deals with "The Inner Dissolution of Romantic Harmony," a process Kurth attributes to kinetic influences on harmonic progression (*Romantische Harmonik,* 262–313).

CHAPTER 7

Sensuous Harmony

Kurth interprets the extension of chords beyond the seventh to the ninth, eleventh, and thirteenth as a sign of composers' growing appreciation of tertian effects. These effects emphasize the sensuous qualities of harmony, and this emphasis, he reasons, counterbalances the energetic forces pervading harmony. Kinetic-melodic energy penetrates and destabilizes otherwise firm tertian structures; these structures in turn seek to fortify their internal constitution by augmenting their mass, thereby creating greater material resistance.

> [The] interpenetration of energy and acoustical phenomena in harmony is a battle, effect and countereffect heighten one another . . . [C]hords consolidate [themselves] to greater compactness; it is a *countereffect from the harmonic side,* nothing more than the increased resistance which springs up against the disintegrating current.[1]

Chords beyond the triad arise according to "harmonic processes given in Nature," that is, by adding thirds, which are prefigured in the overtone series.[2] In addition to the *natural* phenomenon of the overtone series as a basis for such chords, Kurth also invokes the *psychological* phenomenon of "fusion." By the process of fusion, chordal dissonances added to triads are tempered by means of "sonic assimilation" with the thirds in the basic triadic formation. Stumpf bases his belief that fusion is a psychological phenomenon on empirical evidence gained from a series of laboratory experiments. Kurth treats fusion like a theoretical principle. He applies the results of Stumpf's experiments, which were concerned with context-free intervals and triads, to large tertian formations in context. These massive sonorities press down on their fundamentals, evoking the feeling of weight and increased material resistance.[3]

In Romantic music, triads yield to seventh and ninth chords, which are among the hallmarks of Wagner's style.[4] In Example 6-7 in the previous chapter we have already seen one bit of evidence offered by Kurth to demonstrate Wagner's use of ninths. Kurth cites the passage from *Siegfried* in Example 7-1 to show Wagner's liberal treatment of sevenths.[5] He explains that the sevenths do not resolve, indicating their fusion with the triad and co-equality with other triadic members. Apparently, Kurth rejects the resolutions in voices other than the one that carries the seventh. The seventh in the first and second chords g″, for example, does actually resolve to f″ in the third chord, though it does so in a different voice.[6] The seventh in the third chord, a♭″, does not resolve, however, unless we count the g″ in the last chord as its resolution. A c‴ in the first chord of measure 23 does descend to b♭″, but this b♭″ remains unresolved in the subsequent music. We might say that the unresolved sevenths occur in chords whose function is contrapuntal, that is, passing chords; the lesser structural weight of such chords permits a freer treatment of dissonance. According to such a view, in Example 7-2, which shows the music preceding the chords of Example 7-1, all the chords between the second-inversion C^7 in measure 15 and the first-inversion Cm^7 in measure 23 would be considered passing. We might then argue that Kurth's context is too limited, as we did in certain examples discussed in chapter 6. To take that attitude, however, would be to go beyond the analytical horizon of all of Kurth's contemporaries and, furthermore, to miss Kurth's main point: Wagner freely incorporates sevenths into the texture for their sensuous effect, to the point of disguising or, occasionally, even of omitting their resolutions.

EXAMPLE 7-1. *Siegfried*, I, 1

Kurth could cite many passages from *Tristan* or the *Ring* operas in which sevenths lack a straightforward resolution. Consider the excerpts from *Götterdäm-*

EXAMPLE 7-2.

merung in Examples 7-3 and 7-4.[7] In Example 7-3, Wagner isolates the upper portion of a half-diminished seventh chord on F, F–A♭–C♭–E♭, treats it as an A♭-minor harmony (= G♯ minor!), and initiates the Tarnhelm-Motive. The e♭′, introduced as a seventh with a downward tendency, actually takes on the character of a leading tone and ascends to f♭′. In Example 7-4, a chordal seventh, a♭′, ascends to a♮′ in measure 10, yet another seventh.[8] Even though sevenths do resolve in other voices or in other octaves, a glance at nearly any page of a Wagner score will show that the abundant seventh chords of every sort found there have dissonances that often last for several measures before resolving or being interpreted enharmonically; these chords thereby circumvent resolution. For example, in the music immediately preceding act II, scene 2, of *Tristan,* Wagner dwells at length on an F^9 harmony representing the horn calls of Mark's hunt.[9]

Kurth handles ninth, eleventh, and thirteenth chords as quasi-independent harmonic entities. Although he tends to stress the harmonic aspects of these remote dissonances, he does acknowledge their melodic, suspension-like character. In connection with the $D♭^9$ harmony at "O sink hernieder" in *Tristan,* II, 2, for example, he recognizes a downward-pressing appoggiatura in the e♭″, which he says joins with the "weight" of the sensuous ninth.[10] Kurth's hearing of chords beyond the seventh depends crucially on context. He selects musical examples in which the genesis of

EXAMPLE 7-3. *Götterdämmerung*, I, 2

EXAMPLE 7-4.

such elaborate harmonies is particularly revealing for analysis. Among his more interesting examples are the C^{13} harmony in measures 367–68 of the last movement of Bruckner's Sixth Symphony, and the $F\sharp^{13}$ in measures 103–23 of the first movement of the Seventh Symphony.[11] In the latter passage, as well as in the one at "O sink hernieder," the chords are formed by thirds accumulating gradually, one on top of the other, each new dissonance entering unprepared. The dissonances do eventually resolve in the expected manner, as melodic phenomena. But before they do, they have a pronounced *harmonic* effect precisely because of how they evolve, temporally expand, and thus, to an extent, stabilize. Kurth hears them "sensuously" and so refers to them as "dissonant chord tones" in these tertian structures rather than as suspensions.[12]

Example 7-5 illustrates this process.[13] Kurth observes how the G[7] harmony in the middle of measure 35 gradually acquires its ninth (a♭') at the end of the measure, its eleventh (c″) in measure 36, and finally its thirteenth (e♭″) in measure 37. He argues in favor of calling the sonority at the beginning of measure 36 an eleventh chord because the c″ at the head of measure 36 returns on beat four, as if b' were a neighbor note.[14] Concerning the e♭″ in measure 37, Kurth states that "the obvious climbing motion of the upper voice leads clearly to . . . the sensation of a . . . thirteenth."[15] Kurth satisfies himself with the "sensation" of a thirteenth, primarily a psycho-auditive interpretation of the sonority rather than a structural-syntactic one. This is an important distinction. Kurth is clearly aware of the melodic function of both e♭″ and c″; otherwise, why would he take time to justify his harmonic reading of them? Given a style that capitalizes on such dissonances, especially through exaggerated duration, Kurth is trying to sensitize us to the undeniably rich harmonic color of Wagner's music by emphasizing its sensuous aspects.

EXAMPLE 7-5. *Tristan,* Prelude to act III, mm. 34–37

Kurth identifies another instance of harmonic sensuousness in Wagner's use of "under-thirds," thirds added beneath an established fundamental. He cites the music in Example 7-6 to illustrate under-thirds. Following a clear cadence in F minor, the bass descends in thirds from F to G_1, over which a D-minor triad appears. Registral and timbral distinction set the triad off from the G, so that as the bass descends by thirds a second time, now from D to E_1, Kurth says it is "as if the original root [here a D] remained the fundamental" through measure 13, even though the harmony shifts from d: I to ♮VI and IV, before settling on a: V, rooted a third lower than d: IV.[16] Kurth speculates that in such cases we sense "no actual chord change, but rather a kind of supplementation within the framework of the same chord structure."[17]

Besides affecting the sonic disposition of a single, sustained chord, under-thirds may affect connections between chords. According to Kurth, a falling-fifth progression becomes "deceptive" when an under-third appears simultaneously with the arrival of a root-position tonic. Wagner extends this practice by combining dissonances or chordal alterations with the arrival of an under-third (Exx. 7-7 and 7-8).[18] Example 7-8 illustrates Kurth's idea of "shading" (*Klangschattierung*). In measure 19, we expect an A-major or A-minor chord to follow the E[7] of measure 18. Instead, an F[7] harmony follows, with the e shaded into e♭. Thus, the chord in measure 19 results from two simultaneously applied techniques, one sensuous (under-third), the other energetic (shading).

EXAMPLE 7-6. *Siegfried*, I, 2

EXAMPLE 7-7. *Siegfried*, I, 1 (above)   EXAMPLE 7-8. *Rheingold*, 2 (below)

In addition to the under-third cadences just described, where the chords involved were more or less clearly related, sensuous qualities manifest themselves in certain harmonic progressions where the chords seem only remotely related. The series of chords in the Death-Motive in *Tristan* is a good example. In such cases, it is not always a matter of thirds exerting their influence. A different kind of sensuousness is at work, one that isolates a chord pair from its harmonic surroundings and exploits its bracing aural effect. Not that the Death-Motive chords resist tonal explanation altogether; Kurth is aware that Ab- and A-major harmonies fall into the domain of C major/minor. With regard to such striking harmonic "collisions" (*Aufeinanderprallen*), however, Kurth warns against contrived analyses, which by applying schematic logic seek harmonic-tonal continuity at all cost and disregard the obvious aural discontinuity expressed in these progressions.[19]

For Kurth, beyond the sensuously jolting effect, the real significance of "absolute progressions," as he calls such collisions, is a gradual breakdown of traditional harmonic-tonal continuity. A certain harmonic *fluidity,* freely associating distantly related chords and exploiting the resultant sensuous effect, disrupts harmonic-tonal continuity. Kurth does understand that Wagner broadens tonal continuity to proportions considerably wider than his predecessors, and that many chords and chord progressions, though they may range far afield, are still governed by an overarching tonality. Nevertheless, he believes that absolute progressions indicate breaches in tonal solidity and uniformity.[20]

According to Kurth, every chord has three possible referential modes: tonal referentiality, local referentiality, and self-referentiality. As tonal referents, chords have functions supporting a global scheme; this is the case with tonic, dominant, and subdominant harmonies, as well as with chords related closely to them (VI, III, VII, II). As local referents, chords relate only to their immediate predecessors. Local referentiality may or may not confirm tonal referentiality. When it does not, or does so only indirectly, Kurth speaks of absolute progressions, whose jarring effects set chosen chord pairs in relief against their harmonic environment.[21] The conflict between tonal environment and local referentiality may become so great that a chord becomes isolated unto itself. Such chords are self-referential. Kurth believes that tonal referentiality reinforces tonality. For this reason, he calls it "constructive." By contrast, the other two modes, local referentiality and self-referentiality, undermine tonality and are thus "destructive." At any given moment, a chord may function in one or another referential mode. To Kurth's hearing, local referentiality and self-referentiality are particularly strong in Wagner's music.

The harmonically bracing Death-Motive, featuring chordal roots a second apart, exemplifies one type of absolute progression. Absolute progressions may also employ other striking intervals such as major thirds or even diminished fourths between adjacent chordal roots. Kurth calls these "mediant progressions."[22] The intensity of such harmonic collisions is evident in the distance between adjacent roots. Kurth cites the passage in Example 7-9, from the first movement of a Schubert piano sonata, to illustrate an early nineteenth-century instance of such a progression. The abrupt change, via a diminished fourth, from the local tonic chord, F major, to C♯-minor harmony poignantly announces the ensuing development.[23] Composers of the next generation routinely employ mediant progressions to form cycles of thirds, reinforcing tonal unity. Mediant progressions set the reverent and awesome mood for the waving of the Grail in the first act of *Parsifal* (Ex. 7-10). Later in the opera, Wagner continues the mediant succession to create a complete cycle of thirds (Ex. 7-11).[24] There, the music starts on an E♭-major chord, continues with B-major (= C♭-major) and G-major chords, and completes the cycle of thirds with an E♭-minor chord, acting as a dominant preparation for a cadence in the key of D♭ major.

EXAMPLE 7-9. Schubert, Piano Sonata, D. 960, I, mm. 115–17

EXAMPLE 7-10. *Parsifal*, I, 2

EXAMPLE 7-11. *Parsifal,* III, 2

For Kurth, tertian mediators between chords, as well as supplements above and below chords, attest to the Romantics' predilection for thirds. Thirds affect several musical dimensions at once, acting as chordal connectives, integrative harmonic building blocks, and even melodic building blocks (for example, in the Curse-Motive and Ring-Motive).[25] Kurth maintains that this proliferation of thirds in the late Romantic period has consequences for sensuous as well as energetic aspects of harmony. That interval, more than any other, is the "bearer of energies in harmony," because of its leading-tone effect. As such it is one source of "the whole growth of tension which pervades [Romantic] harmony."[26]

The preceding examples of mediant progressions illustrate one of Kurth's three referential modes, local referentiality, which applies to the relationship between a given chord and its predecessor. A harmonic-tonal rift between two successive chords gives rise to absolute progressions. The startling psycho-auditive effect lies in the progression from a tonally native to a foreign harmony, a kind of harmonic-tonal disjunction that isolates a chord pair. A series of such disjunctions alienates chords from the prevailing tonal background and, ultimately, from their local neighbors. In such a harmonic succession, local referentiality among chords yields to self-referentiality for individual chords. Such harmonic isolation produces what Kurth calls the "absolute effect of a chord," which is "a far-reaching disintegration of [tonal] harmony in the effects of progression [that] leads to a concentration on the individual chord."[27]

Kurth realizes that a chord always owes some of its harmonic effect to its predecessor, and he acknowledges that the boundary between absolute progression and the absolute chord is a flexible one. Still, he does locate several instances where timbral accent, along with a striking harmonic turn, throws a chord into sharp relief against its surroundings. For example, in the second act of *Tristan,* prior to Brangäne's first plea not to extinguish the signal torch, an E♭-minor chord (IV♭) juts out and underscores the word "spy" (*Späher*) (Ex. 7-12). Orchestral effects join with the harmonic-textural coordination to isolate the chords from one another. After a tutti chord in measure 15, the color shifts from the strings (m. 16) to the timbrally darker woodwinds at the E♭-minor chord.[28] Kurth thus hears a strong harmonic disjunction between the A[7], G-minor, and E♭-minor chords. Accordingly, he speaks of the absolute effect of E♭ minor. The effect is evident enough in a chord-to-chord hearing of measures 15–17. Nevertheless, the disjunction is only one-sided. The approach to E♭ minor (B♭:IV♭) is certainly unusual, but the subsequent dominant in B♭ major reorients the progression.[29] Without any far-fetched theoretical "reconstructions," Kurth could have analyzed the whole passage in the key of B♭ major: V/III, VI, IV♭, V. He cautions against such reconstructions when they stretch our tonal sensibilities too far. Here, though, the tonal analysis seems fairly audible. The deceptive progression from V/III to VI, followed by the mixed-mode mediant progression from G minor to E♭ minor, probably caused a gradual isolation of the latter harmony in Kurth's ear. Kurth, suggesting that individual keys possess a distinctive "absolute" identity, alludes not only to the timbral darkening of the woodwinds but to a tonal darkening into remote "flat" regions.[30] For him, the features that isolate E♭ minor outweigh those that integrate it into the progression.

EXAMPLE 7-12. *Tristan,* II, 1

Composers of the generation after Wagner further developed the technique of isolating chords as harmonic-dramatic accents. The music by Strauss in Example 7-13 illustrates this development.[31] An A-minor six-four chord, coming after a V–I progression in the key of F minor, jolts us at the word "tot." As in Example 7-12, the subsequent harmonies, not shown in Example 7-13, help to cushion the recent shock. In the next measure, a V⁹–I progression in the key of D minor integrates the A-minor chord into the passage and thus restores, retroauditively, harmonic-tonal logic. Kurth omits the subsequent measures since he wants us to focus on the arrival of the A-minor harmony, which is self-referential in relation to the preceding music.

EXAMPLE 7-13. Richard Strauss, *Salome,* scene I

In music such as Strauss's, where local referentiality, both retrospective and prospective, may indeed be "weak," referentiality of a broader scale may still be operative. In order to establish some overriding tonal unity, we may need to look at musical contexts larger than those Kurth examines. When documenting the evolution of harmonic techniques, however, we must deal with local details since the localized experiments of one generation of composers often become the stylistic features of the next. In attempting to trace the evolution of harmonic techniques throughout the nineteenth century, Kurth identifies many such experiments, among them the isolation of sonorities, eventually of tones, and the resultant tonal decline.[32] To some readers, Kurth's scope may seem too narrow. This is a fair criticism, one pointed out earlier in connection with Example 6-4. Kurth believes, though, that Wagner's music, as well as that of later composers, develops on a broad scale the implications of techniques applied in local contexts. Such an approach to harmony results in a loosening and, at times, an undermining of familiar harmonic-tonal form.

Given Kurth's purpose in *Romantische Harmonik,* it is unfair to discredit his every analytical decision for shortsightedness. He devotes most of the book to local harmonic details and addresses large-scale tonal and formal procedures only briefly. Kurth reserves architectonic issues for *Bruckner,* in which he refers to discussions in *Romantische Harmonik* as background for understanding the details and historical roots of Bruckner's harmonic style.[33] Even when dealing with limited contexts, many analysts today would argue against Kurth's conclusions. They consider chords with striking aural effects, the self-referential kind, to be contrapuntal events lacking harmonic-structural weight.[34] Kurth, too, recognizing that "absolute" harmonic phenomena in late Romantic music result from the activity of energetic-melodic forces, emphasizes the flow from one absolute chord to the next.

> This process [harmonic collision], with its apparent purely sensuous effect, goes back to the *influence of dynamic energies.*
>
> The *technique consists not just in the individual colors*, but *primarily in the flow of colors.* Everywhere . . . the technique appears in connection with the smooth melodic flow of all chords into one another, as the *alteration style* promoted from the other [i.e., the energetic] side.[35]

It is clear from these statements that Kurth appreciates the importance of melodic processes in the genesis of absolute progressions and chords. Nevertheless, he prefers to stress their sensuous qualities. By treating absolute progressions and chords as sensuous-harmonic rather than energetic-melodic phenomena, Kurth can show how their impact highlights textural, dramatic, and psychological details. Sensuous harmony does this precisely because it possesses the necessary "material resistance" to halt the surge of melodic forces; it does not allow the forces to flow through, as voice-leading analysts would have it.

For Kurth, deciding whether harmonies are of a sensuous or energetic nature often depends as much on extramusical, psycho-dramatic details as on strictly musical ones. No preconceived structural premises guide his ear in determining the nature of a given harmony or group of harmonies. Aural impressions and the dynamic interplay of drama and music, examined on a case-by-case basis, are Kurth's chief analytical criteria. He must necessarily allow sufficient analytical flexibility to account for the flexibility of Wagner's polyphonic homophony. Kurth's critics have equated this flexibility with vagueness. They are only partly correct. Kurth's language, with its psychological slant, is at times vague. Such expressions as "chordal form" instead of chord, and "resolution character" instead of resolution, may irritate modern-day theorists, who prefer unambiguous language. Kurth uses these expressions not to be vague but, on the contrary, to describe as exactly and appropriately as possible harmonies that resist being classified under any clear-cut traditional rubric for "chord," and to describe as accurately as possible "resolutions" that seem to contradict conventional notions of that phenomenon. Thus, Kurth molds his language and analytical method to Wagner's idiom.

Definitive stylistic details that articulate the psycho-dramatic action in Wagner's operas are easily lost in rigorously hierarchical voice-leading analyses. Kurth's approach to analysis, though not as systematic, does call attention to those traits of Wagner's style that distinguish it from other styles. Analyses based on structural hierarchies and aimed at penetrating to deep structural levels often treat such traits as "surface phenomena." For Kurth, too, these traits are surface phenomena, but by "surface," Kurth means the audible, outermost edge of the underlying psychic forces from which music issues, not a surface that embellishes some underlying structural foundation. Because Kurth is interested in the evolution of musical style as a reflection of psychic activity, his surface, with all its stylization, is an end in itself. It is a guide on an evolutionary path, not a guide to deep structure.

NOTES

1. Kurth, *Romantische Harmonik,* 230: "das Ineinanderwirken von Energie und Klang in der Harmonik ist ein Kampf, Wirkung und Gegenwirkung steigern einander . . . die Akkorde ballen [sich] zu grösserer Kompaktheit zusammen; es ist *Gegenwirkung von klanglicher Seite,* nichts als der erhöhte Widerstand, der sich gegen die auflösende Strömung herausbildet."

2. Ibid.: "Es geht nach einem in der Natur der harmonischen Vorgänge gegebenen Prinzip zu."

3. Kurth discusses Stumpf's idea of fusion and its relevance for music theory in *Voraussetzungen,* 13–14, 26, 28–29.

4. Kurth, *Romantische Harmonik,* 122: "From *Wagner* onward, the frequency of seventh and ninth chords becomes a chief hallmark of the harmonic style" ("von *Wagner* an wird die Häufigkeit der Sept- und Nonenakkorde zu einem Hauptmerkmal des Klangstiles"). Kurth uses Wagner's own statements, cited in *Romantische Harmonik,* 238, as evidence of the composer's consciousness of thirds. For example, Wagner writes the following in "The Art Work of the Future" ("Das Kunstwerk der Zukunft," *Gesammelte Schriften,* 3:86): "Harmony grows from below upwards as a perpendicular pillar, by the joining-together and overlaying of correlated tone-stuffs" ("Die Harmonie wächst von unten nach oben als schnurgerade Säule aus der Zusammenfügung und Übereinanderschichtung verwandter Tonstoffe"). In "Opera and Drama" ("Oper und Drama," *Gesammelte Schriften,* 4:156), Wagner expresses a similar thought: "This plumbline is the harmonic chord, a vertical chain of tones in closest kinship, mounting from the ground-tone to the surface" ("Diese Kette ist der harmonische Akkord, der als eine vertikale Reihe nächstverwandter Töne aus dem Grundton nach der Oberfläche zu aufsteigt"). The translations given here are from W. A. Ellis's *Richard Wagner's Prose Works,* 1:115 and 2:296–97.

5. Kurth, *Romantische Harmonik,* 232. Schirmer, 47:21–23.

6. Although Kurth rejects the inner-voice resolutions in Example 7-1, he says on several occasions that symphonic style tolerates dissonances resolving in voices other than those in which they initially appeared (*Romantische Harmonik,* 47, 117, 162).

7. Examples 7-3 and 7-4 are in Schirmer, 84:7-12 and 87:3-11 respectively.

8. The a♮′ eventually moves to a♭ (i.e. removed by one octave), which is then no longer a chordal dissonance. After several more measures, the a♭ finally descends to g. We might re-interpret the B♭⁷ chord in measures 4–5 of Example 7-4 (e♭: V⁷) as a "German" augmented sixth chord in measures 7–8 (d: IV$_3^6$), in order to explain a♭′ (= g♯′) ascending to a♮′.

9. Schirmer, 108; also 109–11, where the ninth (g′) never resolves. One might think of the g′ as a fifth of a C-minor harmony over an F pedal. Still, the *sound* of a ninth remains.

10. Kurth, *Romantische Harmonik,* 240.

11. Kurth discusses the passage from the Sixth Symphony in *Romantische Harmonik,* 240, and the passage from the Seventh Symphony in *Voraussetzungen,* 30–34. The latter music was cited by August Halm in his *Harmonielehre,* 122–23, Ex. 100 (example appendix, xxix–xxxi), as an instance of Romantic chord building in thirds.

12. Lorenz, in his review of *Romantische Harmonik* (see chap. 1, n. 76), points out that elevenths and thirteenths are generally not independent dissonances but rather suspensions. Kurth calls such suspensions "dissonante Akkordtöne" (*Romantische Harmonik,* 240). Many theorists before Kurth

had already divided sharply on this issue. Schenker, in *Harmony*, ed. Oswald Jonas, trans. Elisabeth Mann Borgese (Cambridge, Mass.: MIT Press, 1978), 190–208, rejects V^9 and, by extension, ninth chords on all other fundamentals. The "deceptive effect" of V^9, he explains, derives from the "mutual substitution" of V^7, VII, and VII^7. Their interchangeability gives rise to what appear to be independent ninth chords. But this "independence" is negated, Schenker argues, by the lack of invertibility, a characteristic of genuinely independent sonorities. Eleventh and thirteenth chords have even less claim to harmonic independence. Simon Sechter recognizes what appear to be ninth chords, produced by delayed resolutions of 9–8 suspensions (*Grundsätze*, 1:30–31). He does *not* endorse independent ninth chords, however. The Louis-Thuille team and August Halm, whose works were more familiar to Kurth than Schenker's, accepted an independent ninth chord on V, though they, like Sechter, trace its origin to the delayed 9–8 resolution (Louis and Thuille, *Harmonielehre*, 73–79; Halm, *Harmonielehre*, 118). Schoenberg allows all ninth chords, complete with inversions (*Harmonielehre*, 388–92).

13. Kurth, *Romantische Harmonik*, 239. Schirmer, 216:34–37.

14. Kurth does not say this directly, but he implies it when he says that c″ "asserts itself" (*setzt sich durch*) on the last quarter of measure 36.

15. Ibid., 239–40: "die sinnfällige aufschichtende Bewegung der Oberstimme . . . leitet deutlich . . . zur Empfindung einer . . . Tredezime." Pursuing the same line of thought, Aldwell and Schachter mention the significance of gradual tertian buildups for identifying true harmonies beyond the seventh chord (*Harmony and Voice Leading*, 2:132–33). They limit this practice primarily to the twentieth century but place certain examples from the late nineteenth century into an "intermediate category," presumably halfway between clear suspension chords and twentieth-century third stacks. As an example of the intermediate category, the authors cite a passage from the third movement of Bruckner's Eighth Symphony (mm. 169–75), which features "a melodic sequence rising in thirds over a pedal point."

16. Kurth, *Voraussetzungen*, 38: "als bliebe der ursprüngliche Grundton auch weiter das Fundament." Example 7-6 is in Schirmer, 67:7–15. Kurth takes up under-thirds in *Romantische Harmonik*, 24–52.

17. Kurth, *Romantische Harmonik*, 249: "kein eigentlicher Akkordwechsel wird empfunden, sondern nur eine Art Ergänzung im Rahmen des gleichen Klanggefüges." Example 7-6 makes a good case for Kurth's sensuous harmony; Wotan enters on a dissonant c′ and descends by thirds in imitation of the bass.

18. Ibid., 253; Schirmer, 27:30–32 (Ex. 7-7). Ibid., 260; Schirmer, 69–70:18–19 (Ex. 7-8).

19. Kurth, *Romantische Harmonik*, 264, 266–67. Kurth postulates an "ideal C-minor midpoint" ("idelle c-moll-Mitte"), in which the A-major chord in the Death-Motive is a remote dominant, a dominant by "potentiation" (*Potenzierung*), i.e., V/V/V, etc. Like Kurth, Georg Capellen stresses the aural novelty in the "rending effect of chromatic jolts" ("abgerissene Wirkung chromatischer Rückungen"; "Harmonik und Melodik," 19–20).

20. Kurth, *Romantische Harmonik*, 262 (*absolute Fortschreitung*), 285. Regarding the Death-Motive, Kurth says "it is as if the harsh dissonant abrasiveness of a [melodic] minor second were applied to the phenomenon of harmonic progression, and were magnified to sensuous power" ("es ist, als wäre die harte Dissonanzreibung auf das Phänomen der Klangfortschreitung übertragen und zu klangsinnlicher Macht vergrössert"; ibid., 266). This is interesting to compare with Schoenberg, who analyzes the Death-Motive as a not-so-unusual progression from I to ♭II, a root-position "Neapolitan" in A♭ major. He understands the key of A♭ major as VI in the overriding key of C minor. Schoenberg discusses the Death-Motive in his essay "Brahms the Progressive," printed in *Style and Idea*, ed. Leonard Stein, trans. Leo Black (New York: St. Martins Press, 1975), 403.

21. Kurth, *Romantische Harmonik*, 262–64. Applied dominants are good examples of local referents. They sound striking when they enter, though the following chord usually clarifies their meaning. In Wagner's music, the chord following an applied dominant may not clarify its predecessor, in which case Kurth speaks of a series of absolute progressions, each chord being "self-referential."

vides motivic continuity in an essentially discontinuous harmonic progression. The change of mode, from F-major to C♯-minor harmony, intensifies this mediant progression.

24. Ibid., 276. Schirmer, 91:4–8 (Ex. 7-10), 271:8–10 (Ex. 7-11).

25. Ibid., 175. Kurth states that "the chord contains within itself an impulse toward mediant progressions" ("der Klang enthält in sich ein Streben nach Terzfortschreitungen"; ibid., 261). He finds it significant, psychologically, that the Ring-Motive consists of a chain of thirds (ibid., 245).

26. Ibid., 175: "Träger der Energien in der Harmonik." Ibid., 178: "die ganze Spannungsentwicklung, welche die Harmonik durchsetzt."

27. Ibid., 297: "absolute Klangwirkung"; "eine weitgehende Zersetzung der Harmonik in Fortschreitungswirkungen leitet zur Konzentrierung auf den Einzelklang hin."

28. Ibid., 299. Schirmer, 113:15–18. With its timbral accent, the E♭-minor chord becomes a "harmonic color symbol" (*Klangfarben-Symbol;* ibid., 302).

29. Remember that Kurth hears local referentiality primarily with respect to the preceding harmony, and less to the succeeding one(s).

30. Taking the VI six-four as a dependent appoggiatura chord to III does not unify the chords any more convincingly. In fact, coming after a D-minor harmony the absolute effect of E♭ minor would be all the stronger. The "absolute" identity of keys is discussed at the beginning of chapter 8.

31. Kurth, *Romantische Harmonik,* 302. Boosey and Hawkes vocal score, 6:8–10.

32. We must remember that by "tonal decline" Kurth means the breakdown of traditional tonality, a breakdown that includes associating seemingly disparate chords, chromatic voice leading pushing tonally related chords ever further apart, and unconventional key relationships supporting the overall harmonic form. According to Kurth, all of these techniques undermine conventional tonic-dominant tonality. His "constructive" and "destructive" forces apply to that variety. While Kurth clearly realizes that late nineteenth-century music possesses tonal organization, he holds that it rests on new principles that, although rooted in traditional ones, are nevertheless recognizably different from them.

33. Nowhere in *Romantische Harmonik* does Kurth analyze a whole scene, much less an entire act, from an opera. That is simply not his main concern. Chapter 9 outlines Kurth's ideas on large-scale form as they are discussed in *Grundlagen* and *Romantische Harmonik.*

34. A good example of such an analysis is Felix Salzer's interpretation of a passage from *Tristan,* II, 5 (Schirmer, 211:23 ff.), discussed in *Structural Hearing* (New York: Dover, 1962), 1:188–89, and vol. 2:169, Ex. 404.

35. Kurth, *Romantische Harmonik,* 133: "dieser Prozess mit seinen scheinbar rein klangsinnlichen Wirkungsinhalten geht auf das *Einspielen von Bewegungsenergien* zurück." Ibid., 304: "*die Technik beruht nicht* bloss in den *Einzelfarben,* sondern *vornehmlich im Farbenfliessen.* Überall . . . zeigt sie sich zugleich in Verbindung mit dem leichtflüssigen melodischen Ineinandergleiten aller Klänge, wie es von anderer Seite her der *Alterationsstil* gefördert hat."

CHAPTER 8

Energetic Harmony

Kurth distinguishes between harmonic and contrapuntal processes—that is, between sensuous and energetic forces—based on musical emphasis, not on fixed analytical categories. Although he recognizes the melodic origin of absolute progressions and absolute chords, he believes they exist primarily for their *harmonic* effects. An analysis that minimizes such harmonic effects inadequately reflects our hearing and thus widens the gap between analysis and aural comprehension. Certain harmonic techniques, such as under-third cadences and tertian supplements above or below chords, emphasize sensuous traits in harmony. Other techniques, such as those of the "intensive alteration style," emphasize energetic traits. But for the most part, music intermingles the sensuous with the energetic, the one accompanying or complementing the other.[1] For Kurth, the aural impression is decisive in determining their relative strength and, accordingly, the appropriate analytic slant.

So far, we have dealt with sensuous harmony. In the following pages we will examine various manifestations of energetic harmony and the alteration style. First, we will take up three procedures that blend energetic with sensuous qualities in harmony: "coloring," "contrasting," and "shading."[2] These procedures involve chordal alterations and are thus in a way sensuous in nature. But the chordal alterations themselves arise from melodic impulses that intensify connections between chords, an energetic process. Coloring, contrasting, and shading are relatively mild forms of alteration compared with those found in the intensive alteration style. The intensive style features *melodic* alterations, but it may incorporate chordal alterations as well, along with enharmonic shifts, thereby further heightening the overall level of tension.

The force behind both chordal and melodic alterations is leading-tone energy. In chordal alteration, leading-tone energy affects chordal constituents, often by inflecting major harmony into minor, or vice versa. In more thoroughgoing chordal alterations, leading-tone energy distorts the very essence of a chord, its tertian structure. In melodic alteration, leading-tone energy obscures the identity of a chord by displacing its members with neighbor-note insertions, which may or may not resolve to their referential notes within the duration of the chord. When heaped one on the other, neighbor-note insertions can influence chord succession, even to the point of distorting its syntax altogether.

Among the most common forms of chordal alteration are secondary dominants. Raising a diatonic third chromatically is a rudimentary form of harmonic coloring. Nondiatonic leading tones "sharpen" the progression between chords; "*melodic* considerations infiltrate chordal aspects."[3] Referring to a brief passage featuring a string of secondary dominants, Kurth writes, "We must not lose sight of the fact that these apparent purely harmonic procedures . . . go hand in hand with dynamic phenomena and, in their roots, go back to effects of *linear* tension."[4] The applied diminished seventh chord shows how leading-tone energy encroaches on several melodic strands at once. Lowering the third of a diminished seventh chord produces a diminished third chord, more familiar as an augmented sixth chord. Instead of deriving the German sixth from a first-inversion IV^7 in minor, Kurth derives it from a VII^7/V with a lowered third. In light of Example 8-1, it is easy to understand Kurth's thinking.[5] Harmonic alterations inflecting e′ into e♭′, a′ into a♭′, and f into f♯ intensify dramatically the motion toward the next chord. A single leading tone, created by chromatic alteration, produces an applied dominant. Multiple leading tones occurring simultaneously produce a leading-tone chord: "out of the leading *tone* develops the leading *chord*."[6]

Multiple melodic alterations in the form of neighbor-note insertions affect harmony similarly, except that these alterations strive *into* the chord they displace, while harmonic alterations strive *out of* a chord. Example 8-2 illustrates multiple neighbor-note insertions displacing a chord at the very beginning of a piece. Here, f♯ d♯, and A♭ are neighbor-note insertions that strive into notes of the governing C-major harmony. Kurth uses the expression "fixed pivots" to describe those tones remaining motionless while the neighbor-note insertions resolve.[7] Both Example 8-1 and Example 8-2 involve multiple leading-tone resolutions, but Kurth calls the leading tones in Example 8-1 chordal alterations, the ones in Example 8-2 melodic alterations. Why the distinction? Explaining the F♯ diminished third chord in Example 8-1 by means of neighbor-note insertions would mean a *complete* displacement of the harmonic goal, G-major. Apparently, Kurth was reluctant to allow a total displacement of this sort, preferring instead to hear two separate harmonies. To his ear, then, the chord in Example 8-1 results from chordal rather than melodic alterations.

EXAMPLE 8-1. *Rheingold, 4*

Kurth reminds us often that it is kinetic-melodic forces, embodied most purely in the leading tone, that underlie harmonic procedures like the ones in Examples 8-1 and 8-2. Leading-tone energy exerts and multiplies its influence throughout all chordal connections. Propelled by its force, "everything surges and flows"; "[the] permeation of *dynamic tensions* is the *reason for,* and *origin* of, the *heightened play of colors* and also of greater *chordal resources.*"[8]

EXAMPLE 8-2. Schubert, "Am Meer," *Schwanengesang*

Coloring is not limited to dominant functions or to the upward-striving leading-tone energy that activates those harmonies. Some of the oldest forms of coloring involve subdominant harmony, for example, the minor subdominant in a major key. The chordal third of IV, altered downward to produce IV♭, aims toward scale degree five. Kurth hears a kind of harmonic-tonal "darkening" into subdominant, "flat-key regions" in such progressions.[9] Wagner, for example, employs a root-position Neapolitan in the passage in Example 8-3.[10] In the context of B♭ major, Wagner treats the E♭-major chord in measure 1 (IV) like a Neapolitan in D minor and so executes a transitory modulation to that key. Similar examples of root-position Neapolitan chords occur throughout Wagner's works, for instance at "Bruder" in the music of Example 8-4, from Siegmund's monologue in *Walküre.*[11]

EXAMPLE 8-3. *Tristan*, II, 2

Subdominant coloring and tonal darkening into "flat" regions lead Kurth to the idea of "color contrasting." Color contrasting often points up textual or dramatic

EXAMPLE 8-5. *Siegfried*, I, 1

EXAMPLE 8-4. *Walküre*, I, 3

contrasts, as Examples 8-5 and 8-6 illustrate.[12] During the music around Example 8-5, Siegfried tells how he has seen reflections of the surrounding forest in a clear stream. He has also seen his own reflection, which, he realizes, bears no resemblance whatever to Mime, proving that the dwarf cannot be his father. In Example 8-5, Siegfried sings first of the trees and animals, images of the shadowy forest, in the key of E♭ major. As he sings "Spiegel" (reflection) and turns his attention to the

EXAMPLE 8-6. *Walküre*, I, 3

sun and clouds and their glittering reflection in the stream, the music brightens accordingly to D major. Wagner marks the change in harmonic color with one in orchestral color; he introduces an oboe melody, imitated by Siegfried four measures later. Just prior to Example 8-6, Siegmund, left to ponder Hunding's threat of death, recalls the sword he will find in the moment of greatest need. Suddenly, the fire warming the room flares up and illuminates the sword lodged in the World Ash tree. Siegmund compares its gleam to Sieglinde's glance. At Example 8-6, the flame has died down, and Siegmund sings of the darkness enveloping his life ("Nächtiges Dunkel"), accompanied by G-minor and Eb-major harmonies. Then, amid Eb-major and Ab-major chords, Siegmund remembers Sieglinde's glance ("warmth and daylight"), inspiring a harmonic shift to G-major and D-major chords as he sings of warmth and day (I and V). At "Nächtiges Dunkel," high strings (*forte,* tremolo), introduced previously when the fire cast light on the sword, descend to a low register and continue *pianissimo*. A slight *crescendo* and *diminuendo* accompany Siegmund's remembrance of Sieglinde's glance.[13]

Although color contrasting is particularly useful for highlighting dramatic moments in vocal music, it can be equally useful for shifting moods in instrumental music. Here, timbral contrasts are often coordinated with harmonic contrasts, as illustrated in the passage from Bruckner's Fourth Symphony (1878/80 version) in Example 8-7. A lone flute, registrally distinct, outlines C-major harmony (f: V). It is echoed by the darker timbre of a distant-sounding horn, arpeggiating a Db-major chord (VI). Bruckner contrasts three dimensions simultaneously: timbre, register, and harmony. He assures maximum effect by omitting all accompaniment so that we hear only those two instrumental and harmonic colors.[14]

Understanding these harmonic color contrasts requires a sense of the relationship among chords in a single key; understanding abrupt shifts away from a given key into another, distant key requires a sense of relationships among keys, grouped around the central tonality of C major. Two interdependent historical factors, Kurth holds, have conditioned our ear toward a C-major orientation. First, the system of church modes evolved around the notes of a C-major scale; C major thus very early represented a kind of tonal midpoint and served as a foundation for subsequent development. Furthermore, and far more consequentially, this white-note orientation has long influenced musical training. Over the centuries it has become ingrained in our aural faculty and now occupies a central position in our musical sensibilities. These historical factors produce what Kurth calls the "absolute character of a key," the universe of keys situated around a hypothetical C-major hub.[15] Most musicians would agree that we have a relative tonal sense; given some point of departure, this sense permits us to measure aurally detours into remote tonal regions. Those familiar with Wagner's music in particular no doubt accept the idea of "absolute" referential chords and tonalities.[16]

The color contrasts presented so far involve the juxtaposition of two chords, with distinct roots, whose indirect tonal kinship creates a novel harmonic effect. Shifts in tertian structure above a single root produce a different kind of contrast.

EXAMPLE 8-7. Bruckner, Symphony No. 4, II, mm. 91–95

Chromatic alterations applied to the members of a chord "shade" it from one color into another, often darker, color. The passage in Example 8-8 illustrates this technique. Wagner shades the f″ of the neighbor-note sonority g′–b′–f″ into f♭″. This contrast suits the textual contrast of the pure gold ("Um dich, du klares") with the bitter lament of the Rheinmaidens ("wir nun klagen").[17]

EXAMPLE 8-8. *Rheingold,* 4

Example 8-9 illustrates a similar instance of shading. The A-major chord in measure 27 is shaded into A minor, contrasting the momentary joy of Tristan's awakening with his approaching end.[18] Kurth extends the technique of shading to include those cases where we anticipate a certain chord that undergoes shading as it arrives. The expected chord does not actually occur, then, making the color contrast implicit rather than explicit. Kurth calls the chord in measure 21, Example 8-10, "shaded" E♭ major with an under-third. This interpretation points clearly to a twelve-key system with interchangeable major-minor modality, as opposed to a system of twenty-four independent major and minor keys.[19]

Exchanges between major and minor are perhaps the most common forms of shading; they are certainly one of the most familiar in early nineteenth-century music. Several theorists known to Kurth discussed such exchanges.[20] From the many instances of such major-minor shifts in Wagner's music, Kurth singles out two powerful and dramatically suggestive examples from the *Ring*. Near the end of *Rheingold,* as Donner disappears in a cloud, Wagner shades B♭-major harmony into B♭ minor as the storm gathers. He highlights this modal shift with the entrance of flutes, oboes, clarinets, and horns on a sustained B♭-minor chord. In *Siegfried,* III,

EXAMPLE 8-9. *Tristan*, III, 1

EXAMPLE 8-10. *Tristan*, I, 1

3, at Brünnhilde's awakening, the vocal part outlines an A-major chord as the re-
vived Valkyrie sings "Heil euch, Götter!" At "Heil dir, Welt!" an A-minor chord
replaces A major, thus contrasting the realm of the gods with that of the earth.[21]
Kurth notes that Wagner often associates major and its parallel minor in this way to
depict natural or supernatural phenomena.

All of the techniques described above—coloring, color contrasting, and shading—have a sensuous-harmonic side to them. As mentioned earlier, however, their origins lie in melodic impulses. These impulses inflect upward or downward one or more voices of a given sonority to produce a coloration or shading of that sonority, or to contrast one sonority with another. The subtle intermingling of sensuous and energetic effects is essential to polyphonic homophony. Although Kurth may, in his analyses, isolate one harmonic dimension for discussion, excluding the other, in a summary statement he reminds us that both always work together. Of shading, he remarks that "the downward motion passing lightly through [the chords] lowers the tone and darkens the harmonic color. . . . It is the reaction of harmonies to the most delicate energetic tensions."[22] This characterization of shading applies equally well to color contrasting or to applied dominant coloring, except that in the latter case upward motion would substitute for downward, and we would speak of brightening instead of darkening.

Contemporary discussions of harmony generally rely on various types of "mixture" to explain these techniques. Allen Forte discusses chromatic triads by mixture but does not develop the idea very far.[23] Edward Aldwell and Carl Schachter devote more space to modal borrowing. They suggest three types of mixture—simple, secondary, and double—to account for various ways in which major and minor keys are blended.[24] As we have seen, Kurth does not categorize his findings in the same way. He is more interested in the distinctive harmonic effect issuing from the confrontation of two chords, and he categorizes the phenomena accordingly, assigning them names that reflect this interest: one chord "shades," "contrasts" with, or "colors" another one. Furthermore, as pointed out earlier, he stresses the conflict of tonal regions, as expressed by the chordal relationships, rather than the mutual cooperation of a single pair of keys. While most of Kurth's examples do fall into one or another of Aldwell and Schachter's categories, some do not. The passage from Bruckner's Fourth Symphony (Ex. 8-7), for instance, is a color contrast involving two unaltered chords in a single key.[25]

Aldwell and Schachter, though they do not minimize the harmonic effects of mixture, do distinguish harmonic-structural levels; some chords have a "purely local function," while some "enter into larger tonal relationships."[26] For Kurth, the larger dimension is a dramatic rather than a structural one. Like Kurth, Aldwell and Schachter speak of coloration and intensification of chords affected by mixture, as well as of dramatic and textual motivations, but they evaluate the melodic procedures that produce such chords (chromatic neighbor and passing chords) from more of a syntactic-structural point of view than Kurth does.[27] As noted above, Kurth does acknowledge the voice-leading origins of coloring, contrasting, and shading. He does not, however, always take time to identify specific melodic procedures or to trace the causal melodic strand(s) any further than the localized harmonic event. Instead, he directs our attention to the harmonic outcome and its dramatic or textual motivation. This has led critics to fault Kurth for harmonic oversensitivity, for concentrating too much on "surface phenomena" instead of seeking their "deeper" structural implications.[28] Kurth does recognize deeper roots, but not the same kind that modern-day readers have in mind. Even those who credit him for detecting voice-leading procedures qualify their praise because of his analytical myopia and his failure to integrate his harmonic details into a unified, comprehensive structural hierarchy.

These arguments are well taken, but they are ahistorical. They do not address Kurth and his work as a stage in the history of theory and analysis. If we now presume to "know" how Wagner's harmony operates in all contextual dimensions, Kurth's work seems obsolete. This attitude is questionable for any musical inquiry, historical, analytical, or otherwise. It minimizes the importance of the advances by one generation, on which subsequent generations built and improved. Also, apparently preferring to impose their own aesthetic and cultural dispositions, some contemporary readers disregard those of a past age.

Most of Kurth's analyses are intended to show stylistic features in an ongoing evolution; they are thus necessarily limited in scope and do not always account for global operations. But for Kurth, diverse "surface phenomena" are nothing less than the very stylistic identity of a work, composer, or style period. As a historian and analyst, he observes subtle differences in these phenomena, which amount to the manifold stylistic expressions of the Romantic era. Accepting these musical expressions at face value, Kurth ponders their psycho-dramatic motivations in a sort of psychological investigation of style.[29] Only after establishing definitive stylistic details and explaining their sources will he undertake a study of broad musical contexts.

THE INTENSIVE ALTERATION STYLE

As mentioned earlier, Kurth considers harmonic coloring, contrasting, and shading relatively mild forms of only one type of alteration, chordal alteration, which modifies tertian structure. These forms are mild because the altered chords are often consonant, as in major-minor shifts and the Neapolitan chord, or only moderately dissonant, as in applied dominant seventh chords. Another reason for their mildness is the unidirectional melodic tendency of multiple chordal alterations, which strive conjointly upward or downward. In the intensive alteration style, by contrast, chromatically inflected tones may strive in both directions simultaneously. Melodic chromaticism, manifest in free neighbor-note insertions, joins with chordal chromaticism to heighten harmonic tension further. Enharmonic redefinition of sonorities featuring melodic alterations or chordal alterations or both introduces an extra measure of instability into an already lively interplay of linear and harmonic forces. Collectively, these techniques can thoroughly distort individual chords; more importantly for the development of tonality in the late nineteenth century, they can also distort tonal relationships among chords.[30]

Kurth approaches the intensive alteration style from three angles: chordal chromaticism, melodic chromaticism, and chromatic progression. We have already dealt with several procedures in the first category. Even more than chordal chromaticism, melodic chromaticism occupies Kurth in the analysis of Wagner's music. With the third category, chromatic progression, we enter the domain of nontonal chord successions and "floating" tonality. The following paragraphs outline Kurth's presentation of the second and third categories of chromaticism.

The difference between chordal and melodic alteration was explained above in connection with Examples 8-1 and 8-2. Kurth tends to treat chords that are complete neighbor-note displacements of their successors as independent tertian formations, often exhibiting one or more chordal alterations. In cases of less-than-complete neighbor-note displacement, as in Example 8-11, melodic alteration is at work. The sonority on beat two of measure 2 is a neighbor-note displacement of the F^7 on beat three; E and g♯' are neighbor-note insertions to F and a'.[31] Schumann pits E against e♭', forming a diminished octave, and g♯' against c', forming an augmented fifth, and so creates a powerfully dissonant moment of tension in the very first complete sonority of the piece. The passage from *Die Meistersinger* in Example 8-12 shows how a single pitch class, F♯, operates as a neighbor-note insertion embodying two directional tendencies at once.[32] Kurth calls the chord on beat one of the first complete measure an F^7 (V^7) with the melodic-chromatic alteration f♯' forming an augmented octave over the root. He does not discuss the b♭ in the sonority, which might suggest an eleventh chord with minor ninth, g♭'. The f♯' eventually resolves upward to g', making an F^9. On beat two, an inner voice takes up f♯ (bass clef), which behaves like g♭, resolving downward to f.[33]

EXAMPLE 8-11. Schumann, "Abendmusik," Op. 99, No. 12, mm. 1–3

EXAMPLE 8-12. *Die Meistersinger*, II, 5

Neighbor-note insertions of exaggerated duration, common in the intensive alteration style, can obscure the harmonic structure. In Example 8-13, two melodic-chromatic alterations in a B^7 chord suspend clear articulation of that harmony for nearly two full measures. A g♯′, the only non–chord tone at the beginning of measure 18, finally resolves to f♯′ on the last eighth of the bar, but only after the bass and alto have introduced the neighbor notes c and e. On the last eighth of measure 18, the tertian formation F♯–(A)–C–E (E major/minor: II^7), related by fifth to B^7, is "only apparently a new chord."[34] B^7 (V^7) finally sounds in full at the end of measure 19. The freedom accorded neighbor-note insertions is evident in the way Wolf treats the vocal g♯′ in measure 18, which skips to a chordal b′. The E-major harmony in measure 20 is also delayed by neighbor-note insertions, a free appoggiatura, a♯′, and suspended f♯″ in the vocal line.

The music in Example 8-13 continues with the passage in Example 8-14 (mm. 21–24), which again illustrates how neighbor-note sonorities may look like tertian harmonies with plausible tonal meaning. In measure 22, the configuration E–G–B–D could be considered a shading of the E-major chord at the end of measure 21. As the supposed E-minor seventh chord arrives, the music hints at that possibility. But the second half of measure 22 causes us to revise our hearing. The E-minor seventh becomes a neighbor-note configuration which resolves to a V/II, C♯–E♯–G♯–B, displaced by d″, e′ (d×) and G (F×). Kurth explains the chord this way without mentioning the tonal alternative, involving shading. He does note that the "external form" (*äussere Form*) of measure 21 indicates a diminished seventh chord, when in fact it is a neighbor-note formation.[35] As in Example 8-13, Wolf withholds the underlying harmony until the final eighth note of the bar.

Neighbor-note formations that exhibit plausible tonal forms can be aurally confusing. Is the sonority in question "identical," in Kurth's sense of that word, with its successor, or is it an independent chord? Kurth tends to analyze chords as either identical or independent without considering that we might hear a chord one way as it enters and in a different way retroauditively. The problem lies in saying a chord *is* one or the other based on selected criteria when in fact, depending on aural perspective, it might be both. In the kaleidoscopic flow of harmonies characteristic of late Romantic polyphonic homophony, the aural criteria change continually. Kurth is generally sensitive to this fact. But here, apparently eager to "pin down" ambiguous chords, he momentarily forgets the fluidity inherent in his harmonic "surge and flow."

"Identical" tension chords are a case in point. Take, for example, the passage in Example 8-15, which occurs shortly before the end of act II of *Tristan*.[36] Kurth calls the sonorities of measures 10 and 11 identical; the first displaces the second by a neighbor-note insertion, E, in the bass. The augmented sixth on e♭ in measure 8 may have led Kurth to this analysis, but he does not include that bar in his example, nor does he mention other music preceding his printed example (mm. 10–13 in Ex. 8-15). Still, Kurth's interpretation is believable enough, even without such evidence.[37] Measure 12 of Example 8-15 restates the tension chord, except that now b♭ is really a♯, and the bass G is a neighbor-note insertion, allowing the chord to resolve to an F♯⁷ harmony.

EXAMPLE 8-13. Hugo Wolf, "An den Schlaf," *Mörike-Lieder,* III, mm. 18–20

EXAMPLE 8-14.

EXAMPLE 8-15. *Tristan,* II, 3

The chord in measure 10 of Example 8-15 occurs in the Prelude to act III of *Tristan,* which follows shortly thereafter (Ex. 8-16). In the tonality of the Prelude (F minor), the chord now possesses a clear tonal meaning (VII), though Kurth believes the broad tonal development of the Prelude dictates a different analysis.[38] According to Kurth, measure 32 amounts to a G[7] harmony with neighbor-note insertions of d♭ (c♯) to d♮, b♭ (a♯) to b, and e′ to f′. Kurth calls e′ a neighbor-note note to f′ by analogy to other Love-Motive harmonizations. Measure 32 is thus identical with measure 33, which establishes G[7] more clearly and expands it into G[9]. Kurth does not explain why the d♭ neighbor note in measure 32 skips freely to B♭ (= A♯), also a neighbor note, and then on to G. Perhaps he heard an exchange of nonharmonic tones between the bass and alto. Aside from the question of whether e′ is a neighbor note by analogy, and the problem of leaping neighbor notes, the tonal context allows for another interpretation altogether. Within the key of F minor, we could hear the chord as VII[7], a dominant function. Alternatively, we might consider the chord a II[7], a subdominant function, with e′ as a Love-Motive appoggiatura.

EXAMPLE 8-16. *Tristan,* Prelude to act III, mm. 32–33

A chord explainable as a dominant, a subdominant, and an applied dominant (Kurth's G[9]) must be ambiguous.[39] All three interpretations are audible as we reach measure 32 in Example 8-16, although we would probably reject the II[7] option as measure 33 arrives. The difficulty lies in the brevity of Kurth's example. It is too short to allow an analysis that assumes as much as Kurth's does. Ultimately, in light of the Prelude as a whole, Kurth's G[9] turns out to be the most satisfying hearing of the chord, as we shall see in chapter 9.

Kurth views chromatic progressions as an extension of the neighbor-note technique; the chords involved in a chromatic progression are neighbor-note sonorities pressing onward. Each chromatic neighbor-note formation resolves to a sonority which, though it may have a momentary sensuous quality and may even appear tonal, behaves instead like a neighbor-note formation, and so resolves to yet another such formation, and so on. In referring to the passage in Example 8-17, which illustrates a chromatic progression, Kurth says, "Every chord tone led chromatically takes on leading-tone significance in relation to a tone of the following chord, so that in such chromatic progressions a supple interweaving is brought about."[40] The chords are "not tonal but rather . . . the result of voice leading." Kurth calls the ambiguous chords in such chromatic progressions "extratonal."[41] He stresses the extratonal status of the individual chords in Example 8-17 without addressing their collective function. By omitting commentary at this point on the larger role of extra-tonal progressions, Kurth does not mean to imply that they suspend tonality. He goes on to cite examples in which extratonal progressions link chords with clear tonal meanings.

EXAMPLE 8-17. *Tristan*, II, 2

The Ailing-Tristan-Motive, or Tantris-Motive (Ex. 8-18), illustrates how a chord formed by chromatic passing tones intervenes in an otherwise straightforward tonal progression.[42] In order to understand such passages, Kurth examines the end points, where the voices flow into tonal chords. The first and last chords in Example 8-18, VI and V in A minor, are the "basic pillars" (*Grundpfeiler*), connected by an extratonal chromatic passing formation, an apparent F♯-major chord in measure 3. Kurth remarks that other instances of the Tantris-Motive permit similar analyses. Example 8-19 occurs twenty-four measures after the passage in Example 8-18.[43] Using Kurth's analysis of Example 8-18 as a guide, we can establish the basic pillars in Example 8-19 as I and V in A major/minor, with the B♭-major and D♯ half-diminished seventh chords as chromatic passing formations. In Examples 8-18 and 8-19, tonally clear points of departure and arrival "frame" the chromatic-harmonic flow.[44] The notion of basic pillars framing an extended string of chromatic voice-leading chords is an interesting and very important one for its time.

EXAMPLE 8-18. *Tristan*, I, 3

EXAMPLE 8-19.

When the basic pillars are evaded, the tonality itself enters a state of flux. Any potential harmonic arrival that could initiate a cadence leads instead to renewed chromatic progressions, thus pushing the basic pillars ever further apart. Example 8-20 illustrates how chromatic progressions may disrupt harmonic-tonal syntax.[45] In the key of F minor, Kurth assigns roman numerals VI and V to measures 14 and 15 respectively. He calls the D^7 chord in measure 17 a dominant that leads to a first-inversion C-minor harmony, a deceptive cadence, instead of resolving to a tonic in G minor. Having achieved a chord a semitone higher than the one in measure 14, the music proceeds in measures 18–19 with a sequential repetition of measures 14–15.

EXAMPLE 8-20. *Tristan*, III, 1 (continued on facing page)

The sensuous form of the *Tristan* chord, with a♭ and c♭, occupies the following measures. (N.B. the text: "Longing! To die while I am longing."). Subsequently, chromatic voice leading sets in and draws the harmony downward through several extratonal chords, leading to the chord in measure 11, VI⁷ in F minor, which was the point of departure at the beginning of Example 8-20. Kurth does not trace the harmony through to the restatement of the English horn's "alte Weise" in the last measure of Example 8-20, but the analysis offered here follows from his idea of basic pillars.

The idea of basic pillars is not new with Kurth. As explained earlier, in chapter 5, theorists from the late eighteenth century onward had already discussed the connection of two diatonic harmonies by one or more "nonessential" chords. Compared with the ideas of earlier writers, though, Kurth's notion of extended extratonal progressions linking basic pillars is quite advanced. He may have derived his ideas on the subject from the work of the Louis-Thuille team, or perhaps from Josef Schalk.[46] Rudolf Louis and Ludwig Thuille, blending elements of figured-bass theory with "function" theory, described various types of diatonic passing chords. In 1905, when the relationship between harmony and counterpoint was not clearly understood, they disentangled the two well enough to distinguish between chords that appear to be fundamental harmonies but operate as passing formations and those that are truly fundamental harmonies. In general, Louis and Thuille allow no more than two successive passing chords, but in highly chromatic music they allow numerous passing chords to intervene between points of tonal stability. In Example 8-21, which illustrates their approach, they explain all the chords between the initial augmented chord, substituting for the dominant, and its resolution chord in measure 3 as "pure chromatic motion." The passage is especially instructive, they believe, because it shows "how within such apparently completely extratonal chromaticism the tonality, despite everything else, can be maintained."[47]

EXAMPLE 8-21. Strauss, *Till Eulenspiegel* (rehearsal 19 + 1)

In a series of four articles published about twenty years before the Louis-Thuille *Harmonielehre,* Josef Schalk, a student of Bruckner and ardent Wagnerian, deals with unitary tonality in Wagner's music. Schalk discredits analyses, like those of Jadassohn, that invoke numerous modulations to explain unconventional chord progressions. He tries to show that anomalous, nondiatonic chords can be explained as nonessential passing chords within a single key.[48] Though he does make significant progress toward understanding chromatic harmony, Schalk, still very much a chord-to-chord analyst, does not go very far beyond Bruckner's ideas, nor beyond those of Karl Mayrberger. He recognizes the crucial role of melody in difficult chromatic passages, thereby broadening the concept of harmony, and in contrast to his contemporaries, he also insists on mono-tonality, restricting modulations to longer sections that firmly establish a new key. But his examples include only a few successive nonessential chords and thus do not permit us to imagine how he would have explained passages like the ones in Examples 8-20 and 8-21. As a theorist, Schalk is certainly forward-looking, but as analyst, Schalk may not have had a wide enough harmonic scope to deal with passages discussed by Kurth and the Louis-Thuille team.

By 1906, Heinrich Schenker had developed concepts to explain the coordination of scale steps and mediating contrapuntal chords. In *Harmony* he outlines and illustrates his early ideas on scale steps, which, at this stage of Schenker's thinking, play a role similar to that of Kurth's basic pillars. Using excerpts from compositions by Bach, Chopin, Schumann, and Wagner, he explains how scale steps, like "beacons and lights," guide the harmonic succession on a firm tonal path.[49] All of Schenker's examples, except the opening passage from Chopin's E-Minor Prelude, Op. 28, No. 4 (Ex. 124), are basically diatonic and involve single passing or neighboring chords, which are usually dominant harmonies embellishing two statements of the governing scale step. Only the Chopin excerpt contains an extended chromatic passage, which exhibits up to four successive passing chords before reaching a scale step. Schenker's omission of more elaborate chromatic passages in *Harmony* is, of course, not a weakness in itself. Nevertheless, it does show that, except for Schenker's few discussions of limited chromatic progressions, Kurth was on new ground.

In straightforward diatonic music, Kurth does tend to analyze every chord as a fundamental harmony instead of applying the idea of basic pillars. In this respect, he was not unlike many other authors of his day, who were still very much under the influence of conventional chord-by-chord analysis. He was able to free himself from that influence only under certain conditions. In Wagner's music, too, in places where today we might distinguish between dependent and independent chords, Kurth may assign most of them equal harmonic value, save those he considers basic pillars. Still, his observations on chromatic progression broaden considerably the concepts of harmony and tonality. That is particularly so with his awareness of successive extratonal progressions and basic pillars. His achievements in this area are important since they came at a time when a view of harmony that largely neglected melodic forces as determinants in harmonic progressions held sway. The writings of Alfred Lorenz and Hermann Erpf, for instance, attest to the lasting influence of Riemann's tri-functionalism. Even with all of its advances over previous modes of harmonic analysis, Riemann's approach remains basically vertical. Erpf in particular, with his excessive analytic symbology, presses the idea of harmonic derivatives from the primary tonal functions to such dubious extremes that one must sometimes question the aural relevance of his analyses.[50] Kurth, by contrast, avoids an intellectualized approach in his discussion of chromatic progression, melodic alteration, and the intensive alteration style, and thus sets aural relevance above theoretical uniformity.

NOTES

1. The second half of the present chapter deals with the intensive alteration style (*Intensiver Alterationsstil*), which Kurth discusses in *Romantische Harmonik,* 183–228.
2. Kurth, *Romantische Harmonik,* 130 (*Farbentönung*), 150 (*Farbenkontraste*), 159 (*Klangschattierung*). The *Tristan* chord is a good example of how sensuous and energetic qualities combine.
3. Ibid., 102: "melodische Rücksichten sind vorgebrochen über akkordliche Gesichtspunkte."
4. Ibid., 106: "man darf . . . nicht aus dem Auge verlieren, dass diese scheinbar rein klanglichen Vorgänge hängen in Wirklichkeit . . . mit Bewegungserscheinungen zusammen und gehen in ihren Wurzeln auf *lineare* Spannungen zurück." Kurth says this in connection with a passage from Schumann's *Nachtstück,* Op. 23, No. 2, measures 1–2.
5. Ibid., 110. Schirmer, 170:5.
6. Kurth, *Romantische Harmonik,* 109: "aus dem Leit*ton* wird Leit*akkord.*"
7. Ibid., 189: "feste Angelpunkte." Aldwell and Schachter, *Harmony and Voice Leading,* 1:201, cite this same passage as an example of what they call "chromatic embellishing chords."
8. Kurth, *Romantische Harmonik,* 228: "Alles drängt und flutet"; ibid., 110: "Durchdringen von *Bewegungsspannungen* . . . ist der *Anlass* und *Ursprung erhöhten Farbenspiels* und auch grösseren *Akkordreichtums.*"
9. Ibid., 143: "eindunkelndes Hinüberwenden gegen die Be-Tonartsregionen." Most authors explain such chords by referring to modal "mixture." Kurth emphasizes subdominant key regions, varying in tonal "distance" from the tonic, as the source of such altered chords.
10. Ibid., 148. Schirmer, 144:1–3. In major, the Neapolitan derives from two alterations of the subdominant, one harmonic (6♮ becoming 6♭) and one melodic (chromatic neighbor-note displacement of $\hat{1}$). Kurth explains the neighbor-note alteration producing the Neapolitan chord in *Romantische Harmonik,* 145.
11. Schirmer, 56:10–12, 57:1–2.
12. Kurth, *Romantische Harmonik,* 150–51, "Effects of Color Contrasts" ("Wirkungen der Farbenkontraste"). Schirmer, 33:4–8 (Ex. 8-5); Schirmer, 40:19–23, 41:1–3 (Ex. 8-6).
13. Prior to this music, where the fire flares up (Schirmer, 39), the Sword-Motive enters in C major, contrasting with E major as Siegmund sings "Blitz" ("flash") and "Blick" ("sight"). Wagner enhances this harmonic contrast with *fp* accents. Kurth also finds several instances of harmonic color contrasting linked with timbral contrasts in *Tristan,* for example, near the beginning of act III, scene 1, at Tristan's words "was weckt sie mich?" Here, the preceding F-minor lament in the English horn gives way to a fleeting A-major harmony (horn), signifying Tristan's awakening (Schirmer, 220).
14. Kurth, *Romantische Harmonik,* 152. A passage from the Scherzo of the same work, measures 27–32, offers a similar juxtaposition of harmonic and timbral colors. At measure 27, Bruckner interrupts a long tonic pedal in B♭ major with three heavily accented *fortissimo* chords in the low brass, G♭ major, D♭ major, and E♭ major. Accompanied by a tremolo F in the high winds and strings, the horn continues (m. 29) with tonic harmony. Cf. also measures 31 ff.
15. Kurth, *Romantische Harmonik,* 298 n: "absoluter Tonartscharakter."
16. Kurth refers to specific keys in Wagner's music that possess an absolute character, e.g., A♭ major in *Parsifal,* A major in *Lohengrin,* C major and E♭ major among others in the *Ring.* Robert Bailey points out some referential keys in Wagner's music in "The Structure of the *Ring,*" 51–53. He calls this technique "associative" tonality.
17. Kurth, *Romantische Harmonik,* 164. Schirmer, 217:2–4. The enharmonic reading of G–B–F♭ as an E-minor triad, juxtaposed with an A♭ triad, faintly suggests the family of motifs associated with the Tarnhelm, and hence the idea of transformation and change.
18. Schirmer, 220:21–28. Note 13 above mentions the color contrast of A major with the foregoing F-minor tonality. That Tristan awakens to an A-major chord is ironic, since that same harmony had just the opposite meaning in act I, as part of the Death-Motive.

19. Kurth, *Romantische Harmonik,* 103, 159. Schirmer, 7:18–21. Example 7-10 above also shows an instance of shading combined with the use of an under-third. Concerning a system with twelve as opposed to twenty-four keys, see Robert Bailey, "Wagner's Sketches and Drafts For the First Act of *Tristan and Isolde*" (Ph.D. dissertation, Princeton University, 1969), 149. Gregory Proctor also discusses this issue in "Technical Bases of Nineteenth-Century Chromatic Tonality: A Study in Chromaticism" (Ph.D. dissertation, Princeton University, 1978), 131.

20. Kurth was familiar with the following works, among others: Moritz Hauptmann, *Die Natur der Harmonik und Metrik,* 39–41, 62–64 (*The Nature of Harmony and Meter,* trans. W. E. Heathcote [London: Swan Sonnenschein and Co., 1888], 21–23, 42–44); Hugo Riemann, *Harmony Simplified,* trans. H. Bewerung (London: Augener, 1896), 44; and Louis and Thuille, *Harmonielehre,* 145–47.

21. Kurth, *Romantische Harmonik,* 172. Schirmer, 299.

22. Kurth, *Romantische Harmonik,* 160: "die leicht durchziehende Abwärtsbewegung erniedrigt den Ton und drückt auf die Klangfarbe. . . . Es ist ein Reagieren der Klänge auf zarteste energetische Spannungen."

23. Allen Forte, *Tonal Harmony in Concept and Practice,* 3d ed. (New York: Holt, Rinehart and Winston, 1979), 498–99. Forte lists the possible chordal borrowings between major and minor keys and cites some examples from the late nineteenth-century repertoire.

24. Aldwell and Schachter, *Harmony and Voice Leading,* 2:47–59, 186–93. In simple mixture, a given key borrows from its parallel major or minor companion. Secondary mixture produces non-diatonic triads containing notes borrowed from keys other than the parallel. Double mixture combines the procedures of simple and secondary mixture to produce remotely related triads.

25. Example 8-5 (coloring) illustrates secondary mixture, Example 8-10 (shading), simple mixture. The juxtaposition of F minor and A major (color contrasting), mentioned in notes 13 and 18 above, exemplifies double mixture.

26. Aldwell and Schachter, *Harmony and Voice Leading,* 2:187.

27. Ibid., 48, 58, 188, 193.

28. Patrick McCreless criticizes Kurth along these lines in his article "Ernst Kurth and the Analysis of the Chromatic Music of the Late Nineteenth Century," *Music Theory Spectrum* 5 (1983): 66–67. McCreless's criticisms are not entirely fair, though, since he is really more interested in what he can do with Kurth's ideas than in what Kurth himself did. See chapter 10, note 58.

29. See chapter 5, note 32, and the beginning of chapter 6 for some comments on Kurth's approach to analysis as a mechanism for understanding style. Many statements in *Romantische Harmonik* make it clear that, for Kurth, the main business of analysis is to illuminate the psychology of style. He devotes the entire second chapter of part 1 to "The Psychological Foundation of Romantic Harmony" ("Die psychologischen Grundlagen der romantischen Harmonik," 14–43). The goal of theory, "observing the transformation of certain tension processes into sound," clarifies Kurth's aims beyond a doubt (see my chapter 6, note 5). At one point, during a discussion of endless melody, he even uses the expression "style psychology" (*Stilpsychologie; Romantische Harmonik,* 536). Note also the subtitle to Kurth's article "Zur Motivbildung Bachs: Ein Beitrag zur Stilpsychologie" ("A Contribution to the Psychology of Style").

30. The intensive alteration style does not, of course, exist apart from some hypothetical "moderate" style. For didactic reasons, Kurth isolates various harmonic techniques and presents them in an ordered manner, beginning with relatively conservative forms of alteration and progressing to the most radical ones. The intensive alteration style incorporates all of the techniques presented so far, as well as others to be discussed presently. Interestingly, Kurth did not use *Romantische Harmonik* as a text. Even without specific reading assignments, though, Kurth's students realized that he expected them to read the book in order to understand his approach and terminology.

31. Kurth, *Romantische Harmonik,* 189. Louis and Thuille discuss chromatic appoggiatura chords similar to the one in Example 8-11 (*Harmonielehre,* 272–75). Their Ex. 284 *l*) illustrates a chord featuring neighbor-note insertions. They also give examples of chromatic passing chords (Ex. 285)

and "interpolated chords" (*eingeschobene Akkorde;* ibid., 275), the latter shown only in diatonic settings (Ex. 286). One could interpret Schumann's chord as passing from a C-minor to an F^7 harmony, via e♭–e–f and g′–g♯′–a′. This reading is complicated by the texture and the heard metric structure of the passage.

32. Kurth, *Romantische Harmonik,* 190. Schirmer, 287:9–11.

33. We might prefer to call the g′ a passing tone to a′. Kurth calls it a chordal ninth. The Schirmer vocal score notates the F♯'s of Example 8-12 as G♭'s in both treble and bass clefs. The Eulenberg orchestral score, vol. 1, pp. 677–78, also has two F♯'s. Kurth used the Buelow piano transcription, which was unavailable for comparison.

34. Kurth, *Romantische Harmonik,* 200: "nur scheinbar ein neuer Akkord."

35. August Halm discusses appoggiatura formations that have an "apparent chordal image (*akkordliches Scheinbild; Harmonielehre,* 98).

36. Kurth, *Romantische Harmonik,* 206. Schirmer, 214:7–13.

37. Perhaps Kurth expects us to discover the correctness of his reading by studying the passage and its context more thoroughly than is possible in the space he allows himself for any one example.

38. Kurth, *Romantische Harmonik,* 58. Schirmer, 216.

39. A similar ambiguity arose in connection with Example 6-2.

40. Schirmer, 144:8-11. Kurth, *Romantische Harmonik,* 220: "Jeder chromatisch weitergeführte Akkordton gewinnt Leittonbedeutung gegenüber einem Ton des nachfolgenden Akkords, wodurch das schmiegsame Ineinanderdringen in solchen chromatischen Klangfolgen hervorgerufen wird." August Halm speaks similarly of chromatic progressions: "The possibility of interpreting every tone as a leading tone yields the possibility of chromatic progressions and modulations by half step" ("Die Möglichkeit, jeden Ton als Leitton zu deuten, gibt die Gelegenheit zu chromatischen Akkordfolgen und Modulationen um einen halben Ton"; *Harmonielehre,* 100). His Ex. 80-bb (Ibid., xxiii), from the Scherzo of Bruckner's Seventh Symphony (mm. 41–53), illustrates this technique.

41. Kurth, *Romantische Harmonik,* 221: "nicht tonal, sondern . . . Stimmführungsergebnis"; "extratonal chord connections" ("aussertonale Akkordverbindungen"). Alfred Lorenz disagrees altogether with Kurth's reading of Example 8-17. He hears the passage as "completely tonal, with passing semitones" ("ganz tonal mit durchgehenden Halbtönen"; *Tristan,* 92n). Lorenz analyzes the harmonic functions in A major as follows: ⑤, 𝇈 (m. 1), T^7 (m. 2), 𝇈$_{5>}^9$ (m. 3), D (m. 4). Kurth would call Lorenz's interpretation an artificial, mental "reconstruction." Lorenz's reading, plausible though it may be, undervalues the dynamic forces that engender the passage to begin with.

42. Kurth, *Romantische Harmonik,* 224. Schirmer, 34:3–4.

43. Schirmer, 35:5–10. Kurth gives only the one example (8-18). Example 8-19 is my own selection.

44. Kurth uses the expression "tonal framing chords" (*tonale Gerüstakkorde*) synonymously with basic pillars (*Romantische Harmonik,* 375).

45. Schirmer, 249:4–19, 250:1–11. Kurth's Example 222 (*Romantische Harmonik,* 373–74) comprises measures 14–18 of Example 8-20.

46. Robert Wason outlines the evolution of ideas on nonessential harmonies in his article "Schenker's Notion of Scale-Step in Historical Perspective: Non-Essential Harmonies in Viennese Fundamental Bass Theory," *Journal of Music Theory* 27.1 (1983): 49–59. He takes up Schalk and the Louis-Thuille team on pp. 60–65.

47. Louis and Thuille. *Harmonielehre,* 354–55: "reine Durchgangsbewegung"; "wie innerhalb einer solchen scheinbar ganz aussertonalen Chromatik die Tonalität trotz allem gewahrt bleiben kann." On pp. 367–68, Louis and Thuille cite a passage from Chopin's Ballade, Op. 38 (mm. 186–87), which also features a string of chromatic passing chords. The Strauss example occurs on p. 27 in the Kalmus pocket score, one measure after rehearsal 19.

48. Schalk's essays are collectively entitled "Das Gesetz der Tonalität," *Bayreuther Blätter* 11 (1888): 192–97, 381–87; 12 (1889): 191–98; 13 (1890): 65–70.

49. Schenker, *Harmony*, 174. Schenker proposes the idea of scale steps in section 2, chapter 1, "Scale Steps and Harmony," 133–53. Pages 154–74 deal with "Scale Step and Counterpoint." In the pamphlets of Schenker's periodical *Tonwille* (1921–24) and his yearbook *Das Meisterwerk in der Musik* (1925, 1926, and 1930), the notions of scale step and contrapuntal prolongation gradually evolve until they achieve their final form in *Der freie Satz* (1935). All of these works appeared years after Kurth published *Romantische Harmonik*.

50. Hermann Erpf, *Studien zur Harmonie und Klangtechnik der neueren Musik* (Leipzig: Breitkopf und Härtel, 1927).

CHAPTER 9

Kurth's Concept of Form

In *Grundlagen* and *Romantische Harmonik,* Kurth devotes relatively little space to musical form as a separate topic. In a sense, though, much of what he says in those two volumes deals in one way or another with form. His discussions of *Fortspinnung,* endless melody, developmental motives, and overriding lines in *Grundlagen* all begin by examining local details but lead ultimately to revealing something about the broad organizational design of a work. Similarly, his presentation of numerous localized harmonic details and chord connections in *Romantische Harmonik* builds gradually toward the notion of extratonal progressions and framing chords, in order to show how larger harmonic units are formed. The stress throughout is on motion, from motive to *Bewegungszug,* from absolute chord to extratonal progression. The ebb and flow of psychic motion, once actualized in sound, guarantees continuity. A piece of music, then, is *shaped* psychic motion. The particular shape that motion takes in a work amounts to its musical form.

The idea of musical form as motion is, of course, not new with Kurth. Among nineteenth-century writers, the aesthetician Eduard Hanslick comes immediately to mind. His well-known statement about music being sonorous form in motion certainly resembles Kurth's line of thought.[1] Eighteenth- and early nineteenth-century authors had also spoken of music as motion, expressed first as a series of "affections" and later as hypermetrically organized phrase and period constructions. These theories of form highlighted the finished product, the motion arrested in a particular arrangement of affections, themes, or keys. An important difference between Kurth and his predecessors is that he conceives of musical form as a state of tension rather than repose—tension between becoming (*Werden*) and being (*Sein*), between movement and rigidity. Kurth observes, "Form is . . . not a concept of repose but rather [one] of tension . . . musical form is always the *reciprocal action,* held in suspension, *between force and its subjugation in* [external] *contours.*"[2] Kurth understands form neither as a mold, as did August Reismann, for example, nor purely as the completion of anterior rational processes, as did Adolf Bernhard Marx. Rather, he understands form as the transition between mold and process.

Form is neither the pure streaming of the formation process nor the pure
fulfillment of borders, but rather the transition, the active transformation
of the former into the latter. . . . In music . . . form is neither movement
nor its synoptically grasped rigidity, neither flux nor outline, but rather
the lively struggle to grasp something flowing by holding on to something
firm.[3]

Kurth's notion of form is much like his idea of polyphonic harmony. Just as the
individual lines in a polyphonic network coalesce and reach consummation in the
interrelated chords of tonality, so the collective stream of melody, harmony, and
rhythm reaches consummation in the completed work, when flux and the evolved
form achieve equilibrium in what we call form. "Form is not the point from which
the stream of creativity emanates but rather the goal into which it flows."[4] A better
word than "form" here would be "forming" (*Formung*), the active shaping of sound.
Kurth means the *shaping* process when he says form. His formal analyses, like his
melodic and harmonic ones, attempt to illuminate this evolutionary shaping process.
Just as the composer evolves a work, so the analyst in a sense re-evolves it as he
listens in order fully to comprehend its form.

In volume 1 of *Bruckner,* Kurth lays the conceptual groundwork for the extensive analyses of Bruckner's symphonies in volume 2. The basis of his analytical
approach is the idea of dynamic waves. Every musical segment, as a sonorous embodiment of psychic motion, fulfills a dynamic function. Short-range formal segments consist of localized surges called "constituent waves," which contribute to
more broadly paced "developmental waves." These in turn mount toward huge "symphonic waves." After a tension "discharge," a formal apex, the tension gradually
subsides during a counterwave, usually accompanied by "reverberating waves" in
the wake of the recent discharge, and "after-waves" echoing the previous buildup.[5]

We can all live comfortably with Kurth's notion of musical form as dynamic
flux. Compared with the static partitioning schemes that prevailed in the nineteenth
century, Kurth's view is refreshingly musical and intuitively satisfying. Nevertheless, certain problems with the basis of his theory have hindered discussion and acceptance of his ideas. Kurth relied on texts of Bruckner's works that were so heavily
edited by the composer's proponents that, in some cases, the music may no longer
embody Bruckner's intentions at all. His well-meaning editors, striving to suit the
tastes of late nineteenth-century Viennese audiences, did not shy away from altering
harmony and orchestration, omitting large sections, or even adding newly composed
material.[6] A reader today studying Bruckner's Fifth Symphony in Leopold Nowak's
edition, for instance, will discover nearly 120 measures unaccounted for in Kurth's
analysis of the last movement.[7] Kurth worked from orchestral and four-hand piano
editions prepared by Franz Schalk and Ferdinand Löwe, and so could gain only a
limited and, in some cases, distorted picture of Bruckner's work.[8]

The editorial alterations were not restricted to deleted sections only. Löwe in
particular, presuming a Wagnerian backdrop for Bruckner's work, habitually modified the orchestration, freely "smoothing out" Bruckner's ostensible rough edges to

create a fuller, more sumptuous sound. In a formal analysis based on thematic or harmonic-tonal criteria, such reorchestrations would seem unimportant. But with Kurth's dynamic-formal analyses, every detail matters. He sometimes uses timbral distinctions, solo and ensemble, to decide formal junctures. Editorial tampering with instrumentation could thus alter the formal conception. In the edited scores, timbres that shift before or after they actually do in Bruckner's original scores, or timbres that differ altogether from the composer's intention, may lead to a different dynamic-formal image. Consequently, Kurth's delicate arrangements of dynamic waves no longer hold up.

Despite the problems, contemporary writers on Bruckner still refer to Kurth's work, and justifiably so. Kurth was not the first to write about Bruckner's symphonies. Several authors preceded him, including Max Auer, August Halm, and Oskar Lang, all of whom he regarded highly. Kurth *was* the first, however, to go beyond topographical analyses and to delve into the very philosophical and artistic fiber of the music.[9] For this reason, Stefan Kunze, who currently holds the chair of musicology at Bern, downplays the superiority of one version of Bruckner's work over another and lauds Kurth's *Bruckner.* "Important books do not go out of date," Kunze says, "And even their errors remain more relevant than a thousand trivial accuracies."[10] The question of the "versions" has hampered progress in historical and analytical research on Bruckner's music. The problem is a musicological one: to sort out the various versions of the symphonies and, more importantly, to determine which alterations Bruckner made himself—or at least officially sanctioned—and which he did not. In a book dealing primarily with Kurth's ideas on harmony and counterpoint, it is unwise to deal additionally with a work so large as *Bruckner,* lest the discussion be superficial. A critical presentation of the monograph goes beyond the scope of the present study; indeed, it merits a separate, detailed investigation that can deal adequately with the textual as well as the music-analytical issues.

Let us return, then, to *Grundlagen* and *Romantische Harmonik,* where Kurth discusses form in the music of Bach and Wagner. Unlike *Bruckner,* neither book analyzes a complete piece. Furthermore, they consider fewer questions of form. Predictably, *Grundlagen* deals chiefly with melody as a formal determinant, *Romantische Harmonik* with harmony. The following pages offer a sampling of Kurth's analyses as a framework for presenting the ideas on form contained in those two volumes.

Form in *Grundlagen*

In *Grundlagen,* Kurth looks to overarching linear development as a guide to form in Bach's music. By linear development, Kurth does not mean melodic development, which, at least in the everyday sense of melody, amounts to the external thematic form: the number, order, and interaction of motives and themes in a work. Rather than external *thematic* form, Kurth explores the internal *dynamic* form of a work.

This dynamic form, the "shape," is embodied in the composite thrust of all linear strands that course through a work, carrying it deliberately over several dynamic arcs.

Kurth does speak of an overarching tonal foundation accompanying these dynamic arcs, but his comments are brief and keep to the familiar cyclical plan: tonic, dominant, modulatory development/retransition, and return to tonic. He organizes these harmonic stages into a tripartite plan. Then, characteristically infusing the plan with directional energies, he implies a dynamic-formal progression resembling the following diagram.

Dynamic:

Tonal: tonic-dominant   dominant/modulations   tonic

As a general formal outline, Kurth's description and the above interpretive diagram provide a basis for coordinating the tonal and dynamic dimensions of many common-practice works. Because it is so general, however, the plan cannot account for important stylistic details of tonal structure or, further, for subtle and personal artistic traits. For example, the modulatory section, ranging over various related and sometimes unrelated keys, usually dwells for a comparatively extended period of time on one key. This key often acts as a large-scale dominant preparation (VI, IV, II), analogous to the local phenomenon. Of course, Kurth's plan does not try to account for specific modulatory schemes, and the dynamic-tonal arc remains intact whatever schemes are used. It is the instability and *turbulence* characterizing the modulatory section that are foremost in his mind. The specific harmonies there are an attribute of the dynamic form and are subsumed under an overriding arc.

As mentioned above, the tonal dimension of Bach's music occupies Kurth only briefly, almost peripherally, compared with the linear dimension.[11] The dynamic intensification, which builds across approximately two-thirds of a piece (in Kurth's estimation), derives its energy mainly through various linear resources. In monophony, the intensification is implemented through techniques such as progressive rhythmic agitation (quarters, eighths, sixteenths), contour turbulence (increasingly wider melodic leaps, dissonant melodic intervals), and chromaticism. In polyphony, intensification comes about through gradual addition of voices, expanding register, contour turbulence, rhythmic agitation among voices, and climactic wedgelike developments, and through the familiar stock of Baroque compositional devices, such as augmentation, diminution, inversion, and stretto.[12] Curvilinear developments, with their broadly unfolding linear continuities, may supplement any of these techniques. Following the climactic tonic, any of the techniques may occur in reverse as a means of de-intensification.

In polyphony, the chief weight of dynamic-formal development falls to the "episode," or as Kurth prefers to call it, the "transitional passage," or linking passage (*Zwischenspiel*).[13] He prefers the expression "linking passage" to "episode" because the latter implies something parenthetical or secondary to thematic expositions.

Only a point of view that, clinging to an *external* conception, created the
current theory of musical form is capable of defining the linking passage
as an "episode," of seeing in it only the idea of something "secondary"
because it does not belong to the thematic sections of the form.[14]

Kurth hears in such passages more than just incidental sections, more than just "sequences" modulating, however deliberately, between thematic expositions. For him,
linking passages are integral formal components promoting the ebb and flow of the
overarching linear unfoldment; they thus vivify the formal process as a whole. The
resolute, integrative linear thrust of linking passages, rather than their harmonic features, interests Kurth. To his mind, linking passages lie at the very heart of the formal process. Using motives derived from main themes, they carry ascending and
descending waves begun in surrounding thematic expositions to their conclusions
and lead ultimately to renewed thematic exposition. They alone are used to integrate
expository segments with developmental ones by coordinating successive phases of
dynamic intensification and de-intensification, and in so doing to balance the composite linear thrust.

The task of the linking passage lies in a balancing of motion, in the continuation of an ongoing development, in the subtle equalization of [dynamic-
formal] intensifications and gradual resolutions of tension; it serves the
intermeshing of motions and the connection of larger complexes within
the entire form.[15]

Example 9-1 illustrates an integrative dynamic link. The soprano in measures
14–17 presents the entry of the fifth voice in the first thematic exposition. Observe
how the bass in the linking passage (mm. 17–19) rises steadily and so balances the
previous linear descent of the soprano, alto, and quintus in measures 16–17. The
soprano, too, having completed its brief descent on beat one, measure 17, reaches
beyond the aborted cadence there and ascends, with the bass, up to a climactic e″,
coinciding with the awaited C♯-minor harmony. The bass ascends further to e and
thus sustains the linear intensification up to the thematic entrance in the tenor
(m. 19). The upward-directed linking passage counterbalances the descent of the preceding thematic exposition and leads effectively to new thematic entries.[16]

Example 9-2 illustrates a different kind of linking passage, one that first executes a linear downswing, then reverses itself and builds toward the next thematic
entrance. Beginning at measure 22 and ending at measure 24 with E♭ in the bass, a
linking passage draws the dynamic-formal action downward. From there, the linear
thrust rises gradually toward a thematic entrance on the last eighth of measure 25
(bass). Compared with the brief unidirectional dynamic link in Example 9-1, Example 9-2 is more complex, first slackening the tension and then rebuilding it in
order to point up a thematic entry.

EXAMPLE 9-1. Bach, C♯-Minor Fugue, *WTC* I, mm. 14–20

EXAMPLE 9-2. Bach, E♭-Major Fugue, *WTC* I, mm. 22–26

From the preceding examples it is clear that thematic-motivic and tonal analysis alone cannot satisfactorily explain the internal shape of a work. Charting themes and their motivic breakdown over the course of a piece, or uncovering routine Baroque contrapuntal devices, though not unimportant, are but a first step toward understanding form. Kurth does not dispute the utility of those analytical tasks, but he does question their efficacy when they are isolated from the essential formal process supporting the musical features they aim to explain. The dynamic contour of a work is not the *outcome* of its peculiar thematic-tonal development. Rather, the dynamic contour, unfolding in stages through a work, *informs* the thematic-tonal development stage by stage and gives it direction and meaning. The linking passages are a kind of "overriding *Fortspinnung*," a comprehensive spinning forth, which embraces all linear strands.[17]

Linking passages, with their special dynamic-formal task, have a unique effect on the melodic material they incorporate. As they forge bonds and balance the linear drives among thematic expositions, they tend to simplify the motivic material down to elementary melodic gestures reflecting the overall directional thrust, thereby facilitating their work from within. These elementary melodic gestures are Kurth's developmental motives, discussed in chapter 3. A certain thematic flexibility characterizes linking passages, dominated as they are by developmental motives, which themselves are melodically very elastic. Thematic expositions, by contrast, are characterized by stable, distinctive themes. In analyzing polyphonic form, Kurth thus distinguishes between two types of sections based on their essential content: those that present straightforward themes and those that fragment the themes and from them distill the elements of their basic linear designs. A kind of thematic "consolidation" marks the first type, a thematic "dissolution" the second.[18] Exploring passages of thematic dissolution leads Kurth to the discovery of developmental motives, which for him are a product of the dynamic-formal process. Examining and interpreting developmental motives apart from their role in the dynamic-formal process ignores their essential meaning and reduces them to undistinguished polyphonic happenstance.

Bach's E♭-major fugue, *WTC* I, effectively shows the significance of developmental motives in linking passages. After the close of the last thematic entry in the exposition (Ex. 9-3, m. 7, beats 1–3), a linking passage sets in. Thematic dissolution simplifies the embellished downward arpeggiation of the beginning of the fugue subject (see Ex. 9-5) into an unembellished downward arpeggiation, which carries the linear development steadily downward toward the next thematic statement, beginning in measure 11 (soprano).[19] Example 9-4, by contrast, illustrates an upswing. Following a downward trend in the measure preceding Example 9-4 (Ex. 9-2, mm. 22–23), a compensatory two-measure upswing in Example 9-4 leads to a thematic entrance. Observe the developmental motives, in the bass and soprano, that power the ascent. The process of thematic dissolution isolates and simplifies those elements of the subject and countersubject that push upward. The subject and countersubject are shown in Example 9-5; square brackets mark the relevant motives. Note also the downward linear drive of the alto in Example 9-4; this drive provides a counterthrust to the general upswing of the passage and thus intensifies it internally as it builds toward the thematic entrance at the end of measure 25.

Examples 9-1 through 9-4 show how developmental motives corroborate and enhance the dynamic thrust of a linking passage. In some cases, however, the two do not corroborate one another, the developmental motives moving in a direction opposite to that of the linking passage. Example 9-6 illustrates such opposition. Starting on

EXAMPLE 9-3. Bach, E♭-Major Fugue, *WTC* I, mm. 7–11

EXAMPLE 9-4. Bach, E♭-Major Fugue, *WTC* I, mm. 24–26

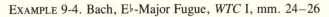

EXAMPLE 9-5.

beat three of measure 6, a linking passage gradually draws the music downward. The rising developmental motives—local melodic and scalar fourths—contrast with the overall descent. Rather than obscuring the dynamic role of the linking passage, the local ascents enhance it by contrasting with its global, curvilinear descent.

EXAMPLE 9-6. Bach, Sinfonia in
A Major, mm. 6–9

The linking passage in Example 9-7, measures 16–18 of the same Sinfonia, employs developmental motives similar to those in Example 9-6, but in a strikingly different manner. The motivic similarities are readily apparent. Like Example 9-6, Example 9-7 includes rising melodic fourths in the soprano and scalar passages in the bass, though the latter are now directed downward. Beginning at measure 17, noteworthy differences appear. The soprano expands its melodic fourth into a sixth, thus heightening the linear tension. Now both soprano and alto execute ascending leaps, unlike the passage in Example 9-6, where the alto counterbalances the rising figures in the soprano (and bass) with a stepwise descent. The most outstanding difference between Examples 9-6 and 9-7, however, is the dynamic action of the curvilinear progression. In Example 9-7 it strives upward toward the primary apex of the piece (mm. 17–18), while in Example 9-6 it strives downward, directing the action away from a preliminary apex. In light of the curvilinear ebb and flow, the joint melodic drives of the soprano and alto in Example 9-7 appropriately and effectively dramatize the final buildup toward the main climax.

The preceding examples demonstrate clearly the sometimes cooperative, sometimes competitive relationship between the local motivic content of linking passages and their curvilinear thrust. Two dynamic-formal levels emerge, analogous to the bi-dimensional linear structure that Kurth perceives in Bach's polyphony. Developmental motives, corresponding to the local level of the actual voice, represent one dynamic-formal level. Linking passages, corresponding to the apparent voice (curvilinear developments), represent a second, "trans-local" level. Both levels participate reciprocally in a play of linear forces guiding and regulating the dynamic-formal action of yet a third level, one that encompasses the action of a musical work as a whole. The local and trans-local makeup of linking passages is designed to suit the evolutionary stage of the dynamic form as a work unfolds.

EXAMPLE 9-7.

FORM IN *ROMANTISCHE HARMONIK*

Kurth exchanges the dynamic-linear view of form posited in *Grundlagen* for a dynamic-tonal one in *Romantische Harmonik*. Unlike *Grundlagen, Romantische Harmonik* looks to broad tonal movement as a guide to formal organization. The far-reaching modulatory and sequential schemes, unusual key arrangements, and apparent lack of large-scale tonic return in Romantic music lead Kurth to focus attention entirely on tonal form.[20] His ideas on Romantic tonal form take as their point of departure the familiar notion of tonal symmetry or "tonal closure" (*tonartliche Geschlossenheit*).[21] By this, Kurth means the return at form junctures of the tonic key from some contrasting key, for example, the dominant. Several closely related keys cluster about the mainstays, thus guaranteeing tonal variety and overall unity. It is precisely this tendency toward tonal closure, Kurth believes, that differentiates late Romantic form from that of earlier styles. Even where late Romantic style exhibits closure, its essential spirit aims at tonal expansion rather than delimitation, at turbulent harmonic surges and unexpected turns rather than a smooth, balanced tonal profile.

> One can characterize the opposition of late Romanticism and Classicism in that the latter, with all expansion of proportions and with modulations reaching so far, emphasizes the closed arch form, tonal *integration,* while Romanticism, by contrast, . . . [emphasizes] the flowing forces, the end-less *possibilities of modulation.* . . . Therefore even in closed forms, which return to the main key, it is often only a remote substructure, concealed and overrun with digressions.[22]

In the analysis of form in late Romantic music, then, Kurth is not so much concerned with the mere presence of tonal closure as with the relative emphasis on closure in the formal process. In Classical music, closure is a normative and consciously pursued element of the style, a definitive formal priority. The tonal narrative of a Classical work is about the departure from and deliberate return to a tonic key. The tonal narrative of a late Romantic work, by contrast, is about the remote and continuous modulatory digressions. According to Kurth, tonal closure is here a subconscious rather than a conscious objective. This fundamental difference in approach to tonal form results in two distinctive types of tonal disposition, which Kurth calls "centripetal" and "centrifugal." [23] The centripetal disposition characterizes Classical music, where tonal forces strive "inward," as it were, converging on an organizing tonic key. The centrifugal disposition characterizes Romantic music, where the forces strive "outward," away from the organizing tonic key. In late Romantic style, the centrifugal disposition manifests itself in two types of tonal "expansion" (*Dehnung*), which obscure and weaken tonal clarity. Kurth describes these two types as "exterior" and "interior" expansion. [24]

When several chromatic passing chords link those harmonies necessary for establishing a tonality, Kurth speaks of exterior tonal expansion. The tonally definitive chords may be widely separated from one another, as is the case with harmonic pillars. In such instances, tonality undergoes an expansion, or broadening, of its cohesive forces, allowing it to incorporate passages foreign to the prevailing key. Protracted nontonal progressions are good examples of exterior expansion. When the local chord succession or the harmonic pillars exhibit mediant or other, more remote relationships, Kurth speaks of interior expansion. The enlarged stock of available chords and chordal relationships expands the tonality by incorporating chords drawn from keys other than the prevailing one. [25] Exterior and interior tonal expansion join with two other techniques that obscure a tonality and yet, paradoxically, help to maintain an overarching sense of tonal orientation. Both involve the tonic. In one technique, the music outlines a tonality with its related keys, all the while carefully evading the tonic *key* itself. In the second technique, the tonic key is not evaded but the tonic *chord* is left unstated. By avoiding the tonic key or harmony, the tonal flow remains "unclosed" without being altogether suspended. The tonic is present by implication, though always elusive.

All of these tonal phenomena—exterior and interior expansion as well as implicit tonic key and harmony—result in a new and distinctive kind of tonality, a typically Romantic kind, which we might call "tension tonality." In contrast to other types of tonality, predicated on the presence of certain crucial elements such as a "tonic" mode or tonic harmony, tension tonality depends on the evasion or absence of that very element, the tonic. Romantic sensibility prefers the deliberate striving toward and allusions to an ideal but unstated tonic.

> The importance of the *sound* is completely supplanted by the importance
> of the *tension*. The *sound* [of tonic] is no longer necessary if the *striving*

of the will directed toward it is present. It [the striving] suffices for the sensation of key and tonic, not only suffices but rather in much greater, more intensive measure is its bearer.[26]

In part 5 of *Romantische Harmonik,* "Paths of Tonal Development," Kurth presents the ideas of tonal form outlined above and applies them to instrumental sections of *Tristan,* the preludes to acts I and III. The wealth and depth of ideas Kurth offers in connection with these pieces far outweigh his short, twenty-page presentation. The analyses themselves are brief and, in the case of the Prelude to act I, fragmentary. The largest and most detailed analysis, covering roughly fifty measures, is of the Prelude to act III.[27]

Kurth's analysis of the Prelude to act III of *Tristan* illustrates well his ability to discern a coherent, unified structure unfolding slowly over an extended span of music that incorporates extratonal progressions. The music is given in Example 9-8. Kurth divides the large-scale tonal movement into six sections.

	1		2		3		4		5		6	
mm.	1	10	11	15	16	25	26	30	30	37	38	52
	IV^7	V	III	V	IV^7	VI	VI	V/V	V/V		V	I

Certain of the harmonies asserted here were questioned earlier in this study, specifically those of measures 1 and 30.[28] In the present discussion, in order to avoid losing sight of Kurth's objective, we will accept the sketch as it stands.

According to Kurth, the first section unfolds a progression from IV^7 to V (mm. 1–10). At the level of harmonic analysis Kurth has chosen here, the suitability of a long-range subdominant-dominant progression spanning measures 1–10 is debatable. Even though measure 1 does contain a subdominant, according to Kurth B♭–D♭–F–A♭, its harmonic consequent seems to lie more in the local tonic harmony of measure 2 than in the dominant harmony concluding the segment. When the subdominant harmony recurs in measures 3 and 5, it presses similarly toward the subsequent tonic in the manner of an upbeat. The sonorities themselves and, further, the dynamic indicators in measures 1–2 strenthen the arsis-thesis feeling, so that the broad harmonic development gives the impression of *tonic*-to-dominant rather than of subdominant-to-dominant. In favor of Kurth's reading, we might point out that the tonic is presented rather weakly; after it is delayed for three beats by an accented passing tone, it then lasts for only one beat.[29] Furthermore, if we count two-bar phrases beginning with measure 1, we find that the delayed tonic of measure 2 is hypermetrically weak. Nevertheless, as stated above, the relative consonance of measure 2 compared with measure 1, along with the prominent bass resolution and *crescendo* into measure 2, puts the hypermetric weight on measure 2, resolving the appoggiatura feeling of measure 1. Accordingly, I to V, rather than IV to V, better describes the overall harmonic activity of measures 1–10.[30]

The problem is one of levels. As in other instances, discussed earlier in various contexts, Kurth does not always distinguish clearly between levels of harmonic and melodic structure. He proposes the theoretical notion of large-scale harmonic pillars but does not work out an analytical method in sufficient detail to distinguish conceptually and to integrate analytically the hierarchic levels implied by harmonic pillars. Nevertheless, as we shall see, Kurth does offer important insights into the fundamental tonal unity of Wagner's chromatic style.

In section 2, covering measures 11–15, Kurth hears a progression from III to V, with an intervening extratonal sequence.[31] An initial motive descends by chromatic

EXAMPLE 9-8. (continued on facing page)

sequence, accompanied by chromatically descending thirds. The steadily falling voices gain momentum up to measure 14, where the melodic sequence in the upper part succumbs to the pervasive linear forces and thus continues in a purely chromatic descent, culminating in the C^7 harmony of measure 15.

> The melodic motive of the sequence disintegrates. Consequently, at the end [of the passage] the sequence plainly undergoes a dissolution into freely streaming voices and with them also the chords. Everything begins to flow and streams downward into the final chord.[32]

In explaining the harmonies of measures 11–14 as a chromatic sequence, Kurth justly denies them structural-harmonic significance, which would be artificial and would confuse the tonal meaning of the passage.

Sections 3 and 4 (mm. 16–25, 26–30) are a varied repetition of sections 1 and 2. Section 3 moves from IV⁷ to VI, instead of to V as in section 1, and section 4, departing from the VI, leads to V/V. This applied dominant occupies section 5 entirely (mm. 30–37), preparing for the dominant in section 6, which leads ultimately to the tonic in measure 52. Coming after twenty-two measures of slow preparation through a colorfully modified applied dominant and dominant, the tonic arrival releases a tremendous store of accumulated tonal tension.

Having established the framing chords that mark out the basic tonal shape of the piece, Kurth calls attention to the simplicity and manifest tonal character of the work as a whole.

> The large *tonal* continuity is . . . preserved by the initial and concluding chords [of each section]. . . . Together, these chords represent a highly simple, rounded [set of] cadences in F minor, with an applied dominant . . . [and] otherwise exclusively with chords of the main tonality itself.[33]

According to Kurth, the overall tonal form is thus an expansion of the harmonies forming a basic cadence, an expansion in the sense that a cadential chord pair is telescoped "to larger proportions" through the interpolation of extratonal passages bounded by the chord pair. This principle of telescoping chord pairs is already evident, Kurth points out, in Protestant chorales. There, local chord progressions lead into and out of cadential fermatas whose nonadjacent harmonic relationships often exhibit those of adjacent chords.[34]

Wagner exploits the expansion technique by transforming the framing chords themselves, normally clear tonal goals, into applied dominants or other chromatic chords, which may then carry the music into remote tonal regions. In this way, one key area becomes subordinate to another, creating tonal hierarchies at the global level similar to harmonic hierarchies at the local level. Kurth calls this tonal "nesting"; "instead of single chords, whole developments nest between the actual tonal harmonies."[35]

This statement, as well as the analysis of the Prelude to act III as a whole, shows clearly that Kurth recognizes the hierarchical structure of tonality in Wagner's music. By applying his ideas of basic pillars and extratonal, chromatic sequences, Kurth is able to demonstrate how the many chromatic digressions support an overarching, rather simply expressed tonality. Both exterior and interior expansion come into play. The widely separated but clearly articulated framing chords exemplify exterior expansion. The unfolded applied dominant of measures 30–37 exemplifies interior expansion, albeit in a relatively mild form. Although Kurth does not go on to illustrate these procedures of expanded tonality with longer passages of music, he does acknowledge that the Prelude to act III represents "a principle whose generalization follows from itself and which, in its particulars, embraces a thousand possibilities for application." [36]

The only other extended analysis in *Romantische Harmonik* is of excerpts from the Prelude to act I of *Tristan*. In the first excerpt, Example 9-9, Kurth hears a dominant/goal relationship between the pair of harmonies in measures 2–3, and again between the pair in measures 6–7. In the key of A minor, he reads the following harmonies. [37]

Example 9-9.

EXAMPLE 9-9.

The first harmony of each pair is altered, its fifth lowered by a half step. Suggestively, the pair of harmonies in measures 10–11 changes the relationship between its members from dominant/goal to subdominant/goal. (This change "darkens" the harmonic mood, aptly preparing for the Fate-Motive in measures 16–17.)

Note that the subdominant cadential effect in measures 10–11 depends on the local relationship of the two chords only, apart from the governing key of A minor, which requires an analysis of $V^7–V^7/V$. In summary, the opening music projects three points of harmonic repose, V, VII (= V/III), and V/V.

After successfully bringing each of the chord pairs in measures 1–13 under the control of a single key, Kurth argues that the analysis is insufficient because it does not account for the genesis of the overall harmonic succession.

> This would be an explanation that proceeds more analytically than synthetically, for even though it is an expression of the present harmonic relationships, . . . [it is] not, however, the demonstration of their *genetic* continuity that led precisely to this series of functions.[38]

The genetic continuity, he says, lies in the bass progression, from e (m. 3) to g (m. 7), and finally to b (m. 11), which unfolds a "*broad dominant upbeat.*"[39] In seeking the genetic continuity of the three chord pairs, Kurth has uncovered a large-scale bass arpeggiation. The notion of a dominant upbeat outlined in measures 1–13 is particularly insightful since the resolution of that expansive dominant is, fittingly, a frustrating nontonic harmony, a deceptive cadence to a VI chord in measure 17. The bass note of this would-be tonic (f) returns us unexpectedly to the music-dramatic stage of measure 2. Comparing measures 2–3 with measures 16–17, we see that the bass motion has been reversed. The progression from e to f in measures 16–17, arriving on a tonic substitute, turns out to be no more satisfying a cadence than the one from f to e in measures 2–3, leaving off on a dominant seventh chord.

Kurth's discovery of large-scale bass arpeggiation as an organizational principle in Wagner's music was, in 1920, a genuine breakthrough. Of the many writers who had tried their hands at analyzing the sphinxlike *Tristan* Prelude, none had offered so lucid and convincing a way of explaining its opening harmonic gestures. With the idea of an unfolded dominant upbeat, Kurth managed to unify linear and harmonic dimensions. Momentous as it was, Kurth's discovery seems nevertheless to have gone largely unacknowledged.[40] This is perhaps because of the unexpected conclusion he drew from it. For instead of emphasizing the tonal and formal unifying power of the bass arpeggiation, he does just the reverse. In the piecemeal exposure of the dominant, Kurth hears a decentralization and destabilization of tonality rather than a consolidation of it. Furthermore, for him the dissonant altered seventh chords above each element of the unfolded dominant point clearly toward a weakening of tonal unity.

> While the simple observation of the harmonic functions establishes more the coherence of the three resolution chords and shores up the loosened harmonic development on a tonal foundation, the decentralizing paths leading to [tonal] expansions are highlighted more in the explanation of the dominant progression contained in the resolution tones [of the three chords].[41]

We see that Kurth addresses measures 1–13 of the Prelude from two different points of view, which are for him apparently antagonistic. On the one hand, he presents three resolution chords, which fit handily into the framework of A minor. On the other hand, he stresses the genetic bass arpeggiation, which remains "concealed" (*verborgen*). For us, these two views complement each other in establishing the key of A minor at two structural levels. For Kurth, however, they seem to conflict. Kurth expected tonality, in the Classical sense, to operate according to certain accustomed norms. Having to rely on basic pillars to explain the passage, rather than on the chord-to-chord succession, meant there was an "exterior" expansion of tonality, which for him necessarily implied a nascent breakdown of tonality. Although Kurth did begin to modify and even to revise the traditional conception of tonality with ideas such as exterior/interior expansion and tension tonality, he continued to measure the music against familiar tonal standards in order to show fundamental changes in the compositional approach to, and stylistic evolution of, tonality. Kurth's remarks must be understood, then, in light of the style-historical attitude and objectives in *Romantische Harmonik*.

Content with his reading of measures 1–13, Kurth continues his analysis by partitioning measures 17–32 into three sections, delineated by key (Ex. 9-10). The first of these projects the subdominant key (mm. 17–21), the second projects the dominant (mm. 21–24), and the third returns to the subdominant (mm. 25–30). He aims at showing how the music evades the tonic key, all the while implying tonic by means of alternating subdominant and dominant key areas.[42] The two accessory tonalities circumscribe a central but unstated tonality that unifies the whole.

> The tonal development here appears expanded in that *not individual chords,* as in small contexts, *but rather larger proportions,* whole sections of music, relate to the overall tonality. . . . [I]nstead of simple tonal chords, entire passages encircle the tonic.[43]

The notion of an implied tonality ("tension tonality") is interesting and certainly appropriate to analysis of late Romantic music. An elusive tonic suits the many veiled references to unspoken desires and emotions in *Tristan*. Furthermore, the alternation of subdominant and dominant keys, a whole step apart, is structurally significant. The harmonic sequence up a whole step in measures 21–23, from A-major to B-major harmony, for example, as well as the elegant melodic sequence down a whole step in measures 25–28, balancing the previous sequence, attests to the motivic importance of these alternating keys.

Kurth's analysis of measures 17–32, perceptive though it is, presents some problems. He gives the roman-numeral analysis of measures 17–21 shown in Example 9-11. It is clear to Kurth that the music is in D minor by measure 21. How the music arrived there from A minor is another matter. After the deceptive cadence on a: VI in measure 17, Kurth continues analyzing the music in A minor for the next two bars. As his roman numerals indicate, he hears two IV⁷s, both with ♯6, separated by a III (mm. 18–19). The second IV⁷ leads by falling-fifth progression to

EXAMPLE 9-10.

V/III, an applied dominant that resolves to C major, suggesting the relative major key.[44] But Kurth looks beyond the tonicization of III to the continuation of the phrase, which to his ear modulates to D minor, overriding the recent pass at C major.

a: VI   IV⁷   III   IV⁷   (V)   III
                                              d: VII   IV VII⁷   I

EXAMPLE 9-11.

We might ask whether D minor is the tonality within which the C-major harmonies operate subordinately or, vice versa, whether C major is the tonality within which D minor becomes tonicized by an applied dominant. Kurth chooses D minor as the governing key, probably because, after the cadence on D-minor harmony in measure 21, the modulation is confirmed by a half cadence in measure 22. Further, cadences in D minor at measures 32 and 36 frame a second pass at C major, analogous to the first one. For the first modulation to D minor (m. 20), Kurth designates the C-major chord as the pivot; III in A minor becomes ♮VII in D minor (Ex. 9-11, m. 20). But ♮VII in a minor key nearly always functions as a V/III, with an ensuing move to the relative major. Using ♮VII as the pivot chord to swing the harmony into a (not yet established) subdominant key seems an unlikely interpretation of our hearing. Kurth's problem is finding a satisfactory pivot chord for the modulation to D minor. His analysis asserts a somewhat artificial diatonic modulation. One solution would be to reach D minor by means of a chromatic modulation, as shown in Example 9-12. Although various texts known to Kurth—for example, the Louis-Thuille *Harmonielehre*—deal with chromatic modulation, he does not explore that option.[45]

a: III   VII⁷/IV
    d: VII⁷   I

EXAMPLE 9-12.

Certain other details of Kurth's roman-numeral analysis of Example 9-11 are debatable. Kurth reads the six-four chords in measure 18 and measure 20 literally as second-inversion representatives of root-position harmonies. The interpretation of six-four chords has long been a stumbling block for theorists, as the legacy of conflicting opinions left by various authors attests.[46] Here, though, where the chords occupy metrically weak positions, their role seems clear. The III$^6_4$ chord in measure 18, G–C–E, is a passing chord expanding the applied dominant, IV$^7_{\sharp6}$ (V/V/III), which resolves normally to a V/III. Similarly, the six-four in measure 20, D–G–B♭, links the C-major harmony on beat one with its chromatically inflected companion in the modulation to D minor (Ex. 9-13).[47]

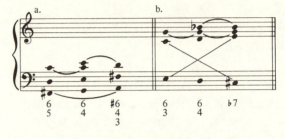

EXAMPLE 9-13.

In support of Kurth's reading, we might consider the tempo marking of the Prelude, "Langsam und schmachtend." At such a slow pace, we do clearly hear the C-major and G-minor harmonies (Ex. 9-11, mm. 18 and 20). Additionally, the shift to pizzicato in the double basses lightens the bass line considerably at measure 18, thus softening the impact of the six-four position. Given the tempo and timbre, Kurth registers the aural impression of the tone combinations, creating a: III and d: IV. This analysis addresses the sensuous implications of the chords but neglects their energetic, that is, voice-leading, implications. In overlooking their voice-leading role, Kurth cannot account for the functional uniqueness of those chords as they interact hierarchically with others.[48]

Kurth's neglect of the energetic-harmonic qualities involved here is troublesome because the success of his large-scale tonal plan hinges on the success of his chord-to-chord analysis. Although his basic intuitions are sound, without a systematic way of dealing with harmonic hierarchies Kurth cannot demonstrate logically how the overall key scheme he has in mind emerges out of the local harmonic activity.

Despite Kurth's problem in asserting the plan logically, his analysis is appealing from a music-dramatic as well as structural point of view. Dramatically, the nontonic appearances of A-major harmony are provocative and only partly gratifying, reflecting the story line of the opera. Further, the D-minor/E-major tonal tension adds to the unsettled feeling of the music. Lorenz's and Mitchell's more sober analyses stress tonic steadiness and thus lack the restlessness of Kurth's tonal fluctuation.[49] Structurally, the sequences ascending and descending by whole step in measures 21–23 and 25–28 (Ex. 9-10) follow from the D-minor/E-major fluctuation. Additionally, measures 17–21, moving toward D minor, and measures 25–28, in E major/minor, reappear in measures 32–36 (D minor) and 45–50 (E major/minor). The ascending whole-step sequence of measures 21–23, including the subsequent cadence on A-major harmony (m. 24), also returns, recast and extended, in measures 36–44 (see for example the poignant return of A-major harmony in the deceptive cadence of measure 44!). The tonal fluctuation based on the whole step thus continues over a large portion of the Prelude.

Absent from Kurth's formal analysis of the *Tristan* Prelude are references to its leitmotifs. For a theorist so attentive to melody and linear design, this seems curious. Lorenz, by contrast, attempts to incorporate leitmotifs into his analysis by coordinating them, throughout the opera, with his tonal periods. Perhaps Kurth chose not to review available and acknowledged motivic analyses of the Prelude.[50] This is not to say that he ignores leitmotifs altogether. Throughout the lengthy discussion of "endless melody," Kurth closely examines their use in *Tristan*—how they are deployed compositionally, how they become fragmented and interlocked, and most importantly, how they achieve dramatic impact through psychological associations. In those discussions, harmony does not figure prominently.

Whether he is focusing on melody or on harmony, Kurth assumes the reader will integrate one phase of his analytical work with another, previously outlined phase. He apparently did not feel obligated to correlate different sets of analytical findings, even though they might be suggestively complementary. For instance, one example of harmonic-melodic cooperation would be Kurth's "subdominant" cadence in measures 10–11, E^7 to B^7 harmony, as a harmonic "darkening" that leads to the Fate-Motive. Also, the passage beginning in measure 18, with the hint at C major and eventual shift to D minor, is marked by a motivic shift away from the chromatic Love-Motive to the diatonic Glance-Motive.

When commenting on form, Kurth does not assemble all of his observations into a practical analytic method. He introduces various approaches, applies them selectively, and then suggests further applications, variations, and avenues of investigation. He himself does not always fully develop his ideas theoretically or analytically. Perhaps he did not have enough time in the three short years between publishing *Grundlagen* and *Romantische Harmonik* to work out all the details and implications of his ideas, or to test them on large sections of Wagner's music. He may already have been studying Bruckner's symphonies and planning the *Bruckner* monograph, which does work out and apply certain notions only suggested in *Romantische Harmonik*. In *Romantische Harmonik*, Kurth generalizes about large-scale form based on limited model analyses. He no doubt also relied on his unpublished investigations; for years of listening experience surely guided his analytical work.

It was left for Alfred Lorenz to confirm or dispute Kurth's findings through extensive macro-formal analysis. In areas of mutual interest, Kurth and Lorenz largely agree. Comparing the two theorists is difficult, however, since they deal with wholly different levels of the music. Lorenz organizes key areas of broad formal "periods" to reveal logical and coherent large-scale tonal structures, while Kurth analyzes chord-to-chord movements, organizing these to reveal a single uniform key area.[51] Another, even more fundamental, difference between Kurth and Lorenz is that the latter insists on certain fixed organizational schemes in Wagner's music, such as arch and bar forms. Without denying the possibility of such schemes, Kurth claims they are not the chief objective of formal analysis. He maintains that in *Tristan* "there are only a few parts which are uniformly rounded over long musical stretches." He attributes this lack of tonal closure to the nature of the drama. According to Kurth, the drama encouraged

> a compositional principle which, in contrast to Classicism and early Romanticism, . . . indulged more in a free modulatory development.

> Romanticism absolves itself from the return to the main key and sees its *main content* in the *modulatory transitions*.[52]

In an interesting metaphor, he likens eighteenth- and early nineteenth-century tonality to a "primary color," which in the late nineteenth century diffracts into a "play of colors."

Kurth's analyses—melodic, harmonic, and formal—seek to illuminate dramatic-poetic motivations, which in turn lead back to psychic motivations. His work is particularly revealing of Wagner's music precisely because it tries to relate word, tone, and action as they combine to produce the *Gesamtkunstwerk*. In this respect, Kurth stands out from among other theorists of his day, who concentrated more on technical aspects of melody and harmony than on their dramatic or psychological motivations. Lorenz, for example, is very specific about excluding such extramusical references from his work.[53] Kurth would argue that dissociating the poetry, events, personages, and so on from the music strips it of its essential meaning. The question is what one considers "purely musical." If individual harmonies are "reflexes from the unconscious," then the sum of all musical events, the form or shape of a piece, is a sonic record of the enduring psyche, an episode lifted from the stream of mental life.

NOTES

1. Eduard Hanslick, *Vom Musikalisch-Schönen*, 8th ed., rev., enl. (Leipzig: J. A. Barth, 1891; 1st ed., 1854), 74: "Der Inhalt der Musik sind *tönend bewegte Formen*." Hanslick's characterization of music as the nonspecific movement inherent in emotions, rather than as the specific emotions themselves (pp. 28, 32–33), closely resembles Kurth's views. Werner Abegg explains Hanslick's often misunderstood thesis in *Musikästhetik und Musikkritik bei Eduard Hanslick*, Studien zur Musikgeschichte des 19. Jahrhunderts, vol. 44 (Regensburg: Bosse, 1974), 47–48. Both Hanslick and Kurth reverse Friedrich W. Schelling's characterization of architecture as frozen music (*erstarrte Musik*) in "Besonderer Theil der Philosophie der Kunst," (1802–3; *Sämmtliche Werke* [Stuttgart und Augsburg: J. G. Cottáscher Verlag, 1859], 5:576). Goethe, too, in *Conversations with Eckerman* (March 23, 1829) had observed that "architecture is frozen music" ("Die Baukunst ist eine erstarrte Musik"). In *Bruckner*, 1:235n, Kurth attributes a similar description of music to Friedrich Schlegel but gives no reference.

2. Kurth, *Bruckner*, 1:234: "Form ist . . . kein Ruhe- sondern Spannungsbegriff . . . musikalische Form ist stets die in Schwebe gehaltene *Wechselwirkung von Kraft und deren Bezwingung in Umrissen.*"

3. *Bruckner*, 1:239: "Form ist weder das blosse Quellen der Gestaltung noch ihre blosse Ausrandung, sondern der Übergang, die wirkende Umsetzung von jener in diese. . . . In der Musik . . . ist Form weder Bewegung noch ihre überblickhaft gefasste Erstarrtheit, nicht Fluss noch Umriss, sondern der lebendige Kampf um die Erfassung des Fliessenden durch Halt am Festen." Contrast Kurth's views with August Reismann's: "Form is delimitation" ("Form ist Begrenzung"; *Lehrbuch der musikalischen Komposition*, vol. 1 [Berlin: Guttentag, 1866], 2). August Reismann's work is discussed briefly in Birgitte Moyer's study "Concepts of Musical Form in the Nineteenth Century with Special Emphasis on Adolf Bernhard Marx and Sonata Form" (Ph.D. dissertation, Stanford University, 1969), 132.

4. Kurth, *Bruckner*, 1:233: "Form ist nicht das wovon der Strom des Schaffens ausgeht, sondern worein er mündet."

5. Although Kurth employs the terms given here fairly consistently, he does not define them strictly. They are found in *Bruckner*, 1:281 (*Teilwelle*), 279 (*Entwicklungswelle* and *symphonische Welle*), 301 (*Entladung*), 305 (*Tiefenwelle*), 322 (*Nachwelle*). Kurth warns that these expressions are only descriptive analogies and are not to be taken as literal comparisons with natural phenomena (ibid., 253).

6. Hans Hubert Schönzeler gives a full account of the various versions of Bruckner's symphonies, including a history of their evolution, in his *Bruckner* (New York: Grossman Publishers, 1970), 80, 171–78. The *New Grove Dictionary of Music and Musicians*, s.v. "Bruckner," 3:360–62, provides a summary of the various editions of the symphonies. Recent information on the versions is available in Franz Grasberger, ed., *Bruckner Symposium: "Die Fassungen"* (Linz: Anton Bruckner Institute, 1981).

7. The missing sections correspond to measures 322–53 and 374–459 (pp. 141–45 and pp. 148–58) in Nowak's 1951 edition. The fourth movement of the Fourth Symphony also underwent a significant abbreviation, amounting to about forty measures (Nowak ed., mm. 383–430).

8. In *Bruckner*, 2:603n, Kurth explains his use of piano transcriptions and pocket-scores editions, and adds "We must reckon with the possibility that entire sections of symphonies have been omitted in the printed scores as a result of misguided recommendations from Bruckner's students. Just how far this proves correct is impossible to determine until a *scholarly edition of the complete works* brings the original versions to light" ("Es ist dabei mit der Möglichkeit zu rechnen, dass ganze Symphonieteile in den gedruckt Partituren infolge missverstehender Ratschläge von Bruckners Schülern fortgeblieben sind. Wie weit dies zutrifft, entzieht sich wohl noch so lange der Feststellbarkeit, bis eine *wissenschaftliche Gesamtausgabe* die Urfassungen ans Licht fördert").

9. Schönzeler compliments Kurth for his "excellent work" but dutifully qualifies his remarks because of the edited scores Kurth used (Schönzeler, *Bruckner*, 179). Kurth's *Bruckner*, 2:1317–19, praises Max Auer's *Anton Bruckner* (Zurich: Amalthea-Verlag, 1923), Oskar Lang's *Anton Bruckner* (Munich: Beck, 1924), and above all, August Halm's *Die Symphonie Anton Bruckners* (Munich: Müller, 1914). On pp. 1313–25, Kurth provides a selective, annotated bibliography of works dealing with Bruckner.

10. Stefan Kunze, "Bruckner und Bern: Ernst Kurth zu Ehren," *Info, Zeitschrift der Bernischen Musikgesellschaft* (June 1980): "Bedeutende Bücher veralten nicht. Und sogar ihre Irrtümer bleiben aktueller als tausend triviale Richtigkeiten."

11. Kurth, *Grundlagen*, 408: "With polyphonic forms, the [linear aspect] is . . . always the primary and determinative factor" ("Bei den Formen der Polyphonie ist . . . stets [das Lineare] das Primäre und Bestimmende").

12. Kurth describes and demonstrates these procedures in *Grundlagen*, 251–56, 395–408.

13. Ibid., 409–10.

14. Ibid., 411: "Das Zwischenspiel als eine 'Episode' zu definieren, in ihm nur den Begriff von 'neben-

sächlichem,' weil nicht der thematischen Durchführung angehörigem Formteil zu sehen, das vermochte nur eine Betrachtungsweise, die in Anklammerung an die *äussere* Anschauung die gangbare musikalische Formenlehre schuf."

15. Ibid., 411: "Die Aufgabe des Zwischenspiels liegt in einem Ausgleich von Bewegungen, in der Fortsetzung einer angebahnten Entwicklung, dem subtilen Gleichgewichtsspiel von Steigerungen und allmählichen Spannungslösungen; es dient dem Ineinanderführen von Bewegungen und der Verbindung von grösseren Komplexen innerhalb der ganzen Form." Hugo Riemann expresses a similar thought in his *Katechismus der Fugen-Komposition,* vol. 1, v.

16. Ibid., 415. The linking passage in measures 5–7 of the Fugue in C Minor, *WTC* I, functions similarly, here as a descent leading to a renewed thematic exposition.

17. Kurth, *Grundlagen,* 411: "The linking passage is nothing more than an overriding *Fortspinnung* encroaching upon the *polyphonic* linear developments" ("Das Zwischenspiel ist nichts als eine über die Linienentwicklungen der *Mehr*stimmigkeit übergreifende *Fortspinnung*").

18. Ibid., 408–38, on "Consolidation and Dissolution of Thematic Movement" ("Verdichtung und Auflösung der thematischen Bewegung"). Kurth discusses "The Process of Thematic Dissolution in the Melody of Linking Passages" beginning on page 417.

19. The tail of the fugue subject (m. 2 of the fugue, beats three and four) already simplifies the initial indirect arpeggiation that characterizes the head motive of the subject.

20. In *Romantische Harmonik,* Kurth does hint at the dynamic implications of tonal form, but he does not develop the idea very far. For example, he states that "the tonal development flows freely *in waves*" (emphasis mine), and likens the persistence of one key in Romantic music to a pedal point, employed "usually at the onset and preparation of large buildups" (p. 329: "Die Tonartsentwicklung strömt frei in Wellen aus"; p. 330: "meist als Ansatz und Vorbereitung grosser Steigerungen"). He also identifies the basis of form as "development, intensification, transition, and tension discharge" (ibid., 333), all dynamic concepts, without documenting them by musical example. He discusses these and other dynamic interpretations of tonal phenomena in *Bruckner.*

21. Kurth, *Romantische Harmonik,* 315. Kurth also calls this tendency a tonal "rounding off" (*Rundung;* ibid., 314).

22. Ibid., 328–29:

> Man kann den Gegensatz der Spätromantik zum Klassizismus so kennzeichnen, dass dieser bei aller Vergrösserung der Proportionen und bei noch so weitgehenden Tonartsausweichungen die geschlossene Bogenführung, die tonale *Zusammengehörigkeit* betont, die Romantik hingegen . . . die ausflutenden Kräfte, die unendlichen *Ausweichungsmöglichkeiten.* . . . Daher ist selbst bei geschlossenen Formen, die in die Haupttonart zurückkehren, diese vielfach nur mehr in die Ferne gerückter Untergrund, verdeckt und überwuchert durch alle Abschweifungen.

23. Ibid., 332.

24. Ibid., 280. Kurth also speaks of tonal "extension" (*Weitung*). He discusses these processes also on pp. 306 and 328. Interior and exterior expansion usually occur together and so complement one another.

25. Kurth's Example 131 (*Romantische Harmonik,* 226), the Sleep-Motive from *Walküre,* II, 3 (Schirmer, 297–98), illustrates an interior expansion. The harmonic pillars there, spaced at two-measure intervals, are related by thirds. Kurth's description of exterior and interior expansion might be extended to include other tonal phenomena. Exterior expansion, for example, might also be invoked to associate related key areas that stand at considerable distance from one another, with one or more subordinate key areas intervening. Alfred Lorenz relies on just such exterior expansions when demonstrating tonal unity in *Das Rheingold* (*Das Geheimnis der Form bei Richard Wagner,* vol. 1 [Berlin: Hesse, 1924], 27), and even in the whole of the *Ring* cycle (p. 48). Interior expansion might also be used to describe relationships among chords in immediate succession, as in absolute progressions.

26. Kurth, *Romantische Harmonik,* 327: "die Bedeutung des *Klanges* wird durch die Bedeutung der

Spannung ganz verdrängt. Des *Klanges* bedarf es nicht mehr, wenn nur die gegen ihn gerichtete *Willensstrebung* vorhanden ist. Sie genügt für das Tonarts- und Tonikaempfinden, genügt nicht nur, sondern ist in viel höherem, intensiverem Masse sein Träger."

27. Ibid., 314–83, "Tonale Entwicklungslinien." Part 5 consists of two chapters. The first one, "Paths of Harmonic Expansion" ("Harmonische Entwicklungslinien"), which covers tonal form, is the shorter of the two (pp. 314–33). Chapter 2 is entitled "Paths of Melodic Incursion" ("Melodische Durchbrechungswege"); it covers sequential techniques and other melodic phenomena as they influence harmonic procedures.

28. The reader may refer to Examples 6-3 and 8-16 for discussion and analyses of the chords.

29. For Kurth, this amounts to a calculated weakening of tonic harmony (*Romantische Harmonik*, 318).

30. The emphasis on tonic in measures 7–9 further clarifies this harmonic interpretation. Kurth, however, hears allusions to VI^7 and IV^9 in measures 7–9 (ibid., 251). IV^9 in measures 8–9 would, of course, support Kurth's argument for a subdominant-dominant progression over measures 1–10.

31. Kurth discusses extratonal sequences in *Romantische Harmonik*, 350–53. Extratonal sequences resemble extratonal progressions with the linear network being governed by a sequential pattern.

32. Ibid., 353: "Das melodische Motiv der Sequenz zersetzt sich; diese erfährt demnach am Schluss schlechtweg eine Auflösung in freies Weiterströmen der Stimmen und damit auch der Klänge, alles gerät ins Fliessen und strömt bis zur Einmündung in den Schlussakkord abwärts." Note that the falling fourth in the bass, from f to c with *crescendo* (mm. 14–15), imitates the B♮–F₁ falling fourth, with *crescendo,* in measures 1–2. This similarity lends support to Kurth's reading of a IV^7–I progression in measures 1–2.

33. Ibid., 317: "Der grosse *tonale* Zusammenhang ist . . . durch die Anfangs- und Endakkorde gewahrt. . . . Jene Akkorde stellen untereinander ein höchst einfaches, abgerundetes Kadenzieren in f-moll dar, mit einer Zwischendominante . . . [und] sonst mit lauter Akkordstufen der Haupttonart selbst."

34. Ibid., 317.

35. Ibid., 318: "statt einzelner Akkorde ganze Entwicklungen nisten zwischen den eigentlichen Tonartsklängen ein."

36. Ibid., 318: "ein Prinzip, dessen Verallgemeinerung sich von selbst ergibt, und das tausenderlei Durchführungsmöglichkeiten im einzelnen umfasst."

37. I review Kurth's analysis here, first given in chapter 6, simply for ease of reference.

38. Ibid., 320: "dies wäre eine Erklärungsweise, die mehr analytisch als synthetisch vorgeht; denn sie ist zwar der Ausdruck der vorliegenden Klangverhältnisse, . . . nicht aber die Darstellung ihres *genetischen* Zusammenhanges, der gerade zu dieser Reihenfolge der Funktionen führte."

39. Ibid., 319: "These initial measures of the Prelude are, tonally, nothing more than a *broad dominant upbeat*" ("diese ersten Takte des Vorspiels bilden in tonaler Hinsicht nichts anderes als einen *breiten dominantischen Auftakt*"). In a well-known contemporary analysis of this music, William Mitchell explains measures 1–13 of the Prelude in the same way. Mitchell's work appears in "The Tristan Prelude: Techniques and Structure," *The Music Forum*, vol. 1 (New York: Columbia University Press, 1967), 169.

40. Neither Alfred Lorenz nor Hugo Leichtentritt, who published important studies on form in the 1920s, mentions Kurth's prophetic analysis (Lorenz, *Tristan*, 13–15; Leichtentritt, *Musikalische Formenlehre*, 3d ed. [Leipzig: Brietkopf und Härtel, 1927], 367–70).

41. Kurth, *Romantische Harmonik*, 320–21: "Während die blosse Betrachtung der Klangfunktionen mehr den Zusammenhalt der drei Lösungsakkorde festlegt und die Abstützung der gelockerten harmonischen Entwicklung gegen den Boden der Tonalität hin rekonstruiert, sind mit der Erklärungsweise von der in den Lösungsgrundtönen enthaltenen dominantischen Entwicklung mehr die zu Weiterungen leitenden, dezentralisierenden Wege herausgehoben."

42. Ibid., 322–24.

43. Ibid., 324–25: "die tonale Entwicklung zeigt sich hier dadurch geweitet, dass *nicht,* wie in kleinen

Zusammenhängen *einzelne Klänge, sondern grössere Proportionen,* ganze Satzpartien auf die Gesamttonalität Bezug haben. . . . an Stelle einfacher Tonartsakkorde ganze Satzpartien die Tonika umspielen."

44. Kurth declines to call the G-major harmony in measure 19 a VII in A minor since, as he says, it clearly refers to the relative major. The resolution to C-major harmony is the strongest arrival since the deceptive cadence in measure 17. Beginning in that bar, the soprano line proceeds diatonically for the first time, pointing clearly toward the key of C major.

45. Louis and Thuille, *Harmonielehre,* 240–61, specifically 246. August Halm's *Harmonielehre,* also well known to Kurth, discusses chromatic modulation on pp. 100–102.

46. David Beach gives a historical survey of eighteenth- and nineteenth-century theoretical views of the six-four chord in "The Function of the Six-Four Chord in Tonal Music," *Journal of Music Theory* 11.1 (1967): 4–11.

47. Max Arend recognized the contrapuntal function of the G-minor six-four chord: "The G-minor triad of the third eighth [in m. 20] is only a passing chord" ("Der g-moll-Dreiklang des 3. Achtels ist blosser Durchgangsakkord"; "Tristanvorspiel," 164). Several theorists from Kirnberger onward cite examples resembling Example 9-13. J. A. P. Schulz comments on the eighteenth-century treatment of the passing six-four chord in *"The True Principles for the Practice of Harmony,"* 176–77. Simon Sechter gives a nineteenth-century view in *Grundsätze,* 1:39–40. Georg Capellen, writing in the early twentieth century, offers a uniquely creative account of the six-four chord in "Der Quartsextakkord, seine Erklärung und seine Zukunft," *Sammelbände der Internationalen Musikgesellschaft* 3 (1901–2): 167–83.

48. Kurth says specifically that in assigning roman numerals he ignores chordal inversions since "they have no organic meaning" ("sie haben keine organische Bedeutung"; *Romantische Harmonik,* 45). In light of this statement, Kurth's analysis becomes more understandable, but the ramifications of his remark, equalizing all positions of a chord under all circumstances, are extreme.

49. Lorenz, *Tristan,* 17, says Kurth goes "too far" in asserting that the tonic is missing altogether in the Prelude. He analyzes the music in measures 18–24 in A minor, with the last chord in measure 24 as a tonic variant (T^+). Max Arend, on the other hand, writing twenty years before *Romantische Harmonik,* agrees with Kurth's hearing of the A-major chord in measure 24 as a subdominant ("Tristanvorspiel," 165). Observe that the music does turn clearly toward E major/minor in measure 23, confirming it in measures 25–26.

50. Analyses of the time include Karl Grunsky, "Das Vorspiel und der I. Akt von 'Tristan und Isolde,'" *Richard Wagner-Jahrbuch* 2 (1907): 207–84; and Siegfried Anheisser, "Das Vorspiel zu 'Tristan und Isolde' und seine Motivik," *Zeitschrift für Musikwissenschaft* 3 (1920–21): 257–304. Motivic analyses of the Prelude continue today; see, for example, Roland Jackson's "Leitmotive and Form in the *Tristan* Prelude," *Music Review* 36 (1975): 42–53.

51. Lorenz distinguishes himself from Kurth in *Tristan,* 10–11. He credits Kurth with uncovering and describing better than anyone "the many elegant features of the music of *Tristan*" ("die vielen feinen Züge der Tristanmusik"). Lorenz, by contrast, sets out to explain the "skeleton" (*Knochengerüst*), the foundation of the work as a whole. Kurth's *Romantische Harmonik* and Lorenz's *Tristan* thus complement one another, as Lorenz himself notes.

52. Kurth, *Romantische Harmonik,* 315: "nur noch wenig Teile sich finden, die auf lange Vertonungsstrecken einheitlich gerundet sind"; "ein Vertonungsprinzip förder[t], das im Gegensatze zu Klassizismus und Frühromantik . . . sich mehr einer freien modulatorischen Entwicklung hingab"; ibid., 329: "die Romantik löst sich von der Rückleitung in die Haupttonart . . . und erblickt in den *modulatorischen Übergängen* den *Hauptinhalt.*"

53. Lorenz, *Tristan,* 4: "Only when one first frees himself from the association to the poetry can one hope for advancement in understanding the purely musical value of the music drama" ("nur so, wenn man sich zunächst von der Beziehung zur Dichtung freimacht, kann man für die Erkenntnis der rein musikalischen Werte des Musikdramas Förderliches erhoffen").

CHAPTER 10

Conclusion

Chapter 1 of this study provides information on the sources of Kurth's ideas in musical as well as nonmusical writings from the late nineteenth and early twentieth centuries. This final chapter supplements the first by adding to and interpreting the historical context of Kurth's work in order that his place in the history of music theory may be better understood.[1] First, we will take a look at the relationship between his writings and those of his contemporaries. That discussion will lead us to distinguish between theory and analysis both in Kurth's work and in general. Finally, we will complete the historical context by identifying the influence of Kurth's ideas, or at least their spirit, in certain early twentieth-century and modern-day writings, and by offering some possible reasons for his eclipse as a theorist in the decades after his death.

Around the turn of the century, the compendious work of Hugo Riemann dominated the music-theoretical arena. By 1900, this one incredibly prolific scholar had published numerous studies in the areas of speculative and practical theory. In the early 1890s he had crystallized his theory of tonal functions in *Vereinfachte Harmonielehre* (1893; trans. 1896), and in 1902 he came out with the first volume of *Grosse Kompositionslehre*. A few years earlier, he had brought together his extensive historical, theoretical, and paleographical investigations in what was the first and, until recently, the only history of music theory. In 1900, Riemann was acknowledged as a leading authority.[2] Around that time, though, there were already rumblings against his rigorously formal style of theory and analysis.

As mentioned in chapter 1, an antipositivist wave was on the rise at the turn of the twentieth century. Rather than examining only external, acoustical, or syntactical evidence in music as a basis for theory and analysis, certain authors in the years just after 1900 were turning toward internal, psychic evidence. One such author was Hermann Kretzschmar, who proposed a "hermeneutic" style of analysis. Kretzschmar sought to reveal the "mental content" (*geistiger Inhalt*) of musical art works and criticized formalist aestheticians, such as Hanslick, for hindering progress in that area of musical analysis.

Taking aim at theorists like Riemann, Kretzschmar gibes that purely technical analysis of music "distracts from the essence of the thing with formal hocus-pocus."[3] The aesthetician Karl Grunsky, writing in 1907, claims that "we barely pay attention to Hanslick any longer" since most musicians "admit and defend" music as an "expression of mental life."[4] Arnold Schering, a student of Kretzschmar, adopted and worked out in greater detail the hermeneutic approach. He, too, tried to establish connections between musical processes and those of psychic life in order to achieve through analysis a "psychic resonance" with the forces of tension and release, which for him characterize all music.[5] Besides reacting to formalism in music theory at the end of the nineteenth century, Kretzschmar, Schering, and later Kurth all reacted to Helmholtz's physio-acoustical and Carl Stumpf's psycho-acoustical approaches to music theory.

Given their search for psychic content in music and their attempts to heighten the re-creative listening process, the aural *experience* of music through analysis, we might describe Kretzschmar's, Schering's, and Kurth's theories as "experiential." We might then describe Helmholtz's and Riemann's theories as "material," since their premises rest on the physical and syntactical interpretation of materials, such as scales, intervals, chords, rhythm, and meter. All of these materials interact in a logical, quasi-scientific manner to produce coherent musical structures.[6]

Different from the "material" theories, and yet unlike the experiential ones, are those of Heinrich Schenker and the team of Rudolf Louis and Ludwig Thuille. The latter co-authors explicitly distinguish their work from a "purely scientific" approach to music; such an approach, they say, can lead to substituting "arbitrary constructions of the mind for real things and, instead of explaining these, [occupying] itself with contrivances of its own roaming imagination."[7] Schenker, too, disliked schematic, intellectualized explanations, but he had an even greater distaste for the then prevailing brand of "conservatory theory," such as that of Ernst Friedrich Richter, who becomes the butt of Schenker's criticism in *Harmony.*[8]

Riemann, Schenker, and Louis and Thuille, their ideological and methodological differences notwithstanding, all share a common concern for isolating and explaining the objective syntactical processes governing tonal relationships. They are all "material" in their theoretical dispositions, not in the sense that they emphasize purely acoustical matters, but rather that they emphasize technical matters of the object itself. Kretzschmar, Schering, and Kurth, as "experientialists," treat music as more than abstract sound structures. All of these men are, of course, interested in the structure of the sound. But while material theories are concerned chiefly with the structure of sound per se experiential theories are concerned with the structure of music as it relates to aural *experience* of it. To Kretzschmar, for instance, "absolute" music is no more feasible than absolute poetry, whose content, he muses, would presumably exhaust itself in rhyme and meter schemes.[9] Further, consider how Kurth defines the basic components of music: "Melody is motion"; "Harmonies are reflexes from the unconscious"; "Form is the subjugation of force through space and time." These definitions grow out of a psychological disposition toward music, a disposition that is absent or at least less pronounced in the "material" theories.[10]

The distinction I have made here between material-theoretic and experiential-theoretic approaches to music brings up another important distinction, the one between theory and analysis as they apply to these two approaches. Roughly speaking, theory generalizes while analysis individualizes. The two overlap, of course, because in the act of explaining and individualizing musical events, the analyst often tacitly relies on certain generalized ideas about how tones, chords, rhythms, and so on combine to produce the individual events in the first place. The question, then, is where the emphasis lies, on the individual event as an example or validation of an explicit generalized notion (theory), or on the individual event itself, and its unique effect and role in a particular context.[11]

Our question here is what role theory and analysis play within the two branches of music study distinguished above, material and experiential. Does Kurth have a theory of music, and if he does, what is it and how does his experiential-theoretic disposition relate to it? If not, how then do we respond to his various analyses and analytical strategies?

In an article of around fifteen years ago, William Thompson says several things about the nature of analysis that might apply to both material and experiential-theoretic modes. In order to get at the nature and goals of analysis, Thompson wonders about aspects of music not inherent in the tones themselves, and about the role of a listener perceiving and mentally constructing music. He writes:

> It would seem . . . that the essential thrust of analysis must be toward the kind of human personal attunement that renders us more capable of apprehending that which lies potential within the musical object. And a part of successful apprehension has very much to do with what the apprehender brings with him. . . . [T]he central role of analysis is to intensify and perfect our individual preoccupations with the decoding of the musical message as auditory images.[12]

Now if we assume that the potentialities "within the musical object" are abstract syntactical structures, we are dealing with a material-theoretic attitude. Analysis, then, will "intensify and perfect our individual preoccupations with the decoding of the musical message" as idealized sound structures. Such analysis is, in Dahlhaus's words, "theoretically oriented." It seeks out the individual to the extent that it confirms the presence and expected behavior of such idealized structures, thus in turn validating the theory. With such a material-theoretic stance, analysis may assume the character of a science or an ideology, as Joseph Kerman implies of "formalistic" criticism, and Thompson of "style analysis."[13]

But if we assume that Thompson's potentialities are psycho-auditive structures of the sort that interest Kurth, and not abstract syntactical structures, then we are dealing with an experiential-theoretic stance. Here, too, analysis seeks out the individual, but instead of idealizing it, analysis highlights its uniqueness as an affective event embedded in an overall psycho-auditive structure manifested in the piece. The results of this sort of "aesthetically oriented" analysis (Dahlhaus) may produce a general theory about how melody and harmony operate, without necessarily producing a theoretical *system* that prescribes or predicts details of their behavior.

In an experiential-theoretic mode, Kurth does theorize about music in various ways. For example, he establishes some important melodic and harmonic procedures. Recall Kurth's ideas of apparent voices, overriding lines, and curvilinear developments in Bach's music, as well as his general notion of polyphonic harmony with its implication of kinetic-linear energy. Kurth's conception of polyphonic homophony in Wagner's music, with its sensuous and energetic aspects, includes the ideas of neighbor-note insertion and other techniques of the alteration style, as well as those of extratonal progressions and basic pillars. All of these are theories of how melodies and chords behave, and of how we might orient our hearing toward them. Kurth identifies these procedures and tries to establish how and to what purpose they are applied compositionally. But he does not build a normative mechanism governing those procedures. He is a systematic researcher, but he does not systematize.

Furthermore, Kurth theorizes about the philosophical roots of music. Humanist that he is, Kurth lavishes much attention on this part of his writings. His idealist conception of music and its link with his psychological theories were discussed in chapter 1; suffice it to say here, then, that these philosophical and psychological ideas are essential to Kurth's analytical activity. They are, therefore, also essential to our understanding of him.

At the end of his publishing career, Kurth finally theorizes about the cognitive processes involved in understanding the various musical processes he had explored in *Grundlagen, Romantische Harmonik,* and *Bruckner.* In *Musikpsychologie,* he assembles his various lines of inquiry and builds an overall theory of music; it is a psychological theory, with different, perhaps less utilitarian goals than someone of a material-theoretic persuasion might prefer. Studying *Musikpsychologie* will enlighten those interested in human cognitive activities but may not necessarily lead to better "structural" analysis of music from the material-theoretical standpoint.

Using language introduced here, we should perhaps differentiate Kurth's work from that of one of his most important contemporaries, Heinrich Schenker. In chapters 2 and 4, I briefly contrasted their views on trans-local melodic continuities. I tried to show that, although the results of their analyses appear at times to be similar, the conceptual foundations of their analytical approaches are essentially different. According to our classification of basic theoretical attitudes, Schenker belongs in the material-theoretic camp; he is interested in music as syntactical structure. His analyses are "theoretically oriented," are of the rigorously generalizing and systematic type, and are aimed at validating idealized sound patterns. Kurth, by contrast, is interested in psycho-auditive patterns. His analyses are "aesthetically oriented" and are of the individualizing type. They are meant to exemplify possible realizations of the musical procedures he identifies and to validate certain psycho-auditive theories, not idealized syntactical ones.

Even with these basic conceptual differences, Kurth's and Schenker's analytical interests do overlap, which has led readers to compare the two men, often to Kurth's disadvantage. Two cases in point are their mutual interests in broadly unfolding melodic continuities (Kurth's overriding lines, Schenker's linear progressions) and in large-scale harmonic progressions (Kurth's basic pillars, Schenker's scale steps). Chapter 4 compares overriding lines and linear progressions; it is the apparent overlap between these two analytical findings that has spawned the most criticism of Kurth.[14] The differences between the two points of view, however, are a specific manifestation of the general difference between experiential and material-theoretic viewpoints. What is "right" according to the one viewpoint may prove "wrong" from the other or, in less categorical instances, the two viewpoints may complement one another, affording a broader perspective than was possible with a single approach.

Little attention has been drawn to the overlap between Kurth's basic pillars and Schenker's scale steps. Kurth develops his idea in a search for points of tonal stability in music featuring extratonal progressions, where the harmony is given over to extended chromatic motion. Schenker proposes his idea of scale steps primarily in connection with clearly diatonic music. In all of his examples, save one, he is pointing out the difference between higher-level scale steps and lower-level chords, which relate directly to the scale steps in a clear diatonic way, as local dominants or applied dominants.[15] In Kurth's examples, for the most part the subsidiary chords have no direct tonal relationship with the surrounding basic pillars. They are chromatic-contrapuntal connectors leading from pillar to pillar. In *Harmony* (1906), Schenker's language already hints at the idea of prolongation; a harmony is "unfolded" (p. 143) by several related chords. Kurth's examples in *Romantische Harmonik* are very different. His pillars are not "prolonged." Rather, chromatic voice-leading chords, often in sequences (extratonal sequences), bridge the distance between pillars without "unfolding" them.[16]

Kurth and Schenker share some similar philosophical views, but they differ in their theoretical expressions of those views. William Pastille, and others before him, have pointed out Schenker's German idealist roots. Kurth, too, is an idealist. But Schenker's idealism manifests itself in the distinction between the readily apparent foreground ("appearance") and the less apparent, concealed middleground and background levels of a piece ("reality").[17] Kurth's idealism, on the other hand, manifests itself in the distinction between sonic music and its psychic roots—between the twists and turns of a melody, or different shades of harmony, and their psychic motivations. Here again, we have a contrast between a material and an experiential-theoretic disposition.

In addition to idealism, Pastille identifies a second important characteristic of Schenker's thinking, morphology, the "science of change and transformation."[18] Morphology is the ideological basis on which rests Schenker's important theory of structural levels, and the technique of reduction is the means by which Schenker illustrates morphological evolution. The reductive technique takes us systematically from the foreground to the first and "higher" levels of middleground until, in the final reductive stage, we reach the background (*Ursatz*). Scanning "down" rather than "up" these levels, we can see the morphological evolution as we trace it from the idealized primordial kernel to the particularized surface of the music.

Kurth's notion of melodic and harmonic levels is not as elaborate as Schenker's. First, Kurth posits only two levels: local and trans-local. Second, and more importantly for distinguishing the two men, Kurth's levels are not related morphologically, the way Schenker's are, but rather psycho-auditively. Because Kurth's analytical criteria for deriving apex lines are so different from Schenker's criteria for moving between the foreground and even the lowest level of middleground, comparing him with Schenker is misleading, even though superficially their ideas appear similar.[19] Kurth's bi-dimensional melody and harmonic pillars lack the systematic morphological integration of Schenker's structural levels. This is less an apology for Kurth than an observation that different theoretical premises may lead to different analytical results.[20]

Throughout my discussion, I have invoked a distinction between material and experiential-theoretic premises. I have related Kurth's experiential premises to the hermeneutics of Kretzschmar and Schering, and to the aesthetic ideas of Grunsky. I have not yet mentioned what was, I believe, more of a guiding influence on Kurth than the writings of any of these men. I am thinking of the wave of educational reform and its ideological foundations which took hold in Germany during the decade before the First World War. The reform movement arose in reaction to the mechanical, personality-stifling education common in Bismarck's Empire. In chapter 1, I discussed Kurth's one-year stint as a teacher in the Free Community School at Wickersdorf, modeled after Hermann Lietz's country boarding schools (*Landerziehungsheime*). Under Gustav Wyneken and later Martin Luserke, Wickersdorf became one of the leading experimental grade-schools during the prewar height of educational reform in the areas of cultural and especially music education.[21] I should mention, too, that Kretzschmar's and Schering's early work on hermeneutics grew out of a dissatisfaction with music education in primary and secondary schools, and out of a desire to raise the level of understanding and appreciation for art music among middle-class citizens.

Advocates of the "new" or "progressive" education, as it was called in the 1920s, emphasized experience as the most effective mode of learning. The battle cry of prewar reformers was "Begin with the child."[22] They adopted the philosophy of Johann Pestalozzi (1746–1827), who a century earlier had placed experience and self-directed activity at the heart of education. Pestalozzi's approach was carried on by Johann F. Herbart (1776–1841) and Friedrich Froebel (1782–1852), who trained at Pestalozzi's Yverdon Institute, and who directly inspired late nineteenth- and early twentieth-century reformers like Georg Kerschensteiner, Hermann Lietz, and Wyneken in Germany, as well as Francis W. Parker (of the "Quincy Movement") in the United States.

In 1930, nearly two decades after he left Wickersdorf, Kurth wrote about his work there. I have already described his approach to music instruction, which avoided technical language and instead made effective use of imagery and metaphor to teach grade-school pupils about music's complexities. Kurth's music instruction, like his colleagues' teaching of other subjects in Wickersdorf and elsewhere, stressed intuitive experience as the path to understanding. Reflecting back on Wickersdorf, Kurth wrote:

> Personal involvement becomes the focus, the actual playing of music is just one part. Supported by discussion, it serves the musical *experience* [emphasis mine].
>
> The understanding of music can . . . be built up gradually from the pure training of instinct.[23]

Simple as this method may sound, in practice, Kurth remarks, it takes a gifted pedagogue. According to his students, Kurth was such a teacher.

The experiential approach to analysis that I have attributed to Kurth is, in a loose sense, phenomenological, if we understand phenomenological to mean an active experiencing (*Erleben*) and consciousness (*Bewusstsein*) of musical works. The connection with Kurth's work seems plain enough, and timely, too, since Edmund Husserl's writings were gaining recognition in the decade from 1910 to 1920, when Kurth wrote *Voraussetzungen, Grundlagen,* and *Romantische Harmonik.* In the context of experiential analysis, phenomenological inquiry entails selective (often tacit) reliance on ideas inherited from traditional music theory as a means of describing musical events, but not as the sole means, and certainly not to the end of validating some aspect of traditional theory. In the years around 1920, several musicians tried to apply phenomenological thinking to the study of music. Hans Mersmann, for example, published an "Essay on Phenomenology of Music" in 1922, and Paul Bekker an *Outline of a Phenomenology of Music* in 1925.[24] Just months before Mersmann's article appeared, Arthur W. Cohn's essay "Musical Understanding: New Goals" was published posthumously in the same journal. In it, Cohn decries the overmechanization and intellectualization of culture, and calls for a new type of musical "understanding," one based on phenomenological principles which he sketches out. It is noteworthy that both Cohn and Mersmann, the first writers to connect phenomenology explicitly with music study, mention Kurth, among others (Kretzschmar, Schering, Halm, Grunsky), as exemplifying their ideas.[25]

Now although Kurth's work does exemplify a phenomenological attitude, it is not *strictly* phenomenological, not in Husserl's sense or, indeed, in Mersmann's or Cohn's. In the same way Taylor Greer shows that Thomas Clifton departs from Husserl's principles, we too can show that Kurth is not genuinely phenomenological.[26] For instance, Kurth does not consciously disengage himself, philosophically or analytically, from preconceptions about music (Husserl's *epoche*). Consequently, he cannot arrive at true Husserlian "essences." Perhaps such orthodoxy is too much to ask of a thinker dealing with music, which is burdened with so many ideas, both intra- and extramusical. But even under Cohn's and Mersmann's modified guidelines for phenomenology, Kurth does not qualify unconditionally. Cohn, for instance, says that musical understanding must be achieved without interpreting musical events as "symbols of any sort of psychic motions of its creator." Similarly, Mersmann demands that phenomenological inquiry, in contrast to psychological inquiry, remove its object (the art work) from all "I-relations" (*Ichbeziehungen*).[27] Kurth's psycho-auditive premises do not comply with either of these requirements. His approach to analysis, while not exactly "psychologistic," is perhaps more psychological than phenomenologists would allow.

Kurth's style of analysis does fall within the framework of current thinking in musical phenomenology, conceptually at least, as exemplified in essays by Philip Batstone and Lawrence Ferrara.[28] Batstone calls his "ad hoc" analysis phenomenological because it is concerned with "perceived *relationships*," not just with sensuous responses, and because "it leads back to the music rather than providing conclusions." He wishes to focus on the particularities of music as aural phenomena, "without a priori worrying about what we think we can or do hear."[29]

Ferrara, like Kurth before him, seems to be reacting to analytical formalism. Invoking Michael Polanyi's notion of "personal knowledge," Ferrara questions scientific objectivity in general and asserts that traditional methods of musical analysis do not "objectify the conclusions drawn by the analyst." He goes on to complain about the "dominant position of the method in relation to the work," and about the restrictiveness of such a method, which "[forces] what one can know and report about [a] work into the matrix of categorical characteristics that constitute the method."[30] Although Ferrara may not know Kurth's work, like Kurth, he takes the music to be

> a dynamic interplay of the world of the composer symbolically transformed into a musical language. . . . It is this polyphonic texture of syntactical, semantic, and ontological meanings that is an important part of any functioning, *experiential* work [emphasis mine].[31]

I have discussed at length Kurth's relationship to trends of his day in an attempt to build a historical context for his work. Kurth, along with several other authors, belongs to an early twentieth-century branch of reform which produced a genre of music-theoretical literature that is relatively unfamiliar today. His influence is alive, though, in certain writings that are more familiar to us. Because Kurth was widely read by musicians in both academic and nonacademic circles in the 1930s and 1940s, we can expect to see some effect of his ideas on writers active in the immediately following decades. This is indeed the case, although tracing Kurth's influence is not easy. The basis of his work, dynamism, was and still is widely acknowledged, making it difficult to demonstrate specific influences. Unless a writer speaks of musical dynamism in language resembling Kurth's, we may only be dealing with a common appreciation for dynamic qualities of music by theorists, composers, performers, and critics. It would be misleading, then, to single out Kurth as the source of such ideas. Still, the work of several authors, notably composers, exhibits ties to Kurth's mode of thought and expression.

Grundlagen, stressing as it did melodic independence and complex polyphonic textures, confirmed for composers of the 1920s the spirit of the then prevalent Back-to-Bach movement. Proponents of the newly emerging style invoked the principles expounded in *Grundlagen,* to Kurth's great annoyance, as theoretical justification for their music.[32] Ernst Krenek clearly had "linear counterpoint" in mind when he wrote to Kurth in 1921 to ask for guidance in teaching counterpoint. When he visited Kurth a few years later, Krenek was disappointed to learn that Kurth was not an "apostle of modernism."[33] Still, in the eyes of early twentieth-century composers, Kurth had established a link with the past by sketching so convincingly the stylistic continuity from Bach through Wagner and Debussy. He thereby verified the evolutionary character of their music and, in a sense, gave it academic and aesthetic respectability. If music academics found Kurth's ideas too unorthodox, composers found them philosophically and technically instructive.

Ernst Toch (1887–1964) was one such composer. Toch's first publication, a theory of melody, shows a strong kinship with Kurth, but the relationship goes further than that.[34] In his book *The Shaping Forces in Music,* Toch discusses the natures of harmony, melody, counterpoint, and form. His ideas closely resemble those laid out in *Grundlagen* and *Romantische Harmonik.* For instance, about melody Toch says:

> The truth is that the melodic impulse is primary, and always preponde-
> rates over the harmonic [impulse]; that the melodic, or linear, impulse is
> the force out of which germinates not only harmony but also counterpoint
> and form. For the linear impulse is activated by *motion,* and motion
> means life, creation, propagation and formation.[35]

The language and tone of these general remarks clearly derive from Kurth. Specific ideas likewise can be traced to Kurth's works. For example, Toch combines Kurth's developmental motives and curvilinear developments to produce what he calls ascending, descending, and encircling "wave lines." The *Anschwung* characterizing the turn ornament in *Grundlagen* becomes Toch's "wind-up."[36] Concerning the genesis of harmony, Toch observes:

> Although harmony may still be defined as the combination of three or
> more tones, it has to be interpreted beyond this concept as a momentary
> situation brought about by moving voices; as the cross-section arising at
> times of arrested motion; or briefly and plainly as *arrested motion.*[37]

His "arrested motion" is a variation of Kurth's potential energy. Concerning form, Toch, like Kurth, cautions against confusing "form" with "forms." Forms are static organizational schemes, which according to Toch are the result, not the origin, of form. Further, along with Kurth Toch stresses the dynamic quality of form, whose essence he defines as "the *balance between tension and relaxation.*" [38]

Another composer who seems to have found much of interest in Kurth is Paul Hindemith. The very style of Hindemith's music, with its strong linear currents unfolding the harmonies, betokens a similarly high regard for melodic forces. There is in fact some documentation supporting Kurth's influence on Hindemith. In a letter of October 12, 1926, the composer recommended Kurth's "newer opinions on musical matters" to Fritz Jöde as alternatives to the dry, academic presentations Hindemith had heard at a Donaueschingen conference. David Neumeyer's recent authoritative book on Hindemith's music speculates that the composer's sharp criticism of Fux may go back to Kurth's diatribe against Fux for teaching counterpoint harmonically and thus destroying its linear essence. [39]

The clearest connection between Kurth and Hindemith is the latter's notion of "step-progression," the stepwise linkage of nonadjacent pitches. Neumeyer, in his exhaustive research on Hindemith's theories, cannot establish definitively whether Schenker's linear progressions or Kurth's overriding lines were the source of the composer's ideas. Given the nature of step-progression, though, in which the pitches do not require harmonic support and are not limited to particular intervals, or even to diatonic notes, Neumeyer leans heavily toward Kurth, rather than Schenker, as Hindemith's source. [40] Regarding melody, Hindemith follows Kurth's idea of an overarching primal melodic continuity, the phase of motion (*Bewegungszug*), out of which resolve individual melodic tones at a later stage of development. Hindemith articulates his version of this idea in the "Introductory Remarks" to the revised edition of *Marienleben* (1948): "Melody . . . does not remain confined to the explicit interval steps from each tone to the next, but is laid out in advance over longer periods, and then subdivided." [41] Here we can see that Hindemith the composer approaches the comprehensive *Bewegungszug* from a practical rather than theoretical point of view when he speaks of laying it out in advance. Still, Hindemith's view of melody for the most part corresponds to Kurth's notion of a *Bewegungszug*.

In general, Hindemith's ideas, like Kurth's, are rooted in dynamism. Hindemith speaks of the "will toward intensified motion dominat[ing] the contrapuntal structure in all its aspects," of the slow "waves of harmonies" rolling beneath and following the "surface-rooted melodic intervals." Further, concerning large-scale rhythmic form, Hindemith refers to the "powerful metric and rhythmic pulsating that organize the general temporal outlines of a musical form and divide it into movements and sections, peaks and valleys of intensity, and so on down to the very smallest subordinate units." [42] Hindemith's "peaks and valleys of intensity" sound very much like Kurth's dynamic-formal "waves."

The contemporary author who dealt most extensively with issues raised by Kurth, and who is ideologically closest to him, is Victor Zuckerkandl (1897–1965). Like Kurth, Zuckerkandl held that the "properly musical quality of tones" was their dynamic quality. For Zuckerkandl, music *proper* transcends the tones, which are essentially "dynamic symbols," indicators of directional forces. The essential content of music, then, is motion.

> Tones are elements of a musical context because and in so far as they are
> conveyors of a motion that goes through them and beyond them. When
> we hear music, what we hear is above all motions.[43]

Like Kurth, Zuckerkandl postulates a continuum of dynamic forces, a "dynamic field," which endows the tones with directional energies.

> The tones of our tonal system are events in a dynamic field, and each
> tone, as it sounds, gives expression to the exact constellation of force
> present at the point in the field at which the tone is situated.[44]

Tones within the field represent directional forces of varying intensity. They move either away from or toward scale degrees one and eight, which Zuckerkandl calls scalar "anchors." Within this framework, scale degree five acts as a kind of crossroads, a point of equilibrium where movement away from one anchor becomes movement toward the other.[45]

Besides Zuckerkandl, a few other noncomposers pursued Kurth's ideas. Kurt Huber, for instance, published a study on "elementary musical motives" in 1923, just three years after *Romantische Harmonik* appeared. Huber builds on Kurth's notion of "primordial motives" (*Urmotive*).[46] Kurth's concept of form shows up in the writings of Kurt Westphal, who contrasts "forms" with "forming." Like Kurth, Westphal understands form as a psycho-auditive, dynamic process, a holistic phenomenon best characterized as an "evolutionary curve" (*Verlaufskurve*). Once revealed, such a curve illuminates the creative process itself.[47] Kurt von Fischer, in his first full-scale published work, examines the relationship between developmental motives and form in Beethoven's music. Although Fischer's developmental motives are broader in scope than those of Kurth, his debt to Kurth is clear.[48]

In addition to furnishing a point of departure for the European authors discussed above, Kurth's ideas also provide a foundation for a few contemporary American writers. Leonard Meyer's ideas of "gap" and "fill," for example, designed to show melodic continuity, are based on the same kind of Gestalt-psychological concepts as Kurth's "overriding lines."[49] The implication/realization model of analysis, proposed by Meyer and then taken up by his student Eugene Narmour, identifies global melodic continuities according to psycho-auditive criteria similar to those that underlie Kurth's curvilinear developments. Like Kurth, Meyer traces the musical relationships he finds to a "complex and subtle cognitive activity." We experience the implicative stimuli as "kinetic tension"; the realization of the stimuli resolves the tension. Accordingly, implicative relationships are a matter of "feeling and affect."[50]

Over the last several years, Alexandra Pierce has evolved a mode of analysis for revealing phrase structure at various hierarchic levels. Pierce explores hierarchic phrase structures using the sensation of motion as a "fundamental research tool." The "dynamic interplay" between what she calls "structure" (quasi background) and "ornament" (quasi foreground) in music produces a certain "quality of movement within the sound." [51] Pierce relies primarily on kinesthesia for interpreting phrase structure. She suggests transforming this kinesthesia into physical movements so that, in performing, a musician might get a better feeling for shaping all levels of phrase structure in a piece. Her "fountaining" and "arcing" movements, for example, carry the arms and body through motions that span broad dynamic intensifications and de-intensifications resembling Kurth's "waves." Here, perhaps without realizing it, Pierce has given physical expression to Kurth's theory of form. [52]

Kurth's main influence preceded World War II. During the Nazi period, his works were banned because of his Jewish descent. In neutral Switzerland, his influence remained strong, if localized, and to some extent the end of the war brought a reemergence of his work in Europe. Nevertheless, the resurgent interest did not reach prewar proportions. Reprints of Kurth's most popular books did appear, but their impact was not the same as it had been in the 1920s and 1930s. [53] Several obstacles stood in the way of a full-fledged revival. Kurth's style of theory and its very language, so bound up in turn-of-the-century culture, lapsed with the generation that grew to maturity in Kurth's day. After 1945, Kurth was no longer read as an innovator but rather as an important and interesting historical figure. At the height of his popularity, Kurth's prose style was culturally understood by his contemporaries, and his success was surely due in part to his special gift for vividly describing musical and psycho-auditive processes that had eluded most other authors. Today, however, compared with the prose of modern theorists, Kurth's style appears flowery and turgid. What was an effective communicational vehicle has become a barrier to modern readers.

Another barrier, for English-language readers at least, is the lack of translations. Even for experienced nonnative German readers, tackling Kurth in the original is a difficult and time-consuming task. A potential translator must consider the sheer length of Kurth's books before undertaking the job. And if Kurth were eventually published in English, the translator or editor would have to caution readers about certain off-putting elements. Like most writers of the past, if Kurth is to teach us anything, we must read him with an eye to both his cultural milieu and practical value, sifting out the useful elements from the less useful ones.

One element in Kurth's writing that easily offends modern-day readers is his historical viewpoint. Kurth, and others with strong Romantic sensibilities, viewed Classical music as "simple," a sort of way station between Baroque and Romantic music. Donald Francis Tovey, writing in 1903, complains about the low appreciation for Mozart and scoffs at those "who still believe that Mozart is a childishly simple composer." [54] Our appreciation of Kurth's work is further hindered by his romanticization of Bach. Besides listening to romanticized performances of this composer, with an ear already full of Wagner's music, Kurth may have been influenced by Albert Schweitzer's highly subjective study of Bach.[55] By modern standards, both the undervaluation of Classical music and the romanticization of Bach's works are questionable. Because current musicians and scholars have rejected such views, Kurth's outlook now hinders a neutral reading of his work. We must try to look beyond such opinions, however, if we are to take advantage of his rich analytical insights.

The secondary literature on Kurth has done little to help introduce his ideas to English-speaking audiences. Dolores Hsu published the first of the few available studies dealing with Kurth. Her essay "Ernst Kurth and His Concept of Music As Motion" (1966) sketches Kurth's biography and introduces the reader to some of his leading ideas by translating and interpreting several key passages. In a dozen pages she presents the conceptual framework of Kurth's writings. In so small a space, though, she of course cannot take time to illustrate the analytical implications of that framework.[56] Ira Lieberman followed Kurt von Fischer's lead by trying to apply some of Kurth's ideas, as well as Fischer's extensions of them, in analyses of Beethoven's music. Unfortunately, Lieberman occasionally misinterprets Kurth's ideas owing to faulty translations.[57]

Patrick McCreless recently published an essay that shows a better grasp of Kurth's ideas, but his presentation and critique of them clearly set his own ideas before Kurth's.[58] McCreless extends and transforms certain of Kurth's analytical principles only to criticize Kurth for failing to discover those modifications himself. Such curiously ahistorical criticisms are all too common. By such criteria, one can freely attack the work of Tinctoris, Zarlino, Kirnberger, or indeed any theorist one chooses. McCreless does admit that he intends "no evaluation of [Kurth's] historical position relative to other theorists of his time." But that disclaimer does not authorize him to criticize Kurth's work relative to other theorists *not* of his own time.[59]

Stylistic and linguistic barriers, changed historical attitudes, and a dearth of helpful secondary literature have blocked the path to a wider audience for Kurth outside of Europe.[60] Add to these obstacles an increasing tendency, since the 1950s, toward scientism in musical analysis and it becomes clear that Kurth's comparatively unscientific style of analysis has appealed little to the modern community of theorists. A growing number of writers, however, have begun to approach music as more than autonomous sound structures, having recognized that a full understanding of music must take its affective impact as well as psycho-auditive factors into account. As an "aural cognitive activity" and the product of "subjective construction," music does not exhaust itself in abstract structural norms, and neither should our understanding of it.[61] Depending on *how* we listen and *what* we are listening for, one mode of analysis or another may better suit our objectives. A pluralistic approach, then, rather than a monistic one, may be the best way to account for a multifaceted musical experience.[62]

In listening to and thinking about music, Kurth strives to balance intuition with intellect, to blend individualizing, aesthetically oriented analysis with selected theoretical ideas inherited from his predecessors. He allows intuition to inform the intellect. Then, through analysis, he tries to find the way back to intuition in order to achieve both an intellectually and a psycho-auditively satisfying musical reportage. This reciprocity between intuition and intellect demands a keen aural sensitivity, analytical flexibility to accommodate any set of musical events, and the talent to verbalize the nature of those events. Kurth excels in all of these skills. But most importantly, by approaching music theory with an experiential-theoretic disposition rather than with a material-theoretic one, Kurth restores the human element to listening and analytical reflection as no other theorist of his time does.

Kurth originated many of his ideas with little precedent. In some cases, the spirit of his work came to fruition years after his major works had appeared, when for reasons outlined above, his seminal writings were beginning to fade from interest. Clearly, Kurth is an influential figure in the development of music-theoretical ideas. At a time when music theory needed revision, he synthesized the results of previous musical inquiries in several areas, directing these inquiries away from a material approach toward an experiential one; in doing so he gave a new direction and impetus to a stalled discipline. His work effectively expands and deepens the insights of his predecessors and lays the foundation for several modern-day authors. Kurth stands between important writers in nineteenth- and twentieth-century music theory, aesthetics, and psychology. His work links the large-scale linear harmonic analyses of Riemann with those of Hindemith, and the music-aesthetic ideas of Karl Grunsky with those of Zuckerkandl, as well as the psychological researches of the early Gestaltists with the psycho-auditive theories of Meyer. In order to understand fully the history of music theory, it is our responsibility to read Kurth carefully and familiarize ourselves with the innovative contributions of one of the most extraordinarily creative thinkers in our century.

NOTES

1. My thoughts here on Kurth's place in the history of music theory are based primarily on my review of his ideas in *Grundlagen* and *Romantische Harmonik*. I also take into account the evolution of his work in *Bruckner* and *Musikpsychologie*, even though I have touched only briefly and selectively on ideas in those volumes and may not always cite them specifically in the following discussion.

2. Hugo Riemann, *Geschichte der Musiktheorie im IX.–XIX. Jahrhundert* (Leipzig: Hesse, 1898); idem, *History of Music Theory*, trans. R. Haggh, books 1, 2 (Lincoln: University of Nebraska Press, 1962); W. Mickelsen, trans., *Hugo Riemann's Theory of Harmony and History of Music Theory, Book 3* (Lincoln: University of Nebraska Press, 1977), 105–238. Mickelsen gives a classified, chronological listing of Riemann's publications on pp. 26–27.

3. Hermann Kretzschmar, "Anregungen" (see chap. 1, n.26), 49–50 (Hanslick), 51–52; idem, "Neue Anregungen," 85: "lenkt mit formalem Hokuspokus vom Wesen der Sache ab."

4. Karl Grunsky, *Musikästhetik* (see chap. 1, n.82), 22: "That music is an expression of mental life is today admitted, defended, demanded from nearly all sides, since we barely pay attention to Hanslick any longer" ("Dass Musik Ausdruck seelischen Lebens sei, wird heutzutage, da man Hanslick kaum mehr beachtet, fast von allen Seiten zugegeben, verfochten, verlangt").

5. See chapter 1, pp. 7–8.

6. In his last years, Riemann, too, re-oriented his thinking toward an experiential-theoretic outlook. In an essay on "tone conceptions" (*Tonvorstellungen*), Riemann says, "The Alpha and Omega of

musical art is not the actually sounding music but rather the mental conception of tone relationships which arise in the imagination of the composer . . . and, once again, in the imagination of the listener. Both the notation of musical creations and the acoustical performance of the works are only the means to transplant the musical experience from the imagination of the composer into that of the listener." Further, he remarks that "every musical art work is [a] psychic experience, not only in its origin in the creative fantasy of the composer but also . . . in the receptive and re-creative fantasy of the listener" ("Ideen zu einer Lehre von den Tonvorstellungen," *Jahrbuch der Musikbibliothek Peters* 21/22 [1914–15]: 2, 10). Due to the war, Riemann's essay did not appear until May 1916, *after* Kurth's *Grundlagen* had gone to press. A second essay on the subject (*Jahrbuch* 23 [1916]: 1–22) did not appear until April 1917, after *Grundlagen* was in print (Kurth, *Musikpsychologie,* 46 n). In 1913, long before *Grundlagen,* Kurth had in fact already set a psychological course in his approach to music theory (*Voraussetzungen,* 6, 53; see my chapter 1). In a 1918 critique of *Grundlagen,* Riemann observed that a "significant change in the basic views of the nature of music" was on the rise. He noted the emergence of a "new branch of music-theoretical literature" in his essay "Die Phrasierung im Lichte einer Lehre von den Tonvorstellungen" (see chap. 1, n. 61), 29.

7. Louis and Thuille, *Harmonielehre,* v–vi: "rein wissenschaftliche Bearbeitungen"; "willkürliche Gedankenkonstruktionen an die Stelle der realen Dinge setzen und statt diese zu erklären mit den Ausgeburten seiner eigenen ausschweifenden Phantasie sich beschäftigt."

8. Schenker, *Harmony,* 175–77.

9. Kretzschmar, "Anregungen," 53.

10. The psychological disposition has its origins, in turn, in philosophical and aesthetic outlooks, for example, those of Schopenhauer, Bergson, and Lipps, as explained in chapter 1.

11. David Lewin provides a good discussion of theory and analysis and their relationship in "Behind the Beyond," *Perspectives of New Music* 7.2 (1969): 60–64. His article is a response to Edward T. Cone's "Beyond Analysis," *Perspectives of New Music* 6.1 (1967): 33–50. Cone answers in "Reply to Lewin," *Perspectives of New Music* 7.2 (1969): 70–72. Carl Dahlhaus discusses the relationship between theory and analysis in *Analysis and Value Judgment,* trans. Siegmund Levairie, Monographs in Musicology, vol. 1 (New York: Pendragon Press, 1983), 7–10, and in *Die Musiktheorie im 18. und 19. Jahrhundert,* vol. 1 (1984), 28–33.

12. William Thompson, "Style Analysis: Or the Perils of Pigeonholes," *Journal of Music Theory* 14.2 (1970): 193. In a roundabout way, Thompson echoes Lewin's belief that the goal of analysis is "to hear the piece better, both in detail and in the large" (Lewin, "Behind the Beyond," 63).

13. Joseph Kerman, "How We Got Into Analysis and How to Get Out," *Critical Inquiry* 7.2 (1980): 313–14; idem, *Contemplating Music: Challenges to Musicology* (Cambridge: Harvard University Press, 1985), 66–67; Thompson, "Style Analysis," 194; Dahlhaus, *Analysis and Value Judgment,* 9. It seems to me that Kurth's style of analysis is a good example of what Kerman is getting at when he contrasts analysis with criticism (*Contemplating Music,* 67–68, 73, 94, 112, 122–23, 154). Kerman, though, apparently wants to draw some evaluative conclusions from "his" criticism. Kurth does not, at least not in the sense that Kerman means. (Kurth does evaluate styles, giving preference to the Baroque and Romantic styles and leaving the Classical style stranded in between.) Kurth's work is, then, perhaps closer to Leonard Meyer's idea of "critical analysis," which dispenses with evaluation (*Explaining Music,* ix, 6, 18).

14. I mentioned a few of Kurth's critics earlier. These include Schenker, Oswald Jonas, Helmut Federhofer, Friedrich Neumann, and John Rothgeb. See the end of chapter 4.

15. Only in his Example 124, the beginning of Chopin's Op. 28, No. 4 (*Harmony,* 148), does Schenker show an instance of the kind of chromatic passing chords that Kurth deals with in Wagner's extratonal progression.

16. The same is true of curvilinear apexes as compared with the notes of a Schenkerian linear progression.

17. Pastille, "*Ursatz*" (see chap. 4, n. 59), xii, 16–42.

18. Ibid., 73–108. Schenker's morphological tendency is linked to his organicist outlook. Organicism is the third of three elements that, according to Pastille, characterize Schenker's theories.

19. In the essay "Resumption of *Urlinie* Considerations" (*Das Meisterwerk in der Musik,* vol. 1), Schenker seems to be distinguishing his linear progressions from Kurth's apex lines when he says, "The highest tones of the upper voice tend to tempt and attract our curiosity, and because they are the highest tones they are also forever thought to be tones of the urlinie." The translation here is from Sylvan Kalib's "Thirteen Essays from the Three Yearbooks *Das Meisterwerk in der Musik* by Heinrich Schenker: An Annotated Translation," vol. 2 (Ph.D. dissertation, Northwestern University, 1973), 135. Schenker goes on to give some examples in which the highest tones do not correspond to those of the *Urlinie.*

20. Carl Dahlhaus comments on Kurth's aesthetically oriented analytical conclusions, as compared with theoretically oriented ones, in his article on counterpoint in the *New Grove Dictionary of Music and Musicians,* 6th ed., 4:848.

21. See chapter 1.

22. Thomas Alexander and Beryl Parker, *The New Education in the German Republic* (New York: John Day Co., 1929), 4. This book, based on travels through Germany from 1908 to 1913, is an excellent source of information on the period.

23. Kurth, "Schulmusik," 346: "Die Selbsttätigkeit wird zum Mittelpunkt, die Wiedergabe selbst ist ja überhaupt nur ein Teil; sie dient, gestützt durch die damit verbundene Erörterung, dem Musikerlebnis." Ibid., 349: "Das Verständnis der Musik . . . kann man allmählich von der reinen Instinktschulung . . . aufbauen."

24. Hans Mersmann, "Versuch einer Phänomenologie der Musik," *Zeitschrift für Musikwissenschaft* 5 (1922): 226–69. Paul Bekker, *Von den Naturreichen des Klanges: Grundriss einer Phänomenologie der Musik* (Stuttgart/Berlin: Deutsche Verlagsanstalt, 1925). Mersmann summarizes his 1922 article in "Zur Phänomenologie der Musik," *Zeitschrift für Ästhetik und allgemeine Kunstwissenschaft* 19 (1925): 372–97. It is noteworthy that Mersmann developed his phenomenological style of analysis in a continuing-education course (*Volkshochschule*) for musical amateurs, just as Schering had done in a similar course, and Kurth did at Wickersdorf. See Mersmann's "Versuch," 261–62 n, and Schering's *Musikalische Bildung,* 5 ("Vorwort").

25. Arthur Wolfgang Cohn, "Das musikalische Verständnis: Neue Ziele," *Zeitschrift für Musikwissenschaft* 4 (1921): 135; Mersmann, "Versuch," 227 n.

26. Taylor A. Greer, "Listening As Intuiting: A Critique of Clifton's Theory of Intuitive Description," *In Theory Only* 7.7 (1984): 3–22, specifically 8–9. Greer is responding to several of Clifton's essays including, among others, "Some Comparisons Between Intuitive and Scientific Descriptions of Music," *Journal of Music Theory* 19.9 (1975): 66–110; and "Music as Constituted Object," *Music and Man* 2.1 (1976): 73–98. In *Music As Heard: A Study in Applied Phenomenology* (New Haven: Yale University Press, 1983), Clifton goes far beyond the work of Philip Batstone and Lawrence Ferrara (see note 28 below).

27. Cohn, "Verständnis," 132; Mersmann, "Versuch," 227.

28. Philip Batstone, "Musical Analysis As Phenomenology," *Perspectives of New Music* 7.2 (1969): 94–110; Lawrence Ferrara, "Phenomenology as a Tool for Musical Analysis," *Musical Quarterly* 70 (1984): 355–73.

29. Batstone, "Musical Analysis," 94–95, 110.

30. Ferrara, "Phenomenology," 355–56. Michael Polanyi, *Personal Knowledge: Towards a Post-Critical Philosophy* (Chicago: University of Chicago Press, 1958), vii, 3–17 (on "Objectivity"). Both Ferrara and Batstone apply their methods to nontonal music, perhaps because it is not burdened with as many theoretical and aural preconceptions as is tonal music, and so allows more readily unbiased listening and analysis.

31. Ferrara, "Phenomenology," 356–57, 359–60. By "syntactical," Ferrara means sound as sound itself (sensuous), and sound as structure. "Semantic" refers to symbolic and referential meanings, and "ontological" to the historical world of the composer.

32. Kurth, responding to some composers' claims, says that the expression "linear counterpoint" was "unscrupulously misused to cover a harmony-free, experimental patchwork of tone lines in new harmonic realms" ("skrupellos zur Deckung eines harmoniefreien, in neuen Klangbereichen experimentierenden Zusammenflickens von Tonlinien missbraucht"; *Grundlagen,* xiii). Kurth speculates that this erroneous interpretation "originated with the defenders of atonality" ("scheint von den Verfechtern der Atonalität ausgegangen"; ibid.).

33. Letter from Ernst Krenek to Kurth, April 13, 1921; letter from Krenek to this author, September 10, 1981.

34. Ernst Toch, *Melodielehre* (Berlin, 1923), originally a Ph.D. dissertation entitled "Beiträge zur Stilkunde der Melodie" (Heidelberg, 1921).

35. Toch, *The Shaping Forces in Music* (New York: Criterion Music Corporation, 1948), 5.

36. Ibid., chap. 5 ("The Wave Line"), and p. 95 ("wind-up").

37. Ibid., 21. Chapter 2 of *Shaping Forces* explores the idea of "Harmony as Arrested Motion," 24–31.

38. Ibid., 157. Compare Toch's characterization of form with Kurth's, cited in chapter 9, notes 2 and 3.

39. David Neumeyer, *The Music of Paul Hindemith* (New Haven: Yale University Press, 1986), 47 n. Kurth gives his opinion on Fux in *Grundlagen,* 103–16, 128–31.

40. Neumeyer, *Hindemith,* 47–48 n, 67. In pointing out Kurth's use of the word *Zug* in *Grundlagen* (1917) as a possible source for Hindemith's ideas, instead of Schenker's *Zug* in the 1920 edition of Beethoven's Piano Sonata Op. 101, Neumeyer places Kurth ahead of Schenker in the use of that important term. It also appears that Hindemith's "harmonic pillars" (*harmonische Hauptstützpunkte*) derive from Kurth's basic pillars rather than from Schenker's scale steps (ibid., 14).

41. Ibid., 29.

42. Hindemith, *Übungsbuch für den dreistimmigen Satz,* ed. Andres Briner, P. Daniel Meier, and Alfred Rubeli (Mainz: Schott, 1970), 199; idem, *Elementary Training for Musicians* (New York: Associated Music, 1946), 158. Neumeyer explains the origins and contents of the *Craft,* vols. 1–3, in *Hindemith,* 21–34. He cites the passages quoted here on pp. 29–30.

43. Victor Zuckerkandl, *Sound and Symbol: Music and the External World,* trans. W. R. Trask, Bollingen Series, vol. 44 (Princeton: Princeton University Press, 1956), 76. Compare Zuckerkandl's statement here with Kurth's characterization of motion streaming over the tones (see chapter 1, p. 13, p. 27 n 57).

44. Ibid., 36–37.

45. Ibid., 95–98. Kurth gives his version of the "dynamic field" in *Grundlagen,* 43. See also his *Musikpsychologie,* 204–9.

46. Kurt Huber, *Der Ausdruck musikalischer Elementarmotive* (Leipzig: J. A. Barth, 1923). Huber's book is a revision of his inaugural thesis, written in 1920, when Kurth published *Romantische Harmonik.* Kurth introduces primordial motives in *Romantische Harmonik,* 465–66.

47. Kurt Westphal, *Der Begriff der musikalischen Form in der Wiener Klassik* (Leipzig: Kister und Siegel, 1935; reprint, Biebing: Katzbichler, 1971), 11, 48–50, 52–53. Westphal quotes liberally from Kurth's works. His book is a revised version of his inaugural dissertation (1933).

48. Fischer, *Form und Motiv* (see chap. 3, n. 48). Fischer acknowledges Kurth in the introductory chapter.

49. Meyer, *Emotion and Meaning in Music,* 130–35 on "Structural Gaps," and 138–43 on "Melodic Completeness and Closure." Meyer expands and refines this material in *Explaining Music,* 145–57.

50. Meyer, *Explaining Music,* 110–13 ("implicative relationships" defined), 114–30 (annotated musical examples with graphs demonstrating implication/realization analyses). Eugene Narmour, *Beyond Schenkerism* (Chicago: University of Chicago Press, 1977), 122–66 (chapter 10, "An Alternative: Toward an Implication-Realization Model").

51. Alexandra Pierce, "Structure and Phrase, Part I," *In Theory Only* 4.5 (1978): 24–25.

52. Pierce, "Structure and Phrase, Part II," *In Theory Only* 5.3 (1979): 3–24; idem, "Climax in Music: Structure and Phrase, Part III," *In Theory Only* 7.1 (1983): 3–30. "Fountaining" and "arcing"

are discussed in "Climax," 12–15. Margret Allen, in *Guides to Creative Musicianship* (Ardmore, Pa.: Dorrance and Co., 1979), takes a similar, though less physically elaborate, approach to feeling motion in music. Her ideological link with Kurth surfaces throughout her book in statements such as "that which happens between the tones . . . is the all important thing" (p. 3); "Music is the sound of energy release" (p. 10); or "Music is the sound of motion" (p. 113).

53. Reprints of *Grundlagen* appeared in 1948, 1956, and 1977; of *Romantische Harmonik* in 1968 and 1975; and of *Bruckner* in 1971.

54. Donald Francis Tovey, "The Classical Concerto," *Essays in Musical Analysis,* vol. 3 (London: Oxford University Press, 1936; orig. 1903), 22. Also: "[Mozart's] work has for the past fifty years been treated with neglect and lack of intelligent observation, for which we at the present time are paying dearly with a notable loss both of ear for fine detail and of grasp of musical works as definite wholes" (p. 3).

55. Albert Schweitzer, *Johann Sebastian Bach* (Leipzig, 1907; orig. Paris, 1905). Leo Schrade discusses Schweitzer's work in "Schweitzer's Aesthetics: An Interpretation of Bach," *The Albert Schweitzer Jubilee Book* (Cambridge, Mass., 1945). Friedrich Blume surveys the changing views of Bach in *Two Centuries of Bach: An Account of Changing Taste,* trans. Stanley Goodman (London: Oxford University Press, 1950).

56. Dolores Hsu, "Ernst Kurth and His Concept of Music As Motion," *Journal of Music Theory* 10 (1966), 2–17. The organization of Hsu's essay, as well as some of her material, seems to be based on Kurt von Fischer's article "In Memoriam Ernst Kurth" (see chapter 1, note 3). Occasionally, she appears to paraphrase or translate Fischer without crediting him. For example when she observes that, according to Kurth, "music is not to be considered merely as the accumulation of sounds . . ." (p. 7), she comes very close to Fischer's statement that begins "Musik stellt keine Summierung von Toneindrücken dar . . ." (p. 235).

57. Ira Lieberman, "Some Representative Works from Beethoven's Early Period Analyzed in Light of the Theories of Ernst Kurth and Kurt von Fischer" (Ph.D. dissertation, Columbia University, 1968). By translating *schlechtweg,* for instance, as "unfortunately" instead of "simply" or "plainly" (p. 27), Lieberman inadvertently reverses Kurth's meaning. Furthermore, *gleichschwebende Temperatur* is "equal temperament," not "temperature changes" (p. 26).

58. Patrick McCreless, "Ernst Kurth" (see chap. 8, n. 28), 56–75.

59. Ibid., 56. McCreless also states that he approaches Kurth's ideas "subjectively" and plans to impose on them foreign ideas (p. 57). In light of such a personally oriented approach to Kurth's work, McCreless's criticism of him is all the more unfounded.

60. Kurth's ideas are known in Russia from a translation of *Grundlagen* into Russian (1931) by the musicologist-composer Boris V. Asaf'yef. Asaf'yef's book *Musical Form As Process* (Moscow, 1947), which was translated into German in 1976, shows strong links to Kurth's ideas.

61. Mary Louise Serafine discusses the issue of music as an "aural cognitive activity" in her article "Cognition in Music," *Cognition* 14 (1983): 156–57, 165. She gives a full account of her research in *Music As Cognition: The Development of Thought in Sound* (New York: Columbia University Press, 1988). Chapters 2 and 3 incorporate material from the 1983 article. Kerman points out analysts' neglect of concerns other than "structural" ones in *Contemplating Music,* 73.

62. Ferrara outlines such a pluralistic approach in "Phenomenology," 365. Sounding much like Kerman, Ferrara says, "If the work functions at levels of meaning other than syntax, then so must the analysis. Musical analysis must not be limited to a discussion of formal elements" (p. 373).

APPENDIX: LIST OF MUSICAL EXAMPLES

JOHANN SEBASTIAN BACH

Well-Tempered Clavier, vol. 1
    C-Major Fugue: 3-6, 3-9
    C♯-Minor Prelude: 3-21
    C♯-Minor Fugue: 3-18, 9-1
    E♭-Major Fugue: 9-2, 9-3, 9-4, 9-5
    G-Major Fugue: 3-16*a-c,* 3-17, 3-20
    B-Minor Fugue: 3-4*a,b*
Well-Tempered Clavier, vol. 2
    C♯-Minor Fugue: 5-4
    E-Minor Fugue: 4-6
    F♯-Major Fugue: 3-7
    B-Major Fugue: 3-5, 3-22
Violoncello Suites
    No. 1 in G Major: 4-3 (Allemande), 4-4 (Allemande), 4-8 (Prelude)
    No. 2 in D Minor: 4-7 (Prelude), 4-22 (Allemande), 4-35 (Allemande)
    No. 3 in C Major: 2-6 (Prelude), 4-19 (Prelude), 4-27 (Allemande), 4-32 (Gigue)
    No. 4 in E♭ Major: 4-1 (Prelude), 4-10 (Allemande), 4-23 (Courante)
    No. 6 in D Major: 2-1 (Courante)
Violin Sonatas/Suites
    Sonata No. 1 in G Minor: 4-18 (Presto), 4-20 (Presto), 4-34 (Fugue)
    Suite No. 1 in B Minor: 4-11 (Double 2), 4-13 (Double 1), 4-24 (Double 2)
    Sonata No. 2 in A Minor: 4-28 (Allegro), 4-29 (Allegro)
    Suite No. 2 in D Minor: 4-31 (Allemande)
    Sonata No. 3 in C Major: 4-15 (Allegro), 4-33 (Allegro)
    Suite No. 3 in E Major: 2-2*a–d* (Prelude)

Inventions

   Two-Part

         No. 3 in D Major: 3-11*b*, 5-2*a,b*

         No. 8 in F Major: 3-11*c*

         No. 13 in A Minor: 5-5

   Three-Part (Sinfonias)

         No. 12 in A Major: 9-6, 9-7

Miscellaneous

   Art of the Fugue, No. 3: 5-1*a,b*

   Partita No. 1 in B♭ Major: 5-7 (Allemande)

   French Suite No. 1 in D Minor: 3-19 (Allemande)

   Little Fugue in C Major, BWV 952: 3-23

   Little Fugue in E Minor, BWV 900: 3-11*a*

   Organ Sonata in C Minor, BWV 526: 5-6 (Allegro)

   Clavier Fugue in A Minor, BWV 944: 5-10

   Italian Concerto: 5-14 (1st movement)

   Chorale Variation, BWV 768 ("Sei gegrüsset, Jesu gütig"): 5-13

   Menuet in F Major, Anh. 113 (Notenbüchlein für A. M. Bach): 5-11*a,b*, 5-12

ANTON BRUCKNER

Symphony No. 1: 3-26 (2d movement)
Symphony No. 4: 8-7 (2d movement)

HEINRICH MARSCHNER

Der Vampyr: 3-28 (act II, Finale)

FRANZ SCHUBERT

Piano Sonata, D 960: 7-9 (1st movement)
"Am Meer," *Schwanengesang,* No. 12: 8-2

ROBERT SCHUMANN

"Abendmusik," Op. 99, No. 12: 8-11

RICHARD STRAUSS

Salome: 7-13 (scene 1)
Till Eulenspiegel: 8-21

RICHARD WAGNER

Tristan und Isolde (scene given in parentheses)
    Prelude to act I: 6-1, 6-2, 6-8, 9-9, 9-10, 9-11
    Act I: 2-7(1), 3-27(4), 3-29(3), 3-30(3), 3-32(1), 3-33(4), 6-4(5), 6-7(3),
        6-9*a*(3), 6-9*c*(2), 8-10(1), 8-18(3), 8-19(3)
    Act II: 2-15(2), 7-12(1), 8-3(2), 8-15(3), 8-17(2)
    Prelude to act III: 6-3, 7-5, 8-16, 9-8
    Act III: 2-13(1), 2-14(1), 2-17(1), 6-9*b*(1), 8-9(1), 8-20(1)
Rheingold
    Scene 2: 7-8
    Scene 3: 2-9, 2-11
    Scene 4: 8-1, 8-8
Siegfried
    Act I: 2-8(1), 7-1(1), 7-2(1), 7-6(2), 7-7(1), 8-5(1)
Walküre
    Act I: 3-31(3), 8-4(3), 8-6(3)
    Act II: 3-25(5)
Götterdämmerung
    Act I: 7-3(2), 7-4(2)
Parsifal
    Act I: 7-10(2)
    Act III: 7-11(2)
Die Meistersinger
    Act II: 8-12(5)
Wesendonck-Lieder: 3-24

HUGO WOLF

"An den Schlaf," *Mörike-Lieder,* III: 8-13, 8-14

BIBLIOGRAPHY

Books

Abegg, Werner. *Musikästhetik und Musikkritik bei Eduard Hanslick.* Studien zur Musikgeschichte des 19. Jahrhunderts, vol. 44. Regensburg: Bosse, 1974.

Adler, Guido. *Der Stil in der Musik,* 2d ed. Leipzig: Breitkopf und Härtel, 1929; 1st ed., 1911.

———. *Wagner.* Leipzig: Breitkopf und Härtel, 1904.

———. *Wollen und Wirken: Aus dem Leben eines Historikers.* Vienna: Universal, 1935. `

Albrechtsberger, Johann G. *Gründliche Anweisung zur Komposition.* Leipzig: J. G. I. Breitkopf, 1790.

Aldwell, Edward and Carl Schachter. *Harmony and Voice Leading,* 2 vols. New York: Harcourt Brace Jovanovich, 1979.

Alexander, Ian W. *Bergson: Philosopher of Reflection.* Studies in Modern European Literature and Thought. New York: Hillary House, Inc., 1957.

Alexander, Thomas and Beryl Parker. *The New Education in the German Republic.* New York: John Day, 1929.

Allen, Margaret. *Guides to Creative Motion.* Ardmore, Pa.: Dorrance and Co., 1979.

Asaf'yef, Boris V. *Musical Form as Process.* Moscow, 1947.

Bekker, Paul. *Von den Naturreichen des Klanges: Grundriss einer Phänomenologie der Musik.* Stuttgart/Berlin: Deutsche Verlagsanstalt, 1925.

Bellerman, Heinrich. *Der Contrapunkt,* 4th ed. Berlin: Julius Springer, 1901; orig. 1862.

Bergson, Henri. *Mind Energy,* trans. H. Wildon Carr. New York: Hoyt and Co., 1920.

Bernsdorf, Eduard. *Neues Universal-Lexikon der Tonkunst,* Supplement. Offenbach: Andre, 1865.

Bimberg, Siegfried, ed. *Handbuch der Musikästhetik.* Leipzig: VEB Deutscher Verlag für Musik, 1979.

Blume, Friedrich. *Two Centuries of Bach: An Account of Changing Taste,* trans. Stanley Goodman. London: Oxford University Press, 1950.

Boyd, William and Wyatt Rawson. *The New Education.* London: Heinemann, 1965.

Cherubini, Luigi. *Theorie des Contrapunkts und der Fuge,* trans. Franz Stöpel. Leipzig: Kistner, 1835.

Clifton, Thomas. *Music as Heard: A Study in Applied Phenomenology.* New Haven, Conn.: Yale University Press, 1983.

Copleston, Fredrick C. *Arthur Schopenhauer: Philosopher of Pessimism,* 2d ed. New York: Search Press, 1975.

Dahlhaus, Carl. *Analysis and Value Judgment,* trans. Siegmund Levarie. Monographs in Musicology, vol. 1. New York: Pendragon Press, 1983.

————. *Die Musiktheorie im 18. und 19. Jahrhundert, Erster Teil: Grundzüge einer Systematik.* Geschichte der Musiktheorie, vol. 10. Darmstadt: Wissenschaftliche Buchgesellschaft, 1984.

————. *Untersuchungen über die Entstehung der Tonalität.* Saarbrückener Studien zur Musikwissenschaft, vol. 2. Kassel: Bärenreiter, 1968.

Dahlhaus, Carl and Lars Ulrich Abraham. *Melodielehre.* Musik-Taschen-Bücher, vol. 13. Cologne: Hans Gerig Verlag, 1972.

Davis, John B. *The Psychology of Music.* Stanford, Ca.: Stanford University Press, 1978.

Deutsch, Diana, ed. *The Psychology of Music.* New York: Academic Press, 1982.

Dilthey, Wilhelm. *Gesammelte Schriften,* 21 vols. Leipzig: Tübner, 1914– .

————. *Von deutscher Dichtung und Musik.* Leipzig: Tübner, 1933.

Ellis, Willis D. *A Source Book of Gestalt Psychology.* London: Routledge and Kegan Paul, 1955.

Erpf, Hermann. *Studien zur Harmonie- und Klangtechnik der neueren Musik.* Leipzig: Breitkopf und Härtel, 1927.

Federhofer, Helmut. *Akkord und Stimmführung in den musiktheoretischen Systemen von Hugo Riemann, Ernst Kurth und Heinrich Schenker.* Veröffentlichungen der Kommission für Musikforschung, vol. 21. Vienna: Verlag der österreichischen Akademie der Wissenschaften, 1981.

Finck, Henry T. *Wagner and His Works,* 2 vols. New York: Scribner, 1893.

Fischer, Kurt von. *Die Beziehung von Form und Motiv in Beethovens Instrumentalwerken.* Zurich: P. H. Heitz, 1948.

Fordham, Frieda. *An Introduction to Jung's Psychology,* 3d ed. Middlesex, England: Penguin Books, 1966.

Forte, Allen. *Tonal Harmony in Concept and Practice,* 3d ed. New York: Holt, Rinehart and Winston, 1979.

Gatz, Felix M. *Musik-Ästhetik in ihren Hauptrichtungen.* Stuttgart: Verlag von Ferdinand Enke, 1929.

Grasberger, Franz, ed. *Bruckner Symposium: "Die Fassungen."* Linz: Anton Bruckner Institute, 1981.

Grout, Donald J. *A Short History of Opera,* 2 vols. New York: Columbia University Press, 1947.

Grunsky, Karl. *Musikästhetik.* Berlin: Göschen, 1907.

Haagh, Raymond. *History of Music Theory, Books 1 and 2 by Hugo Riemann.* Lincoln: University of Nebraska Press, 1962.

Halm, August. *Die Symphonie Anton Bruckners.* Munich: G. Müller, 1914.

———. *Einführung in die Musik.* Berlin: Deutsche Buchgemeinschaft, 1926.

———. *Von Form und Sinn der Musik,* ed. Siegfried Schmalzriedt. Wiesbaden: Breitkopf und Härtel, 1978.

———. *Harmonielehre.* Leipzig: Göschen, 1905.

———. *Die Symphonie Anton Bruckners.* Munich: Georg Müller Verlag, 1913; rev. enl. 1923; rep. Hildesheim: Olms, 1975.

———. *Von zwei Kulturen der Musik,* 3d ed. Stuttgart: Klett, 1947; 1st ed. G. Müller, 1913.

Hanslick, Eduard. *Vom Musikalisch-Schönen: Ein Beitrag zur Revision der Aesthetik der Tonkunst.* Leipzig: Barth, 1854; 8th ed. rev. enl., Leipzig: Barth, 1891.

Hasse, Karl. *Johann Sebastian Bach.* Bielefeld und Leipzig: Velhagen und Klasing, 1925.

Hauptmann, Moritz. *Die Natur der Harmonik und Metrik.* Leipzig: Breitkopf und Härtel, 1853; trans., ed. W. E. Heathcote. London: Swan Sonnenschein and Co., 1888.

Heinichen, Johann D. *Der Generalbass in der Composition.* Dresden, 1728.

Helmholtz, Hermann von. *On the Sensations of Tone as a Physiological Basis for the Theory of Music,* 2d ed., rev. to conform to the 4th and last German ed. of 1877, trans. Alexander J. Ellis. New York: Dover, 1954.

Hodges, Donald A., ed. *Handbook of Music Psychology.* Lawrence, Kan.: National Association for Music Therapy, 1980.

Hodges, Herbert A. *The Philosophy of Wilhelm Dilthey.* Westport, Conn.: Greenwood Press, 1974; rep. of London: Routledge and Paul, 1952.

———. *Wilhelm Dilthey: An Introduction.* New York: Oxford University Press, 1944.

Huber, Kurt. *Der Ausdruck musikalischer Elementarmotive.* Leipzig: J. A. Barth, 1923.

Hughes, Henry Stuart. *Consciousness and Society: The Reorientation of European Social Thought, 1890–1930.* New York: Octagon Books, 1976.

Jacobi, Dr. Jolan. *The Psychology of C. G. Jung,* trans. K. W. Bash. London: Kegan Paul, Trench, Trubner and Co. Ltd., 1942.

Jadassohn, Salomon. *Lehrbuch der Harmonie.* Leipzig, 1883; 23d ed., 1923.

———. *Melodik und Harmonik bei Richard Wagner.* Berlin: Verlagsgesellschaft für Literatur und Kunst, 1899.

———. *Treatise on Single, Double, Triple and Quadruple Counterpoint,* trans. G. Wolff. New York: Schirmer, 1877; orig. German, 1884.

Janik, Allan and Stephen Toulmin. *Wittgenstein's Vienna.* New York: Simon and Schuster, 1973.

Jonas, Oswald. *Das Wesen des musikalischen Kunstwerks: Eine Einführung in die Lehre Heinrich Schenkers.* Vienna: Universal, 1935; trans. John Rothgeb. *Introduction to the Theory of Heinrich Schenker.* New York: Longman, 1982.

Jung, Carl G. *The Structure and Dynamics of the Psyche, Collected Works,* vol. 8, ed. Sir H. Read, et al.; trans. R. F. C. Hull. Bollingen Series, vol. 20. New York: Bollingen Foundation, 1960.

Kant, Immanuel. *Kritik des Urteils,* ed. J. H. von Kirchmann. Philosophische Bibliothek, vol. 3. Berlin: Heimann, 1896; orig. Berlin: Lagardes, 1790.

Keller, Hermann. *Die musikalische Artikulation insbesondere bei Bach.* Augsburg: Bärenreiter, 1925.

Kerman, Joseph. *Contemplating Music: Challenges to Musicology.* Cambridge, Mass.: Harvard University Press, 1985.

King, Alexander Hyatt. *Mozart in Retrospect.* London/New York: Oxford University Press, 1955.

Kirnberger, Johann P. *Die Kunst des reinen Satzes in der Musik.* Berlin: 1776–79; rep. Hildesheim: Olms, 1968; trans. David Beach and Jurgen Thym, *The Art of Strict Composition.* Yale Translation Series, vol. 4. New Haven, Conn.: Yale University Press, 1982.

Kistler, Cyrill. *Harmonielehre für Lehrer und Lernende.* Munich, 1879.

Köhler, Wolfgang. *Gestalt Psychology.* New York: Liveright, 1947.

Koffka, Kurt. *Principles of Gestalt Psychology.* New York: Harcourt Brace and Co., 1935.

Krause, Karl. *Anfangsgründe der allgemeinen Theorie der Musik nach den Grundsätzen der Wesenslehre,* ed. Victor Strauss. Göttingen: Dieterichschen Buchhandlung, 1838.

Krehl, Stephan. *Kontrapunkt.* Leipzig: Göschen, 1908.

Kurth, Ernst. *Bruckner,* 2 vols. Berlin: Hesse, 1925; rep. Hildesheim: Olms, 1971.

———. *Grundlagen des linearen Kontrapunkts: Bachs melodische Polyphonie.* Bern: Drechsel, 1917; Berlin: Hesse, 1922, 1927; Bern: Krompholz, 1946, 1956.

———, ed. *Johann Sebastian Bach: Sechs Sonaten und Sechs Suiten für Violine und Violoncello solo.* Munich: Drei Masken Verlag, 1921.

———. *Musikpsychologie.* Berlin: Hesse, 1931; Bern: Krompholz, 1947.

———. *Romantische Harmonik und ihre Krise in Wagners "Tristan."* Bern: Haupt, 1920; Berlin: Hesse, 1922, 1923; repr. Hildesheim: Olms, 1975.

———. *Die Voraussetzungen der theoretischen Harmonik und der tonalen Darstellungssysteme.* Bern: Drechsel, 1913; rep. Schriften zur Musik, vol. 14. Munich: Katzbichler, 1973.

Lach, Robert. *Studien zur Entwicklungsgeschichte der ornamentalen Melopöie.* Leipzig: C. F. Kahnt Nachfolger, 1913.

Larabee, Harold, ed. *Selections from Bergson.* New York: Appleton-Century-Crofts, 1949.

Leichtentritt, Hugo. *Musikalische Formenlehre.* Leipzig: Breitkopf und Härtel,

1920; 3d ed. rev. enl. Handbücher der Musiklehre, vol. 8. Leipzig: Breitkopf und Härtel, 1927.

Lerdahl, Fred and Ray Jackendoff. *A Generative Theory of Tonal Music*. Cambridge, Mass.: MIT Press, 1983.

Lessing, Theodor. *Schopenhauer, Wagner, Nietzsche: Einführung in die moderne deutsche Philosophie*. Munich: C. H. Beck'sche Verlagsbuchhandlung, 1906.

Liebe, Annelise. *Die Ästhetik Wilhelm Diltheys*. Bleichrode: Carl Nieft, 1938.

Lipps, Theodor. *Grundlegung der Ästhetik*, 2 vols. Hamburg: Leopold Voss, 1903–05.

———. *Psychologische Studien*, 2d ed. enl. Leipzig: Dürr'schen Buchhandlung, 1905; trans. Herbert C. Sanborn, *Psychological Studies*. Baltimore: Williams and Wilkins Co., 1926; rep. Psychology Classics, vol. 2. New York: Arno Press, 1973.

Lobe, Johann C. *Lehrbuch der musikalischen Komposition*. Leipzig: Breitkopf und Härtel, 1860.

Lorenz, Alfred. *Das Geheimnis der Form bei Richard Wagner*, 4 vols. Berlin: Hesse, 1924–33.

Lotze, Hermann. *Grundzüge der Ästhetik*. Leipzig: Hirzel, 1884.

Louis, Rudolf and Ludwig Thuille. *Harmonielehre*. Stuttgart: Carl Grüninger, 1907.

McCreless, Patrick. *Wagner's "Siegfried": Its Drama, History and Music*. Ann Arbor, Mich.: University Microfilms Press, 1982.

Marpurg, Friedrich W. *Handbuch bey dem Generalbass und der Composition*, 4 vols. Berlin: G. A. Lange, 1755–60.

Marx, Adolf B. *Compositionslehre*, 2d ed. rev. enl., 4 vols. Leipzig: Breitkopf und Härtel, 1841.

Mattheson, Johann. *Der vollkommene Capellmeister*, ed. M. Reimann. Documenta Musicologica, vol. 5. Kassel: Bärenreiter, 1954; orig. 1739; trans. Ernest C. Harriss, *Johann Mattheson's "Der vollkommene Capellmeister": A Revised Translation With Critical Commentary*. Ann Arbor, Mich.: University Microfilms Press, 1981.

Mayrberger, Karl. *Lehrbuch der musikalischen Harmonik*. Pressburg: G. Heckenast, 1878.

Mendel, Hermann. *Musikalisches Conversations-Lexikon*, 11 vols. Berlin: Heimann, 1870–79.

Mersmann, Hans. *Angewandte Musikästhetik*. Berlin: Hesse, 1926.

Meyer, Kathi. *Bedeutung und Wesen der Musik*. Sammlung musikwissenschaftlicher Abhandlungen, vol. 5. Leipzig: Heitz, 1932; rep. Baden-Baden: Körner, 1975.

Meyer, Leonard. *Emotion and Meaning in Music*. Chicago: University of Chicago Press, 1956.

———. *Explaining Music*. Berkeley: University of California Press, 1973.

———. *Music, the Arts and Ideas*. Chicago: University of Chicago Press, 1967.

Moos, Paul. *Moderne Musikästhetik in Deutschland*. Leipzig: Seemann Nachfolger, 1902.

————. *Die Philosophie der Musik von Kant bis Eduard v. Hartmann,* 2d ed. enl. Stuttgart: Deutsche Verlags-Anstalt, 1922.

Murphy, Gardner and Joseph K. Kovach. *Historical Introduction to Modern Psychology,* 3d ed. New York: Harcourt Brace Jovanovich, 1972.

Neumeyer, David. *The Music of Paul Hindemith.* New Haven, Conn.: Yale University Press, 1986.

Pfrogner, Hermann, *Lebendige Tonwelt: Zum Phänomen Musik.* Munich: Langen-Müller, 1976.

————. *Musik: Geschichte ihrer Deutung.* Freiburg: Alber, 1954.

Polanyi, Michael. *Personal Knowledge: Towards a Post-Critical Philosophy.* Chicago: University of Chicago Press, 1958.

Rameau, Jean-Phillip. *Treatise on Harmony,* trans. Paul Gossett. New York: Dover, 1952; orig., Paris, 1722.

Reismann, August. *Lehrbuch der musikalischen Komposition.* Berlin: Guttentag, 1866.

Richter, Ernst F. *Lehrbuch der Harmonie,* 13th ed. Leipzig: Breitkopf und Härtel, 1878; orig., 1853.

————. *Lehrbuch des einfachen und doppelten Kontrapunkts.* Leipzig: Breitkopf und Härtel, 1872.

Riemann, Hugo. *Catechism of Musical Aesthetics,* trans. H. Bewerung. London: Augener and Co., 1895.

————. *Geschichte der Musicktheorie im IX.–XIX. Jahrhundert.* Leipzig: Hesse, 1898; trans. Raymond Haggh *History of Music Theory, Books 1 and 2.* Lincoln: University of Nebraska Press, 1962; trans. William C. Mickelsen *Hugo Riemann's Theory of Harmony and History of Music Theory, Book 3.* Lincoln: University of Nebraska Press, 1977.

————. *Grosse Kompositionslehre,* 2 vols. Berlin/Stuttgart: Spemann, 1902–03.

————. *Handbuch der Musikgeschichte,* 2 vols. Leipzig: Breitkopf und Härtel, 1919; 3d ed., ed. Alfred Einstein. Leipzig: Breitkopf und Härtel, 1923.

————. *Harmony Simplified,* 3d ed., trans. H. Bewerung. London: Augener, 1899; orig. London, 1893.

————. *Katechismus der Fugenkomposition,* 2 vols. Leipzig: Hesse, 1890–91; trans. J. S. Shedlock. *Analysis of J. S. Bach's Wohltemperiertes Clavier,* 2 vols. New York: Schirmer, 1890–91.

————. *Lehrbuch des einfachen, doppelten und imitierenden Kontrapunkts.* Leipzig: Breitkopf und Härtel, 1888.

————. *Musikalische Dynamik und Agogik: Lehrbuch der musikalischen Phrasierung.* Hamburg: Rahter, 1884.

————. *Musik-Lexikon,* 7th ed. Berlin: Hesse, 1909.

————. *Präludien und Studien: Gesammelte Aufsätze zur Ästhetik, Theorie und Geschichte der Musik.* Nendeln, Liechtenstein: Krause Reprint, 1976; orig. 1901.

————. *Systematische Modulationslehre als Grundlage der musikalischen Formenlehre.* Hamburg: J. F. Richter, 1887.

Rubin, Edgar. *Synsoplevede Figurer.* Copenhagen, 1915; trans. Peter Collett. *Visuell wahrgenommene Figuren.* Copenhagen/Berlin, 1921.

Salzer, Felix. *Structural Hearing,* 2 vols. New York: Dover, 1962; orig., 1952.

Schäfke, Rudolf. *Geschichte der Musikästhetik in Umrissen.* Berlin: Hesse, 1934.

Schenker, Heinrich. *Erläuterungsausgabe der letzten fünf Sonaten Beethovens.* Vienna: Universal, 1913–20; ed. Oswald Jonas, Vienna: Universal, 1970–71.

———. *Der Freie Satz.* Neue musikalische Theorien und Phantasien, vol. 3. Vienna: Universal, 1935; 2d ed. rev. Oswald Jonas, 1956; trans. Ernst Oster, *Free Composition.* New York: Longman, 1979.

———. *Harmonielehre.* Neue musikalische Theorien und Phantasien, vol. 1. Vienna: Universal, 1906; trans. Elisabeth Mann Borgese *Harmony,* ed. Oswald Jonas. Chicago: University of Chicago Press, 1956; Cambridge, Mass.: MIT Press, 1978.

———, ed. *J. S. Bach, Chromatische Phantasie und Fuge, Erläuterungsausgabe.* Vienna: Universal, 1909; trans. Hedi Siegel, New York: Longman, 1984.

———. *Kontrapunkt,* 2 vols. Neue musikalische Theorien und Phantasien, vols. 2/1–2. Vienna: Universal, 1910, 1922.

———. *Das Meisterwerk in der Musik,* vol. 1. Vienna: Drei Masken Verlag, 1925.

———. *Der Tonwille.* Vienna: Albert Gutmann, 1921–24.

Schering, Arnold. *Vom musikalischen Kunstwerk,* 2d ed., ed. Friedrich Blume. Leipzig: Köhler und Amelang, 1951; orig., 1949.

———. *Musikalische Bildung und Erziehung zum musikalischen Hören.* Leipzig: Quelle und Meyer, 1911.

Schoenberg, Arnold. *Harmonielehre.* Vienna: Universal, 1911; trans. Roy Carter, *Theory of Harmony.* Berkeley: University Press, 1978.

———. *Style and Idea,* ed. Leonard Stein, trans. Leo Black. New York: St. Martins Press, 1975.

Schönzeler, Hans Hubert. *Bruckner.* New York: Grossman, 1970.

Schopenhauer, Arthur. *Die Welt als Wille und Vorstellung,* 4 vols. Sämtliche Werke, ed. Wolfgang F. von Löheneysen. Cotta-Verlag, n.d.; orig. 1819; trans. R. B. Haldane and J. Kemp as *The World as Will and Idea.* Boston: J. R. Osgood, 1866.

Schorske, Carl. *Fin-de-siècle Vienna: Politics and Culture.* New York: Knopf, 1979.

Schuh, Willi, ed. *Schweizer Musikbuch.* Zurich: Atlantis, 1939.

Schulz, Johann A. P. *Die wahren Grundsätze zum Gebrauch der Harmonie.* Berlin: Königsberg: G. J. Pecker and G. L. Hartung, 1773; trans. David Beach and Jurgen Thym, "The True Principles for the Practice of Harmony," *Journal of Music Theory* 23.2 (1979), 163–225.

Schwanzara, Ernst, ed. *Vorlesungen über Harmonielehre und Kontrapunkt an der Universität Wien.* Vienna: Österreichischer Bundesverlag für Unterricht, Wissenschaft und Kunst, 1950.

Schweitzer, Albert. *Johann Sebastian Bach,* 2 vols., trans. Ernst Newman. London:

A. and C. Black Ltd., 1923; orig. Eng. ed., London: Breitkopf and Hartel, 1911.

Sechter, Simon. *Die Grundsätze der musikalischen Komposition,* 3 vols. Leipzig: Breitkopf und Härtel, 1853–54.

Serafine, Mary Louise. *Music as Cognition: The Development of Thought in Sound.* New York: Columbia University Press, 1988.

Stachura, Peter. *The German Youth Movement, 1900–1945.* London: Macmillan, 1981.

Stein, Jack. *Richard Wagner and the Synthesis of the Arts.* Detroit: Wayne State University Press, 1960.

Strunk, Oliver. *Source Readings in Music History.* New York: Norton, 1950.

Stumpf, Carl. *Die Anfänge der Musik.* Leipzig: J. A. Barth, 1911.

———. *Tonpsychologie,* 2 vols. Leipzig: Hirzel, 1883, 1890.

Toch, Ernst. *The Shaping Forces in Music.* New York: Criterion Music Corp., 1948.

Tovey, Donald Francis. *The Classical Concerto, Essays in Musical Analysis,* vol. 3. London: Oxford University Press, 1936; orig. 1903.

Vogel, Martin. *Der Tristan-Akkord und die Krise der tonalen Harmonielehre.* Orpheus Schriftenreihe zu Grundfragen der Musik, vol. 2. Düsseldorf: Gesellschaft zur Förderung der systematischen Musikwissenschaft, 1962.

Vogler, Abbé. *Handbuch der Harmonielehre.* Prague, 1802.

Wagner, Manfred. *Der Wandel des Konzepts: Zu den verschiedenen Fassungen don Bruckners Dritter, Vierter und Achter Sinfonie.* Vienna: Musikwissenschaftlicher Verlag, 1980.

Wagner, Richard. *Gesammelte Schriften,* 4th ed. Leipzig: Breitkopf und Härtel/Siegel, 1907; trans. William A. Ellis as *Richard Wagner's Prose Works.* London: Routledge and Kegan Paul, 1899.

Wagner, Wieland, ed. *Hundert Jahre Tristan: Neunzehn Essays.* Emsdetten: Lechte, 1965.

Wallaschek, Robert. *Anfänge der Tonkunst.* Leipzig, 1903.

Walther, Johann G. *Musikalisches Lexikon.* Leipzig: Wolffgang Deer, 1732; facs. ed., ed. Richard Schaal. Kassel: Bärenreiter, 1953.

Wason, Robert. *Viennese Harmonic Theory from Albrechtsberger to Schenker and Schoenberg.* Ann Arbor, Mich.: University Microfilms Press, 1985.

Weber, Gottfried. *Versuch einer geordneten Theorie der Tonsetzkunst,* 3 vols. Mainz: Schott, 1817–21; trans. James F. Warner as *Theory of Musical Composition.* Boston: Diston, 1851.

Wellek, Albert. *Musikpsychologie und Musikästhetik.* Frankfurt am Main: Akademische Verlagsgesellschaft, 1963.

Werker, Wilhelm. *Studien über Symmetrie im Bau der Fugen und die motivische Zusammengehörigkeit der Präludien und Fugen des 'Wohltemperierten Klaviers' von Johann Sebastian Bach.* Abhandlungen der sächsischen staatlichen Forschungsinstitut zu Leipzig, vol. 3. Leipzig: Breitkopf und Härtel, 1922.

Wessley, Othmar, ed. *Bruckner-Studien: Festgabe der österreichischen Akademie*

der Wissenschaften zum 150. Geburtstag von Anton Bruckner. Veröffentlich-
    ungen der Kommission für Musikforschung, vol. 16. Vienna: Verlag der öster-
    reichischen Akademie der Wissenschaften, 1975.

Westphal, Kurt. *Der Begriff der musikalischen Form in der Wiener Klassik.* Leipzig:
    Kister und Siegel, 1935; rep. Biebing: Katzbichler, 1971.

Williams, Leslie P. *The History of Science in Western Civilization,* 3 vols. Washing-
    ton, D.C.: Washington University Press of America, 1977–   .

Wundt, Wilhelm. *Grundzüge der physiologischen Psychologie,* 6th ed. Leipzig: En-
    gelmann, 1908–11.

Zarlino, Giosoffe. *The Art of Counterpoint. L'Istitutione harmoniche,* Part 3 (1558),
    trans. Guy Marco and Claude Palisca. New York: Norton, 1968.

Zuckerkandl, Victor. *The Sense of Music.* Princeton, N.J.: Princeton University
    Press, 1959.

———. *Sound and Symbol: Music and the External World,* trans. W. R. Trask.
    Bollingen Series, vol. 44. Princeton, N.J.: Princeton University Press, 1956.

Zuckerman, Elliot. *The First Hundred Years of Wagner's Tristan.* New York: Co-
    lumbia University Press, 1964.

Articles

Adler, Guido. "Umfang, Methode und Ziel der Musikwissenschaft," *Vierteljahres-
    schrift für Musikwissenschaft* 1 (1885), 5–20.

Anheisser, Siegfried. "Das Vorspiel zu 'Tristan und Isolde' und seine Motivik,"
    Zeitschrift für Musikwissenschaft 3 (1920–21), 257–304.

Arend, Max. "Harmonische Analyse des Tristanvorspiels," *Bayreuther Blätter* 24
    (1901), 160–69.

Bailey, Robert. "The Structure of the *Ring* and Its Evolution," *Nineteenth Century
    Music* 1.1 (1977), 48–61.

———. "Visual and Musical Symbolism in German Romantic Opera," *Papers
    of the Congress of the International Musicological Society.* Berkeley, 1977,
    436–44.

Barford, Philip. "Music in the Philosophy of Schopenhauer," *Soundings* 5 (1975),
    29–43.

Barry, Elizabeth W. "What Wagner Found in Schopenhauer's Philosophy," *Musical
    Quarterly* 11 (1925), 124–37.

Batstone, Philip. "Musical Analysis As Phenomenology," *Perspectives of New Mu-
    sic* 7.2 (1969), 94–110.

Beach, David. "The Function of the Six-Four Chord in Tonal Music," *Journal of
    Music Theory* 11.1 (1967), 2–31.

Bekker, Paul. "Kontrapunkt und Neuzeit," *Frankfurter Zeitung,* vol. 62, Erstes
    Morgenblatt, March 27, 1918, 1.

Bennett, Victor. "Referring to Schopenhauer," *Music Review* 11 (1950), 195–200.

Bergson, Henri. "Introduction à la métaphysique," *Revue de la métaphysique et de morale,* vol. 11 (1903), 1–36; trans. T. E. Hulme, *Introduction to Metaphysics.* Library of Liberal Arts, vol. 10. New York: Liberal Arts Press, 1949.

———. "The Perception of Change," *The Creative Mind,* trans. M. Andison. New York: Greenwood Press, 1946, 1968.

Blume, Friedrich. "Fortspinnung und Entwicklung," *Jahrbuch der Musikbibliothek Peters* 36 (1929), 51–70.

Bregman, A. S. and J. Campbell. "Primary Auditory Stream Segregation and Perception of Order in Rapid Sequences of Tones," *Journal of Experimental Psychology* 89 (1971), 244–49.

Bowarzik, D. et al. "Einige Bemerkungen über Ostwalds Verhältnis zur Atomik," *Sitzungsbericht der Akademie der Wissenschaften der DDR* 13N (1979), 103–12.

Bücken, Ernst. "Kurth als Musiktheoretiker," *Melos* 4 (1924–25), 358–64.

Capellen, Georg. "Exotische Rhythmik, Melodik und Tonalität als Wegweiser zu einer neuen Kunstentwicklung," *Die Musik* 6.3 (1906–07), 216–27.

———. "Der Quartsextakkord, seine Erklärung und seine Zukunft," *Sammelbände der Internationalen Musikgesellschaft* (1901–02), 167–83.

———. "Harmonik und Melodik bei Richard Wagner," *Bayreuther Blätter* 25 (1902), 3–23.

———. "Vierteltöne als wesentliche Tonleiterstufen," *Die Musik* 42.11 (1911–12), 334–41.

Clifton, Thomas. "Music as Constituted Object," *Music and Man* 2.1 (1976), 73–99.

———. "Some Comparisons Between Intuitive and Scientific Descriptions of Music," *Journal of Music Theory* 19 (1975), 66–110.

Cohn, Arthur W. "Das musikalische Verständnis: Neue Ziele," *Zeitschrift für Musikwissenschaft* 4 (1921), 129–35.

Cone, Edward T. "Beyond Analysis," *Perspectives of New Music* 6.1 (1967), 33–50.

———. "Reply to Lewin," *Perspectives of New Music* 7.2 (1969), 70–72.

Dahlhaus, Carl. "Bach und der 'lineare Kontrapunkt'," *Bach-Jahrbuch* 49 (1962), 55–79.

———. "Review of *Romantische Harmonik,*" *Die Musikforschung* 25 (1972), 225.

———. "Zur Geschichte der Syncope," *Die Musikforschung* 12 (1959), 385–91.

Deutsch, Diana. "Music Perception," *Musical Quarterly* 66 (1980), 165–79.

———. "Two-Channel Listening to Musical Scales," *Journal of the Acoustical Society of America* 57.2 (1975), 1156–70.

Dowling, W. J. "The Perception of Interleaved Melodies," *Cognitive Psychology* 5 (1973), 322–37.

Ehrenfels, Christian von. "Die musikalische Architektonik," *Bayreuther Blätter* 19 (1896), 257–63.

———. "Über Gestaltqualitäten," *Vierteljahresschrift für wissenschaftliche Phi-*

losophie 14 (1890), 249–92.

Eimert, Herbert. "Bekenntnis und Methode," *Zeitschrift für Musikwissenschaft* 9 (1926–27), 95–109.

Federhofer, Helmut. "Heinrich Schenkers Bruckner-Verständnis," *Archiv für Musikwissenschaft* 39.3 (1982), 198–218.

Ferrara, Lawrence. "Phenomenology as a Tool for Musical Analysis," *Musical Quarterly* 70 (1984), 355–73.

Fischer, Kurt von. "Ernst Kurth †," *Schweizerische Musikzeitung* 86.10 (1946), 373–74.

———. "In Memoriam Ernst Kurth," *Der Musik-Almanach,* ed. Viktor Schwarz. Munich: K. Desch, 1948, 228–52.

Fischer, Wilhelm. "Zur Entwicklung des Wienerklassischen Stils," *Studien zur Musikwissenschaft* 3 (1915), 24–84.

Forster, Walter von. "Heutige Praktiken im Harmonilehrunterricht an Musikhochschulen und Konservatorien," *Beiträge zur Musiktheorie im 19 Jahrhundert,* ed. Martin Vogel. Studien zur Musikgeschichte im 19. Jahrhundert, vol. 4. Regensburg: Bosse, 1966, 257–80.

Forte, Allen. "Schoenberg's Creative Evolution: The Path to Atonality," *Musical Quarterly* 64.2 (1978), 133–76.

Frank, P. L. "Wilhelm Dilthey's Contribution to the Aesthetics of Music," *Journal of Aesthetics and Art Criticism* 15 (1956–57), 477–80.

Grave, Floyd. "Abbé Vogler's Theory of Reduction," *Current Musicology* 29 (1980), 41–69.

Green, Dunton. "Schopenhauer and Music," *Musical Quarterly* 16 (1930), 199–206.

Greer, Taylor A. "Listening as Intuiting: A Critique of Clifton's Theory of Intuitive Description," *In Theory Only* 7.7 (1984), 3–22.

Griesbach, Karl-Rudi. "Errungenschaften und Grenzen neuer Musiktheorie," *Musik und Gesellschaft* 18.7 (1968), 454–58.

Grunsky, Karl. "Das Vorspiel und der erste Akt von 'Tristan und Isolde'," *Richard Wagner-Jahrbuch* 2 (1907), 207–84.

———. "Wagner als Sinfoniker," *Richard Wagner-Jahrbuch* 1 (1906), 242.

Halm, August. "Bruckner als Melodiker," *Der Kunstwart* 18.2 (1905), 242–47.

———. "Über den Wert Brucknerschen Musik," *Die Musik* 6.1 (1906–07), 3–20.

Handschin, Jacques. "De différentes conceptions de Bach," *Schweizerisches Jahrbuch für Musikwissenschaft* 4 (1929), 7–35.

Hartmann, Hans. "Schopenhauer und die Musikphilosophie—zur 100. Wiederkehr seines Todestages," *Musica* 14 (1960), 557–60.

Hasty, Christopher. "Rhythm in Post-Tonal Music: Preliminary Questions of Duration and Motion," *Journal of Music Theory* 25.2 (1981), 183–216.

Herbst, Kurt. "Musikpsychologie und Musikwissenschaft: eine grundsätzliche Betrachtung über Ernst Kurths *Musikpsychologie,*" *Acta Musicologica* 3 (1931), 64–68.

Hornbostel, Erich von. "Melodischer Tanz: Eine musikpsychologische Studie," *Zeitschrift der Internationalen Musikgesellschaft* 5 (1903–04), 482.

———. "Studien über das Tonsystem und die Musik der Japaner," *Sammelbände der Internationalen Musikgesellschaft* 4 (1902–03), 302–60.

Hsu, Dolores M. "Ernst Kurth and His Concept of Music as Motion," *Journal of Music Theory* 10 (1966), 2–17.

Husmann, Heinrich. "Verschmelzung und Konsonanz, Den Manen Carl Stumpfs," *Deutsches Jahrbuch der Musikwissenschaft* (1956–57), 66–75.

Hynais, Cyrill. "Die Harmonik Richard Wagners in Bezug auf die Fundamenttheorie Sechters," *Neue musikalische Presse* 4 (1901), 50–52; 5:67–69; 6:81–82; 7:97–100.

Jackson, Roland. "Leitmotive and Form in the *Tristan* Prelude," *Music Review* 36 (1975), 42–53.

Jöde, Fritz. "Die Anfänge der Jugendmusikbewegung," *Die Wandervogelzeit,* ed. Werner Kindt. Düsseldorf: Diederichs, 1968.

Jorgensen, Dale. "A Résumé of Harmonic Dualism," *Music and Letters* 44 (1963), 31–42.

Kerman, Joseph. "How We Got Into Analysis and How To Get Out," *Critical Inquiry* 7.2 (1980), 311–31.

Kreidler, Walter. "Ernst Kurth † am 2. April [*sic*], 1946," *Die Musikforschung* 2 (1949), 9–13.

Kretzschmar, Hermann. "Allgemeines und Besonderes zur Affektenlehre," *Jahrbuch der Musikbibliothek Peters* 18 (1911), 63–78; 19 (1912), 65–78.

———. "Anregungen zur Förderung musikalischer Hermeneutik," *Jahrbuch der Musikbibliothek Peters* 2 (1902), 45–66.

———. "Neue Anregungen zur Förderung der musikalischen Hermeneutik," *Jahrbuch der Musikbibliothek Peters* 5 (1905), 75–86.

Krüger, Fritz. "Review of Meyer's 'Contributions to a Psychological Theory of Music'," *Zeitschrift für Psychologie* 29 (1902), 152–54.

Kunze, Stefan. "Bruckner und Bern," *Info* (Zeitschrift der Bernischen Musikgesellschaft) June, 1980.

Kurth, Ernst. "Bruckner," *Die Musik* 16.12 (1924), 861–69.

———. "Bruckners Fernstand," *Musikblätter des Anbruchs* 6 (1924), 351–57.

———. "Julius Bittners grosse Messe mit Te deum in D," *Die Musik* 18.12 (1925–26), 878–83.

———. "Der musikalische Formbegriff," *Melos* 4 (1924–25), 364–70.

———. "Die Schulmusik und ihre Reform," *Schweizerische Musikzeitung* 70.9 (1930), 341–51; orig. *Schulpraxis* 19 (1930).

———. "Symbolische und dynamische Primitivformen," *Die Musik* 23.2 (1930), 81–86.

———. "Zur 'ars cantus mensurabilis' des Franko von Köln," *Kirchenmusikalisches Jahrbuch* 21 (1908), 39–47.

———. "Zur Motivbildung Bachs, ein Beitrag zur Stilpsychologie," *Bach-Jahrbuch* (1917), 80–136.

———. "Zum Wesen der Harmonik," *Musik-Blätter des Anbruchs* 2.16–17 (1920), 539–43; 568–71.

————. "Zur Stilistik und Theorie des Kontrapunkts," *Zeitschrift für Musikwissenschaft* 1 (1918), 176–82.

Leichtentritt, Hugo. "Arnold Schönbergs Op. 19," *Die Musik* 25.1 (1932–33), 405–13.

Lenneberg, Hans. "Johann Mattheson on Affect and Rhetoric in Music," *Journal of Music Theory* 2 (1958), 47–84; 193–236.

Lerdahl, Fred and Ray Jackendoff. "Generative Music Theory and Its Relation to Psychology," *Journal of Music Theory* 25.1 (1981), 45–90.

Lewin, David. "Behind the Beyond," *Perspectives of New Music* 7.2 (1969), 59–69.

Lipps, Theodor. "Zur Theorie der Melodie," *Zeitschrift für Psychologie* 27 (1902), 225–63.

Lorenz, Alfred. "Review of *Romantische Harmonik*," *Die Musik* 16.4 (1924), 255–62.

————. "Ernst Kurths *Musikpsychologie*," *Die Musik* 23 (1930), 182–87.

Mayrberger, Karl. "Die Harmonik Richard Wagners," *Bayreuther Blätter* 4 (1881), 169–80.

Mersmann, Hans. "Versuch einer Phänomenologie der Musik," *Zeitschrift für Musikwissenschaft* 5 (1922–23), 226–69.

————. "Zur Geschichte des Formbegriffs," *Jahrbuch der Musikbibliothek Peters* 37 (1930), 32–48.

————. "Zur Phänomenologie der Musik," *Zeitschrift für Ästhetik und allgemeine Kunstwissenschaft* 19 (1925), 372–97.

Meyer, Max. "Elements of Psychological Theory of Melody," *Psychological Review* 7 (1900), 241–73.

————. "Some Points of Difference Concerning the Theory of Melody," *Psychological Review* 10 (1903), 534–50.

Mitchell, William. "The Tristan Prelude: Techniques and Structure," *The Music Forum*, vol. 1. New York: Columbia University Press, 1967, 162–203.

Morgan, Robert P. "Schenker and the Theoretical Tradition," *College Music Symposium* 18 (1978), 72–96.

Müller, Siegfried F. "Auseinandersetzung mit der dualistischen Harmonielehre," *Schweizerische Musikzeitung* 77 (1937), 469–73.

Münnich, Richard. "Konkordanz und Diskordanz," *Zeitschrift der Internationalen Musikgesellschaft* 13 (1911), 49–56.

————. "Von der Entwicklung der Riemann'schen Harmonielehre und ihrem Verhältnis zu Öttingen und Stumpf," *Riemann-Festschrift*. Leipzig: Hesse, 1909, 60–76.

McCreless, Patrick. "Ernst Kurth and the Analysis of the Chromatic Music of the Late Nineteenth Century," *Music Theory Spectrum* 5 (1983), 56–75.

Neumann, Friedrich. "Das Verhältnis von Melodie und Harmonie im dur-molltonalen Tonsatz, insbesondere bei J. S. Bach," *Die Musikforschung* 16 (1963), 22–31.

Niemöller, Klaus W. "Zur Musiktheorie im frühen 20. Jahrhundert: Georg Capellens Ideen einer Erneuerung des Tonsystems," *Festschrift Karl Gustav Fellerer*. Cologne: Arno-Volk Verlag, 1973, 402–08.

Pierce, Alexandra. "Juncture," *In Theory Only* 3.6 (1977), 23–34.

———. "Structure and Phrase," *In Theory Only* 4.5 (1978), 22–35; 5.3 (1979), 3–24; 7.1 (1983), 3–30.

Platen, Emil. "Review of *Die Voraussetzungen der theoretischen Harmonik,*" *Die Musikforschung* 29 (1976), 226.

Riemann, Hugo. "Konsonanz und Dissonanz," *Zeitschrift der Internationalen Musikgesellschaft* 13 (1912), 96–97.

———. "Ideen zu einer 'Lehre von den Tonvorstellungen'," *Jahrbuch der Musikbibliothek Peters* 21–22 (1914–15), 1–26.

———. "Neue Beiträge zu einer Lehre von den Tonvorstellungen," *Jahrbuch der Musikbibliothek Peters* 23 (1916), 1–22.

———. "Die Phrasierung im Lichte einer Lehre von den Tonvorstellungen," *Zeitschrift für Musikwissenschaft* 1.1 (1918), 26–39.

———. "Das Problem des harmonischen Dualismus," *Neue Zeitschrift für Musik* 72.1 1, 2, 3, 4, 5 (1905).

Rothgeb, John. "Review of Helmut Federhofer's *Akkord und Stimmführung in den musiktheoretischen Systemen von Hugo Riemann, Ernst Kurth und Heinrich Schenker,*" *Music Theory Spectrum* 4 (1982), 131–38.

Rufer, Josef. "Begriff und Funktion von Schönbergs Grundgestalt," *Melos* 38.7–8 (1971), 281–84.

Schalk, Josef. "Das Gesetz der Tonalität," *Bayreuther Blätter* 11 (1888), 192–97, 381–87; 12 (1889), 191–98; 13 (1890), 65–70.

Schering, Arnold. "Das kolorierte Orgelmadrigal des Trecento," *Sammelbände der Internationalen Musikgesellschaft* 13 (1911–12), 172–204.

———. "Zur Grundlegung der musikalischen Hermeneutik," *Zeitschrift für Ästhetik und allgemeine Kunstwissenschaft* 9 (1914), 168–75.

Schrade, Leo. "Schweitzer's Aesthetics: An Interpretation of Bach," *The Albert Schweitzer Jubilee Book*, ed. Roback. Cambridge, Mass., 1946.

Schünemann, Georg. "Review of *Bach-Jahrbuch,* 1914–17," *Zeitschrift für Musikwissenschaft* 1 (1918–19), 364–69.

———. "Carl Stumpf," *Archiv für Musikforschung* 2 (1937), 1–7.

Schuh, Willi. "Ernst Kurth zum 60. Geburtstag," *Schweizerische Musikzeitung* 86.7 (1946), 302.

Schumann, E. "Die Förderung der Musikwissenschaft durch die akustisch-psychologische Forschung Carl Stumpfs," *Archiv für Musikwissenschaft* 5 (1923), 172–76.

Serafine, Mary Louise. "Cognition in Music," *Cognition* 14 (1983), 119–83.

Spencer, Herbert. "The Origin of Music," *Mind* 15 (1890), 449–68.

Stein, Jack. "The Influence of Schopenhauer on Wagner's Concept of the *Gesmatkunstwerk,*" *Germanic Review* 22 (1947), 92–105.

Strieburg, L. "Die philosophische Konzeption Wilhelm Ostwalds," *Sitzungsbericht der Akademie der Wissenschaften der DDR* 13N (1979), 113–22.

Stumpf, Carl. "Lieder der Bellakula-Indianer," *Vierteljahresschrift für Musikwissenschaft* 2 (1886), 405–26.

———. "Origin of Music," *Zeitschrift für Psychologie* 1 (1890), 511.

Tovey, Donald F. "The Classical Concerto," *Essays in Musical Analysis,* vol. 3. London: Oxford University Press, 1936, 3–26.

Wason, Robert. "Schenker's Notion of Scale-Step in Historical Perspective: Non-Essential Harmonies in Viennese Fundamental Bass Theory," *Journal of Music Theory* 27.1 (1983), 49–59.

Weinmann, Fritz. "Zur Struktur der Melodie," *Zeitschrift für Psychologie* 35 (1904), 340–79, 401–53.

Wellek, Albert. "Der gegenwärtige Stand der Musikpsychologie und ihre Bedeutung für die historische Musikforschung," *Report of the Eighth Congress of the International Musicological Society,* vol. 1. Kassel: Bärenreiter, 1961, 121–32.

———. "Gegenwartsprobleme systematischer Musikwissenschaft," *Acta Musicologica* 41.3–4 (1969), 213–35.

———. "Review of *Musikpsychologie,*" *Acta Musicologica* 5.2 (1933), 72–80.

Wertheimer, Max. "Experimentelle Studien über das Sehen von Bewegungen," *Drei Abhandlungen zur Gestalttheorie.* Erlangen: Verlag der philosophischen Akademie, 1925, 1–105; orig. in *Zeitschrift für Psychologie* 60–61 (1911–12).

Westphal, Kurt. "Ernst Kurths *Musikpsychologie,*" *Schweizerische Musikzeitung* 72 (1932), 233–46.

Wetzel, Hermann. "Zur Stilforschung in der Musik: Bemerkungen und Betrachtungen zu Ernst Kurths *Romantische Harmonik,*" *Die Musik* 16.4 (1924), 262–69.

Wilks, Samuel. "The Origin of Music," *Medical Magazine* (1894), 503–11.

Unpublished Materials

Bailey, Robert. "The Genesis of 'Tristan und Isolde' and a Study of Wagner's Sketches for the First Act," Ph.D. diss., Princeton University, 1969.

Kalib, Sylvan. "Thirteen Essays from the Three Yearbooks *Das Meisterwerk in der Musik* by Heinrich Schenker: An Annotated Translation," 3 vols. Ph.D. diss., Northwestern University, 1973.

Lieberman, Ira. "Some Representative Works from Beethoven's Early Period Analyzed in Light of the Theories of Ernst Kurth and Kurt von Fischer," Ph.D. diss., Columbia University, 1968.

Mennicke, Carl H. "Hasse und die Gebrüder Graun als Symphoniker," Ph.D. diss., Leipzig University, 1905.

Moyer, Birgitte. "Concepts of Musical Form in the Nineteenth Century with Special Reference to A. B. Marx and Sonata Form," Ph.D. diss., Stanford University, 1969.

Pastille, William A. "*Ursatz:* The Musical Philosophy of Heinrich Schenker," Ph.D. diss., Cornell University, 1985.

Proctor, Gregory M. "Technical Bases of Nineteenth-Century Chromatic Tonality: a Study in Chromaticism," Ph.D. diss., Princeton University, 1978.

Rothfarb, Lee A. "Ernst Kurth's *The Requirements for a Theory of Harmony:* An Annotated Translation with an Introductory Essay," Masters Thesis, University of Hartford, Hartt School of Music, 1979.

Solie, Ruth. "Metaphor and Model in the Analysis of Melody," Ph.D. diss., University of Chicago, 1977.

INDEX